A Collection of Surveys on Savings and Wealth Accumulation

A Collection of Surveys on Savings and Wealth Accumulation

Edited by Edda Claus and Iris Claus

WILEY Blackwell

CONTENTS

1

SAVINGS AND WEALTH ACCUMULATION: MEASUREMENT, INFLUENCES AND INSTITUTIONS[1]

Edda Claus

Wilfrid Laurier University and CAMA

Iris Claus

International Monetary Fund and University of Waikato

> The financial crisis and the Great Recession demonstrated, in a dramatic and unmistakable manner, how extraordinarily vulnerable are the large share of American families with very few assets to fall back on. (J. L. Yellen, 2014)[2]

We tend to not think about savings and wealth accumulation when times are good and incomes are rising. But when income growth stops and rainy days arrive, savings and wealth jump back to the forefront of our minds, as individuals, policy makers and researchers.

Developments over the past twenty-five years are a case in point. During the boom years of the 1990s and early 2000s, incomes grew rapidly reflecting sustained high growth rates of economic activity and an unprecedented rise in commodity prices. Furthermore, historically low interest rates in many advanced economies reduced the return on savings and lowered the cost of borrowing, contributing to higher household consumption and indebtedness and low savings rates.[3] Savings rates, measured as the difference between income and consumption, have not only been low and indebtedness rising at the household level, but also at the country level, demonstrated by large and sustained current account deficits and rising debt in many advanced economies.

When the boom ended with the onset of the global financial crisis in 2007, it became clear that much of the wealth created over the previous two decades was all but on paper and individuals and countries had very few assets to fall back on. Chair Yellen's quote at the beginning of this article is applicable not only to American families but to families and governments around the world. The lack of assets has played an important part in the painfully slow economic recovery post crisis. Consumers have been hesitant about spending and high government indebtedness has raised concerns about debt sustainability. This has hindered fiscal expansions and worsened the economic downturn through a full blown sovereign debt crisis in Europe.

Moreover, many countries, some high and some medium income economies, are experiencing a demographic transition with an aging population and falling fertility rates, raising concerns about the adequacy of people's retirement savings and the sustainability of public pension funds.

It is therefore high time that we turn our attention to savings and wealth accumulation, which is the theme of this book. The nine papers presented here critically review topical issues in the recent policy and research debates ranging from the effects of access to credit, the rise of Islamic finance and sovereign wealth funds, the measurement of wealth inequality and genuine savings, the distribution of wealth across generations and retirement savings.

A fundamental principle in economics is that of utility maximization–each period people choose a bundle of consumption goods and services, including leisure, to maximize lifetime utility. The way in which people maximize lifetime utility, which represents their preferences over goods and services, is by ensuring a balance between consumption and savings during the different phases of their life. Generally people prefer stable levels of consumption to large variations, meaning that similar levels of consumption today, tomorrow and the day after are preferred to a pattern that more closely matches a person's lifetime income of no or low income when young and when retired and high earnings during working years. This desire to smooth consumption and maintain accustomed living standards typically leads to three stages of savings and wealth accumulation during the lifetime of an individual. The first stage is a period of dis-savings or borrowing in early adulthood that is marked by post-secondary education expenditures, low income and debt accumulation. The second stage is a period of savings when income is high and assets are accumulated. The third stage again is a period of dis-savings and a decline in assets during retirement when earnings are low.

Access to credit is an essential tool for consumption smoothing and the topic of the first two articles in this book. The first article by Igor Livshits (2015) reviews "Recent developments in consumer credit and default literature." Consumer credit rose sharply during the 1980s but this increase in personal debt coincided with an acceleration in bankruptcy filings in the United States and other countries with personal bankruptcy systems. The dramatic rise in household indebtedness and default raised concerns with policy makers and became a focus of attention for economists seeking to understand the driving forces behind them. Since then the quantitative literature on unsecured consumer debt and default has made great strides. In the basic model of default the key assumption is that borrowers face an interest rate that is a function of the amount borrowed and that includes a risk premium–the risk premium reflects the probability of default and is also a function of the amount borrowed. Underlying the design of bankruptcy systems is a basic tradeoff between the partial insurance of being able to walk away from debts (i.e., greater ability to smooth consumption across states of the world) and the inability to commit to repaying loans in future, which makes borrowing more expensive and reduces the scope for consumption smoothing over time. There are four possible explanations for the rise in personal bankruptcies and consumer credit. The first is increased risk exposure of borrowers: Existing borrowers face more adverse shocks. The second is increased risk exposure of lenders: Lenders advance loans to riskier borrowers. The third explanation is compositional changes in the population and the fourth is greater willingness of borrowers to file for bankruptcy. The empirical evidence reviewed by Livshits suggests that the rise in personal bankruptcies and consumer credit was due to two reinforcing factors: a decline in the cost of bankruptcy and a decline in the cost of lending as a result of interest rate deregulation and improvements in information processing technology. Moreover, welfare analysis suggests that information improvements have raised average welfare despite leading to greater bankruptcy rates. Livshits also discusses delinquency and informal default, debt restructuring and collection, and the cyclical behavior of credit and bankruptcy. He concludes with key challenges and future research directions including the need to model the interaction of borrowers with multiple lenders and combining secured and unsecured debt.

The second article by William Elliott and Melinda Lewis (2015) focuses on "Student debt effects on financial wellbeing: research and policy implications". Student debt has been rising since the mid-1980s in the United States and the authors conjecture that wealth inequality has become a more pressing problem among young adults than income inequality. Presently about 75% of young adults in the United States aged 30–40 years have higher incomes than their parents had, but only about 36% have accumulated more wealth than their parents did. A contributing factor to the lower wealth accumulation is student debt–young adults with student debt are more likely to have less wealth than their parents had despite earning higher incomes. Student debt started rising when needs based financial aid and state support for public, higher education institutions were reduced, shifting the cost of tertiary education from the government to individuals. This has had important effects on wealth accumulation. Households with student debt tend to have lower net worth and lower retirement savings than those without student debt. They also tend to have lower credit scores making it more difficult for them to gain access to productive capital to finance wealth creation, in the form of homeownership or business development. Student debt also influences other lifetime decisions. For instance, it can affect career planning (driving graduates away from lower paying, public sector jobs) and it can lower the probability of marriage and delay having children. The authors contend that schemes designed to prevent student debt burdens, such as income based repayment and pay as you earn plans, may in fact be *adding* to the student loan problem rather than solving it. They argue that the rebuilding of the U.S. financial aid system must begin with a more complete accounting of the true costs of student loans, both to students and to the larger economy. They also advocate for more research to be done in particular on how much debt is too much debt.

Access to credit is rising around the world including in Islamic countries and Pejman Abedifar, Shahid Ebrahim, Philip Molyneux and Amine Tarazi (2015) examine in the third article in this book the recent empirical literature on "Islamic banking and finance: recent empirical literature and directions for future research". In Islamic banking and finance the key underlying principles are the prohibition of *Riba* (narrowly interpreted as interest) and the adherence to other *Shariá* (Islamic law) requirements. A ground breaking experiment of incorporating Islamic principles into financial transactions was conducted during the 1960s in Egypt and the first Islamic financial institution with "bank" in its name was established in 1971. Since then the Islamic financial industry has developed as an alternative model of financial intermediation and Islamic banking is practiced by conventional commercial banks (via Islamic windows), traditional Islamic banks as well as non-bank financial institutions and multinational financial institutions (like the Islamic Development Bank). Reviewing the empirical literature on the performance of Islamic versus conventional banks the authors conclude that apart from key exceptions, there are no major differences between Islamic and conventional banks in terms of efficiency, competition and risk features although small Islamic banks are found to be less risky than their conventional counterparts. However, there is suggestive evidence that Islamic banking and finance may aide inclusion in wealth accumulation to a greater extent than conventional financial institutions, which may, at least in part, reflect the core principles of Islam of social justice, inclusion and sharing of resources. However, much more research is needed on the features and (socio)economic effects of Islamic financial instruments and institutions.

Frank Cowell and Philippe Van Kerm (2015) expressly examine the distribution of wealth. In their article "Wealth inequality: a survey" they address three main questions. What is the appropriate definition of wealth? How does the measurement of wealth inequality differ from that of income inequality? What are the appropriate procedures for analyzing wealth data and drawing inferences about changes in inequality? To answer these questions Cowell and Van Kerm summarize the main issues concerning wealth data, inequality estimation and inference. They outline standard methods, practical solutions and convenient remedies for potential problems and illustrate some of the concepts and methods using data from the Eurosystem Household Finance and Consumption Survey. The authors propose that the most appropriate definition of wealth in empirical analysis is current net worth or net wealth, measured as the difference between assets and debts. A particular feature of current net worth or net wealth is that a large proportion of households or individuals have negative net wealth. Furthermore, wealth distributions are characterized by skewness and fat tails resulting in sparse, extreme data in typical samples. These features of wealth distributions render traditional measures of inequality inadequate and require adjustments in measurement, estimation and inference. Making the appropriate adjustments wealth inequality typically is found to be (much) larger than income inequality. Moreover, life cycle dynamics tend to be more pronounced in the case of wealth inequality compared to income distributions. The authors conclude that measuring wealth inequality is beyond estimations of wealth concentration among the extremely wealthy, which recently have become popular measures of inequality, and should take into account entire distributions. However, taking into account entire distributions requires a broader set of concepts and tools than are used in income inequality measurements.

Beyond consumption smoothing and wealth accumulation at the individual or household level, intergenerational equity considers the extent to which living standards are equalized across generations. In this respect, government expenditures and savings are important influences. Public expenditures that are financed by issuing government debt are a transfer of obligations from current to future generations. Such transfer of obligations may be appropriate, for example, to finance the purchase of assets that are used by current as well as future generations or if sustained economic growth over time means that better off future generations are more able to afford the cost of repaying inherited debt. Respectively, future obligations may be met by generations accumulating assets to prefund future payments, such as pension payments, or to share revenues from the extraction of non-renewable resources with future generations, e.g. sovereign wealth funds.

The measurement of government debts and deficits is the topic of the article by Timothy Irwin (2015) "Defining the government's debt and deficit". Irwin notes that despite international accounting standards, there are still many differences in how governments measure debts and deficits. They can be defined for central government, general government and the public sector, and, for any definition of government, there are different measures of debt and deficit, including those generated by four kinds of accounts–cash, financial, full accrual and comprehensive accounts. The different measures of debt and deficit all contain different information about public finances and they all are susceptible to mismeasurement. Narrow definitions of government encourage the shifting of spending to entities outside the defined borders of government, while narrow definitions of debt and deficit encourage operations involving off balance sheet assets and liabilities. Broad measures of debt and deficit on the other hand are susceptible to the mismeasurement of on balance sheet assets and liabilities. Moreover, measures of debt and deficit are more likely to be manipulated if they are subject to binding fiscal rules or targets. In contrast, governments with greater budgetary transparency are less likely to engage in budgetary manipulations as these are more likely to be discovered and publicized. Irwin concludes with two lessons for accountants, statisticians and budget officials. First, he advocates that debt and deficit measures need protection from manipulation, such as independent measurement, independent auditing, the use of standards set by independent bodies and the publication of the assumptions underlying the measurements so that calculations can be verified. Second, several measures of the deficit and debt should be produced and reconciled to provide more complete assessments of public finances and to help reveal manipulation in targeted measures.

William Megginson and Veljko Fotak (2015) in "Rise in the fiduciary state: a survey of sovereign wealth fund research" review the literature on sovereign wealth funds (SWFs), which are investment vehicles that transfer wealth from current to future generations. Since January 2008 more than 25 countries have launched or proposed to set up sovereign wealth funds–usually to preserve and protect new monetary inflows from transfers of oil (and natural gas) revenues or from transfers of excess foreign exchange reserves earned from exports. Norway's Government Pension Fund Global (GPFG) is the largest sovereign wealth fund and the second largest pension fund after Japan's Government Employees Pension Fund. Almost without exception all of the recently established funds are modeled after the GPFG with respect to organizational design, transparency, managerial professionalism and investment preference for listed shares and bonds of international companies. The defining characteristic of SWFs is that they are state owned and Megginson and Fotak discuss the existing literature on state ownership and what it predicts about the efficiency and beneficence of government control of SWF assets. Findings from a review of the empirical literature suggest that private funds generally outperform sovereign wealth funds across the board in their investments. Moreover, announcement period abnormal returns associated with SWF stock purchases are positive but they are significantly lower than those observed for private sector investments. This finding implies the presence of a sovereign wealth fund "discount", which the authors suggest is due to the state ownership. They conclude with unresolved issues in SWF research. With the notable exception of the activities of Norway's GPFG, they argue, far too little is known about the details of SWF investments and the returns that the investments achieve. It is also unclear what will be the long-term impact and effects of sovereign wealth funds. In particular, they question whether it is reasonable to expect markets to efficiently and accurately assess the value impact of investments which are intentionally kept opaque by a group of funds that are themselves often little understood.

Nick Hanley, Eoin McLaughlin and Louis Dupuy (2015) consider "Genuine savings and sustainability". Genuine savings is an empirical indicator of sustainable development and hence intergenerational well-being. It measures how a nation's total capital stock changes from year to year, where capital includes all assets (or instruments of wealth) from which people obtain well-being. It comprises physical capital (machines, buildings, infrastructure), human capital, natural capital (renewable and non-renewable resources, ecosystems) and social capital (institutions, social networks). The literature distinguishes between weak sustainability, which requires non-declining total wealth, and strong sustainability, which requires non-declining natural wealth. Genuine savings is typically viewed as an empirical measure of the weak sustainability of an economy. It is forward looking and provides information about the sustainability of a given consumption path or pattern of resource use and hence future sustainability. Genuine savings thus gives an indication about variation in intergenerational well-being. Estimates are available for many countries and regions but the authors find that they are typically not directly comparable because of different concepts of genuine savings being used across countries. However, as a general rule, the results suggest that economic development is probably sustainable in many countries over the long run when accounting for all instruments of wealth including human capital and total factor productivity growth. Moreover, longer time horizons and the addition of measures of the gradual improvement of productivity and technology tend to enhance the ability of genuine savings to predict future consumption. The authors conclude that genuine savings is a useful concept but its measurement requires further improvement. An interesting area of future research they suggest would be the investigation of the impact of an asymmetric distribution of wealth instruments on sustainability.

The last two articles in this book focus on retirement issues. In the context of retirement income policies, intergenerational equity implies that government services received by generations throughout their lifetime match the amount of taxes they have paid. A recent wave of pension reforms in several countries has led to cuts in public pension programs partly because pension policy had tended to favor current over future generations. Moreover, rising pension expenditures as a result of ageing populations have exacerbated the problem of unsustainable government finances.

In "Savings in times of demographic change: lessons from the German experience" Axel Börsch-Supan, Tabea Bucher-Koenen, Michela Coppola and Bettina Lamla (2015) discuss how German households have adjusted their retirement and savings behavior in response to far reaching pension reforms. Germany, which was the first country to introduce a formal national pension system in the 1880s, embarked on a series of reforms between 1992 and 2007. The reforms encompassed three features. They raised the statutory retirement age, they decreased public pension replacement rates and they transformed the monolithic public pension system into a multi-pillar system by fostering private and occupational pensions. The authors conclude that most Germans have adapted to the changes with both actual and expected retirement ages increasing and the proportion of households without any source of supplementary income in retirement decreasing sharply. But there is a large heterogeneity in the responses. Households with higher income and education responded strongly, while a substantial fraction of households, in particular those with low education, low income and less financial education, did not respond at all. The evidence also suggests important information gaps. For instance, Germans on average underestimate their life expectancy by a substantial margin, women by 7 years and men by 6.5 years, which corresponds to roughly a third of life spent in retirement. The authors conclude with a call for better informing people by providing easier to understand information about life expectancy as well as the eligibility for private and occupational pension schemes and their high subsidy rates. Better informed individuals may also help counter reform backlash, which is appearing in the political climate.

Retirement, which marks the end of labor earnings and the beginning of a drawdown of retirement resources, is probably the most important financial decision people make and Courtney Coile (2015) in "Economic determinants of workers' retirement decisions" reviews the theory and evidence on the influences that have been found important. She discusses the impact of private and public pensions, wealth and savings, health and health insurance and labor demand and concludes with thoughts about future retirement behavior. A persistent trend in labor markets that is expected to continue in the future is the steady increase in the number of older women. It has occurred mainly because of a societal trend of greater female labor force participation and has offset any movement towards earlier retirement by women. Moreover, economic activity is shifting into the services sector away from manufacturing and other traditional blue-collar industries. The services sector typically requires computer literate workers and the evidence suggests that having computer skills is associated with an increase in the probability of continuing to work at older ages. However, the importance of this factor is expected to abate over time as the gaps in computer use by age are declining. Regarding pension plans, retirement ages have been rising and benefits have been declining for public pensions, while private plans have been shifting from defined benefit to defined contribution plans. At the same time, more responsibility is being put on workers to decide whether or not to participate in a pension plan, how much to contribute, where to invest those contributions, and how to draw down savings in retirement. With respect to the influence of health factors on retirement decisions, continuing health improvements are anticipated to further reduce the number of workers being forced into retirement earlier than planned because of adverse health shocks. However, as Coile points out more research is needed on the effects of retirement on health and well-being. Finally, the impact of equity markets and house prices on retirement decisions has not been strong and is expected to remain moderate.

Savings and wealth accumulation are once again at the forefront of policy and research debates. The nine articles presented here provide critical reviews of some of the most topical private and public sector aspects and discuss policy implications. However, many challenges and unanswered questions remain underlining the need for more analysis and research.

Notes

1. The views expressed in this article are those of the authors and do not necessarily represent those of the International Monetary Fund (IMF), IMF policy, its Executive Board or IMF management.
2. Speech Chair Janet L. Yellen, At the 2014 Assets Learning Conference of the Corporation for Enterprise Development, Washington, D.C., September 18, 2014; http://www.federalreserve.gov/newsevents/speech/yellen20140918a.htm accessed 24 April 2015.
3. This is the substitution effect. The income effect works in opposite direction to the substitution effect for savers, i.e., lower interest rates reduce income from interest earning assets thus increasing savings. For borrowers the substitution and income effects reinforce each other, i.e., lower interest rates increase disposable income because of lower debt payments. Other factors contributing to low savings rates are demographic changes.

References

Abedifar, P., Molyneux, P. and Tarazi, A. (2015) Islamic banking and finance: recent empirical literature and directions for future research. *Journal of Economic Surveys* 29(4): 637–670.

Börsch-Supan, A., Bucher-Koenen, T., Coppola, M. and Lamla, B. (2015) Savings in times of demographic change: lessons from the German experience. *Journal of Economic Surveys* 29(4): 807–829.

Coile, C. (2015) Economic determinants of workers' retirement decisions. *Journal of Economic Surveys* 29(4): 830–853.

Cowell, F. and Van Kerm, P. (2015) Wealth inequality: a survey. *Journal of Economic Surveys* 29(4): 671–710.

Elliott, W. and Lewis, M. (2015) Student debt effects on financial well-being: research and policy implications. *Journal of Economic Surveys* 29(4): 614–636.

Hanley, N., McLaughlin, E. and Dupuy, L. (2015) Genuine savings and sustainability. *Journal of Economic Surveys* 29(4): 779–806.

Irwin, T. (2015) Defining the government's debt and deficit. *Journal of Economic Surveys* 29(4): 711–732.

Livshits, I. (2015) Recent developments in consumer credit and default literature. *Journal of Economic Surveys* 29(4): 594–613.

Megginson, W. and Fotak, V. (2015) Rise of the fiduciary state: a survey of sovereign wealth fund research. *Journal of Economic Surveys* 29(4): 733–778.

2

RECENT DEVELOPMENTS IN CONSUMER CREDIT AND DEFAULT LITERATURE

Igor Livshits

University of Western Ontario, Federal Reserve Bank of Philadelphia and BEROC

1. Introduction

The last two decades of the 20th century witnessed a dramatic increase in personal bankruptcy filings, which continued into the new millennium. The phenomenon was not limited to the USA, and was present in other countries where the institution of personal bankruptcy is present.[1] Annual personal bankruptcy filings in the USA crossed the 1 million mark in the 1990s, with annual Chapter 7 filings alone exceeding that level in the 2000s. That is, about 1% of American households file for bankruptcy every year.[2] These rising bankruptcy trends in North America seem to have been broken only by the reforms of the bankruptcy system (BAPCPA in the USA in 2005, and reforms of the 1990s in Canada). Not surprisingly, personal bankruptcy received attention not only from policy makers concerned about the large number of filers, but also from economists seeking to better understand the key mechanisms of household debt and default, and the driving forces behind the dramatic rise in both debt and filings. The research in this area has been both very active and very fruitful in the last 10 years, and yet, the only survey of bankruptcy models, Athreya (2005), predates most of these contributions. The current survey aims to highlight the key questions, contributions, and theoretical developments in this burgeoning literature.

The recent bankruptcy models have built on the theoretical foundations that had already been in place. The single most important building block in this literature is the incomplete-market model of Eaton and Gersovitz (1981). The key idea, which has been almost universally adopted in the quantitative bankruptcy literature, is that the interest rates (which explicitly depend on the loan size) reflect the probability of an individual borrower's default and compensate lenders in non-default states for the losses they suffer in default. Furthermore, the most basic tradeoff associated with the design of bankruptcy systems – that between the partial insurance afforded by the ability to walk away from debts on the one hand and the inability to commit to repaying loans in the future, which hampers intertemporal smoothing, on the other hand – has been understood since Zame (1993).[3] So, a lot of the recent contributions have been quantitative in

A Collection of Surveys on Savings and Wealth Accumulation, First Edition. Edited by Edda Claus and Iris Claus.
Chapters © 2016 The Authors. Book compilation © 2016 John Wiley & Sons, Ltd. Published 2016 by John Wiley & Sons, Ltd.

nature, with quantitative models by Chatterjee *et al.* (2007a) and Livshits *et al.* (2007) being the standard references. But this quantitative research has in turn posed new theoretical questions, and has led to the development of new theoretical models. These quantitative findings and theoretical developments are the subject of this survey. I will forego the discussion of the personal bankruptcy system and characteristics of a typical bankruptcy filer, referring the reader instead to White (2007) and Sullivan *et al.* (2000).[4] For a detailed description of the consumer credit industry and its evolution, please see Evans and Schmalensee (1999) and Livshits *et al.* (2015).[5]

The survey is organized as follows: Before going into specific questions and agendas, the next section lays out the key mechanisms and tradeoffs associated with consumer credit and bankruptcy, and presents the key features of the standard models employed. Section 3 discusses the papers dedicated to explaining the rise in bankruptcies and debt over the last few decades. Improvements in information processing technology figure prominently in this literature, and thus, Section 4 follows up on the importance of information in the consumer credit markets. Section 5 discusses welfare implications of various bankruptcy regimes (including the effects of personal bankruptcy rules on entrepreneurship), as well as those of the recent developments in consumer credit markets. Section 6 turns to papers that study delinquency and informal default, as well as debt restructuring and collection. Section 7 discusses papers on the cyclicality of debt and default. Lastly, Section 8 presents some challenges moving forward and some promising directions for addressing them.

2. Basic Models, Mechanisms, and Tradeoffs

The starting point for a successful model of bankruptcy involves having default on debt occur with positive probability as part of (the equilibrium path of) the model outcome. This seemingly trivial statement rules out a large set of models that study debt under the *threat* of default (most standard references being Kehoe and Levine (1993), Kocherlakota (1996), and Alvarez and Jermann (2000)). The basic idea is exceedingly simple: No rational lender would advance a loan that will certainly not be repaid. In a complete market setting, where every loan is obtained by issuing a promise to pay in a specific state only, lenders will not accept such liabilities if the borrower will not repay in that future state of the world, because they will not be repaid in any other state of the world either. Thus, a complete market setting fails to generate a model of equilibrium default.[6] However, if the markets are (exogenously) incomplete, and loans are not made contingent on the realizations of (idiosyncratic) uncertainty, then lenders may be willing to advance a loan that is *sometimes* not repaid – as long as they are compensated for the losses by a higher interest rate (when the loan is repaid).[7] Thus, the standard approach in the default literature has been to model the debt markets as maximally incomplete, where the only form of debt is a (borrower-specific) non-contingent one-period bond. Of course, the option of default generates some "state dependence" – the return on the bond is constant only across the states where the borrower does not default.

The basic model of equilibrium default goes back to Eaton and Gersovitz (1981). The key assumption in that model and in the literature that followed is that a borrower faces an interest rate *schedule* that makes the rate an explicit function of the amount borrowed. In a competitive setting with risk-neutral lenders, the interest rates include a risk premium, which reflects the probability of default as a function of the amount borrowed (and possibly, the expected recovery rate in the event of default). Such pricing makes the borrower fully take into account the effect of the debt level on the probability of default,[8] and generates an endogenous borrowing constraint – maximum amount a borrower can receive in exchange for a pledge of future income.

From the most basic model of bankruptcy, let's move on to the most basic tradeoff – the one associated with the concept of bankruptcy itself. Unlike in models with complete markets, full enforcement of debt contracts is not necessarily *ex ante* optimal in the incomplete market models of default. In complete market models, inability to commit to future payments unequivocally shrinks the *ex ante* choice set available to the borrower (and thus, lowers welfare). In contrast, such lack of commitment is associated with a meaningful *ex ante* tradeoff in incomplete market models. The ability to walk away from one's debt in some states of the world introduces some (partial) insurance into the setting where no other insurance is available. Of course, on the other hand, risk of default makes borrowing more expensive (and this is not just a matter of shifting payments from one state of the world to the other ones – at least, not as long as there is some deadweight loss associated with bankruptcy); and the lack of commitment makes certain debt levels simply unattainable. This basic tradeoff was first clearly laid out in Zame (1993), and of course, has been central to the welfare analysis in most subsequent papers (see, for example, Chatterjee *et al.* (2007a) and Livshits *et al.* (2007), where commitment is basically equated to the severity of the bankruptcy "punishment").

Another way of formulating this key tradeoff is as a choice between greater ability to smooth consumption over time, which is supported by greater commitment (equivalently, greater cost of bankruptcy to the borrower), and greater ability to smooth across states of the world, which is facilitated by the ability to walk away from debts (i.e., lower bankruptcy cost). Phrasing the tradeoff this way helps understand, for example, the finding in Livshits *et al.* (2007) that the implications of income uncertainty for the choice of optimal bankruptcy system depends on the exact nature of the income uncertainty. While greater variance of persistent income shocks makes lower bankruptcy costs more attractive (as the demand for smoothing across states increases), the same does not hold for transitory income shocks. Households can quite effectively smooth transitory income shocks over time, as long as they are able to borrow (sufficient amounts and at good interest rates). Thus, greater variance of transitory income shocks makes lower bankruptcy costs less attractive, as they limit the borrowers' ability to commit to repayment and make intertemporal smoothing more difficult.

Before discussing specific research topics, I think it is useful to highlight several key mechanisms that are embedded in bankruptcy models, and thus come up in the discussions of a number of topics. The first of these recurrent themes is precautionary savings. The concept, which dates back to Leland (1968), is a very intuitive one – in the absence of perfect insurance markets, risk-averse households "save for a rainy day" (i.e., accumulate more savings than they would if perfect insurance were available). Precautionary savings arise not only in incomplete market settings (Aiyagari (1994) is the most standard reference for this point), but also in models with complete but imperfect markets. That is, when markets are subject to enforcement (or other) frictions, perfect insurance may not be attainable, and thus there is the need to save for the rainy day. This mechanism is present, for example, in the Kehoe and Levine (1993) economy.[9] And naturally, these forces arise in models which have both frictions – both the market incompleteness and the inability of borrowers to commit to repaying their loans. One example of why precautionary savings are important to keep in mind is that an increase in the frequency or size of adverse shocks doesn't simply translate into a greater frequency of default in this class of models, as households respond by accumulating precautionary savings (and reducing their debts).

One consequence of this phenomenon is that a typical quantitative model with a realistic income shock process struggles to generate the observed frequency of defaults. As a result, most of the quantitative models of bankruptcy introduce some additional idiosyncratic uncertainty that drives some households into bankruptcy. Livshits *et al.* (2007) introduce what they call "expense shocks," which affect households' balance sheets directly and are meant to capture out-of-pocket medical expenses and costs of family shocks, such as divorce and unwanted children. Chatterjee *et al.* (2007a) add a preference shock which makes households particularly "hungry" in some periods and serves the same basic purpose. These assumptions of additional shocks are not only useful, but also quite realistic, as a large fraction of filers report expense shocks as (part of) the reason they ended up in bankruptcy (see Domowitz and Sartain, 1999; Warren *et al.*, 2000; Sullivan *et al.*, 2000).

Another model ingredient necessary to reconcile a typical bankruptcy model with the data is some transaction cost of making loans. The gap between the average interest rates charged on unsecured debt and the (risk-free) savings interest rate in the economy is just too large to be attributed solely to the risk-premium on unsecured debt. Again, these transaction costs are not only useful from the model perspective, but also quite realistic (and several recent papers study mechanisms that comprise such transaction costs – see, for example, Drozd and Nosal, 2008; Sanchez, 2010; Livshits *et al.*, 2011; Drozd and Serrano-Padial, 2014). Furthermore, in a setting that has nothing to do with default, Mehra *et al.* (2011) argue that such transaction costs are both realistic and important.

One other common theme in this literature is the "democratization of credit" (including what Drozd and Serrano-Padial (2014) call "revolving revolution") – the extension of credit to new (and seemingly riskier) borrowers in the recent decades. This phenomenon is clearly present in the data, and arises quite naturally in many different models, both in response to various improvements in information technologies (e.g., Sanchez, 2010; Athreya *et al.*, 2012; Narajabad, 2012; Drozd and Serrano-Padial, 2014; Livshits *et al.*, 2015) and even in response to lower costs of advancing loans (Drozd and Nosal, 2008; Livshits *et al.*, 2015). The mechanism is usually quite intuitive – lending to the best (safest) borrowers generates the largest surplus, and thus, takes place even when (information) technology is underdeveloped. As lending technology improves, it makes lending to riskier types (associated with greater expected deadweight losses from default) profitable. Note that this increased average riskiness of the debt is associated with higher welfare in all these models, as it arises from realizing new gains from trade (and comes from the newly realized trades being the relatively risky ones).

To conclude this section, I will use the comparison of the two key quantitative models, Chatterjee *et al.* (2007a) and Livshits *et al.* (2007), to highlight the basic modeling approaches and their respective benefits. First of all, Chatterjee *et al.* (2007a) is a full general equilibrium model, where the risk-free interest rate (as well as individual borrowing rates) is determined endogenously. Livshits *et al.* (2007) argue that, since unsecured consumer credit is just a small part of the overall financial market, a partial equilibrium approach is justified. That is, while individuals' borrowing rates are determined endogenously (as in Eaton and Gersovitz, 1981), the risk-free rate is taken as given. The partial equilibrium approach makes computation of the model less demanding, but may not be appropriate, of course, if one considers general equilibrium effects potentially important (and thinks that financial markets are closed to international capital movement). A second important distinction between the two models concerns the life-cycle of borrowers. Whereas Chatterjee *et al.* (2007a) model individuals as (potentially) infinitely lived, Livshits *et al.* (2007) have overlapping generations of households with an explicit life-cycle both in their earnings and in their family size, which allows them to explicitly study the age profile of both unsecured debt and bankruptcy filings. The assumption of finite life further reduces computational costs as, instead of looking for a fixed point of a stationary value function (as in Chatterjee *et al.*, 2007a), the model of Livshits *et al.* (2007) can be simply solved by backward induction. The last important distinction I will point to is the choice of a key empirical target for calibration – debt. Chatterjee *et al.* (2007a) map debt in the model to negative net worth in the data, while Livshits *et al.* (2007) interpret it as gross unsecured debt in the data. Of course, the distinction is absent in the model as it has just a single asset (and thus, no distinction between gross and net debt). On the one hand, the negative net worth is the more natural measure of households' indebtedness. But on the other hand, it is the gross unsecured debt that can be discharged in bankruptcy (while some assets are exempt from seizure by the lenders). The literature has not really settled on which data moment is the right target for a model to match; but fortunately, most key findings seem robust to the alternative mappings of debt to the data.

3. The Rise in Personal Bankruptcies and Consumer Credit

The rise in bankruptcy filings has been almost uniformly cited as a motivation for studying default in the consumer debt markets, even in papers that did not address the issue directly. It is not surprising, as in the USA, for example, the personal bankruptcy rate has increased more than three-fold in the last two decades of the last millennium. And while there has been no shortage of proposed explanations for this phenomenon, this is still a very active area of research. As Livshits *et al.* (2010) argue, the mechanisms that are easy to quantify (increases in uncertainty, demographic changes, etc.) account for just a fraction of the rise in filings (and a smaller increase in debt), and one is left with explanations that are much harder to quantify, such as a fall in the "stigma" of bankruptcy and a fall in intermediation costs. Thus, this quantitative paper helps set the stage for future research more than provide specific answer(s). And a number of subsequent papers have offered specific stories that are consistent with the key observations.

The proposed explanations can be loosely categorized into four types: increased risk exposure of borrowers (i.e., existing borrowers face more adverse shocks), increased risk exposure of lenders (i.e., lenders advance loans to riskier borrowers), compositional changes in the population (population of borrowers can thus become riskier without any change in lending standards), and lastly, greater willingness of borrowers to file for bankruptcy. The first category includes both increase in household income risk (as suggested, for example, by Barron *et al.* (2000) and Hacker (2006)), and increase in out-of-pocket medical spending (pointed to by Warren and Warren Tyagi (2003)). The increased willingness of lenders to advance riskier loans may have also come from several sources. It could have been a consequence of changes in the regulation – specifically, the U.S. Supreme Court's 1978 *Marquette* decision, which effectively lifted interest rate ceilings, is most often cited (e.g., Ellis, 1998) as being critical in enabling lenders to go after riskier borrower pools (and be appropriately compensated for it with higher interest rates). Additionally, credit market innovations (such as the development and spread of credit scoring and securitization) may have lowered the cost of lending and/or improved accuracy of targeting specific groups of borrowers, thereby leading to more borrowing and potentially more defaults (Ellis, 1998, Barron and Staten, 2003).[10] Many of the specific mechanisms that have recently been suggested along these lines are rooted in improvements in information technologies (Sanchez, 2010; Livshits *et al.*, 2011; Athreya *et al.*, 2012; Narajabad, 2012; Drozd and Serrano-Padial, 2014), and I will come back to them in the next

section. Dick and Lehnert (2010) combine the last two channels, arguing that banking deregulation (lower barriers to inter-state banking) had led banks to adopt information-intensive
technologies, facilitating greater extension of credit to both existing and new customers. The
importance of the composition changes in the population (such as the passing of the baby-
boomers through the prime bankruptcy ages, and a larger share of unmarried borrowers who
have higher default probabilities) was highlighted by Sullivan et al. (2000). Possibly the most
commonly suggested explanation is that the cost of filing for bankruptcy has declined (e.g.,
Gross and Souleles, 2002). This can be a result of amendments to the U.S. bankruptcy code,
which had made bankruptcy more attractive to borrowers (as suggested by Shepard (1984)
and Boyes and Faith (1986)) or of the increased willingness of lenders to advance new loans
to borrowers with a record of bankruptcy[11] (Han et al. (2013) document the availability of
new credit to recent filers). The more common version of this explanation is that the "stigma"
attached to bankrupts has weakened (e.g., Buckley and Brinig, 1998; Fay et al., 2002), or as
the then Chairman of the Federal Reserve Board Alan Greenspan had put it in his testimony
before Congress in 1999, "personal bankruptcies are soaring because Americans have lost
their sense of shame."[12]

Several papers, including Moss and Johnson (1999), Athreya (2004), and Gross and Souleles
(2002), have analyzed several alternative explanations at the same time. Livshits et al. (2010)
attempt to combine all these mechanism in a single quantitative model in an attempt to assess the
importance of individual channels. They found that increased uncertainty faced by households
(emphasized in Warren and Warren Tyagi (2003) and SMR Research (1997) summarized in
Luckett (2002)) played a relatively small role in explaining the rise in bankruptcies. Changes
in expense uncertainty (due primarily to medical expenses) account for at most 20% of the
increase in filings (and likely less than 10%). Changes in income risk faced by borrowers do not
lead to a significant increase in bankruptcies either, primarily because more uncertainty leads
to an increase in precautionary savings, or conversely, a decrease in debt. In their quantitative
model, an increase in the variance of the transitory income shock has practically no effect on
the bankruptcy rate, while an increase in the variance of the persistent shocks leads to a very
modest increase in filings, accompanied by a dramatic fall in debt levels. Livshits et al. (2010)
also find that the demographic changes contribute very little to the rise in bankruptcy rate.[13]
In fact, all four studies examining multiple explanations (Moss and Johnson, 1999; Gross and
Souleles, 2002; Athreya, 2004; Livshits et al., 2010) come to much of the same conclusion –
the rise in bankruptcies is not primarily driven by the increase in uncertainty, but rather by
changes in the consumer credit market.

There is less consensus on the exact changes in the consumer debt market that drove the
rise in filings. Moss and Johnson (1999) argue that changes in regulation (both of bankruptcy
and of lending) were the critical factor, while Athreya (2004) argues that a decline in the
transactions cost of borrowing alone could have been responsible for the increase in filings.
On the other hand, Gross and Souleles (2002) find that the dramatic increase in the default
rate in their data set (of credit card accounts from 1995 to 1997) is consistent with a decline
in the cost of bankruptcy. Finally, Livshits et al. (2010) argue that, in order to match the key
observations (large increase in filings, smaller increase in debt, and roughly constant average
real interest rates on unsecured loans), one needs a combination of these stories. Specifically,
a combination of a decline in the cost of bankruptcy with a decline in the cost of lending
(accompanied by the interest rate deregulation) is capable of reproducing the observations in
the U.S. unsecured credit market between the late 1970s and the late 1990s. The reason why
a combination of stories is needed is intuitive – a reduction in the "stigma" of bankruptcy

by itself does increase the default rate, but leads to an increase in borrowing interest rates (to compensate lenders for the default losses) and a decline in debt levels. Lower lending costs (either due to a reduction in transaction costs or simply due to lower prevailing interest rates) can offset the latter effects, inducing households to borrow more, and thus further contribute to the rise in filings. Admittedly, these "stories" are not deeply rooted in a specific microeconomic theory and are more of a black box (or "reduced-form proxies" as Livshits *et al.* (2010) referred to them). Thus, one result of this quantitative research has been a call for more formal modeling of changes in the consumer debt markets, with a particular emphasis on the impact of the improvements in information technology (IT). And the very active research program that followed (Drozd and Nosal, 2008; Sanchez, 2010; Livshits *et al.*, 2011; Athreya *et al.*, 2012; Narajabad, 2012; Drozd and Serrano-Padial, 2014) is the subject of the next section.

Before moving on to discuss the specifics of these information-related mechanisms proposed, it is worth highlighting one more key empirical distinction related to the rise in unsecured debt and bankruptcies – that between the intensive margin of existing borrowers carrying larger debt balances (or being more prone to default on their existing balances) on the one hand, and the extensive margin of new borrowers gaining access to unsecured credit on the other hand. Both channels are clearly present in the data (the extensive margin of debt expansion is cited, for example, in Bird *et al.* (1999), Black and Morgan (1999), Durkin (2000), Moss and Johnson (1999), and Sullivan *et al.* (2000)), but sorting through them is not trivial. Livshits *et al.* (2015) do a decomposition exercise, which attributes about a quarter to a third of the rise in bankruptcies to the extensive margin (which they call "democratization of credit"), while the remainder is attributed to "existing" borrowers. Interestingly, a further decomposition of the intensive margin yields a result similar to that of Gross and Souleles (2002) – most of the intensive margin portion is due to a greater propensity of existing borrowers to file for bankruptcy, rather than greater debt burdens.

4. The Importance of Information

While complete information models of bankruptcy discussed thus far are useful benchmarks for quantitative analysis, informational frictions definitely play an important role in the unsecured debt market – it is easy, for example, to think of situations where a borrower is more informed of their risk profile (probability of default) than a lender, leading to an adverse selection problem (Ausubel (1999) and Agarwal *et al.* (2010) provide systematic empirical evidence of the presence and importance of adverse selection in the credit card market).[14] A number of recent papers incorporate such information frictions and explore the implications of the improved information technology for the credit market. But before highlighting the papers dealing with the changes in the IT and their impact, I think it is important to highlight the paper by Chatterjee *et al.* (2007b), which provides a basic model of *credit scoring*. Credit score in this context is a borrower-specific summary statistic, based on the borrower's repayment history, which captures the likelihood that the borrower is of a low-risk type.[15] The model is intuitive, captures the basic idea of the credit score quite nicely, and is able to generate the relevant empirical phenomena, like that documented by Musto (2004).

Dealing with asymmetric information (adverse selection, specifically) is notoriously tricky technically – think of the non-existence of an equilibrium in the screening environment of Rothschild and Stiglitz (1976) (arising from the inability of competitive equilibria to support cross-subsidization between the types, even when both types prefer a pooling allocation) or the multiplicity of equilibria in a signaling environment. Some of the ways to get around these problems include discretizing the space of possible asset holdings as in Chatterjee *et al.* (2007b), an additional timing assumption as in Hellwig (1987) and Livshits *et al.* (2011) to support the pooling equilibria in a screening economy,[16] or introducing a refinement as in Athreya *et al.* (2012) to pick a specific equilibrium in a signaling setting.

The progress in IT impacts the consumer credit market in several distinct ways – improving availability and accuracy (timeliness) of information about individual borrowers, dramatically reducing the cost of processing such information, lowering the cost of both identifying and targeting pools of borrowers based on their (risk) characteristics (see, for example, Mann, 2006; Baird, 2007). The specific mechanisms suggested by the recent papers are quite distinct as well. Narajabad (2012) points to an improved accuracy of signals received by lenders regarding their potential borrowers' types (their idiosyncratic default costs). Greater signal accuracy leads to more favorable interest rates for the "good" type borrowers, which in turn leads to them taking on larger loans, and increases the probability of default among these "good" borrowers. The mechanism is somewhat similar to that in Athreya *et al.* (2012), who highlight the effects of the informational frictions in a signaling model by comparing it to a full information benchmark. In the presence of adverse selection, "good" borrowers signal their type by taking on smaller loans. Getting rid of the informational asymmetry increases "good" type's borrowing, and thus the default rate. The screening contracts in Sanchez (2010), while technically quite different, tell a similar story – relaxing informational asymmetries increases borrowing by "good" type borrowers, exposing them to a higher risk of default. Mechanics are quite different in Sanchez (2010) though – lenders have a choice of using a costly "screening" technology which reveals a borrower's type or designing a separating contract to deal with the adverse selection. As the cost of the information technology falls, more lenders switch to technological screening (away from contractual screening), thus generating more (risky) borrowing by the good type of borrowers. In all three of these papers, the key mechanism works along a similar intensive margin – some of the existing (good) borrowers take on larger loans, which increases their probability of default.

The mechanism presented in Livshits *et al.* (2015) is quite different and emphasizes the extensive margin of extending credit to new (and riskier) borrowers. Unlike the paper discussed above, which model improvements in information quality and lower cost of obtaining such information, Livshits *et al.* (2015) emphasize technological improvements in lenders' ability to *process* such information. They highlight the spread of credit score cards and other statistical tools lenders employ to assess riskiness of potential borrowers (see Barron and Staten (2003), Berger (2003), and Evans and Schmalensee (1999) for a deeper discussion).[17] These new technologies have been enabled by the rapidly declining costs of computing and data storage. Livshits *et al.* (2015) model the costs of processing information as a cost of designing a contract in the model (corresponding to developing a specific credit card product, for example). This mechanism (as well as the ones discussed above, as a matter of fact) is thus consistent not only with the basic macro-level observations of higher debt and bankruptcy rates, but also with additional empirical evidence of greater dispersion of interest rates (see Livshits *et al.*, 2011; Athreya *et al.*, 2012) and more accurate risk-based pricing of unsecured debt (see Edelberg, 2006). While the basic story may have implications for the intensive margin of borrowing, Livshits *et al.* (2015) choose to concentrate on the extensive margin, the "democratization of credit," which arises from lenders' choosing to develop credit products for higher risk categories of borrowers, the credit products that generate relatively little surplus and were not profitable when the cost of designing contracts were high. Another paper where the extensive margin of the expansion of borrowing is present is Drozd and Nosal (2008), who consider a fall in lenders' costs of reaching a specific type of potential borrower, both in the data and in the context of a search model. A decline in the search friction leads to greater competition among lenders, a smaller transaction wedge in interest rates, and more borrowers getting loans.

Another information-based explanation has recently been advanced by Drozd and Serrano-Padial (2014) – they point to the IT advancements in the debt collection industry. Unlike the previous studies, which mostly focus on the improvement in the *ex ante* information available to lenders (based on which loans are advanced), this paper suggests that improvements in the *ex post* information regarding delinquent borrowers can have similar aggregate implications. Having better information (signals) about reasons for delinquency allows lenders to better target their collection efforts *ex post*, while still providing both the insurance against "distress" shocks to affected borrowers and the right incentives to repay the loans to the non-distressed borrowers. This greater *ex post* efficiency in collections improves the *ex ante* contractual environment and supports more loans *ex ante* (while still being consistent with a greater *ex post* bankruptcy rate).

5. Welfare Implications

One important commonality among all of these papers on the effects of IT improvements in the consumer credit market is that all of these information improvements lead to greater average welfare in the model economies, despite the fact that they all (by construction) lead to greater bankruptcy rates (see Livshits *et al.* (2015) and Athreya *et al.* (2012) for an explicit discussion of welfare gains).[18] How can more frequent default (typically thought of as failure) be associated with welfare improvements? This somewhat counter-intuitive result comes from models with rational (and sophisticated) borrowers and lenders realizing newly accessible gains from trade; and the *ex post* default is a foreseen consequence of the *ex ante* desirable arrangement in an incomplete market environment.[19] Deviating from the standard assumption can easily change the welfare assessment of these recent changes in the debt market – Nakajima (2013) shows that in a model with temptation preferences the rise in debt (and bankruptcy) can be driven by consumers' over-borrowing, and can thus be associated with welfare losses (and the calibrated version of the model does indeed imply a welfare loss arising from the relaxation of borrowing constraints).[20]

More generally, the welfare analysis in models of bankruptcy goes back to Zame (1993), who points out another key and possibly counter-intuitive result – more commitment does not necessarily make borrowers *ex ante* better off in models with incomplete markets. A more severe bankruptcy punishment, which provides borrowers with a greater level of commitment to future repayment, lowers their cost of borrowing and expands their endogenous credit limit, but it comes at a cost – it takes away from the bankruptcy's role as partial insurance against bad otherwise uninsurable shocks. The key tradeoff associated with bankruptcy regimes is then that between intertemporal consumption smoothing, which is improved under a strict bankruptcy regime, and intratemporal smoothing, which is facilitated somewhat by a lax bankruptcy code. Any policy recommendations have to come from a quantitative assessment of this tradeoff.

Not surprisingly then, the welfare assessments of bankruptcy regimes and reforms have been quite wide-ranging: In an Aiyagari (1994)-like endowment economy, Athreya (2002) finds "only modest" effects of means-testing in bankruptcy, but finds that eliminating the bankruptcy option altogether leads to a large welfare gain. On the other hand, Li and Sarte (2006) argue that accounting for general equilibrium effects in a model with production reverses this finding – they find that completely eliminating bankruptcy would lead to a significant welfare loss (though the effect of means-testing are also found to be small). Livshits *et al.* (2007) reformulate the question from entirely eliminating the default option to the choice of the basic bankruptcy regime – eliminating default altogether is simply not plausible in their model, since they introduce "expense shocks" that some borrowers are simply incapable of paying. Livshits *et al.* (2007) thus compare a "Fresh Start regime" representing the U.S. Chapter 7 bankruptcy with a European-style "No Fresh Start regime," in which defaulting borrowers cannot discharge their loans and remain liable for the debts indefinitely. They find that the welfare comparison between the two regimes is very sensitive to the exact nature and magnitude of the uncertainty faced by households. When the model is calibrated to the U.S. economy, the Fresh Start regime is (slightly) preferred from the *ex ante* perspective.[21] Chatterjee and Gordon (2012) do a similar exercise in a model with explicit garnishment and come to the opposite conclusion – they find that eliminating the Fresh Start option would be welfare improving. Chatterjee *et al.* (2007a) evaluate a bankruptcy reform that basically amounts to means-testing in their quantitative model and find that it can generate large welfare gains. Gordon (2014) also argues that a simple means-tested bankruptcy system is capable of generating large welfare gains. The reason for the large dispersion of findings comes not so much from the differences in the underlying exercise, but rather from the different parameterizations of the economies, as discussed in detail in Livshits *et al.* (2007). The findings are very sensitive not just to the relative magnitudes of the income uncertainty, the expense shocks, and the life-cycle borrowing motive, but also to the nature of income uncertainty – while a greater volatility of persistent income shocks makes the easy discharge option more attractive, a greater transitory income uncertainty swings the welfare comparison the other way, making loose bankruptcy regimes less attractive (since, unlike persistent income shocks, transitory shocks can be quite effectively smoothed across time).

The discussion of the welfare implications of personal bankruptcy regimes would be incomplete without mentioning the effects they have on entrepreneurs. Since entrepreneurs rely quite heavily on using personal wealth and personal loans to finance their businesses, the availability of personal bankruptcy is quite important to them (as is evidenced by the self-employed being over-represented among personal bankruptcy filers).[22] In fact, in what was probably the first quantitative assessment of a bankruptcy regime in a heterogeneous-agent macro model, Zha (2001) analyzed the effects of exemption levels on entrepreneurial financing (finding that some exemption can be welfare improving). More recently, key empirical contributions by Fan and White (2003), Berkowitz and White (2004), and Armour and Cumming (2008) have documented a positive relationship between leniency of the bankruptcy code and the level of entrepreneurial activity. This spurred a number of macroeconomics models which analyze the effect of bankruptcy code on occupational choice (of whether to become an entrepreneur), including Akyol and Athreya (2011), Herranz *et al.* (forthcoming), Jia (2015), Meh and Terajima (2008), and Mankart and Rodano (2012). In these papers, the familiar tradeoff (between the partial insurance *ex post* and the inability to commit to repayment that hampers borrowing *ex ante*) takes on a new dimension – it now affects an individual's decision to become an entrepreneur. The partial insurance provided by lax bankruptcy law makes entrepreneurship more attractive to the riskiest potential entrants (marginal entrepreneurs), thus generating an extensive margin effect. On the other hand, generous bankruptcy exemptions limit the ability of *all* entrepreneurs to commit to repaying their loans, thus possibly hampering financing of many inframarginal projects. Welfare evaluation can then depend not only on the assessment of the risk factors faced both by workers and entrepreneurs, but also on the relative importance of these extensive and intensive margins of entrepreneurial activity.

6. Delinquency, Informal Bankruptcy, Debt Restructuring, and Collection

Formal bankruptcy (Chapter 7 filings in the USA, more specifically) has been the focus of most of the papers discussed so far. Considering this subset of defaults has big advantages – the institutional framework is well-defined and rather well-understood, measurement is clear and rather precise (since filers have to inform the court about all their assets and income), and the event of default itself is clearly binary (the filing either took place or it didn't). But restricting attention to this formal bankruptcy procedure (and a specific chapter) misses a large share of defaults, as well as an important part of the interaction between lenders and distressed borrowers. Dawsey and Ausubel (2004) report that about half of all defaults (charge-offs, or credit losses) in their sample occurred without a bankruptcy being filed (and point to several surveys that put this estimate even higher). Within the formal bankruptcy system in the USA, about 30% of all bankruptcies are filed under Chapter 13, which involves a multi-year repayment plan, often fails, and thus, lacks the simple binary nature of Chapter 7 filings. But before a borrower ends up in a formal or informal bankruptcy, a rich set of options is available to both the distressed borrowers and their lenders. These may result in debt restructuring (or partial debt forgiveness) on the one hand or wage garnishment and asset seizure on the other hand. Or, of course, these may result in bankruptcy. Fortunately, these important interactions and other finer details of default are now subject of active and fruitful research.

The discussion of the various possible scenarios associated with distressed debt and default could be structured around the following event tree (you could almost think of this as an extensive form game). The first "stage" of default, the first sign of financial distress, is *delinquency*, which is defined as a borrower being late on a payment by X days, where X is typically 60, 90, or 120 days. Delinquency typically triggers some form of penalty, such as late fees or higher interest rates. But it is the lenders' response beyond the automatic contractual penalties that I will think of as the second "stage" of the default "game."

Lenders can respond to delinquency in a number of ways. First, they can do nothing and just wait for the borrower to pay back the loan with the additional charges and penalties. Such recoveries do indeed occur and are referred to as "self-cures." In the case of 60-day delinquent mortgages, Adelino *et al.* (2013) found that the "self-cure" rate was in excess of 60% in 2005–2006 (see also Herkenhoff and Ohanian (2012) for a nice summary of empirical facts regarding transitions of mortgages into and out of delinquencies). Second, at any point during delinquency, lenders can pursue collection efforts, which range from repeated phone calls to the borrower to obtaining court judgments allowing the lenders to garnishee the borrower's wages (the importance of debt collection is highlighted in Dawsey *et al.* (2009), Chatterjee and Gordon (2012), and Drozd and Serrano-Padial (2014)). The collections can be pursued by the original lender or "outsourced" to specialized collection agencies (which typically purchase distressed debt from lenders).[23] These third-party collection agencies are a rather large industry employing about 150,000 people in the USA, and that number does not include those involved in "in-house" collection efforts.[24] The collection efforts increase the overall recovery rates, but they risk driving a distressed borrower to bankruptcy (which is often referred to as bankruptcy *protection* as it protects filers from harassment by the lenders/collectors). Thus, lenders may choose to pursue yet another, third, approach – they may renegotiate the terms of the loan. This is referred to as debt restructuring or debt settlement.

Distressed borrowers, in turn, have a number of avenues open to them (in what could be thought of as the third "stage"). They can, of course, repay the debt, if their financial situation improves. This can mean honoring either the original debt contract or a restructured one, if such were offered by the lender in the previous stage. Second, borrowers can also "do nothing," and just put up with collectors' harassment and/or wage garnishment indefinitely, without ever going through the legal process of bankruptcy. This is referred to as informal bankruptcy. And last but not least, the borrowers have the option of declaring bankruptcy. But even the bankruptcy itself comes in two different flavors in North America. In the USA, filers can choose between Chapter 7 and Chapter 13.[25] The former is a rather straightforward and quick process of discharging debts (in which the borrower surrenders any non-exempt assets), which has been the focus of most papers in this survey.[26] On the other hand, Chapter 13 filing involves a 3- to 5-year repayment plan, but allows the borrower to keep her assets.[27] However, as Eraslan et al. (2007) document, Chapter 13 filings do not share the binary (and rather certain) nature of Chapter 7 filings – about a fifth of all Chapter 13 proposals are not approved by the court, and of those approved, more than half fail (that is, they do not ultimately lead to a discharge, typically due to borrowers missing their prescribed payments). And the recent empirical study by Dobbie and Song (2015) suggests that this added uncertainty is costly – the financial state of dismissed (i.e., unsuccessful) Chapter 13 filers deteriorates significantly.

With the basic framework of the "stages" of default in place, I will now highlight some of the contribution in the specific areas. I will begin with delinquency, which I prefer to think of as a transitory state of a distressed borrower, rather than an absorbing state of default or a radical fresh start afforded by Chapter 7 bankruptcy. In fact, Herkenhoff (2012) makes a compelling case that a delinquency can sometimes be thought of as a substitute to new loans, especially when such new loans are not available when they are needed most (following a job loss, for example, as discussed in Sullivan (2008)). This transitory view of delinquency is well captured in Chatterjee (2010), where "financial distress" is explicitly modeled as a period when the delinquent debtor is actively pursued by creditors, and when the debtor is choosing between the form of default (formal or informal) or repayment.

Some borrowers, however, never exit this state, neither recovering nor filing for bankruptcy. These are the "informal bankrupts." Dawsey and Ausubel (2004) should probably get credit both for coining the phrase "informal bankruptcy" and for bringing the phenomenon to the forefront of bankruptcy research. Dawsey and Ausubel (2004) study the choice between formal and informal bankruptcy, arguing that the two should be thought of as substitutes from borrowers' perspective (they nicely utilize cross-state variation in garnishment and exemption laws to make that point). Dawsey and Ausubel (2004) think of informal bankruptcy as an absorbing state, and Drozd and Serrano-Padial (2014) find some support for that view in their analysis of data from Experian – the long-term default state appears very persistent, with almost 80% of defaulters neither recovering nor filing for bankruptcy in a 2-year window. By "long-term defaulter" I am referring to those who have already been in default for 2 years, as opposed to newly delinquent borrowers. Though notably, in the data reported in Drozd and Serrano-Padial (2014), almost two-thirds of delinquent borrowers end up in this persistent default state (with the rest roughly equally split between formal bankruptcy and recovery) after 2 years. This finding is in marked contrast with the high "self-cure" rates reported in Adelino et al. (2013) for roughly the same period. Notably though, they apply to different types of debt – while Adelino et al. (2013) are concerned with mortgages, Drozd and Serrano-Padial (2014) are looking at credit card debt.

Lastly, I want to highlight the recent literature on debt restructuring (i.e., renegotiation of debt contracts between borrowers and lenders). Kovrijnykh and Livshits (2015) offer a theoretical model where delinquency, debt restructuring, and bankruptcy all arise with positive probability in an optimal screening mechanism that deals with a single adverse selection friction – the lender cannot observe the borrower's income.[28] Benjamin and Mateos-Planas (2012) and Athreya *et al.* (2012) propose quantitative models (with symmetric information) where delinquency, debt renegotiation, and bankruptcy are also present. In Benjamin and Mateos-Planas (2012), renegotiation occurs with an exogenously given probability upon delinquency, and this possibility of renegotiation leads to an endogenous distinction between delinquency and bankruptcy. In Athreya *et al.* (2012), delinquency also triggers debt restructuring, but deterministically so. The coexistence of bankruptcy and delinquency in Athreya *et al.* (2012) arises from the fact that, unlike bankruptcy filers, delinquent borrowers are subject to income garnishment. Athreya *et al.* (2012) can thus study how borrowers select into the two forms of default, and find that delinquency is often used by borrowers with the worst labor income shocks (which is very consistent with the basic idea in Herkenhoff (2012)).

7. The Cyclical Behavior of Credit and Bankruptcy

One aspect of bankruptcy and consumer debt that has received relatively little attention until recently is their cyclical properties. Yet, the cyclicality of bankruptcy is very pronounced – filings are strongly counter-cyclical (go up during recessions) and volatile. The same holds true for the charge-off rate. The picture is less clear-cut when it comes to consumer debt in the USA. Until the 1990s, consumer debt exhibited a clearly pro-cyclical behavior – it increased in expansions and contracted during recessions. That pattern was broken in the 1990s, when debt did not decline during recessions. But the pattern seems to have resumed in the new millennium, with debt rising during the expansion and shrinking during the Great Recession. See Fieldhouse *et al.* (2014) for a detailed macro-level data discussion. Exploiting regional variation, Agarwal and Liu (2003), Garrett and Wall (2014), and Fieldhouse *et al.* (2012) document similar trends – bankruptcies and delinquencies increase during recessions and, more specifically, increase with unemployment rates.[29]

The standard quantitative models of bankruptcy with the usual parameterizations of income shocks over the cycle have struggled to reproduce the key macro observations. The model in Nakajima and Ríos-Rull (2005) generates pro-cyclical filings (and pro-cyclical debt), while the model in Fieldhouse *et al.* (2014) generates counter-cyclical debt (but counter-cyclical filings). Both models fail to reproduce the large volatility of filings observed in the data. The problem is rather fundamental – if debt is used to smooth negative income shocks, and the negative income shocks are more prevalent during recessions, then consumer debt should be counter-cyclical (and it is in the model, but not in the data).

One explanation for the pro-cyclicality of consumer debt is that it could be used to finance (pro-cyclical) purchases of consumer durables. For example, Iacoviello (2008) and Iacoviello and Pavan (2013) generate pro-cyclical debt in a model with housing. But that mechanism should mostly affect secured, rather than unsecured debt; yet, unsecured debt seems to have the same pro-cyclical pattern. Another alternative, suggested by Luzzetti and Neumuller (2015) (who also point out the inability of the standard model to match the cyclical observations), is assuming that both borrowers and lenders use adaptive learning to form expectations about the future.[30] This departure from rational expectations generates a boom-bust cycle in consumer debt and increases volatility of bankruptcies. Lastly, a rather mechanical alternative resorted to in Fieldhouse *et al.* (2014) is a "financial intermediation shock," which increases the risk-free interest rate (e.g., through an increase in transaction cost of making loans) during recessions.

A very recent paper by Nakajima and Ríos-Rull (2014) seems to have overcome the most basic challenge in a much more satisfactory fashion. The model generates counter-cyclical and volatile filings, as well as pro-cyclical debt, without relying on any non-standard assumptions or exogenous variation in model parameters (besides those governing the idiosyncratic income uncertainty, of course). Two forces are the key to this success. The first is the assumption about the income process over the business cycle, which the authors refer to as "counter-cyclical earnings risk" – recessions are associated with increased risk of very bad earnings shocks. The second key force is the response of the pricing of debt (the lending standards) to the recession. Increased earnings risk in a recession leads to much higher risk-premia demanded by lenders, and thus to a contraction of consumer debt (and yet greater filing volatility due to the inability of some borrowers to roll over their existing loans).

The cyclical behavior of consumer debt and bankruptcies is much more than just a testing ground for the quantitative models. Gordon (forthcoming) makes a compelling argument that explicitly modeling aggregate fluctuations is essential for the welfare analysis of bankruptcy policy. And the bankruptcy model, in turn, can inform our understanding of the driving forces of the business cycle, as Athreya *et al.* (forthcoming) aptly demonstrate in the case of the Great Recession.

8. Challenges Going Forward

In closing, I want to highlight what I see as the key challenges and promising directions of research related to personal bankruptcy and credit.

One key challenge that I don't think has been successfully addressed yet is modeling a consumer credit market where borrowers deal with multiple lenders. All of the papers discussed in this survey assume exclusive relations in debt, i.e., that a borrower can only accept credit from a single lender. There is a very good technical reason for this assumption – the alternative generates a very unpleasant (and rather unsatisfactory) prediction of debt dilution. As Bizer and DeMarzo (1992) clearly establish, in the absence of exclusivity, equilibrium allocation involves sub-optimally large levels of borrowing and very high default rates, as any other allocation with actuarially fair pricing would be diluted by an additional loan with an additional lender. Some of the debt dilution is clearly present – pay-day loans are a prime example of a diluting lender (see Skiba and Tobacman, 2011). Yet, the reality is hardly as gloomy as the theory (Bizer and DeMarzo, 1992) would suggest. Cooperation of lenders (facilitated by credit reporting agencies) could certainly be a factor, but it would presumably require a deal of cartel-like behavior. Of course, borrowers would be happy to avoid the debt dilution problem by committing to dealing with a single lender, but such commitment is hardly available.

One possible approach to model borrowers' interactions with multiple lenders could be a search model, like the one used in Drozd and Nosal (2008). Though admittedly, pay-day loans and other ways of diluting one's debt are not that hard to find; and it could be argued that search frictions are becoming less relevant. On the other hand, the search model of Drozd and Nosal (2008) has another nice feature – it generates a meaningful distinction between credit lines (limits on how much can be borrowed) and amounts of outstanding debt. Most models in this literature forego this distinction entirely. Notably, the search model is not the only way to model this distinction. One can think of the credit lines as commitments on the part of the lender – see Mateos-Planas (2013) and Mateos-Planas and Ríos-Rull (2009). Note also that either way of modeling the longer-term relations between borrowers and lenders (which is essential for thinking about credit lines) could have major implications for the analysis of the unsecured credit market. One important example is the thesis of Athreya *et al.* (2009) that the unsecured credit market is not very effective at smoothing income shocks as borrowing terms are at their worst exactly when a borrower needs the loan the most. Credit lines (or other commitments of a lender) could thus drastically alter the way we think of the consumer credit market.[31]

Lastly, I want to point to yet another promising direction of research – explicitly combining secured and unsecured debt in a quantitative model. It is certainly more computationally demanding than modeling the two types of debt separately, but the interaction between the two forms of debt can be non-trivial and important (as perhaps best illustrated by Mitman (2014)). The first batch of bankruptcy models with multiple assets was used to study the effects of asset exemptions in bankruptcy (thus, requiring co-existence of assets and debts). These include Athreya (2006), Pavan (2008), and Mankart (2014). More recently, several papers, including Li and White (2009), Li *et al.* (2011), Luzzetti and Neumuller (2014a), and Mitman (2014), have investigated the relation between bankruptcy and mortgage defaults.

Acknowledgements

The views expressed herein are those of the author and not necessarily those of the Federal Reserve Bank of Philadelphia or the Federal Reserve System. Comments from Viktar Fedaseyeu, Jim MacGee, Makoto Nakajima, and three anonymous referees have been instrumental in improving this survey.

Notes

1. Moreover, some countries that did not have personal bankruptcy systems were compelled to introduce one in that period. Germany, for example, introduced personal bankruptcy in 1999. Until then, borrowers unable to repay their loans ("overindebted" borrowers) in Germany remained liable to the lenders indefinitely.
2. See White (2007) for an excellent summary.
3. I should note that Zame (1993) attributed the basic model to Dubey *et al.* (2005), which had been circulated as a working paper in 1988.
4. Fieldhouse *et al.* (2012) provide a rather detailed picture of the characteristics of filers (and how they change over a business cycle) using the administrative dataset of Canadian filers between 2007 and 2011.
5. Note that these studies focus on the revolving debt, i.e., credit cards. More generally, the bankruptcy literature has been largely concerned with just the unsecured household debt, rather than total household debt (thus abstracting from mortgages and other secured loans). This is typically justified by the fact that unsecured loans are simply discharged in bankruptcy, while secured loans can only be eliminated at the cost of losing the collateral. By the same logic, students loans, which are not dischargeable in the U.S. bankruptcy system, are also often abstracted from. Within the unsecured debt, credit cards have become the dominant form of debt (see Livshits *et al.*, 2010), and thus, the focus on the revolving debt is fairly natural.
6. Kehoe and Levine (2006) argue against this basic observation (and their own statements in Kehoe and Levine (2001)) and claim that "complete contingent claims [in Kehoe and

Levine (2001)] are, in practice, . . . implemented not through Arrow securities, but rather through a combination of non-contingent assets and bankruptcy."

7. The assumption of the (exogenous) market incompleteness is often justified by referring to some underlying informational frictions, like costly state verification in Townsend (1979) and Gale and Hellwig (1985), which generate "standard debt contracts," which basically amount to non-contingent debt with a "verification" or "punishment" (as in Diamond (1984)) regions of state space that loosely correspond to default or bankruptcy states. Grochulski (2010) explicitly demonstrates that bankruptcy which involves some discharge of unsecured debt is part of a market implementation of an optimal allocation that is subject to moral hazard on the part of the borrower. Hopenhayn and Werning (2008) show that an optimal contract involves default in equilibrium when the value of default to the borrower is random and unobserved by the lender. Also along these lines is the finding of Krasa and Villamil (2000) that the optimal contract between an investor and an entrepreneur in a no-commitment environment with costly enforcement is a standard debt contract. Most of the papers discussed in this survey (with the notable exception of the papers discussed in Section 4 and Kovrijnykh and Livshits (2015)) do not explicitly model the underlying informational frictions, and simply take the incompleteness of the market as exogenous. Similarly, the bankruptcy option *per se* is also taken as an exogenously specified (institutional) alternative, and is not derived as part of an optimal arrangement.

8. One additional assumption that is key to generating this result is the exclusivity of the borrower–lender relation. If a borrower is able to borrow from multiple lenders at the same time (or sequentially), an externality arises, that I will refer to as debt dilution, and which is discussed in Section 8.

9. The mechanism is also present in Krueger and Perri (2006), who offer a quantitative assessment of an increase in income uncertainty in both an incomplete market economy, and an economy with enforcement frictions.

10. While the bankruptcy papers discussed in this section view securitization as a way of lowering the cost of funds for the lenders, empirical literature on mortgages points to another important effect of securitization, which could have led to an increase in bankruptcies. Keys *et al.* (2010) offer compelling evidence that lenders are less careful in their screening of borrowers when the loans are securitized (and that this shirking leads to more defaults). Loutskina and Strahan (2011) point to a similar effect of geographic diversification of lenders' portfolios – diversified lenders do not screen as carefully as those who are geographically specialized.

11. This increased willingness of lenders to overlook a past bankruptcy can in turn be a result of the improvements in the quality of information available to them (as discussed in the next section).

12. While the stigma is inherently difficult to measure, the bankruptcy spillovers documented in Scholnick (2013) and Dick *et al.* (2008) (though evidence is somewhat mixed in the latter) can be viewed as evidence of the presence of stigma or informational cascades. Note that the informational cascades (of borrowers learning about bankruptcy by observing others filing) are bundled with stigma both from a model standpoint and empirically – the two stories are rather indistinguishable in the data.

13. One reason why Sullivan *et al.* (2000) found demographics important is that they attributed the contribution of the overall population growth to the rise in the *number* of bankruptcies to the demographic component. Of course, the overall population growth had no effect on the bankruptcy *rate*.

14. Note, however, that Dobbie and Skiba (2013) do not find evidence of adverse selection in their study of payday lending.
15. I think that this type of a model can actually serve as a basis for modeling endogenous stigma of bankruptcy. In the absence of other information, an observation of default is given a lot of weight in the calculation of the credit score, and the informational cost (stigma) of default is high. As other sources of information become available, a single event of default becomes less important in lenders' calculations, and the stigma of default falls. This is further amplified by the fact that more "low-risk type" borrowers now choose to file for bankruptcy, further diluting the default signal. An alternative, though related, idea of "stigma" is present in Chatterjee *et al.* (2008), where a default on an unsecured loan reveals something about the borrower's type in an insurance market.
16. The challenge here is to prevent a "cream skimming" deviation by a competing lender, which would only be preferred to the pooling allocation for the "good" type of borrower, thus destroying pooling as an equilibrium. Hellwig (1987) introduced a timing assumption, which allows a lender offering a pooling contract to exit if a cream-skimming contract is observed (it nicely formalizes the idea of Wilson (1977) to put some added discipline on the potential deviations).
17. A similar development in the auto financing market is documented by Einav *et al.* (2013).
18. Of course, if informational frictions have become more severe, as suggested by Keys *et al.* (2010) and Loutskina and Strahan (2011), the growth in debt and bankruptcies may not have been welfare improving overall.
19. Athreya (2001) is one of the few papers to argue that the rise in debt and bankruptcy are associated with welfare losses, based on the premise that the bankruptcy code was too lax, and having access to the debt market made low-income people worse off due to their inability to commit to repaying the loans. More recently, MacGee (2012) has made a point that, while larger consumer debt balances (in Canada) are not detrimental *per se*, they may make borrowers (and the financial system) more vulnerable to aggregate shocks, especially ones associated with sharp increases in interest rates.
20. The finding that the increased indebtedness is associated with welfare losses is also present in Nakajima (2012), where an exogenous relaxation of the borrowing constraints leads to more over-borrowing.
21. In an earlier version of the paper, Livshits *et al.* (2003), the authors also analyzed an alternative calibration of the model that matched key observations in Germany, and found that the No Fresh Start regime was (slightly) preferred in that environment.
22. Key empirical papers documenting the relation between bankruptcy codes and levels of entrepreneurship include Fan and White (2003), Berkowitz and White (2004), and Armour and Cumming (2008).
23. The prevalence of the outsourcing of collections is somewhat surprising, given that the third-party collectors face many more legal restrictions than the originating lenders. Fedaseyeu and Hunt (2014) attempt to explain this rather puzzling observation.
24. See Fedaseyeu (2011), Fedaseyeu and Hunt (2014), Hunt (2007), and Drozd and Serrano-Padial (2014) for more details about the debt collection industry.
25. In Canada, insolvent borrowers have a similar choice – between "bankruptcy," which is the counterpart of the U.S. Chapter 7 bankruptcy, and "consumer proposal," which resembles the U.S. Chapter 13 process. Both alternatives are part of the same legal structure, just as they are in the USA, and both are administered by the same trustees.

26. Following BAPCPA reform of 2005, some high-income borrowers in the USA are no longer eligible for Chapter 7 filings. This only applies to the subset of borrowers whose income is above the state median, and who meet a further "means test" classifying their filing under Chapter 7 as "presumptively abusive."

27. While this basically amounts to a court-imposed restructuring of debt payments, I will reserve the term "debt restructuring" for the voluntary response of the lenders mentioned in the previous paragraph.

28. In an earlier version of the paper, the unobservable characteristic of the borrower was her idiosyncratic bankruptcy cost (or in the case of mortgages, the borrower's personal valuation of the house).

29. Using an administrative dataset of Canadian filers between 2007 and 2011, Fieldhouse *et al.* (2012) provide additional evidence about the changing characteristics of filers during the last recession – there are more filers with "middle class characteristics" during the economic downturn. That is, filers during the recession were slightly older, more educated, more likely to own a home.

30. This adaptive learning is explicitly tied to (backward-looking) credit scoring in Luzzetti and Neumuller (2014b).

31. It could also change the way we think of the welfare implications of increased competition among the lenders or simply lower entry cost for lenders. Rather than increasing efficiency, it could undermine these important long-term relationships, especially if borrowers lack commitment not to exploit newly arriving opportunities to take on additional loans.

References

Adelino, M., Gerardi, K. and Willen, P. (2013) Why don't lenders renegotiate more home mortgages? Redefaults, self-cures and securitization. *Journal of Monetary Economics* 60(7): 835–853.

Agarwal, S. and Liu, C. (2003) Determinants of credit card delinquency and bankruptcy: macroeconomic factors. *Journal of Economics and Finance* 27(1): 75–84.

Agarwal, S., Chomsisengphet, S. and Liu, C. (2010) The importance of adverse selection in the credit card market: evidence from randomized trials of credit card solicitations. *Journal of Money, Credit and Banking* 42(4): 743–754.

Aiyagari, S.R. (1994) Uninsurable idiosyncratic risk and aggregate savings. *Quarterly Journal of Economics* 109(3): 659–684.

Akyol, A. and Athreya, K. (2011) Credit and self-employment. *Journal of Economic Dynamics and Control* 35(3): 363–385.

Alvarez, F. and Jermann, U.J. (2000) Efficiency, equilibrium, and asset pricing with risk of default. *Econometrica* 68(4): 775–797.

Armour, J. and Cumming, D.J. (2008) Bankruptcy law and entrepreneurship. *American Law and Economics Review* 10(2): 303–350.

Athreya, K. (2001) The growth of unsecured credit: are we better off? *Economic Quarterly* 87(3): 11–33.

Athreya, K. (2002) Welfare implications of the bankruptcy reform act of 1999. *Journal of Monetary Economics* 49: 1567–1595.

Athreya, K. (2004) Shame as it ever was: stigma and personal bankruptcy. *Federal Reserve Bank of Richmond Economic Quarterly* 90(2): 1–19.

Athreya, K. (2005) Equilibrium models of personal bankruptcy: a survey. *Federal Reserve Bank of Richmond Economic Quarterly* 91(2): 73–98.

Athreya, K. (2006) Fresh start or head start? Uniform bankruptcy exemptions and welfare. *Journal of Economic Dynamics and Control* 30: 2051–2079.

Athreya, K., Sanchez, J.M., Tam, X.S. and Young, E.R. (2012) Bankruptcy and delinquency in a model of unsecured debt. Federal Reserve Bank of St. Louis Working Paper 2012-042B.

Athreya, K., Sanchez, J.M., Tam, X.S. and Young, E.R. (2015) Labor market upheaval, default regulations, and consumer debt. *Review of Economic Dynamics* 18(1): 32–52.

Athreya, K., Tam, X.S. and Young, E.R. (2009) Unsecured credit markets are not insurance markets. *Journal of Monetary Economics* 56(1): 83–103.

Athreya, K., Tam, X.S. and Young, E.R. (2012) A quantitative theory of information and unsecured credit. *American Economic Journal: Macroeconomics* 4(3): 153–183.

Ausubel, L. (1999) Adverse selection in the credit card market. University of Maryland Working Paper.

Baird, D.G. (2007) Technology, information and bankruptcy. *University of Illinois Law Review* 2007(1): 305–322.

Barron, J.M. and Staten, M. (2003) The value of comprehensive credit reports. In M.J. Miller (ed.), *Credit Reporting Systems and the International Economy* (pp. 273–310). MIT Press, Cambridge, MA, USA.

Barron, J.M., Elliehausen, G. and Staten, M.E. (2000) Monitoring the household sector with aggregate credit bureau data. *Business Economics* 35(1): 63–76.

Benjamin, D. and Mateos-Planas, X. (2012) Formal versus informal default in consumer credit. Mimeo, SUNY Buffalo.

Berger, A. (2003) The economic effects of technological progress: evidence from the banking industry. *Journal of Money, Credit and Banking* 35(2): 141–176.

Berkowitz, J. and White, M.J. (2004) Bankruptcy and small firms' access to credit. *RAND Journal of Economics* 35(1): 69–84.

Bird, E., Hagstrom, P. and Wild, R. (1999) Credit cards debts of the poor: high and rising. *Journal of Policy Analysis and Management* 18(1): 125–133.

Bizer, D.S. and DeMarzo, P.M. (1992) Sequential banking. *Journal of Political Economy* 100(1): 41–61.

Black, S. and Morgan, D. (1999) Meet the new borrowers. *Federal Reserve Bank of New York Current Issues in Economics and Finance* 5(3): 1–6.

Boyes, W. and Faith, R.L. (1986) Some effects of the Bankruptcy Reform Act of 1978. *Journal of Law and Economics* XXIX: 139–149.

Buckley, F. and Brinig, M.F. (1998) The bankruptcy puzzle. *The Journal of Legal Studies* XXVII: 187–207.

Chatterjee, S. (2010) An equilibrium model of the timing of bankruptcy filings. Mimeo, Federal Reserve Bank of Philadelphia.

Chatterjee, S. and Gordon, G. (2012) Dealing with consumer default: bankruptcy vs garnishment. *Journal of Monetary Economics* 59(S): S1–S16.

Chatterjee, S., Corbae, D. Nakajima M. and Ríos-Rull, J.-V. (2007a) A quantitative theory of unsecured consumer credit with risk of default. *Econometrica* 75(6): 1525–1589.

Chatterjee, S., Corbae, D. and Ríos-Rull, J.-V. (2007b) Credit scoring and competitive pricing of default risk. Mimeo, University of Texas.

Chatterjee, S., Corbae, D. and Ríos-Rull, J.-V. (2008) A finite-life private-information theory of unsecured debt. *Journal of Economic Theory* 142: 149–177.

Dawsey, A.E. and Ausubel, L.M. (2004) Informal bankruptcy. Mimeo, UNC Greensboro.

Dawsey, A.E., Hynes, R.M. and Ausubel, L.M. (2009) The regulation of non-judicial debt collection and the consumer's choice among repayment, bankruptcy and informal bankruptcy. John M. Olin Law and Economics Research Paper Series No. 2009-13.

Diamond, D.W. (1984) Financial intermediation and delegated monitoring. *Review of Economic Studies* 51(3): 393–414.

Dick, A. and Lehnert, A. (2010) Personal bankruptcy and credit market competition. *Journal of Finance* 65: 655–686.

Dick, A., Lehnert, A. and Topa, G. (2008) Social spillovers in personal bankruptcies. Mimeo, Federal Reserve Bank of New York.

Dobbie, W. and Skiba, P.M. (2013) Information asymmetries in consumer credit markets: evidence from payday lending. *American Economic Journal: Applied Economics* 5(4): 256–282.

Dobbie, W. and Song, J. (2015) Debt relief and debtor outcomes: measuring the effects of consumer bankruptcy protection. *American Economic Review* 105(3): 1272–1311.

Domowitz, I. and Sartain, R.L. (1999) Determinants of the consumer bankruptcy decision. *The Journal of Finance* 54(1): 403–420.

Drozd, L. and Nosal, J. (2008) Competing for customers: a search model of the market for unsecured credit. Mimeo, University of Wisconsin.

Drozd, L. and Serrano-Padial, R. (2014) Modeling the revolving revolution: the role of IT reconsidered. Mimeo.

Dubey, P., Geanakoplos, J. and Shubik, M. (2005) Default in a general equilibrium model with incomplete markets. *Econometrica* 73(1): 1–38.

Durkin, T.A. (2000) Credit cards: use and consumer attitudes, 1970–2000. *Federal Reserve Bulletin* pp. 623–634.

Eaton, J. and Gersovitz, M. (1981) Debt with potential repudiation: theoretical and empirical analysis. *Review of Economic Studies* 48(2): 289–309.

Edelberg, W. (2006) Risk-based pricing of interest rates for consumer loans. *Journal of Monetary Economics* 53(8): 2283–2298.

Einav, L., Jenkins, M. and Levin, J. (2013) The impact of credit scoring on consumer lending. *RAND Journal of Economics* 44(2): 249–274.

Ellis, D. (1998) The effect of consumer interest rate deregulation on credit card volumes, charge-offs and the personal bankruptcy rate. *FDIC Bank Trends* 98(5).

Eraslan, H., Li, W. and Sarte, P.-D. (2007) The anatomy of U.S. personal bankruptcy under Chapter 13. Federal Reserve Bank of Richmond Working Paper 07-05.

Evans, D.S. and Schmalensee, R. (1999) *Paying with Plastic: The Digital Revolution in Buying and Borrowing*. Cambridge, MA: MIT Press.

Fan, W. and White, M.J. (2003) Personal bankruptcy and the level of entrepreneurial activity. *Journal of Law and Economics* 46: 543–568.

Fay, S., Hurst, E. and White, M.J. (2002) The household bankruptcy decision. *American Economic Review* 92(3): 706–718.

Fedaseyeu, V. (2011) Debt collection agencies and the supply of consumer credit. Mimeo, Bocconi University Working Paper 442.

Fedaseyeu, V. and Hunt, R. (2014) The economics of debt collection: enforcement of consumer credit contracts. Mimeo, Federal Reserve Bank of Philadelphia Working Paper No. 14-7.

Fieldhouse, D., Livshits, I. and MacGee, J. (2012) Income loss and bankruptcies over the business cycle. Insolvency Research Paper, Office of the Superintendent of Bankruptcy Canada.

Fieldhouse, D., Livshits, I. and MacGee, J. (2014) Aggregate fluctuations, consumer credit and bankruptcy. Working Paper, University of Western Ontario.

Gale, D. and Hellwig, M. (1985) Incentive-compatible debt contracts: the one-period problem. *Review of Economic Studies* 52: 647–663.

Garrett, T. and Wall, H. (2014) Personal-bankruptcy cycles. *Macroeconomic Dynamics* 18(7): 1488–1507.

Gordon, G. (2014) Optimal bankruptcy code: a fresh start for some. CAEPR Working Papers 2014-002, Indiana University Bloomington.

Gordon, G. (forthcoming) Evaluating default policy: the business cycle matters. *Quantitative Economics*.

Grochulski, B. (2010) Optimal personal bankruptcy design under moral hazard. *Review of Economic Dynamics* 13: 350–378.

Gross, D.B. and Souleles, N.S. (2002) An empirical analysis of personal bankruptcy and delinquency. *The Review of Financial Studies* 15(1): 319–347.

Hacker, J.S. (2006) *The Great Risk Shift*. Oxford University Press, New York.

Han, S., Keys, B.J. and Li, G. (2013) Unsecured credit supply over the credit cycle: evidence from credit card mailings. Mimeo, Federal Reserve Board Finance and Economics Discussion Paper No. 2011-29.

Hellwig, M. (1987) Some recent developments in the theory of competition in markets with adverse selection. *European Economic Review* 31: 319–325.

Herkenhoff, K.F. (2012) Informal unemployment insurance and labor market dynamics. Federal Reserve Bank of St. Louis Working Paper 2012-057.

Herkenhoff, K.F. and Ohanian, L.E. (2012) Foreclosure delay and U.S. unemployment. Federal Reserve Bank of St. Louis Working Paper 2012-017.

Herranz, N., Krasa, S. and Villamil, A.P. (forthcoming) Entrepreneurs, risk aversion and dynamic firms. *Journal of Political Economy*.

Hopenhayn, H. and Werning, I. (2008) Equilibrium default. Mimeo, MIT.

Hunt, R.M. (2007) Collecting consumer debt in America. *Federal Reserve Bank of Philadelphia Business Review*, pp. 11–24.

Iacoviello, M. (2008) Household debt and income inequality, 1963–2003. *Journal of Money, Credit and Banking* 40(5): 929–965.

Iacoviello, M. and Pavan, M. (2013) Housing and debt over the life cycle and over the business cycle. *Journal of Monetary Economics* 60(2): 221–238.

Jia, Y. (2015) The impact of personal bankruptcy law on entrepreneurship. *Canadian Journal of Economics* 48(2).

Kehoe, T.J. and Levine, D.K. (1993) Debt constrained asset markets. *Review of Economic Studies* 60(4): 865–888.

Kehoe, T.J. and Levine, D.K. (2001) Liquidity constrained markets versus debt constrained markets. *Econometrica* 69(3): 575–598.

Kehoe, T.J. and Levine, D.K. (2006) Bankruptcy and collateral in debt constrained markets. Federal Reserve Bank of Minneapolis Staff Report 380.

Keys, B.J., Mukherjee, T., Seru, A. and Vig, V. (2010) Did securitization lead to lax screening? Evidence from subprime loans. *Quarterly Journal of Economics* 125(1): 307–362.

Kocherlakota, N.R. (1996) Implications of efficient risk sharing without commitment. *Review of Economic Studies* 63(4): 595–609.

Kovrijnykh, N. and Livshits, I. (2015) Screening as a unified theory of delinquency, renegotiation and bankruptcy. Mimeo, Arizona State University.

Krasa, S. and Villamil, A. (2000) Optimal contracts when enforcement is a decision variable. *Econometrica* 68: 119–134.

Krasa, S., Sharma, T. and Villamil, A. (2008) Bankruptcy and firm finance. *Economic Theory* 36: 239–266.

Krueger, D. and Perri, F. (2006) Does income inequality lead to consumption inequality? Evidence and theory. *Review of Economic Studies* 73(1): 163–193.

Leland, H.E. (1968) Saving and uncertainty: the precautionary demand for saving. *Quarterly Journal of Economics* 82(3): 465–473.

Li, W. and Sarte, P.-D. (2006) U.S. consumer bankruptcy choice: the importance of general equilibrium effects. *Journal of Monetary Economics* 53(3): 613–631.

Li, W. and White, M.J. (2009) Mortgage default, foreclosure, and bankruptcy. NBER Working Paper 15472.

Li, W., White, M.J. and Zhu, N. (2011) Did bankruptcy reform cause mortgage defaults to rise? *American Economic Journal: Economic Policy* 3(4): 123–147.

Livshits, I., MacGee, J. and Tertilt, M. (2003) Consumer bankruptcy: a fresh start. Federal Reserve Bank of Minneapolis Working Paper 617.

Livshits, I., MacGee, J. and Tertilt, M. (2007) Consumer bankruptcy: a fresh start. *American Economic Review* 97(1): 402–418.

Livshits, I., MacGee, J. and Tertilt, M. (2010) Accounting for the rise in consumer bankruptcies. *American Economic Journal Macroeconomics* 2: 165–193.

Livshits, I., MacGee, J. and Tertilt, M. (2011) Costly contracts and consumer credit. NBER Working Paper 17448.

Livshits, I., MacGee, J. and Tertilt, M. (2015) The democratization of credit and the rise in consumer bankruptcies. Mimeo, University of Western Ontario.

Loutskina, E. and Strahan, P.E. (2011) Informed and uninformed investment in housing: the downside of diversification. *Review of Financial Studies* 24(5): 1447–1480.

Luckett, C. (2002) Personal bankruptcies. In T. Durkin and M. Staten (eds.), *The Impact of Public Policy on Consumer Credit* (pp. 69–102). Springer US.

Luzzetti, M.N. and Neumuller, S. (2014a) Bankruptcy reform and the housing crisis. SSRN Working Paper.

Luzzetti, M.N. and Neumuller, S. (2014b) The impact of credit scoring on credit spreads and consumption over the business cycle. SSRN Working Paper.

Luzzetti, M.N. and Neumuller, S. (2015) Learning and the dynamics of unsecured consumer debt and bankruptcies. SSRN Working Paper.

MacGee, J. (2012) The rise in consumer credit and bankruptcy: cause for concern? Commentary No. 346, C.D. Howe Institute.

Mankart, J. (2014) The (Un-) importance of Chapter 7 wealth exemption levels. *Journal of Economic Dynamics and Control* 38: 1–16.

Mankart, J. and Rodano, G. (2012) Personal Bankruptcy Law, Debt Portfolios, and Entrepreneurship. Mimeo, University of St. Gallen.

Mann, R.J. (2006) *Charging Ahead: The Growth and Regulation of Payment Card Markets*. Cambridge University Press, Cambridge UK.

Mateos-Planas, X. (2013) Credit limits and bankruptcy. *Economics Letters* 121: 469–472.

Mateos-Planas, X. and Ríos-Rull, J.-V. (2009) Credit lines. Mimeo, University of Southampton.

Meh, C. and Terajima, Y. (2008) Unsecured debt, consumer bankruptcy, and small business. Bank of Canada Working Paper No. 2008-5.

Mehra, R., Piguillem, F. and Prescott, E.C. (2011) Costly financial intermediation in neoclassical growth theory. *Quantitative Economics* 2(1): 1–36.

Mitman, K. (2014) Macroeconomic effects of bankruptcy and foreclosure policies. University of Pennsylvania Working Paper.

Moss, D.A. and Johnson, G.A. (1999) The rise of consumer bankruptcy: evolution, revolution or both? *American Bankruptcy Law Journal* 73: 311–352.

Musto, D.K. (2004) What happens when information leaves a market? Evidence from post-bankruptcy consumers. *Journal of Business* 77(4): 725–749.

Nakajima, M. (2012) Rising indebtedness and temptation: a welfare analysis. *Quantitative Economics* 3(2): 257–288.

Nakajima, M. (2013) A tale of two commitments: equilibrium default and temptation. Federal Reserve Bank of Philadelphia Working Paper 14-1.

Nakajima, M. and Ríos-Rull, J.-V. (2005) Default and aggregate fluctuations in storage economies. In T.J. Kehoe, T.N. Srinivasan and J. Whalley (eds.), *Frontiers in Applied General Equilibrium Modelling: In Honor of Herbert Scarf*. Cambridge University Press, Cambridge UK.

Nakajima, M. and Ríos-Rull, J.-V. (2014) Credit, bankruptcy and aggregate fluctuations. NBER Working Paper 20617.

Narajabad, B.N. (2012) Information technology and the rise of household bankruptcy. *Review of Economic Dynamics* 15(4): 526–550.

Pavan, M. (2008) Consumer durables and risky borrowing: the effects of bankruptcy protection. *Journal of Monetary Economics* 55(8): 1441–1456.

Rothschild, M. and Stiglitz, J. (1976) Equilibrium in competitive insurance markets: an essay on the economics of imperfect information. *Quarterly Journal of Economics* 90: 629–650.

Sanchez, J. (2010) The IT revolution and the unsecured credit market. Federal Reserve Bank of St. Louis Working Paper 2010-022A.

Scholnick, B. (2013) Bankruptcy spillovers between close neighbors. Mimeo, University of Alberta.

Shepard, L. (1984) Personal failures and the Bankruptcy Reform Act of 1978. *Journal of Law and Economics* XXVII: 419–437.

Skiba, P.M. and Tobacman, J. (2011) Do payday loans cause bankruptcy? Vanderbilt University Law School Working Paper.

SMR Research (1997) The Personal bankruptcy crisis: demographics, causes, implications, & solutions. SMR Research, Hackettstown, New Jersey.

Sullivan, J.X. (2008) Borrowing during unemployment: unsecured debt as a safety net. *Journal of Human Resources* 43(2): 383–412.

Sullivan, T.A., Warren, E. and Westbrook, J.L. (2000) *The Fragile Middle Class.* New Haven and London: Yale University Press.

Townsend, R.M. (1979) Optimal contracts and competitive markets with costly state verification. *Journal of Economic Theory* 21(2): 265–293.

Warren, E., Sullivan, T.A., and Jacoby, M.B. (2000) Medical problems and bankruptcy filings. *Norton Bankruptcy Law Advisor* 5(5): 1–12.

Warren, E. and Tyagi, A.W. (2003) *The Two Income Trap: Why Middle-Class Mothers & Fathers Are Going Broke (With Surprising Solutions That Will Change Our Children's Futures).* New York: Basic Books.

White, M. (2007) Bankruptcy reform and credit cards. NBER Working Paper No. 13265.

Wilson, C. (1977) A model of insurance markets with incomplete information. *Journal of Economic Theory* 16: 167–207.

Zame, W.R. (1993) Efficiency and the role of default when security markets are incomplete. *American Economic Review* 83(5): 1142–1164.

Zha, T. (2001) Bankruptcy law, capital allocation, and aggregate effects: a dynamic heterogeneous agent model with incomplete markets. *Annals of Economics and Finance* 2: 379–400.

3

STUDENT DEBT EFFECTS ON FINANCIAL WELL-BEING: RESEARCH AND POLICY IMPLICATIONS

William Elliott and Melinda Lewis

School of Social Welfare,University of Kansas

1. Introduction

According to Shapiro, the American Dream "is the promise that those who work equally hard will reap roughly equal rewards" (Shapiro, 2004, p. 87); that is, the American Dream holds that this country is a meritocracy where effort and ability are the primary determinants of success. Institutions provide the economic conditions that make it possible for people to believe that their hard work and ability will determine their success or failure. This task is facilitated by Americans' strong desire to feel as though their destiny can be controlled and that institutions will "echo" their own contributions, rather than work against them. Primed to look for evidence of this "effort plus ability equals outcomes" equation, Americans cling to this ideal, even as it recedes in reality for many. Today, while there is no evidence that Americans are less capable or less committed than in previous generations, the highly specialized, technology-driven, global context makes the upward mobility that animates the American Dream only possible if effort and ability are combined with institutional might. Paramount among the institutions charged with facilitating this ascension is higher education, yet, today, there are serious questions about the extent to which the organization and, especially, the finance of post-secondary studies, are consistent with these aims.

Post-Great Recession, Americans are surrounded by examples of unsupportive institutions and the crumbling aspirations of those whose effort and ability have failed to yield advancement. These adverse conditions are not just constraining financial progress; they imperil the very foundation of the American Dream. Today, a majority of Americans (63%) no longer believe American institutions are able to facilitate children being better off than their parents (Luhby, 2014). Instead of aspiring to economic mobility, many now hope only for financial security – not dreaming of getting ahead but striving not to fall behind. While some Americans display tremendous capacity to hope against all hope, the average person requires grounds for

A Collection of Surveys on Savings and Wealth Accumulation, First Edition. Edited by Edda Claus and Iris Claus.
Chapters © 2016 The Authors. Book compilation © 2016 John Wiley & Sons, Ltd. Published 2016 by John Wiley & Sons, Ltd.

believing that achieving the American Dream is possible. In this sense, belief in the American Dream as it relates to one's own life is more malleable than the vague ideal one might hold for the country; it can and does readily change depending on one's economic context. This suggests that people see the American Dream as more or less achievable in their own lives based largely on how institutions like the education system, labor market, economic markets, and education system are functioning for them (Hochschild and Scovronick, 2003).

The significance of the education system, in particular, in sustaining the American Dream cannot be overstated. Americans' understanding of "effort and ability" features educational attainment prominently, particularly the higher education widely understood to correlate with superior employment and earnings prospects and, then, upward mobility. Here, too, though, the aspirations of a generation of young people are colliding with the economic realities they confront, contributing to the shaky foundation on which the American Dream stands today. While it is clear that it does pay to get an education, there is plenty of evidence to suggest that it pays off unevenly. First, economically disadvantaged students carry their inferior academic preparation – forged in inferior primary and secondary schools and exacerbated by familial differences in educational investments – into post-secondary education, where it contributes to lower completion rates (Bailey and Dynarski, 2011) and longer paths to degrees because of the need to take remedial classes (Engle and Tinto, 2008). Second, even highly qualified students do not achieve equitably in college, as the economics of higher education strongly influence institutional selection to steer even high-achieving low-income students or students of color to less selective schools that spend less per student on instruction, have lower graduation rates, and yield poorer labor market returns than more competitive institutions (Carnevale and Strohl, 2013). Indeed, analysis of this "undermatching" (Hoxby and Avery, 2012) suggests the existence of two tiers of higher education and powerful forces that track students into one or the other, based more on socioeconomic status than innate ability or even academic preparation. Higher education cannot be an equalizing force if it delivers an unequal product with highly disparate outcomes. As evidence of the gap between different types of institutions, more than half of community college students fail to complete a degree, receive a certificate, or transfer to a four-year institution within six years (National Center for Education Statistics, 2011), considerably poorer interim outcomes than students at more selective, four-year institutions. Yet these institutions serve as a linchpin in the aspirations of millions of Americans whose educational futures are constrained by the high price tag of a college degree.

Even successful college completion does not erase the legacies of inequity. Despite the fact that education nearly always "pays" compared to failure to pursue post-secondary studies, research suggests that the precise level of economic advantage afforded from a higher education depends on school selectivity, major, and chosen occupation. Specifically, the rate of return on a bachelor's degree from a non-competitive four-year private institution is under 6%, while the rate of return on a bachelor's degree at the most competitive public institutions is over 12% (Owen and Sawhill, 2013). While there is certainly an economic need for diverse majors and a case to be made for the non-financial benefits of post-secondary education, the extent to which career choice may be influenced by the student's socioeconomic background also warrants examination, since the lifetime difference in earnings between, for example, a student who majored in engineering and a student who studied arts or humanities can be well over $1 million (Schneider, 2013). Finally, and of primary interest here, even when two students earn the exact same degree from the exact same institution, the real value of that credential may vary depending on the way in which they financed it, as student loan debt may erode asset accumulation for years following degree completion, thus increasing the real cost of the degree (e.g., Hiltonsmith, 2013).

Today, high college costs due in part to diminishing state funding, declining availability of non-repayable financial aid and poorer labor market outcomes may raise doubts in the minds of parents and children about whether the return on college is too risky to justify the investment of required financial and personal resources. In the lives of individual students and in the aggregate for this generation, then, education – one of the most critical institutions shaping opportunity in today's America – may be seen as less capable of facilitating a path to the American Dream.

1.1 Shifting Understanding of Education's Welfare Function in America

Since the beginning of the 20th century, education has become a locus for the emphasis on opportunity, through expanded support for public schools, colleges, and universities, and eventually through provision of government subsidies to facilitate individual access to higher education. In 1976, in talking about the function of education in the American welfare system, Janowitz wrote,

> Perhaps the most significant difference between the institutional bases of the welfare state in Great Britain and the United States was the emphasis placed on public education – especially for lower income groups – in the United States. Massive support for the expansion of public education, including higher education, in the United States must be seen as a central component of the American notion of welfare – the idea that through public education both personal betterment and national social and economic development would take place. (pp. 34 & 35)

Now such an accepted part of the American approach to fostering upward mobility, placing education in this central role was not a foregone conclusion, but instead an explicit and intentional decision about how our nation, specifically, would build policy structures to complement individual effort and ability. While European nations have relied on the "direct redistributive role of the welfare state to reconcile citizenship and markets," the United States has chosen to use education as a lever for ensuring equitable outcomes (Carnevale and Strohl, 2010, p. 83). This distinctly American conviction – that economic disparity can be narrowed through individual effort in school, the pursuit of higher education, and calculated public investments in educational opportunities – runs deep. In the past few decades, though, while there is little evidence that Americans' beliefs about the importance of education as a gateway to opportunity have eroded, there has nonetheless been a repositioning and repurposing of education policies, within a shifting frame of "welfare." Education has been increasingly viewed as a primarily individual, rather than societal good, with the accompanying retrenchment paralleled by cuts in other arenas of welfare policy, as well. In the higher education domain, this shift can be clearly traced by examining political pronouncements about financial aid since the 1965 enactment of the Higher Education Act.

While education is certainly not the only policy sphere where shifts in arrangements between individuals and the government are reshaping opportunities and risks (Hacker, 2008), these trends are seen vividly in higher education, looking, for example, at the evolution of how presidents talk about, specifically, financial aid policy. In talking about the Higher Education Act Reauthorization of 1968 President Lyndon B. Johnson said, "So to thousands of young people education will be available. And it is a truism that education is no longer a luxury. Education in this day and age is a necessity." Here, the federal government's role is understood as making education available to all. Similarly, speaking of the Higher Education Act Reauthorization of 1980 President Jimmy Carter said, "We've brought college within reach of every student in the nation who's qualified for higher education. The idea that lack of money should be no barrier to a college education is no longer a dream – it is a reality." This frame of education as a collective investment in shared prosperity shifted in the mid-1980s. The burden of paying for college shifted inexorably to the individual, evidenced through reductions in state support for public institutions of higher education, declining purchasing power of need-based financial aid, and concurrent increases in college costs. Because relatively few households could finance these new obligations without some external assistance, given the high cost of college, this "risk shift" (Hacker, 2008) necessitated a larger role for student loans, absent policy innovations that would bridge these gaps.

1.2 Economics of Higher Education and Increasing Indebtedness

Significantly, while the research regarding the effects of student debt on individuals' educational outcomes and subsequent financial statuses has primarily centered on student borrowing in the United States, the shifts toward greater reliance on individual and family contributions – and the increasing assumption of student debt, with which to meet these obligations – is witnessed beyond U.S. borders, as well. Taking Canada as a point of comparison, while economic mobility rates are higher than in the United States (Corak, 2010), similar trends toward individual responsibility for college financing and corollary indebtedness may cast these outcomes in doubt. In the late 1970s, federal and provincial funding covered more than 80% of Canadian higher educational institutions' operating budgets (Falvo, 2012). By 2009, only 61% of post-secondary education revenues came from government sources (Statistics Canada, 2011). This drives up tuition at a rate significantly higher than overall inflation. More than 80% of Canadian parents now expect to pay for their child's post-secondary education, evidence that many in the Canadian public have internalized the cost shift (BMO Wealth Institute, 2013). Indeed, tuition increased 22% and student loans increased 28% between 2002 and 2008 (Girdharry *et al.*, 2010).

Structurally, Canada's loan system roughly parallels that in the United States, including zero-nominal interest rates while students are in school and tax credits for interest payments (Usher, 2005). And lending looms large in aggregate higher education financing in Canada as in the United States. In 2013, Canada made $2.46 billion in student loans and only $695 million in grants (Rahman, 2014). Individual student debt loads are increasing in tandem, rising from $14,700 in 1995 to $16,600 in 2005 (Canadian Council on Learning, 2010) and almost $27,000 in 2013 (Canadian Federation of Students, 2013), with debt highest for the 25–44 age group (Falvo, 2012). These effects are observed in households' overall balance sheets. In 1990, the average Canadian household had less than $0.80 of household debt for every one dollar in disposable income, a figure that had increased to more than $1.40 by 2010 (Falvo, 2012). While the United States may be leading the world, then, in reliance on student borrowing as the primary mechanism for higher education financing, the forces of revenue reductions, spending cuts, and cost shifts are not uniquely American, trends which suggest that the observed effects may not be limited to the U.S. landscape, either. A growing evidence base in the United States suggests that these student debt figures are not only of political importance, as they attract headlines about "debt crises," or rhetorical significance, as they change individuals' expectations about what might be possible for their own higher educational futures, but economically, as they change the calculus of return on investment and shape young people's balance sheets well into their economic maturity. While, again, this evidence is most prominent in the United States, the renegotiation of individual and collective investments in human capital can be felt in other national contexts, as well.

1.3 *Research on Student Debt's Effects on Young Adults' Asset Accumulation*

This relatively recent conceptualization of higher education financing has largely presumed that any method of confronting college costs is roughly equivalent to another; the "measure" of a financial aid system has been primarily limited to its adequacy as a payment mechanism, leveraged at the point of college enrollment. Recently, however, researchers have begun to question this accounting, and to expand the metrics by which financing approaches are judged. Specifically, analyses have tested the assumption that, if the student loan program strengthens the education path as an equalizer in society, upon graduating, two students with similar degrees should be able to achieve similar returns on their credentials, holding all else equal (see e.g., Elliott and Nam, 2013). Here, emerging research indicates that student loans may, instead, reduce the return on college. This section discusses some of the research that examines student post-graduation social and economic outcomes, with a focus on research that examines student debt's effects on young adults' asset accumulation. While researchers have not always recognized the distinction between income and assets, scholarship has found that, indeed, they work differently to shape outcomes and even individuals' psychology (Sherraden, 1991). While higher educational attainment may catalyze greater earning potential (Pew Research Center, 2014), wealth inequality may be a bigger problem among young adults than income inequality, and the former may be particularly driven by early disparities in balance sheets. As evidence of the growing disconnect between earnings and wealth building, a new report by Pew Charitable Trusts (2014) finds that about 75% of young adults 30 to 40, Generation X, have higher incomes than their parents did but only about 36% have exceeded their parents' wealth. Those with student debt are particularly likely to fail to match their parents' wealth, even if they out earn them. So, higher incomes are not translating into more mobility, a cornerstone of the American Dream.

1.4 *Career and Social Choices*

Survey data from American Student Assistance (2013) finds that 30% of respondents say that student debt played a role in their career choice. In line with the survey data, Rothstein and Rouse (2011) find evidence that student loan debt drives graduates away from low-paying and public-sector jobs (also see, Minicozzi, 2005). Similarly, Field (2009) finds that the rate of placements in public-interest law is roughly a third higher when law students are given tuition waivers instead of loan repayment assistance. Taken together, what these findings suggest is that borrowers may see their career opportunities differently than non-borrowers, in ways that distort their post-college planning. Given the widespread reliance on student loans across this cohort of college students, these selection pressures may have significant repercussions in the broader economy.

Beyond career decisions, student loans also appear to provide people with an embedded thought process that conveys the message that they should wait to start their social lives. For example, Gicheva (2011) finds that students with outstanding student debt have a lower probability of marriage than students without outstanding debt, among people younger than 37 (also see, Baum and O'Malley, 2003). If they marry, graduates with student debt express less satisfaction with their marriage than students with no debt (Dew, 2008). Moreover, when asked, survey data indicate that 43% of student loan borrowers say they have delayed having children (American Student Assistance, 2013; also see, Baum and O'Malley, 2003).

1.5 *Financial Stress*

Given the above dynamics, it is perhaps not surprising that Fry (2014) discovers that 18- to 39-year-olds with two- or four-year degrees who have outstanding student debt are less satisfied overall with their financial situations than similarly situated young adults without outstanding student debt (70% vs. 84%, respectively). Further, he finds that 18- to 39-year-olds with two- or four-year degrees who have outstanding student debt are less likely to perceive an immediate payoff from having gone to college than similarly situated young adults without outstanding student debt (63% vs. 81%, respectively). Compounding the problem of financial stress associated with repaying student loans may be the evidence of abusive debt collection practices and the lack of enforcement collection agencies face for these excesses (Burd, 2014). Student borrowers face large penalties if they are late or fail to pay back their debt on time, and they may be frustrated in their efforts to better manage their debts by onerous restrictions, many of which are peculiar to this type of consumer borrowing (Consumer Financial Protection Bureau, 2013). Changes in regulations have allowed the assumption of ever-greater levels of debt, in many cases far beyond what would be prudent, given a particular student's likely future earnings. While interest does not accrue while the student is in school, the initiation of payment obligations shortly after college exit – often at the period of the individual's lowest lifetime earnings (Mishel *et al.*, 2012) – can spark repayment difficulties and, increasingly, reliance on alternative repayment schedules (Delisle, 2014), some with long-term financial implications, as discussed below. Denoting the peculiar regulatory context of student borrowing, even the extreme financial event of bankruptcy cannot usually bring relief from delinquent student debt, given special treatment of student loans that deny borrowers opportunities to discharge these obligations (National Association of Consumer Bankruptcy Attorneys, 2012). While media attention and cohort effects may increase the perception of distress among student borrowers, it must be emphasized that the strains felt by many student borrowers today are, indeed, grounded in the economic realities they face.

1.6 *Delinquency and Default*

Considerable popular attention, and significant financial resources, have been dedicated to the problem of student loan delinquency and default. Student loans become delinquent when payment is 60 to 120 days late. In 2011 the U.S. Department of Education spent $1.4 billion to pay collection agencies to track down students whose loans are delinquent or in default (Martin, 2012). While all types of consumer debt have some experiences of repayment difficulty, there is evidence that something about the student loan product, or the context in which it is situated, makes it particularly difficult to service successfully. According to Brown *et al.* (2014), the measured student debt delinquency rate is currently the highest of any consumer debt product. Cunningham and Kienzl (2011) find that 26% of borrowers who began repayment in 2005 were delinquent on their loans at some point but did not default. By 2012, Brown *et al.* (2014) report that just over 30% of borrowers who began repayment were delinquent at some point.

And some of the practices utilized by borrowers and lenders to cope with repayment difficulties may have the perverse effects of deepening loans' negative implications for student borrowers. About 21% of borrowers avoid delinquency by using deferment (temporary suspension of loan payments) or forbearance (temporary postponement or reduction of payments for a period of time because of financial difficulty) to temporarily alleviate the problem (Cunningham and Kienzl, 2011). While this may allow borrowers to stay out of official "trouble" with their loans, by stretching out the period of total indebtedness, these practices may further retard capital development. In total, Cunningham and Kienzl (2011) find that nearly 41% of borrowers have been delinquent or defaulted on their loans. These trends have effects far beyond the cohort of young adults most plagued by student loan difficulties. Accompanying the increase in student loan indebtedness, delinquency is also a growing problem among older adults. Among student loans held by Americans aged 60 or older, 9.5% were at least 90 days delinquent, up about 7.4% from 2007 (Greene, 2012).

Defaults are also on the rise. According to the U.S. Department of Education (2012), the national 2-year student loan default rate was 9.1% in 2010 and the 3-year default rate was 13.4%. Not surprisingly, defaults occur unevenly. Students from lower-income households are more likely to default (Woo, 2002), along with students of color (Herr and Burt, 2005). With fewer familial resources to cushion the payment strain prompted by student loan obligations and greater likelihood of inadequate income upon leaving college (Woo, 2002; Lochner and Monge-Naranjo, 2004), these borrowers may have to confront the failed economics of student loans very shortly after exiting higher education. Critically, responses to the prominent failings of the student loan system – vividly illustrated in delinquency and default rates – may similarly fail, unless policy takes a complete and accurate accounting of both the causes and consequences of student debt's effects.

For example, given rising rates of delinquency and default, some researchers have suggested making loan eligibility determinations on an individual basis, taking into consideration all of the circumstances faced as well as the outlook for future ability to repay (see Akers, 2014). This concept, predicated as it is on the availability of nearly unattainable information, seems born of a desperate attempt to justify the continued existence of the student loan program, while mitigating its most visibly negative effects. That is, there are too many ways in which the student loan program fails (individuals and society), so we try to patch solutions together when the reality is that only reducing the prominence of student borrowing as a part of the financial aid system will address the roots of the problems. In sharp contrast, these patchwork solutions are likely to exacerbate inequality, perpetuating the survival of a program that will continue to fail whole cohorts of aspiring college students, while diverting massive resources that could be deployed toward more promising approaches. Similar critiques can be made of Income-Based Repayment, Pay-as-You-Earn, and other efforts to "soften" the damage associated with student borrowing, discussed in greater detail below.

1.7 Overall Debt

Since recent college graduates' annual earnings are usually much lower than they will be during later, prime earning years, most young adults with student loan debt are forced to rely on credit as a key mechanism for purchasing wealth-building items like a home (Keister, 2000; Oliver and Shapiro, 2006). However, delinquent and defaulted accounts may be reflected in students' credit scores. For many students, this reveals another way in which student loans may haunt them as they embark on financial independence. Research by Brown and Caldwell

(2013) indicates that students with student loans have credit scores that are 24 points lower than students without student loans. This compromised financial position may make it more difficult for student borrowers to gain access to the productive capital from which to finance wealth creation, in the form of homeownership or business development.

Contrary to the idea that student loan borrowers face credit constraints, however, research using data from 2010 or earlier finds that there was a positive correlation between having outstanding student debt and other debt (such as mortgage, vehicle, or credit card), when comparing graduates with and without debt. For instance, Fry (2014) uses 2010 Survey of Consumer Finance data and finds that 43% of households headed by a college graduate with student debt have vehicle debt and 60% have credit card debt. However, using 2012 data, Brown and Caldwell (2013) find that households with student debt have lower over-all debt than households without student debt. They speculate that borrowers post-Great Recession have become less sure about the labor market, causing a drop in the demand for credit. Additionally, lenders may have become more reserved about supplying loans to high-balance student borrowers in the tighter credit markets that followed the financial collapse.

1.8 Asset Accumulation

Student debt's most troubling financial effects may be its constraints not on other borrowing, however, but on asset accumulation, particularly given the emerging understanding about the significance of initial assets as catalysts for later economic mobility (Elliott and Lewis, 2014). Assets reflect ownership power or control over resources that are stored over time and used for human development, social mobility, and intergenerational transmission of wealth and advantage, while income is a flow on a family's balance sheet and represents resources earned over a particular span of time, such as a week or month. A household's ability to leverage income for wealth creation may differ according to its access to institutional supports that cultivate relative advantage (Sherraden, 1991). For example, with respect to the racial wealth gap, Shapiro *et al.* (2013) find that a $1.00 increase in income later translates to a $5.00 increase in wealth for Whites, but only a $0.70 increase for Blacks. Similarly, Elliott and Lewis (2014) find that at the onset of the Great Recession (2007), for each one dollar increase in initial capital income (e.g., income from interest, dividends, and trusts), total household income increased by $1.22 for households at the 25th percentile of capital income but increased by $5.26 at the 75th percentile. At the end of the Great Recession (2011), it increased by $0.58 at the 25th percentile and by $1.29 at the 75th percentile. Then, because assets can be converted back into income (e.g., rent from real estate, dividends from stocks, or interest from bonds), indebted students have less income available as they age.

Here it is clear that, even if incomes are equal, some people receive greater financial benefits from their income than other groups. It might be that student loan debt works in a similar fashion. That is, students who leave college with debt may not be able to earn as much wealth from each dollar earned because, while in college, they were borrowing against their future earnings. So, while they make similar incomes as students who graduate with no student loan debt, they have less of that income for accumulating assets. Critically, this may account for a meaningful amount of the wealth inequality seen later in life between college graduates with and without outstanding student debt. It represents, then, a potentially significant threat to the fundamental calculation of the American Dream, in which two individuals who receive the same degree and achieve similar career heights should see their financial standings similarly advantaged. In this section we will review research on the correlational relationship between student debt and asset accumulation.

Table A1 (Appendix A) provides more detailed information on each of the studies reviewed in this section. Even though researchers have only begun to examine student debt effects on young adults' post-college financial outcomes, Table A1 indicates that researchers are using a variety of methods, data sets, and controls in their investigations. At this point, given methodological complications in this relatively nascent field of inquiry, there are few randomized control trials. However, several researchers have attempted to use instrumental variables to ascertain information about the potential causal link between student debt and financial health. For example, Rothstein and Rouse (2011) use a natural experiment to examine the causal link between student debt and young adults' career choice. Given that it is hard, if not impossible, to assign some students to the student debt condition, using secondary data sets and techniques might be the closest that researchers can come to figuring out whether there is a causal link between student debt and young adults' financial health. In any case, the fact that a variety of methods and data sets are being used, and different researchers are finding similar results, builds confidence in these findings and raises concerns about the student debt program in America.

1.8.1 *Net Worth*

Survey data indicate that 63% of young adults with student debt report delaying purchasing large ticket items such as a car. Therefore, it is no surprise that researchers are finding that young adults with student debt have less net worth (i.e., total assets − total liabilities) than students without student debt. For example, Elliott and Nam (2013) find that families with college debt may have 63% less net worth than those without outstanding student debt. Similarly, over the life course, Hiltonsmith (2013) finds that an average student debt load ($53,000) for a dual-headed household with bachelors' degrees from four-year universities leads to a wealth loss of nearly $208,000. Fry (2014) also finds a net worth loss among households headed by a college-educated (i.e., bachelor's degree or higher) adult younger than 40 who has outstanding student debt. Specifically, he finds that a household headed by a college graduate without outstanding student debt has seven times ($64,700) the typical net worth of a household headed by a college graduate who has outstanding student debt ($8,700).

1.8.2 *Homeownership*

There is evidence to suggest that credit constraints as a result of student loan debt may force young adults with outstanding student debt to either delay purchasing a house or to purchase it at a higher interest rate in the subprime loan market. The higher interest rate may make it harder to earn equity in the house and can price indebted households out of the most desirable real estate markets. For context, Mishory et al. (2012) find that the average single student debtor would have to pay close to half of his or her monthly income toward student loans and mortgage payments. As a result, the debtor would not qualify for an FHA loan or many private loans (Mishory et al., 2012). In line with this, Stone et al. (2012) find that 40% of students graduating from a four-year college with outstanding student loan debt delay a major purchase, including a home.

Quantitative analysis supports descriptive findings. Shand (2007) finds that student debt has a negative effect on homeownership rates when comparing four-year college graduates with and without debt. Hiltonsmith (2013) finds that households with four-year college graduates and outstanding student debt have $70,000 less in home equity than similarly situated households without outstanding student debt. Potentially explaining this gap, Houle and Berger (2014) find that student debt is associated with a delay in buying a home among college graduates with outstanding student debt compared to those without outstanding student debt. Though Houle and Berger's findings are significant but not very strong, they still raise serious concerns, if we expect that the student loan system should contribute to economic prosperity, not just do relatively little harm to the financial well-being of those who use it. Moreover, even though the effects are not strong in the aggregate, some groups of students may be disproportionately affected by these pressures. Significantly, for example, Houle and Berger (2014) find evidence that suggests these effects are much stronger among Black graduates with outstanding student debt. This is important to the question of whether student loans are helping to strengthen the ability of the education path to act as an "equalizer" in society, given the structural barriers Blacks already face in the housing market (e.g., Oliver and Shapiro, 2006).

Raising doubts about options to quickly maneuver away from these adverse outcomes, Shand (2007) finds little evidence to suggest that this wealth loss is the result of credit constraints. That is, the presence of student loans on a household's balance sheet may not render the household unable to obtain a mortgage. Instead, households with outstanding student debt might be averse to obtaining a mortgage for a home. In this manner, student loans may introduce additional levers of inequality into students' post-college lives, artificially constraining home purchase and, then, preventing the development of a powerful asset base (Shapiro *et al.*, 2013). The reason for these differences, with regard to the role of credit constraints, might be due to the different years examined. For example, as discussed above, Brown and Caldwell (2013) find credit scores of student loan borrowers and non-borrowers were essentially the same in 2003, but by 2012 borrowers had lower scores. Further, Brown and Caldwell (2013) show that as credit scores of borrowers declined and student debt per borrower have increased, homeownership rates of 30-year-old student loan borrowers have decreased by more than 5% compared to homeownership rates of 30-year-old non-borrowers. This is a fairly substantial drop, particularly given that the overall homeownership rate for 30-year-olds is below 24%. The Federal Reserve Bank of New York speculates that the drop in housing rates post-Great Recession is due in part, not only to credit score declines, but tighter underwriting standards and higher delinquency rates (Brown *et al.*, 2014).

In the aggregate, these findings on student debt and asset accumulation suggest that student loans are simultaneously more and less alarming for the future of the United States than commonly believed. While student debt may not incite the next financial collapse, despite the sensationalist claims in some popular media coverage (for discussion of this coverage, see Karsten, 2014; Harvey, 2014), the long-term and aggregate effects of these derailed asset aspirations may constrain economic mobility and threaten the financial security of student borrowers throughout their lives, and *these* effects could transmit significant, albeit indirect, economic fallout from student loans. Again, these analyses also suggest measures by which other nations – such as Canada – should assess the possible effects of their own shift to increasingly debt-dependent financial aid. Unfortunately, difficulties in adequately assessing these effects, particularly on a timeline that lends itself to policy deliberations, contribute to the overly narrow frame through which student loans are judged. However, even if some of the corrosive effects of deterring homeownership, for example, may not be felt until today's indebted youth lack the asset foundation with which to leverage a secure retirement (Pew

Charitable Trusts, 2013), that slow-moving threat is no less deserving of our urgent policy attention.

1.8.3 *Retirement Savings*

In the American Student Assistance (2013) survey on young adults with outstanding student debt, 73% of borrowers say they have put off saving for retirement or other investments. In support of this finding, Elliott *et al.* (2013) find that families with outstanding student debt have 52% less retirement savings than families with no outstanding student debt. Hiltonsmith's (2013) results indicate that dual-headed households with a college graduate and median student debt ($53,000) have about $134,000 less in retirement savings in comparison to dual-headed households with a college graduate and no student debt. Similarly, Egoian (2013) finds that four-year college graduates with median debt of $23,300 have $115,096 less in retirement savings than a four-year college graduate with no student loans by the time they reach age 73.

With so many potentially intervening factors unfolding over the next few decades, the full impact may be even worse. For example, Egoian's (2013) estimates assume that 7% of an indebted college graduate's earnings go toward yearly loan repayments. This is more conservative than the recommended cutoff for unmanageable student debt of 8% or 10% (Baum and Schwartz, 2005), and far lower than the actual debt burdens of many college graduates. That is, he finds negative effects that kick in even at levels of indebtedness lower than recommended levels. He also bases his estimates on relatively small amounts of debt – $23,000 – far less than that apocryphal $100,000 and even less than current estimates of average debt loads, yet he finds these relatively large effects. Moreover, his estimates assume that households will pay off their student debts in 10 years. However, current approaches to dealing with escalating student debt largely seek to make unsustainable debt levels more bearable by extending the period of repayment. This makes monthly payments smaller, certainly, but also lengthens the period of depressed capital accumulation, with potentially greater effects on wealth building.

Schemes such as Income-Based Repayment and the Pay-as-You-Earn plans usually require consolidating student loans and have largely been designed to prevent debt burden (how much of the borrower's monthly income has to be devoted to paying back student loans) from becoming excessive. In order to reduce payments, income-driven repayment plans extend the time students typically have to pay off their loans from 10 years to up to 25 years in the case of the Income Contingent Repayment plan. According to the metric of reduced asset accumulation, these payment modifications may *add* to the student loan problem rather than solving it. Even before the growth in use of these types of programs, the length of time borrowers took to pay off loans was increasing. For example, Akers and Chingos (2014) find that the mean term of repayment in 1992 was 7.5 years; it increased to 13.4 years by 2010 largely because of students consolidating their loans. The time it takes to pay off loans is only likely to grow as income-driven repayment plans are "sold" as a way to increase affordability. And utilization of these modifications is growing rapidly, alongside continued increases in concerns about the consequences of student borrowing. In 2013 these programs accounted for 6% of borrowers in repayment and, by 2014, nearly 11% of borrowers were in such a repayment modification (Delisle, 2014). Further, these programs account for almost 22% of the Direct Loan portfolio in repayment (Delisle, 2014). Lauded by many as a great way to manage loan burdens, the fact that so many borrowers require such programs should be a warning sign that the current program is flawed and an example of how minor changes to student loan terms fail to address the problems caused by their prominence in the financial aid landscape. Certainly, if so many borrowers find their regular payment plan to be unbearable, and in fact, such payments are officially deemed to be unbearable, one could reasonably conclude that the United States has a student debt problem. This realization is even more disturbing in light of evidence that the "solution" adopted to address this problem may only intensify the long-term harmful effects of student loans, while reducing the policy momentum for more substantive reforms by easing some of the pressure exerted by overburdened borrowers. As Egoian's (2013) research and others makes clear, putting off asset accumulation for 10 to 20 years may have real consequences; even having to divert 7% of one's income to paying back loans may have a large effect on long-term wealth accumulation, let alone the 10% to 20% required by income-driven repayment plans.

From the evidence discussed in this report, it appears clear to us that the student loan program exacerbates uneven returns on a college degree. This conclusion is all the more convincing when we consider that it is not based on any one study but a body of evidence conducted by a variety of different researchers and ranges across a number of different outcomes (e.g., marriage, homeownership, net worth, financial distress, etc.) using a variety of different methods and samples. Higher education systems in the United States and, to a somewhat lesser extent, other countries as well, have drifted into debt dependence with relatively little consideration of the long-term consequences of these policy changes on the educational, financial, and life outcomes of students. However, it is important to emphasize that, as a whole, this evidence does not suggest that higher education does not pay. Indeed, to the extent to which concern over student borrowing has called into question the value of higher education, those doubts may be less tangible but still significant "costs" of this debt-dependent financial aid system. Human capital is created by student debt, and graduates can leverage their human capital into earnings and wealth accumulation potential. That promise makes these findings, which call into question the soundness of the U.S. financial aid system, all the more alarming, since aspiring students who cannot finance their post-secondary educations from family wealth largely have to choose between foregoing valuable educational investments, on the one hand, or taking on potentially crippling student loans on the other. Faced with these undesirable "options," students' fates seem largely out of their control, contrary to the American ideal of reward for effort and ability. As nations such as Canada shift to a more debt-centric financial aid system, the comparatively robust path to upward mobility enjoyed in those countries may be similarly imperiled. In the end, students with outstanding student debt still end up behind their peers whose family asset stores or other advantages enabled human capital accumulation without significant borrowing.

2. Policy Discussion

The U.S. federal student loan program has received considerable policy attention in recent years, particularly as popular media coverage of repayment woes skyrocketed following the financial collapse (see Levin, 2013; Frizell, 2014; Korkki, 2014) and the associated increase in unemployment for even college graduates (Mishel *et al.*, 2013). However, the policies proposed in the aftermath have almost exclusively focused on softening the blow dealt by student loans, rather than avoiding the damage in the first place. Approaches such as income-based repayment plans, in their various iterations (Talbott, 2014), are designed to help borrowers cope with the consequences of their student borrowing, yet none have been demonstrated to truly avoid the educational, social, and financial hazards of our debt-dependent system. Temporary reductions in interest rates would reduce the cost of borrowing, at least in the short term, but would not address loans' deterrent effects (Baum and O'Malley, 2003), particularly since few prospective students understand the real cost of financing.

Even as understanding of student loans as a dis-equalizing force has permeated popular discussion to some degree (see Thompson, 2014), there has been little reconsideration of the fundamental wisdom of relying on debt to facilitate such an important part of the U.S. path to economic mobility. Indeed, some proposals might exacerbate inequity in higher education. For example, if policy encourages low-income students to enroll in less expensive two-year schools to reduce their expenses (Goldrick-Rab and Kendall, 2014) and, then, need to borrow, but economically advantaged students can choose their schools without such considerations, there is the real risk of creating an explicitly two-tiered structure (Brown-Nagin, 2015), particularly since all institutions are not created equal in terms of educational outcomes.

Reimagining, and, then, rebuilding, the U.S. financial aid system must begin with more completely accounting for the true costs of student loans, to students and the larger economy (see, Hiltonsmith, 2013; Elliott and Lewis, 2013; Dugan and Kafka, 2014). In this light, it is clear that, while current proposals center on reducing monthly payment burdens because these "tweaks" can reduce the incidence of delinquency and default (Sheets and Crawford, 2014), potentially masking the problems, they do little to address the long-term effects of student loans, before and after college, and may even move in the wrong direction. Indeed, innovations that seek to reduce the strain on student borrowers by extending the repayment period or making other modifications may only prolong the harmful effects on financial and life outcomes (e.g., Egoian, 2013). And even this analysis does not fully account for the potentially corrosive effects of student debt on educational outcomes, where evidence suggests that student loans fail to catalyze greater achievement or increase students' engagement in school, threatening their core aim of facilitating educational attainment (Cofer and Somers, 2000; Perna, 2000; Kim, 2007; Heller, 2008; Dwyer *et al.*, 2011; Fry, 2014, among others). There is a growing body of evidence that reveals the dimensions on which student loans endanger the well-being of individual borrowers, the institutions dependent on them, and our macro-economy. Data reveal that disadvantaged students, particularly low-income and students of color, are disproportionately affected by these forces (Fenske *et al.*, 2007). These disparate effects may be particularly unacceptable given the role of higher education in fostering greater equity and upward mobility (Greenstone *et al.*, 2013) in the American welfare system.

2.1 *The Need for Reducing Absolute Borrowing*

This fuller accounting of the effects of student loans reveals not only the different dimensions on which student loans may harm prospective, current, and former college students and their households, but also the serious limitations of any reforms that do not reduce absolute dependence on student borrowing. Contrary to popular belief (Sanchez, 2012), it is not only the extremely "high-dollar" loans – still relatively rare – that should be alarming (Egoian, 2013). Indeed, since some of these loans are incurred by relatively advantaged students pursuing exceptional degrees, these outliers may be far less dangerous than the "routine" assumption of several thousand dollars in debt by millions of Americans. What is increasingly clear is that there is no "safe" level of student loan debt. Analysis reveals negative effects on asset accumulation and subsequent financial well-being at levels even far below "recommended" thresholds, revealing the limitations of efforts to protect students by simply trying to avoid huge loans (Egoian, 2013; Akers, 2014).

Indeed, to the extent to which the collective narrative focuses on high-dollar debt as the problem, typically defined as $100,000 or more (e.g., Edmiston *et al.*, 2012), the psychic toll may be increased for those who wonder why their "small" loans are still crippling. Additionally, while talk of high-dollar debt may be particularly off-putting to debt-averse low-income students, even the prospect of relatively small student loans may deter some prospective college-goers and, certainly, does little to motivate their engagement (Cunningham and Santiago, 2008). It is absolutely true that some students manage to borrow for college and still do fine, at least eventually. It is also true that, in what is becoming a predictable outcome, many students who borrow even fairly small amounts experience disruptions in their college experience, thwarting of their academic aspirations, and/or delay in their life progression (American Student Assistance, 2013; Mishory *et al.*, 2012). With the caveats required before student loans can be safely recommended, America might be wise to focus its policy energies on reducing the utilization of student loans through the most efficient and equitable means possible.

While there are options in terms of the specific routes to reducing debt dependence, the clear objective must be to reduce the cost burden that college poses to individual students and their families. This could include helping to equip American households with the asset foundations with which to confront costs, as in proposals to establish Children's Savings Accounts (CSAs) at birth (Cramer and Newville, 2009), increasing public appropriations as part of an effort to reduce college tuition prices, and increasing the adequacy of need-based financial aid (Rethinking Pell Study Group, 2013; Burd *et al.*, 2013). Indeed, using these strategies in concert could increase their efficacy, as reflected in proposals to, for example, repurpose Pell awards as early deposits in progressively funded CSAs (Rethinking Pell Study Group, 2013), or to leverage federal investments in financial aid to discourage state disinvestment in higher education (Hurley *et al.*, 2014).

But this is admittedly a long-term solution; a short-term solution for those already in debt is also needed. If the U.S. government cannot bring itself to provide young adults whose lifetime chance at financial security and economic mobility is compromised by their indebted starting point with a bailout, while we take a long-term approach toward fixing our broken financial aid system, then it might have to rely on an income-based repayment scheme as a stopgap measure. However, policy should only do so after first immunizing young adults from student debt's potentially negative effects by removing any impact student loans might have on young adults' credit. This underwriting practice may be more tolerable for the providers of student loans if everyone who has student debt is enrolled into an income-based repayment program, reducing the risk for providers.[1] What risk that remains to providers would be further lessened by existing bankruptcy laws that make it almost impossible to discharge student debt.

3. Conclusion

There is need for additional research, to elevate the policy conversation about student loans beyond heated rhetoric about exorbitant balances or, conversely, platitudes about the value of a college degree. There are open questions about the extent to which changes in family composition, asset investments, and career choices can be attributed to student debt, as contrasted to general shifts in generational preferences. Research should attempt to differentiate between the diffuse effects of greater student indebtedness on the expectations and attitudes of even those students who are not, themselves, indebted, compared to those confronting their own financial liabilities. And analysis is needed to examine student debt effects in real time, with the benefit of some distance from the recent recession, particularly as some are eager to dismiss financial setbacks as temporal. Finally, more research is needed to figure out how much debt is too much debt. This is important if programs like the income-based repayment plan are going to be part of the short-term solution. These programs assume that payments of 10% to 15% of a young adult's income will greatly reduce the negative effects associated with outstanding student debt. That is, at a minimum, they are expected to enable borrowers to avoid falling into delinquency or default. However, there is little empirical evidence to support this assumption. With evidence beginning to show that even small amounts of debt are associated with financial harm, more research is needed.

Still, from the body of research existing today, there is very little evidence, if any, to suggest that the student loan program is strengthening the education path as an equalizer (Heller, 2008). And it is to this standard that we should hold a financial aid program that in the 2011–2012 school year cost Americans $70.8 billion (College Board, 2012), from which the federal government earned $41.3 billion in interest payments in 2013 (Jesse, 2013), and from which Sallie Mae (the nation's largest private student loan lender) made $939 million in net profit for 2012 (Hartman, 2013). The depression of asset accumulation that may result in the immediate post-college period as a result of real financial strains of debt repayment may really matter when it comes to understanding the financial well-being of young adults and growing wealth inequality (Elliott and Lewis, 2014).

Acknowledgment

This paper could not have been completed without the generous support of the Kaufmann Foundation.

Notes

1. With regard to enrolling everyone in income-based repayment plans, see http://younginvincibles.org/enroll-all-student-loan-borrowers-in-income-based-repayment-report-says/
2. These are only a few of the assumptions made.

References

Akers, B. (2014) *How Much Is Too Much? Evidence on Financial Well-Being and Student Loan Debt.* Washington, DC: The American Enterprise Institute (AEI). Available at http://www.aei.org/files/2014/05/14/-how-much-is-too-much_100837569045.pdf (Accessed August 12 2014).

Akers, B. and Chingos, M.M. (2014) *Is a Student Loan Crisis on the Horizon?* Washington, DC: The Brookings Institution.

American Student Assistance. (2013) *Life Delayed: The Impact of Student Debt on the Daily Lives of Young Americans.* Washington, DC: American Student Assistance.

Bailey, M.J. and Dynarski, S. (2011) Inequality in postsecondary education. In G. Duncan and R. Murnane (eds.), *Whither Opportunity?* (pp. 117–132). New York: Russell Sage Foundation.

Baum, S. and O'Malley, M. (2003) College on credit: How borrowers perceive their education debt. *Journal of Student Financial Aid* 33(3), article 1. Available at http://publications.nasfaa.org/jsfa/vol33/iss3/1 (Accessed August 17 2014).

Baum, S. and Schwartz, S. (2005) How much debt is too much? Defining benchmarks for manageable student debt. Available at https://www.cgsnet.org/ckfinder/userfiles/files/How_Much_Debt_is_Too_Much.pdf (Accessed August 14 2014).

BMO Wealth Institute. (2013) *Student Tuition and Debt on the Rise: RESPs and Beyond*. Montreal, Canada: Bank of Montreal.

Brown, M. and Caldwell, S. (2013) *Young Adult Student Loan Borrowers Retreat from Housing and Auto Markets*. New York: Federal Reserve Bank of New York.

Brown, M., Haughwout, A., Lee, D., Scally, J. and vander Klaauw, W. (2014) Measuring student debt and its performance. Federal Reserve Bank of New York Staff Reports, no. 668.

Brown-Nagin, T. (2015) The wrong path to higher ed equality. Available at https://www.insidehighered.com/views/2015/02/13/ratings-and-free-community-college-are-wrong-way-end-inequality-essay (Accessed February 18 2015).

Burd, S. (2014) No one is watching over the student loan repo man. Available at http://www.edcentral.org/one-watching-student-loan-repo-man/ (Accessed August 14 2014).

Burd, et al. (2013) *Rebalancing Resources and Incentives in Federal Student Aid*. Washington, DC: The New America Foundation.

Canadian Council on Learning. (2010) State of learning in Canada, 2009–2010. Available at http://www.ccl-cca.ca/pdfs/SOLR/2010/SOLR-2010-Report-FINAL-E.pdf (Accessed February 18 2015).

Canadian Federation of Students. (2013) Student debt in Canada. Available at http://cfs-fcee.ca/wp-content/uploads/sites/2/2013/11/Factsheet-2013-11-Student-Debt-EN.pdf (Accessed February 18 2015).

Carnevale, A.P. and Strohl, J. (2010) How increasing college access is increasing inequality, and what to do about it. In R. Kahlenberg (ed.), *Rewarding Strivers: Helping Low-Income Students Succeed in College* (pp. 1–231). New York: Century Foundation Books.

Carnevale, A. and Strohl, J. (2013) Separate and unequal: How higher education reinforces the intergenerational reproduction of white racial privilege. Available at http://www.issuelab.org/click/download2/separate_and_unequal_how_higher_education_reinforces_the_intergenerational_reproduction_of_white_racial_privilege

College Board. (2012) *Trends in Student Aid 2012: Trends in Higher Education Series*. New York: College Board. Available at http://trends.collegeboard.org/student-aid

Cofer, J. and Somers, P. (2000) A comparison of the influence of debt load on the persistence of students at public and private colleges. *Journal of Student Financial Aid* 3: 39–58.

Consumer Financial Protection Bureau. (2013) Annual report of the CFPB student loan ombudsman. Available at http://files.consumerfinance.gov/f/201310_cfpb_student-loan-ombudsman-annual-report.pdf (Accessed August 10 2014).

Corak, M. (2010) Chasing the same dream, climbing different ladders: Economic mobility in the United States and Canada. Available at http://www.pewtrusts.org/uploadedfiles/wwwpewtrustsorg/Reports/Economic_Mobility/PEW_EMP_US-CANADA.pdf

Cramer, R. and Newville, D. (2009) *Children's Savings Accounts: The Case for Creating a Lifelong Savings Platform at Birth as a Foundation for a 'Save-And-Invest' Economy*. Washington, DC: New America Foundation.

Cunningham, A.F. and Kienzl, G.S. (2011) Delinquency: The untold story of student loan borrowing. Available at http://www.ihep.org/assets/files/publications/a-f/delinquency-the_untold_story_final_march_2011.pdf

Cunningham, A.F. and Santiago, D. (2008) Student aversion to borrowing: Who borrows and who doesn't. Available at http://www.nyu.edu/classes/jepsen/ihep2008-12.pdf

Delisle, J. (2014) Number of borrowers using income-based repayment doubles in one year. Available at http://www.edcentral.org/borrowers-using-income-based-repayment-double-one-year/ (Accessed July 28 2014).

Dew, J. (2008) Debt change and marital satisfaction change in recently married couples. *Family Relations* 57(1), 60–71.

Dugan, A. and Kafka, S. (2014) Student debt linked to worse health and less wealth. Available at http://www.gallup.com/poll/174317/student-debt-linked-worse-health-less-wealth.aspx (Accessed August 12 2014).

Dwyer, R.E., McCloud, L. and Hodson, R. (2011) Youth debt, mastery, and self-esteem: Class-stratified effects of indebtedness on self-concept. *Social Science Research* 40: 727–741. doi:10.1016/j.ssresearch.2011.02.001.

Edmiston, K.D., Brooks, L. and Shepelwich, S. (2012) Student loans: Overview and issues (Working Paper 12-05). The Federal Reserve Bank of Kansas City Community Affairs Department. Available at http://www.kansascityfed.org/publicat/reswkpap/pdf/rwp%2012-05.pdf (Accessed August 20 2014).

Elliott, W., Grinstein-Weiss, M. and Nam, I. (2013) *Student Debt and Declining Retirement Savings (CSD Working Paper 13–34)*. St. Louis, MO: Washington University, Center for Social Development.

Elliott, W. and Lewis, M. (2013) *Are Student Loans Widening the Wealth Gap in America? It's a Question of Equity*. Lawrence, KS: Assets and Education Initiative (AEDI).

Elliott, W. and Lewis, M. (2014) *Harnessing Assets to Build an Economic Mobility System: Reimagining the American Welfare System*. Lawrence, KS: Assets and Education Initiative (AEDI).

Elliott, W. and Nam, I. (2013) *Is Student Debt Jeopardizing the Long-Term Financial Health of U.S. Households?* St. Louis, MO: St. Louis Federal Reserve Bank. Available at https://www.stlouisfed.org/household-financial-stability/events/20130205/papers/Elliott.pdf (Accessed August 14 2014).

Engle, J. and Tinto, V. (2008) *Moving Beyond Access: College Success for Low-Income, First-Generation Students*. Washington, DC: The Pell Institute.

Falvo, N. (2012) Canada's self-imposed crisis in higher education. Available at: http://www.academicmatters.ca/2012/06/canadas-self-imposed-crisis-in-post-secondary-education/ (Accessed February 18 2015).

Fenske, R.H., Porter, J.D. and DuBrock, C.P. (2000) Tracking financial aid and persistence of women, minority, and need students in science, engineering, and mathematics. *Research in Higher Education* 41, 67–94. Available at http://link.springer.com/article/10.1023%2FA%3A1007042413040 (Accessed August 11 2014).

Field, E. (2009) Educational debt burden and career choice: Evidence from a financial aid experiment at the NYU Law School. *American Economic Journal Applied Economics* 1, no. (1): 1–21.

Frizell, S. (2014) Student loans are ruining your life. Now they're ruining the economy, too. Available at http://time.com/10577/student-loans-are-ruining-your-life-now-theyre-ruining-the-economy-too/ (Accessed August 13 2014).

Fry, R. (2014) *Young Adults, Student Debt and Economic Well-Being*. Washington, DC: Pew Research Center's Social and Demographic Trends project.

Gicheva, D. (2011) Does the student-loan burden weigh into the decision to start a family? Available at http://www.uncg.edu/bae/people/gicheva/Student_loans_marriageMarch11.pdf (Accessed September 23 2014).

Girdharry, K., Simonova, E. and Lefebvre, R. (2010) Registered Education Savings Plans –Valuable Opportunities for the Students of Tomorrow. For the Certified General Accountants Association of Canada.

Goldrick-Rab, S. and Kendall, N. (2014) Redefining college affordability: Securing America's future with a free two year college option. *The Education Optimists*. Available at http://www.luminafoundation.org/publications/ideas_summit/Redefining_College_Affordability.pdf (Accessed August 12 2014).

Greene, K. (2012) New peril for parents: Their kids' student loans. *Wall Street Journal*. Available at http://online.wsi.com/article/SB10000872396390444024204578044622648516106.html (Accessed August 19 2014).

Greenstone, M., Looney, A., Patashni, J. and Yu, M. (2013) Thirteen economic facts about social mobility and the role of education. Available at http://www.brookings.edu/research/reports/2013/06/13-facts-higher-education

Hacker, J.S. (2008) *The Great Risk Shift: The New Economic Insecurity and the Decline of the American Dream*. New York: Oxford University.

Hartman, R.R. (2013) Who makes money off your student loans? You might be surprised. Available at http://news.yahoo.com/blogs/the-lookout/makes-money-off-student-loans-might-surprised-093332073.html (Accessed August 14 2014).

Harvey, J.T. (2014) Student loan debt crisis? Available at http://www.forbes.com/sites/johntharvey/2014/04/28/student-loan-debt-crisis/ (Accessed April 28, 2014).

Heller, D.E. (2008) The impact of student loans on college access. In S. Baum, M. McPherson, and P. Steele (eds.). *The Effectiveness of Student Aid Policies: What the Research Tells Us* (pp. 39–68). New York: College Board.

Herr, E. and Burt, L. (2005) Predicting student loan default for the University of Texas at Austin. *Journal of Student Financial Aid* 35(2), 27–49.

Hiltonsmith, R. (2013) *At What Cost: How Student Debt Reduces Lifetime Wealth*. New York: Demos.

Hochschild, J.L. and Scovronick, N. (2003) *The American Dream and the Public Schools*. New York, NY: Oxford University Press.

Houle, J. and Berger, L. (2014) Is student loan debt discouraging home buying among young adults? Available at http://www.appam.org/assets/1/7/Is_Student_Loan_Debt_Discouraging_Home_Buying_Among_Young_Adults.pdf (Accessed August 14 2014).

Hoxby, C.M. and Avery, C. (2012) The missing "one-offs": The hidden supply of high-achieving, low income students. Available at http://www.nber.org/papers/w18586 (Accessed August 12 2014).

Hurley, D., Harnisch, T. and Nassirian, B. (2014) *A Proposed Federal Matching Program to Stop the Privatization of Public Higher Education*. Washington, DC: American Association of Public Colleges and Universities. Available at http://www.aascu.org/policy/publications/policy-matters/federalmatchingprogram.pdf (Accessed February 18 2015).

Janowitz, M. (1976) *Social Control of the Welfare State*. New York: Elsevier Scientific Publishing Co.

Jesse, D. (2013) Government books $41.3 billion in student loan profits. Available at http://www.google.com/url?sa=t&rct=j&q=&esrc=s&source=web&cd=1&ved=0CCAQFjAA&url=http%3A%2F%2Fwww.usatoday.com%2Fstory%2Fnews%2Fnation%2F2013%2F11%2F25%2Ffederal-student-loan-profit%2F3696009%2F&ei=NyX8U7-VIIWOyASC-4CQAg&usg=AFQjCNGf4ACixG4UGZD0cRp46wH6wAEecw&sig2=9OxvkYgT5mXOnTTVlf1N4Q (Accessed August 14 2014).

Karsten, T. (2012) Will student debt lead to a financial crisis? http://www.cnbc.com/id/47159110

Keister, M.P. (2000) *Wealth in America*. Cambridge, MA: Cambridge University Press.

Kim, D. (2007) The effects of loans on students' degree attainment: Differences by student and institutional characteristics. *Harvard Educational Review* 77(1), 64–100.

Korkki, P. (2014) The ripple effects of student debt. *The New York Times*. Available at http://www.nytimes.com/2014/05/25/business/the-ripple-effects-of-rising-student-debt.html?_r=0 (Accessed August 13 2014).

Levin, A. (2013) Politicians, ignore the millennial student loan crisis at your own risk. Available at http://www.huffingtonpost.com/adam-levin/politicians-ignore-the-mi_b_4428230.html (Accessed February 18 2015).

Lochner, L. and Monge-Naranjo, A. (2004) *Education and Default Incentives with Government Student Loan Programs*. Cambridge, MA: National Bureau of Economic Research.

Luhby, T. (2014) The American dream is out of reach. Available at http://money.cnn.com/2014/06/04/news/economy/american-dream/ (Accessed August 14 2014).

Martin, A. (2012) Debt collectors cashing in on student loans. Available at http://www.nytimes.com/2012/09/09/business/once-a-student-now-dogged-by-collection-agencies.html?hp (Accessed January 5 2012).

Minicozzi, A. (2005) The short term effect of educational debt on job decisions. *Economics of Education Review* 24 no. 4: 417–30.

Mishory, J., O'Sullivan, R. and Invincibles, Y. (2012) Denied? The impact of student debt on the ability to buy a house. Available at http://younginvincibles.org/wp-content/uploads/2012/08/Denied-The-Impact-of-Student-Debt-on-the-Ability-to-Buy-a-House-8.14.12.pdf (Accessed November 9 2012).

Mishel, L., Bivens, J., Gould, E. and Shierholz, H. (2012) *The State of Working America* (12th edn). Ithaca, NY: Cornell University Press.

Mishel, L., Bivens, J., Gould, E. and Shierholz, H. (2013) *The State of Working America* (12th edn). Ithaca: NY: Economic Policy Institute Book, Cornell University Press.

National Association of Consumer Bankruptcy Attorneys. (2012) The student loan "debt bomb": America's next mortgage-style economic crisis? Available at http://nacba.org/Portals/0/Documents/Student%20Loan%20Debt/020712%20NACBA%20student%20loan%20debt%20report.pdf (Accessed February 18 2015).

National Center for Education Statistics. (2011) Community college student outcomes: 1994–2009. NCES 2012–253.

Oliver, M.L. and Shapiro, T.M. (2006) *Black Wealth/White Wealth: A New Perspective on Racial Inequality* (Vol. 10th-anniversary edn). New York: Routledge.

Owen, S. and Sawhill, I. (2013) *Should Everyone go to College? (CCF Brief #50)*. Washington, DC: Center on Children and Families at Brookings.

Perna, L.W. (2000) Differences in the decision to attend college among African Americans, Hispanics, and Whites. *The Journal of Higher Education* 71, no. 2 (2000): 117–141.

Pew Charitable Trusts. (2013) Retirement security across generations. Available at http://www.pewtrusts.org/en/research-and-analysis/reports/0001/01/01/retirement-security-across-generations (Accessed February 18 2015).

Pew Charitable Trusts. (2014) *A New Financial Reality: The Balance Sheets and Economic Mobility of Generation X*. Washington, DC: The Pew Charitable Trusts. Available at http://www.pewtrusts.org/en/research-and-analysis/reports/2014/09/a-new-financial-reality (Accessed September 23 2014).

Pew Research Center. (2014) *The Rising Cost of Not Going to College*. Available at: http://www.pewsocialtrends.org/2014/02/11/the-rising-cost-of-not-going-to-college/ (Accessed February 18 2015).

Rahman, A. (2014) *Canada Student Loans Program Overview*. Presentation to U.S. researchers. Gatineau, Quebec: Canada.

Rethinking Pell Grants Study Group. (2013) *Rethinking Pell Grants*. Washington, DC: The College Board. Available at http://m.insidehighered.com/sites/default/server_files/files/RethnkPellGrants_FullReport_Web.pdf (Accessed February 18 2015).

Rothstein, J. and Rouse, C.E. (2011) Constrained after college: Student loans and early-career occupational choices. *Journal of Public Economics* 95 no. (1–2): 149–163.

Sanchez, M. (2012) Student loan debt isn't a crisis. Available at http://careercollegecentral.com/news/student-loan-debt-isn%E2%80%99t-crisis (Accessed February 19 2014).

Schneider, M. (2013) Higher education pays, but a lot more for some graduates than for others. Available at http://www.collegemeasures.org/post/2013/09/View-full-report-here.aspx (Accessed August 20 2014).

Shand, J. M. (2007) The impact of early-life debt on the homeownership rates of young households: An empirical investigation. http://www.fdic.gov/bank/analytical/cfr/2008/jan/CFR_SS_2008Shand.pdf (Accessed August 2 2014).

Shapiro, T. (2004) *The Hidden Cost of Being African-American: How Wealth Perpetuates Inequality*. New York: Oxford University Press.

Shapiro, T., Meschede, T. and Osoro, S. (2013) *The Roots of the Widening Racial Wealth Gap: Explaining the Black-White Economic Divide*. Waltham, MA: Brandeis University, Institute on Assets and Social Policy.

Sheets, R.G. and Crawford, S. (2014) From income-based repayment plans to an income-based loan system. George Washington Institute of Public Policy. Available at: http://www.luminafoundation.org/

publications/ideas_summit/From_Income-based_Repayment_Plans_to_an_Income-based_Loan_
System.pdf (Accessed August 12 2014).

Sherraden, M. (1991) *Assets and the Poor: A New American Welfare Policy.* Armonk, NY:
M.E. Sharpe.

Statistics Canada. (2011) Spending on postsecondary education. Available at http://www.statcan.gc.ca/
pub/81-599-x/81-599-x2011007-eng.pdf (Accessed February 18 2015).

Stone, C., Van Horn, C. and Zukin, C. (2012) *Chasing the American Dream: Recent College Graduates
and the Great Recession.* New Brunswick, NJ: Center for Workforce Development. Available at
http://www.heldrich.rutgers.edu/sites/default/files/content/Chasing_American_Dream_Report.pdf

Talbott, J. (2014) How to pay for school with no student debt. Available at http://www.
huffingtonpost.com/john-r-talbott/how-to-pay-for-school-wit_b_4889633.html (Accessed August
13 2014).

Thompson, C. (2014) Student loan crisis is making inequality worse: Experts. Available at
http://www.huffingtonpost.com/2014/03/27/student-loans-inequality_n_5042197.html (Accessed
August 13 2014).

United States Department of Education. (2012) First official three-year student loan default rates published. Available at http://www.ed.gov/news/press-releases/first-official-three-year-student-loan-
default-rates-published (Accessed February 18 2015).

Usher, A. (2005) Global Debt Patterns: An International Comparison of Student Loan Burdens
and Repayment Conditions. Toronto, Ontario: Educational Policy Institute. Available at http://
educationalpolicy.org/pdf/global_debt_patterns.pdf (Accessed February 18 2015).

Woo, J.H. (2002) *Clearing Accounts: The Causes of Student Loan Default.* Rancho Cordova, CA:
EdFund.

Appendix A

Table A1. Research Examining Student Loan Effects on Young Adults' Post-Graduation Financial Outcomes

Study	Covariates	Methods	Post-Graduation Outcome(s)	Key Findings
1. The short-term effect of educational debt on job decisions				
Minicozzi (2005)	*College Debt*: Debt amount *Primary Controls*: Age, White, 2-year college, 4-year college, graduate school, worked while in school, tenure at job; school ranking; U.S. unemployment rate	*Methods*: Loglinear wage regression; standard wage growth model *Data*: 1987 National Post-secondary Student Aid Survey (contains survey on out of school students) 3,508 men who finished normal schooling by age 35 and pursed a 2- or 4-year college degree	Hourly Wages	Higher educational debt is associated with higher initial wage rate the year after finishing school and lower wage growth over the next 4 years
2. Constrained after college: Student loans and early career occupational choices				
Rothstein and Rouse (2011)	College debt: Simulated loan Primary Controls: GPA; Honors; Post-graduation plans (plans graduate school, plans employment, has a job); Occupation (Consulting/ banking/finance; any high-salary industry; non-profit/govt./ education; & any low-salary industry); Salary (salary below $41,395; 25th percentile); Alumni gifts (pledge for 1st year after graduation; gift in 1st year after graduation)	Methods: Regression-based version of Difference-in-Difference/Wald estimator; combined with instrumental variables Data: A selective university that introduced a "no-loans" policy under which the loan component of financial aid was replaced with grants Policy introduced in 1998 to incoming students and then in 2001 to all students 8,641 student from cohorts graduating in 1999/2001 & 2005/2006 Natural Experiment	Career choice	Debt causes graduates to choose substantially higher-salary jobs and reduces the probability that students choose low-paid public interest jobs

(continued)

Table A1. (*Continued*)

Study	Covariates	Methods	Post-Graduation Outcome(s)	Key Findings
3.	The impact of early life debt on the homeownership rates of young households: An empirical investigation			
Shand (2007)	*College Debt*: Student loan amount debt *Primary Controls*: Credit constraint, poor credit, balance on credit card, both educational and credit card debt, young owner-occupiers, head's education, spouse's education, gender, marital status, race, work status	*Methods*: Bivariate probit model Two underlying models, on that governs whether the household is not credit constrained, and the other that determines if the household would prefer to own a home *Data*: Survey of Consumer Finance (SCF) 1992, 1995, 1998, 2001, and 2004 Repeated-cross-sectional data Households ages 23–32	Homeownership rates	Student loans associated with reduced homeowner-ship rates; Credit constraints do not appear to explain the homeowner-ship gap
4.	Young adult student loan borrowers retreat from housing and auto markets			
Brown and Caldwell (2013)	*College Debt*: Student Debt Use *Primary Controls*: N/A	*Methods*: Do not discuss *Data*: Consumer Credit Panel Examine 30 year olds with regard to homeownership Examine 25 year olds with regard to vehicle purchase and total debt	Homeownership Vehicle Purchase Total Debt	Student debtors were more likely to own a home prior to 2012 but by 2012 they were less likely; same pattern holders in the case of vehicle purchase; Student debtors are borrow less

Table A1. (*Continued*)

Study	Covariates	Methods	Post-Graduation Outcome(s)	Key Findings
5. Is student debt jeopardizing the short-term financial health of U.S. households?				
Elliott and Nam (2013)	*College Debt*: Student loan use; amount of student loan debt *Primary Controls*: Household income; 2007 net worth; 4-year college graduate; age; occupational prestige; marital status; use of welfare; race; health insurance	*Methods*: Quantile regression *Data 1*: Survey of Consumer Finance (SCF) 2007–2009 panel data Household level data (N = 3857) *Data 2*: Only households with 4-year graduate included (*n* = 2,385) *Data 3*: Only households with 4-year graduate with outstanding debt (*n* = 543)	Net Worth (liabilities - assets)	Households with student loan debt and median 2007 net worth of $128828 incur a loss of about 54% of net worth in 2009 compared to their counterparts with no student loans
6. How student debt reduces lifetime wealth				
Hiltonsmith (2013)	*College Debt*: Amount of student debt *Primary Controls*: Assumes inflation 2.5% Real income growth of 2.05% per year for household no student debt 1.6 for households with student debt Assumes student debt to be $53,200 (dual household)[2]	*Methods*: Model estimations *Data*: 2010 Survey of Consumer Finance (SCF) Projects through ages 18–64	Net worth; retirement savings; home equity	Households with student debt vs. households without debt: Lifetime wealth loss of $208,000; $134,000 loss in retirement savings; $70,000 in home equity; income falls behind by age 40

(*continued*)

Table A1. (*Continued*)

Study	Covariates	Methods	Post-Graduation Outcome(s)	Key Findings
7. 73 will be the retirement norm for millennials				
Egoian (2013)	*College Debt*: Amount of Student Debt *Primary Controls*: Median graduate, with median student debt and median starting salary Average 2012 social security benefit, average 2012 401(k) match, 30 year average national salary growth rate, 30 year average inflation rate, 30 year annualized S&P 500 returns, life expectancy, 30 year average personal savings rate, 2012 Stafford loan interest rates, and standard loan repayment terms	*Methods*: Model estimations *Data*: Bureau of Economic Analysis, Bureau of Labor Statistics, Fidelity Investments; National Association of College and Employers; New York Federal Reserve; Pew Research Center; Social Security Administration; World Bank; and Consumer Financial Protection Bureau	Retirement savings	Most college graduates will not be able to retire until 73 due to high debt load; The median debt load of $23,300 will cost student over $115,000 (in today's dollars) by the time they reach retirement age
8. How much is too much? Evidence of financial well-being and student loan debt				
Akers (2014)	*College Debt*: Amount of Student Debt; Monthly Payments *Primary Controls*: Spouse controls and age	*Methods*: Year-fixed effects; Ordinary least squares estimates *Data*: Survey of Consumer Finance (SCF); 2001, 2004; 2007; and 2010 Ages 20 – 40 Repeated cross-sectional data	Financial hardship (i.e., late bill payment)	Highest rates of late bill payment, are observed among household with outstanding debts less than $5000; Nearly one-third of households, regardless of their borrowing behavior, report they have made late payments on bills at least once during the last two years; highest rates of financial distress, as measured by late bill payments, are seen among households with the lowest levels of educational attainment

Table A1. (*Continued*)

Study	Covariates	Methods	Post-Graduation Outcome(s)	Key Findings
9.	Young adults, student debt and economic well-being			
Fry (2014)	*College Debt*: Outstanding Student Debt *Primary Controls*: N/A	*Methods*: Descriptive analysis *Data*: 2010 Survey of Consumer Finance (SCF) Household Level Heads younger than 40 ($n = 1,711$)	Overall Debt Financial Distress Net Worth	Household with student debt have less net worth, more overall debt, and are more likely to be financially distressed; Prior to age 40, income does not differ by student debt status but wealth does
10.	Is student loan debt discouraging home buying among young adults?			
Houle and Berger (2014)	*College Debt*: Amount of Student Debt *Primary Controls*: Average education tuition cost; race; region; living arrangement; parent's education level; marital status; employment household income	*Methods*: Reduced form ordinary least squares regression Linear probability models Instrumental variable (cost of college attended): two-stage leas squares *Data 1*: National longitudinal Study of Youth 1997 (NLSY97) Individual level data Ages 25 and 30 ($n = 11,003$) Replaced missing data with sample mean *Data 2*: Integrated Post-secondary Education Data System (IPEDS) Delta Cost Project –for instrumental variable	Homeownership; holding a mortgage; and the amount of mortgage debt	Find modest evidence that rising student loan debt is predictive of homeowner-ship among young adults; however, the effects are stronger for Blacks than Whites

Note: Articles are listed in ascending chronological order by publication year.

4

ISLAMIC BANKING AND FINANCE: RECENT EMPIRICAL LITERATURE AND DIRECTIONS FOR FUTURE RESEARCH

Pejman Abedifar

School of Management, University of St Andrews

Shahid M. Ebrahim

Durham Business School, Durham University Business School

Philip Molyneux

Bangor Business School, Bangor University

Amine Tarazi

Université de Limoges, LAPE

1. Introduction

The key principles underlying Islamic banking and finance – namely the prohibition of *Riba* (narrowly interpreted as interest) and adherence to other *Shariá* (Islamic law) requirements – are as ancient as religion itself, although it has only been since the 1960's that banks have offered Islamic financial services.[1] These *Shariá* compliant services now sum-up to a global industry amounting to around $2 trillion in assets, of which 80% is accounted for by Islamic banks (including Islamic windows of conventional banks), 15% *Sukuk* (Islamic bonds),[2] 4% Islamic mutual funds and 1% *Takaful* (Islamic insurance) (The Economist, 2014). According to the Islamic Financial Services Board (2013), Iran is the biggest Islamic banking market (accounting for around 40% of global Islamic banking assets) followed by Saudi Arabia (14%), Malaysia (10%) and the United Arab Emirates (UAE) and Kuwait (both with 9% shares). There are few countries that have solely Islamic banks – only Iran and Sudan – in the majority of Muslim countries Islamic banks compete head-on with conventional banks. For instance in places such as Saudi Arabia around 35% of banking sector assets are *Shariá* compliant, figures are lower for UAE (22%), Qatar (20%) and Malaysia (20%). While Islamic

A Collection of Surveys on Savings and Wealth Accumulation, First Edition. Edited by Edda Claus and Iris Claus.
Chapters © 2016 The Authors. Book compilation © 2016 John Wiley & Sons, Ltd. Published 2016 by John Wiley & Sons, Ltd.

banking and financial assets comprise under 1% of total global financial assets (given Credit Suisse's 2013 estimates of world financial assets) it is a sector that has grown faster than conventional (Western) finance since the 2007–2008 banking crisis, and this trend is expected to continue into the near future (The Economist, 2014). In addition to the growth in banking assets there is increasing competition between major financial centres to take the lead in *Sukuk* issuance and to develop a broader array of Islamic investment products (TheCityUk, 2013). In the light of these developments it is timely to provide a review of the recent empirical literature on Islamic banking and finance to highlight the main areas of interest and futures areas for further research.

2. A Brief History

From the earliest stages in Islamic history, Muslims were able to establish a system without interest for mobilizing resources to finance productive activities and consumer needs. The system worked quite effectively during the heyday of Islamic civilization and for centuries thereafter. According to Goitein (1971) the *Mudharabah* partnership (incorporating profit-sharing and loss-bearing – PSLB-features), the Musharakah facility (incorporating profit and loss – PLS-sharing features) and non-interest-based borrowing and lending formed the basis of commerce and industry in twelfth and thirteenth centuries in the Mediterranean region.[3] However, the Protestant Reformation in the Western world provided an impetus to intellectual growth (Hillebrand, 2009). This eventually led to the change in the centre of economic gravity to the West and Western financial institutions (especially banks) became dominant and the Islamic tradition remained dormant. Over the last 50 years or so, however, there has been a revival of interest in developing a modern version of the historic Islamic financial system in the wake of Muslims' desire to stay clear of interest and practice financial transactions consistent with *Shariá* principles.

When commercial banking emerged after the industrial revolution, Muslim scholars expressed reservations with the Western model of financial intermediation due to its reliance on interest and they called for the development of alternative mechanisms to perform a financial intermediation function in Muslim societies (Iqbal and Molyneux, 2005, Molyneux and Iqbal, 2005). Muslims to a significant extent refrained from dealing with commercial banks. However, the growing needs of traders, industrialists and other entrepreneurs in rapidly monetizing economies were pressing and as a consequence Muslim economists and bankers took up the challenge of developing alternative models of financial intermediation. In the early 19th century most of the Muslim world was under colonial rule. When many of these countries gained their independence after World War II, practical experiments in interest-free financing started at a modest scale and gradually expanded in scope.

While credit societies and cooperatives working on an interest-free basis existed in several Muslim countries even during the colonial period, the semblance of banking institutions started emerging in the early 1960s. A pioneering experiment of putting Islamic principles governing financial dealings into practice was conducted in Mit-Ghamr, Egypt, from 1963–1967. Modelled on the German saving banks (Sparkassen), the Mit-Ghamr initiative mobilized small savings from the rural sector largely through savings accounts. No interest was paid to account holders. However, as an incentive they were eligible for small short-term interest-free loans for productive purposes. Account holders were allowed to withdraw their deposits on demand. In addition, investment accounts on the basis of *Mudharabah* were also introduced. The funds so mobilized were invested on the basis of PSLB with entrepreneurs.

The first interest-free institution with 'bank' in its name, Nasser Social Bank, was established in Egypt in 1971.[4] This was the first time a government in a Muslim country provided public support for incorporating an interest-free institution. Even though the objectives of the Nasser Social Bank were mainly social, such as providing interest-free loans to the poor and needy; scholarships to students; and micro-credits to small projects on a PLS basis; the involvement of a public authority in interest-free banking sent important signals to Muslim businessmen having surplus funds. A group of such businessmen established the Dubai Islamic Bank in 1975. This was the first Islamic Bank established on private initiative. However, official support was crucial with the governments of UAE and Kuwait contributing respectively 20% and 10% of the capital (Iqbal and Molyneux, 2005).

Probably one of the most important developments in the history of Islamic banking took place with the establishment of the Islamic Development Bank (IDB) in 1975. The IDB was established as an international financial institution by representatives of member countries of the Organization of the Islamic Conference (OIC) (in 1975 there were 23 members increasing to 57 by 2014). The IDB's main objective is to promote economic and social development in the Muslim world in accordance with the principles of *Shariá* and it has been a major financier and promoter of an array of Islamic banking and finance initiatives since its formation.

Between 1975 and 1990 the Islamic financial industry developed into an alternative model of financial intermediation. The period was marked by the establishment of a substantial number of Islamic financial institutions in the private sector. In addition, governments in three countries, namely, Pakistan, Iran and Sudan, expressed the desire to gradually eliminate interest from their entire economies and substitute it with banking systems based entirely on Islamic principles – by 1983 and 1984 Iran and Sudan had (virtually) achieved these objectives. Even more important was the fact that several multinational banks started offering Islamic financial products. This was a clear recognition of the viability of the new model and its acceptance by international players. The International Monetary Fund and the World Bank also recognized Islamic financial products as alternative means of financial intermediation (Sundararajan and Errico, 2002; World Bank, 2013). During the 1990s, while growth in the Islamic banking industry continued, attention was also given to the development of non-bank financial institutions. Islamic financial institutions other than banks started coming on the scene in increasing numbers. These included insurance companies and investment funds although (as noted earlier) the bulk of Islamic financial assets (80%) are in banking business.

Initiatives for the establishment of some infrastructure institutions supporting the Islamic financial industry also started in the 1990s. In the beginning, Islamic banking institutions had to work within the institutional framework that supported conventional banking and they were at somewhat of a comparative disadvantage because the institutional framework was not specifically geared to Islamic needs. While still in its infancy, a beginning was made towards constructing a network of supporting institutions for the Islamic financial industry.

Nowadays Islamic banking and finance manifests itself in five ways:

1. Banks and financial institutions operate in countries where the promotion of an Islamic financial system receives active government support.[5]
2. Islamic banks and financial institutions operate in the private corporate sector competing with conventional (Western) institutions.
3. Islamic banking is practiced by conventional commercial banks (via Islamic windows), traditional Islamic banks as well as non-bank financial institutions.
4. Multinational financial institutions (like the IDB in Jeddah) operate on *Shariá* principles.

5. Islamic capital market instruments (mutual funds, *Sukuk*), and insurance *(Takaful)* are becoming more important, for instance, *Sukuk* issuance partly funded London's Olympic Village and 'Shard' building.

3. Principle of Islamic Banking and Finance

Islamic banking and finance is based on *Shariá* principles which forbid payment or receipt of *Riba* generally misconstrued as interest (Pryor, 2007).[6] The lending facility encouraged in the medieval era of Islamic society is that of gratuitous loans termed as *Qard Al-Hasan*. It is interesting to note that *Shariá* recognizes the time value of money, since according to Islamic rules the price of a good to be sold on a deferred payment basis can be different from its current value.[7] While *Shariá* recognizes excessive payments in business transactions, it prohibits the same on lending activities (Obaidullah, 2005). Islamic banks typically fund their lending with depositors funds and their equity capital (very rarely do they employ *Sukuk* bonds for such financing). Islamic finance has evolved based on the precedence of transactions conducted specifically in the medieval era and recorded under *Fiqh al-Muamalat*. These can mainly be categorized as: 1) Debt-based financing: where the financier purchases or has the underlying assets constructed or purchased and then this is sold to the client at a mark-up. The sale would be on a deferred-payment basis with one or several instalments. 2) Lease-based financing: the financier purchases or has the underlying assets constructed or purchased and then rents it to the client. At the end of the rental period (or proportionate to the rentals) ownership would be transferred wholly or partially to the client. 3) PSLB financing: the financier is the partner of the client and the realized profit or loss would be shared according to pre-agreed proportions (Khan and Ahmed, 2001). The first two Islamic finance methods are collectively known as 'Non-PSLB' contracts.

Besides restrictions on *Riba*, *Shariá* has various other prohibitions which have to be taken into account. For instance, according to *Shariá* all contracts should be free of '*Gharar*', which is narrowly interpreted as excessive uncertainty.[8] Hence as noted earlier, Islamic financial institutions face some restrictions on application of financial derivatives and other types of contracts (including various forms of insurance policies). In addition, Islamic financial firms are not allowed to undertake business prohibited under Islamic law (known as *Haraam*) such as investing in companies involved with alcohol, gambling, non-Islamic financial services, pornography, tobacco or weapons. However, as many large firms receive a modest proportion of income from such prohibited activities (for instance, hotel chains and alcohol sales), modern *Shariá* scholars tend to allow investment in companies with tolerable proportions of revenues from prohibited activities under the condition of *Haraam* purification. This requires investors to donate equivalent proportion of their distributions from such companies to charities to purify their earnings from prohibited activities (Hoepner *et al.*, 2011). Islamic financial institutions all have *Shariá* supervisory boards composed of executive management as well as Islamic scholars whose role it is to ensure that the firm's activities are undertaken in a *Shariá* compliant manner.[9]

It has been argued that Islamic finance contracts are more complex than conventional contracts (Errico and Farahbaksh, 1998; Dar and Presley, 2000; Sundararajan and Errico, 2002 and Abedifar *et al.*, 2013, discuss the complexity of the *Sharia*-based finance contracts). Generally, in debt-based or lease-based finance, such as *Murabaha*, Islamic banks arrange for the goods/projects to be purchased and then sell or rent them (at a mark-up) to clients. For purchase/implementation of the goods/projects, Islamic banks normally appoint the client as their agent. Such a framework is somewhat complicated as compared to conventional loan contracts. Sundararajan and Errico (2002) note the specific risks attached to various Non-PSLB methods, such as *Salam* and *Ijara*. In the former, Islamic banks are exposed to both credit and commodity price risks; in the latter, unlike conventional lease contracts, Islamic banks cannot transfer ownership and therefore have to bear all the risks until the end of the lease period.

Another area of debate relates to the treatment of default penalties. Some jurisdictions rule that such penalties are not authorized by *Shariá*, so banks make use of rebates instead (Khan and Ahmed, 2001). Here the mark-up on the finance arrangement implicitly covers the return to the banks as well as a default penalty component. If the client repays the loan in a timely manner then they will receive the rebate. While default interest payments are typically calculated over the delayed period in conventional banking, some Islamic banks collect the delayed penalty over the whole financing period. In addition, Islamic banks can also face restrictions regarding the use of derivatives as well as different types of collateral, for instance, they are not authorized to use interest-based assets, like money market instruments or bonds, for security.

In addition to lending, conventional banks also allocate a part of their funds to investments. Such investments normally include purchase of bonds (as well as instruments with shorter maturities) of different types that have risk/return features that help manage portfolio risk. Islamic banks have limited options for such investments since they are not authorized to invest in interest bearing instruments. Alternatively they can invest in short-term *Sukuk* issued by the International Islamic Liquidity Management Corporation (IILM – see Archer and Karim, 2014).[10] Although (like in short-term Islamic money markets) the asset class still remains relatively underdeveloped, limitations on Islamic bank investment opportunities has been weakened over time due to *Haraam* purification as well as the expansion of alternative Islamic financing instruments. Interest rates (in a mixed system) and 'PSLB rates' in a purely Islamic system are typically set by the central bank. The interbank rates based on 'wakalah' (agency) agreements are set on PSLB rates, which usually track market rates.

4. Performance of Islamic versus Conventional Banks

Table 1 illustrates recent empirical literature comparing the performance of Islamic and conventional banks. Early studies focus on single countries, such as those by Bashir (1999) on Sudan, Samad (1999) and Majid *et al.* (2003) on Malaysia, and El-Gamal and Inanoglu (2002) on Turkey, and use a variety of approaches (OLS regression, analysis of variance and stochastic frontier analysis) to compare various performance features of Islamic versus conventional banks. More recent studies tend to be cross-country in nature and use frontier modelling approaches, either parametric (Majid *et al.*, 2003; Mohamad *et al.*, 2008; Gheeraeart and Weill, 2014) or non-parametric (Yudistra, 2004; Bader *et al.*, 2008; Johnes *et al.*, 2014) to model cross-country bank cost and profit efficiency (as well as productivity). Mohamad *et al.* (2008), for instance, analyse a sample of banks operating in 21 OIC member countries between 1990 and 2005 and use the non-parametric Data Envelopment Analysis (DEA) approach to compare the cost, profit and revenue efficiency of conventional banks with Islamic banks. They find no significant difference between the efficiency features of the two kinds of banks. In contrast, Johnes *et al.* (2009) look at banks operating in six Gulf Cooperation Council (GCC) countries between 2004 and 2007 again using DEA, as well as various other performance metrics including the Malmquist productivity index. Johnes *et al.* (2009) find that Islamic banks are significantly less efficient than their conventional counterparts and this result is also confirmed in a later study by Johnes *et al.* (2014) that has a larger sample – banks from countries where more than 60% of the population are Muslim (18 countries in total) over 2004 and 2009.

Table 1. Performance of Islamic versus Conventional Banks – Recent Empirical Evidence.

Authors	Country(ies) of Study	Period	Data Type	Research Focus	Methodology	Main Finding
Bashir (1999)	Sudan	1979–1993	Yearly bank-level accounting data	Asset size and bank performance	Regression – OLS	Larger banks are more profitable yet have higher leverage. Analysis is based on only two Islamic banks.
Samad (1999)	Malaysia	1992–1996	Yearly bank-level accounting data	Cost efficiency	Descriptive statistics and ANOVA	Islamic banks are more efficient than their conventional counterparts.
El-Gamal *et al.* (2002)	Turkey	1990–2000	Yearly bank level accounting data	Production technology	Stochastic Frontier Analysis	Islamic banks have a similar production technology to conventional commercial banks.
Majid *et al.* (2003)	Malaysia	1993–2000	Yearly bank level accounting data	Cost efficiency	Stochastic Frontier Analysis	No statistically significant difference in the level of efficiency between Islamic and conventional banks and no evidence to suggest that ownership influences cost efficiency.
Hassan and Bashir (2003)	Islamic banks operating in 21 countries	1994–2001	Yearly bank level accounting data	Determinants of bank profitability (ROA, ROE, NIM)	Regression – GLS	Controlling for macroeconomic environment, financial market structure, and taxation, the results indicate that high capital and loan-to-asset ratios lead to higher profitability (as does favorable macroeconomic conditions).

Study	Sample	Period	Data	Efficiency	Methodology	Findings
Yudistra (2004)	Islamic banks operating in 12 countries	1997–2000	Yearly bank level accounting data	Technical and scale efficiency	Data Envelopment Analysis (DEA) and OLS regression	Islamic bank inefficiencies appear relatively low (around 10%) compared with those for conventional banks derived from other studies. Small to medium-sized Islamic banks exhibit diseconomies of scale. Islamic banks in the Middle East are less efficient than those operating outside the region.
Al-Jarrah and Molyneux (2005)	Bahrain, Egypt, Jordan and Saudi Arabia	1992–2000	Yearly bank level accounting data	Cost and profit efficiency	Stochastic Frontier Analysis	Islamic banks are found to be the most cost and profit efficient banks compared to conventional commercial and investment banks.
Mohamad et al. (2008)	21 Organization of Islamic Conference (OIC) countries	1990–2005	Yearly bank level accounting data	Cost and profit efficiency	Stochastic Frontier Analysis	No significant difference between cost and profit efficiency of conventional versus Islamic banks, irrespective of size, age and geographical location. Islamic banks based in the Middle East and Turkey are more cost efficient than their African counterparts.

(*continued*)

Table 1. (*Continued*)

Authors	Country(ies) of Study	Period	Data Type	Research Focus	Methodology	Main Finding
Bader *et al.* (2008)	21 OIC countries	1995–2005	Yearly bank level accounting data	Cost, revenue and profit efficiency	Data Envelopment Analysis	No significant difference between cost, revenue and profit efficiency of conventional versus Islamic banks. Note this study uses the same sample as Mohamad *et al.* (2008).
Abdul-Majid *et al.* (2010)	10 countries	1996–2002	Yearly bank level accounting data	Returns to scale and efficiency	Parametric output distance function	Islamic banks are found to have moderately higher returns to scale than conventional banks but appear less efficient due to *Sharia* compliance. Country effects have a significant impact on efficiency differences.
Johnes *et al.* (2009)	GCC – 6 countries	2004–2007	Yearly bank level accounting data	Efficiency and productivity	DEA Malmquist productivity Ratio Analysis	Islamic banks have (significantly) lower efficiency than conventional banks. Modest productivity growth over the study period.
Rashwan (2010)	15 countries	2007–2009	Bank level data	Profitability and efficiency over the banking crisis	Multivariate analysis of variance (MANOVA)	Islamic banks are more profitable and efficient than traditional banks pre-crisis but the opposite is the case post-crisis.

Study	Sample	Period	Data	Focus	Methodology	Findings
Abdul-Majid et al. (2011a,b)	Malaysia	1996–2002	Bank level data	Efficiency and productivity	Stochastic Frontier Analysis	Islamic banks and Islamic window banks are less cost efficient than their conventional counterparts.
Beck et al. (2013)	141 countries (including 22 OIC member countries)	1995–2007	Yearly bank-level accounting data	Efficiency, asset quality, stability and business orientation	Regression – OLS Fixed effects, Robust	Few significant differences are found between Islamic and conventional banks.
Gheeraeart and Weill (2014)	70 countries	2000–2005	Yearly bank-level accounting data and macro data	Examines Islamic banking development and macroeconomic efficiency	Stochastic Frontier Analysis	There is a non-linear relationship between Islamic banking development and macroeconomic efficiency. Islamic banking aids macroeconomic efficiency up to a point and then restricts it thereafter.
Johnes et al. (2014)	Countries where at least 60% of the population is Muslim – 18 countries.	2004–2009	Yearly bank-level accounting data	Efficiency	DEA, meta-frontier, Two-stage approach examining determinants of efficiency	Islamic banks are less efficient, in general, than their conventional counterparts.

Source: Adapted from Abedifar *et al.* (2013) Table 1 and authors updates.

Possibly the most comprehensive study is that by Beck *et al.* (2013) who investigate Islamic bank performance issues using a sample of banks from 141 countries over 1995 and 2007. Using a variety of regression approaches (OLS, fixed effects and robust regression) and comparing risk, efficiency and business model features, they find few significant differences between Islamic and conventional banks.

Despite the focus of performance comparisons to be dominated by efficiency comparisons, no strong consensus emerges from this literature, although a (small) majority of studies find no major difference between Islamic and conventional banks in terms of cost and profit efficiency. Fewer studies focus on the determinants of bank profitability (Hassan and Bashir, 2003, Rashwan, 2010) and here there is some evidence that better capitalised and loaned-out Islamic banks are more profitable. A study by Gheeraeart and Weill (2014) covering 70 countries, interestingly finds a non-linear relationship between Islamic banking development and macroeconomic efficiency – Islamic banking aids macroeconomic efficiency up to a point and then restricts it thereafter.[11]

5. Risks in Islamic Banking?

Islamic banking is characterized by features that appear on the one hand to reduce risk: the religious beliefs of clients may induce greater loyalty and discourage default (it may also reduce deposit withdrawal risk). On the other hand it could increase risk due to such factors as: the complexity of Islamic loan contracts, limited default penalties and moral hazard incentives caused by PSLB contracts. In terms of insolvency risk, the special relationship with depositors could provide Islamic banks with greater capacity to bear losses yet at the same time, operational limitations on investment and risk management activities could make them less stable than their conventional counterparts. Moreover, while interest is forbidden in Islamic banking, those institutions that compete with conventional banks may be forced to mirror their pricing behaviour and as such may be subject to (indirect) interest rate risk.

After the global financial crisis in 2007–2008 there has been increased interest in risk in banking in general as well as in the Islamic world. Table 2 illustrates the most recent literature.

Early studies typically use regression approaches to try and explain various types of risk and to examine differences between conventional and Islamic banks. Čihák and Hesse (2010) study banks operating in 20 OIC member countries over 1993–2004, and Abedifar *et al.* (2013) with a more recent sample from 24 OIC countries over 1999–2009. Both use regression analysis to examine risk (using the Z-score measure) to gauge insolvency risks and typically find that small Islamic banks have lower default risk compared with small conventional banks, but the opposite is the case for larger Islamic banks where insolvency risk is higher. Beck *et al.* (2013), however, using a more comprehensive sample find no such differences. The most recent studies have tended to investigate survivorship of the two types of banks, again cross country, using duration models. Pappas *et al.* (2014), for instance, model the survival rates of Islamic and conventional banks over 1995–2010 using duration analysis and find that Islamic banks have significantly lower failure rates compared to similar conventional banks. Baele *et al.* (2014) use hazard functions to model the loan default rates of small business loan borrowers in Pakistan. Using a unique data sample of 150,000 small business loans (from the Central Bank of Pakistan's Credit Register) over 2006–2008 they find that the default rate on small business Islamic loans is less than half that of conventional loans. The study also shows that small business borrowers that take on loans from both conventional and Islamic banks are more likely to default on the former – this they put down to the moral pressures linked to

Table 2. Risk and Islamic Banking.

Authors	Country(ies) of Study	Period	Data Type	Research Focus	Methodology	Main Finding
Čihák and Hesse (2010)	20 OIC member countries	1993–2004	Yearly bank-level accounting data	Insolvency risk	Regression – OLS and Robust	Small Islamic banks are more stable than small conventional banks; however, large Islamic banks are less stable than their conventional counter-parts.
Hassan and Dridi (2010)	8 countries	2007–2009	Yearly bank-level accounting data	Factors influencing performance, growth and ratings over crisis period	Regression – OLS	The credit and asset growth of Islamic banks was more than that of conventional banks from 2008–2009 'contributing to financial and economic stability', although profits of Islamic banks fell more than conventional banks in 2009 due to limitations in their risk management practices.

(*continued*)

Table 2. (*Continued*)

Authors	Country(ies) of Study	Period	Data Type	Research Focus	Methodology	Main Finding
Abedifar *et al.* (2013)	24 OIC member countries	1999–2009	Yearly bank-level accounting data	Credit risk, insolvency risk, interest rate risk and possibility of extracting religious rent	Regression – random effects	Islamic banks that are small, leveraged and based in countries with predominantly Muslim populations have lower credit risk than conventional banks. Small Islamic banks appear more stable than similar sized conventional banks. During the recent crisis, however, large Islamic banks exhibit lower stability than large conventional banks. Implicit interest income and expense, as well as credit risk of Islamic banks are less responsive to domestic interest rates. Islamic banks do not seem to charge special rents to their clients for offering *Shariā* compliant financial products.
Beck *et al.* (2013)	141 countries (including 22 OIC member countries)	1995–2007	Yearly bank-level accounting data	Efficiency, asset quality, stability and business orientation	Regression – OLS Fixed effects, Robust	Few significant differences are found between Islamic and conventional banks.

Study	Countries	Period	Data	Focus	Method	Findings
Pappas *et al.* (2014)	20 countries	1995–2010	Yearly bank-level accounting data	Survival rates of Islamic and conventional banks	Duration models, hazard rates	Islamic banks have a significantly lower risk of failure both unconditionally and conditionally on time-varying bank characteristics, market structure and macro-economic conditions.
Baele *et al.* (2014)	Pakistan	2006:04–2008:12	150000 Monthly business loans	Loan default rate	Hazard function	Default rate of Islamic loans is less than half the default rate of conventional loans. Islamic loans are less likely to default during Ramadan.
Saeed and Izzeldin (2014)	Bahrain, Bangladesh, Indonesia, Kuwait, Pakistan, Qatar, Saudi Arabia and UAE	2002–2010	Yearly bank-level accounting data	Profit efficiency and default risk	Stochastic Frontier Analysis and distance to default (Merton) model	Profit efficiency is inversely related to default risk for Islamic banks, whereas for conventional banks it is positively linked.
Mollah *et al.* (2014)	Bahrain, Bangladesh, Malaysia, Pakistan, Saudi Arabia, The United Arab Emirates, and The United Kingdom	2006–2009	Yearly bank-level accounting data	Links between risk exposure, governance indicators and bank performance/value	OLS and GMM	Corporate governance (CGI) and financial disclosure (FDTI) indexes have emerged as the key driving forces for risk-taking for Islamic banks. *Shariá* boards do not inhibit risk-taking.

Source: Adapted from Abedifar *et al.* (2013) Table 1 and authors updates.

religious beliefs.[12] Saeed and Izzeldin (2014) take a different slant looking at the link between profit efficiency (derived from parametric stochastic frontier estimates) and distance to default and show that for Islamic banks defaults rates are inversely related to profit efficiency whereas there is a positive relationship for their conventional counterparts.[13] Mollah *et al.* (2014) investigates a variety of determinants of Islamic bank risk-taking across seven countries over 2006–2009. Using accounting risk measures (among other things) they find that corporate governance and financial disclosure issues appear to have the biggest impact on Islamic bank risk-taking whereas the nature of *Shariá* boards does not seem to limit risk-taking. Reviewing the studies in Table 2 one can again see somewhat mixed findings from studies that typically use different bank samples, methodologies and study periods. The majority of the literature appears to suggest that small Islamic banks may be less risky than similar sized conventional banks.

6. Other Topical Banking Issues

6.1 *PSLB versus non-PSLB Types of Finance*

The theory of Islamic banking, emanating from Uzair (1978) conceptualizes an Islamic financial intermediary as a double *Mudharabah* (quasi-equity PSLB) contract. This involves underwriting the contractual relationship on the asset as well as the liabilities side as a *Mudharabah* one twice. This conceptual model of Uzair (1978) is not observed in practice as Islamic banks often tend to deviate from PSLB financing principles and operate similar to conventional banks (see Abedifar *et al.*, 2013). This is because *Mudharabah*: (1) defies the general law of hire and runs afoul of a number of *ahādith*; (2) suffers from an agency issue due to the *fiqh* constraint on *rabb-al-māl* providing 100% capital; and (3) suffers from both adverse selection and moral hazard and thus needs to overcome these problems (Kahf and Khan, 1992; Ebrahim and Sheikh, 2014b). In addition, potential deposit withdrawal risk may persuade management to vary from PSLB principles by paying competitive returns to investment account holders if they are competing with conventional banks. For instance, Chong and Liu (2009) use Malaysian data over 1995–2004 and Granger causality tests to illustrate that monthly investment deposit rates of Islamic banks are closely linked to those of their conventional counterparts. Also, when lending Islamic banks are likely to apply non-PSLB principles due to the risks and complexities associated with the PSLB method. For instance, under PSLB financing, Islamic banks need to determine how to share the realized return for each project which can be complicated due to difficulties in quantifying the characteristics of clients and the proposed business opportunity. Also under PSLB revenue is not guaranteed and since under these types of contracts banks typically cannot collect collateral from clients, they need to put more effort into selection and monitoring so as to ensure that informational rents are not extracted by borrowers.[14] Hence, for short-term financing, it may not always be viable for Islamic banks to use the PSLB method. Moreover, under the *Mudharabah* contract, Islamic banks have limited means to control and intervene in the management of a project.

There is evidence to suggest that Islamic banks typically do not depend on PSLB contracts to undertake their financing activities. Aggarwal and Yousef (2000) show that Islamic banks mainly use Non-PSLB instruments to avoid moral hazard problem associated with PLS financing. Chong and Liu (2009) also find that in Malaysia, only 0.5% of Islamic bank finance is based on PSLB principles and Baele *et al.* (2014) find that the bulk of Islamic financing in Pakistan is not via PSLB. According to the Bank Indonesia Report (2009) PSLB modes of finance account for 35.7% in the financing of Islamic banks operating in the country by the end of 2008, and this they claim to be the highest proportion in any Islamic banking system.[15]

6.2 *Competition*

A handful of studies, noticeably Turk Ariss (2010) and Weill (2011) investigate competition in various countries where Islamic and conventional financial institutions operate together. The former study uses a variety of competition indicators – both concentration ratios, and the non-structural Panzar-Rosse H-statistic and Lerner indexes – to gauge market structure and competition issues. Turk Ariss (2010) uses a sample of 58 Islamic and 192 conventional banks operating in 13 countries between 1992 and 2006 and measures competition using the Panzar-Rosse and Lerner indicators finding that Islamic banks are less competitive than conventional operators. This finding, however, conflicts with Weill (2011) who uses the Lerner index to gauge bank market power in 17 OIC member countries, and he finds that Islamic banks are more competitive. An interesting study by Aysan *et al.* (2014) uses Central Bank of Turkey deposit data and a panel-VAR methodology to investigate depositor responsiveness to interest rate changes. Surprisingly, Islamic depositors seem to respond more to deposit rate changes compared to conventional bank depositors – this provides (perhaps) some indirect evidence that Islamic banks on the deposit-side are more competitive.

6.3 *Small Business Lending and Other Issues*

Other areas covered in the empirical banking literature span a variety of issues. Ongena and Şendeniz-Yüncü (2011) use cross-sectional data for Turkish banks in 2008, and apply multinomial logit analysis to examine bank-firm relationships. Shaban *et al.* (2014) analyze similar relationships in Indonesia over 2002–2010 using Granger causality and dynamic panel modelling approaches (Generalized Method of Moments – GMM). Both studies find that Islamic bank business borrowers are dominated by relatively small and young firms that have multiple bank relationships. Islamic banks have a preponderance of such borrowers and they generate relatively high margins. Other studies cover a range of disparate themes. Imam and Kpodar (2010) model the diffusion (take-up) of banking across 117 countries and find that the probability of the development of Islamic banking increases with a larger Muslim population share, greater income per capita and when the country is an oil exporter. Higher interest rates limit the take-up of Islamic banking. Mallin *et al.* (2014) use a sample of banks from 13 countries to examine how corporate social responsibility (CSR) disclosure of Islamic banks influences performance. They find that there is a positive relationship between CSR disclosure and bank performance (profitability) and a highly significant link between the size of *Shariá* supervisory boards and the level of CSR disclosure. Elnahass *et al.* (2014) use a sample of 74 conventional and 32 Islamic banks over 2006–2011 from Middle East North Africa (MENA) countries to examine the link between loan-loss provisioning (an indicator of credit risk) and shareholder value creation where they find conventional banks are more sensitive to provisioning compared to Islamic banks. A recent interesting study by Gheeraert (2014) uses aggregate financial and economic data from the World Bank's Financial Structure Database from 55 countries over 2000–2005 to examine the finance and growth nexus. The study finds that Islamic banking sector development aids overall banking sector growth. A summary of the areas discussed in this section are summarised in Table 3.

Table 3. Other Islamic Banking Issues.

Authors	Country(ies) of Study	Period	Data Type	Research Focus	Methodology	Main Finding
Chong and Liu (2009)	Malaysia	1995:04–2004:04	Monthly interest rates (rates of return for Islamic banks)	Causality relationship between Islamic banks deposits rates and interest rates in conventional banking.	Granger causality test	Rates of return on the investment deposits of Islamic banks are closely related to rates on conventional banks' deposits.
Imam and Kpodar (2010)	117 countries	1992–2006	Country level data	Determinants of the diffusion of Islamic banking	Regression – Tobit	Probability for Islamic banking to develop in a country rises with the share of the Muslim population, income per capita, and whether the country is a net exporter of oil. Increasing interest rates limit the diffusion of Islamic banking.
Turk Ariss (2010)	13 countries	2000–2006	58 Islamic and 192 conventional banks. Yearly bank accounting data from Bankscope	Competitive conditions in banking markets	Measures of concentration, PanzarRosse H-statistic and Lerner index (market power)	Islamic banks are less competitive compared to conventional banks.

Ongena and Şendeniz-Yüncü (2011)	Turkey	2008	Bank-firm relationships	Firm bank choice	Multinomial logit	Islamic banks mainly have corporate clients that are young, transparent, industry-focused, and have multiple-bank relationships.
Weill (2011)	17 OIC member countries	2001–2007	Yearly bank-level accounting data	Market power	Regression – random effects GLS	Islamic banks have lower market power than conventional banks.
Aysan et al. (2014)	Turkey	2004:03–2012:12	Deposit data	Behavioral aspects of Islamic bank depositors in a dual banking system	Panel vector autoregression (panel-VAR)	Conventional bank depositors are relatively less sensitive to interest rate changes compared to Islamic bank depositors since only the largest depositor groups are found to be significantly responsive to interest rate shocks.
Hassan et al. (2014)	55 OIC countries	1990–2011	Financial inclusion indicators (e.g. ATM usage) and GDP growth measures	Examines the relationship between financial inclusion and economic development in Islamic economies	Panel VAR, forecast error variance decompositions, Panel Granger causality tests	Financial inclusion has a positive link to economic development and the relationship varies across regions.

(continued)

Table 3. (*Continued*)

Authors	Country(ies) of Study	Period	Data Type	Research Focus	Methodology	Main Finding
Shaban *et al.* (2014)	Indonesia	2002–2010	Data on small business lending and other financial data on 107 conventional banks and 7 Islamic banks. Data from the Central Bank of Indonesia	Determinants of small business lending	Dynamic GMM and Granger causality tests	Small and more profitable banks are more likely to focus on small business lending. Islamic banks also have a higher proportion of small business lending on their books from which they earn relatively high margins.
Mallin *et al.* (2014)	13 countries – Bahrain, Bangladesh, Indonesia, Jordan, Kuwait, Malaysia, Pakistan, Qatar, Saudi Arabia, Sudan, Syria, UAE and UK.	2010–2011	Constructs a corporate social responsibility (CSR) disclosure index	Examines the relationship between Islamic bank CSR disclosure and the features of the *Shariá* Supervisory Board on bank performance	OLS and 3SLS	Positive link between *CSR* disclosure and performance. There is also a positive and highly significant link between the *Shariá* supervisory board (*SSB*) size and *CSR* disclosure index.

Elnahass et al. (2014)	Middle East North Africa (MENA) countries	2006–2011	74 Conventional and 32 Islamic banks	Looks at the link between loan loss provisioning (LLP) and value creation	Fixed effects regression	LLP has positive value relevance to investors in both banking sectors. Investors in Islamic banks price the discretionary component relatively lower than their conventional counterparts.
Gheeraert (2014)	55 countries	2000–2005	Aggregate data on banking and financial sector development. Data from the World bank's Financial structure database	Examines the link between Islamic banking and aggregate banking sector development	Regression	Islamic banking sector developments aids overall banking sector development.

7. Islamic Finance

7.1 *Islamic Mutual Funds*

So far, we have discussed the literature that looks at Islamic banking. In this section, we outline recent developments in the study of Islamic finance – typically in capital markets areas. The empirical literature is dominated by work that compares the risk and return features of Islamic mutual funds with various benchmarks including conventional and Islamic market indexes as well as portfolios of conventional bonds. These offer an avenue to observe the risk-sharing aspect of Islamic financial intermediation in practice. The main difference between Islamic funds and their conventional counterparts is that managers have a smaller universe of companies to invest in as they are subject to screening out businesses that are not *Shariá* compliant – this includes (religious) screening out of companies that operate in areas prohibited under Islamic law and screening out firms that cannot achieve certain financial criteria (for instance, exceeding maximum interest payments on debt deemed permissible). All in all, Islamic fund managers have a more limited investment choice.[16] Typically, the Islamic fund literature uses performance metrics – Sharpe ratios, Jensen's alpha, Treynor indexes, Fama and French and related models, to compare the risk-adjusted returns of funds and testing to see if these are statistically different for Islamic and conventional funds. Recent empirical studies, such as Elfakhani *et al.* (2005), Hayat (2006), Abderrezak (2008), Haddad *et al.* (2009) and Hoepner (2011) find no difference in the performance of Islamic equity funds with other conventional funds or index benchmarks. Others, such as Ferdian and Dewi (2007) and Mansor and Bhatti (2011) even find that Islamic funds perform better. There is little evidence, however, that Islamic funds perform worse – Hayat and Kräussl (2011) being the exception. A couple of studies have combined efficiency analysis (that tends to dominate the empirical Islamic banking literature) with analysis of fund returns (Saad *et al.*, 2010; and Abdelsalam *et al.*, 2014a). Saad *et al.* (2010) use non-parametric Data Envelopment Analysis (DEA) and a variety of inputs and outputs to gauge fund efficiency and find that some Islamic funds are more efficient than their conventional counterparts. Abdelsalam *et al.* (2014a) show that the average socially responsible investment fund is more efficient than the average Islamic fund.

7.2 *Sukuk*

A more recent trend has been to examine features of the Islamic bond – *Sukuk* – market. Cakir and Raei (2007) show that *Sukuk* returns are not highly correlated with Eurobond returns and therefore present portfolio diversification opportunities (although Derigs and Marzban, 2008 find no such potential benefits). Both Godlewski *et al.* (2010) and Alam *et al.* (2013) use event study approaches to examine investor reaction to *Sukuk* issuance – they both find evidence of negative market reaction suggesting that investors do not view such activities in a positive light. Finally, Bialkowski *et al.* (2012) also use an event study approach to look at the 'Ramadan effect' – they find that stock returns are higher and less volatile than during the rest of the year. They say, 'Ramadan positively affects investor psychology, as it promotes feelings of solidarity and social identity among Muslims world-wide, leading to optimistic beliefs that extend to investment decisions' (p. 835). Table 4 provides a summary of the recent empirical finance literature.

Table 4. Empirical Evidence from Islamic Finance.

Authors	Sample	Period	Data Type	Research Focus	Methodology	Main Finding
Ismail and Shakrani (2003)	12 Islamic Malaysian mutual funds	May 1999 to July 2001	Monthly mutual fund returns and market benchmark	Examining the link between market risk and fund returns	CAPM and cross-sectional regression	Beta explained most of the variation in Islamic fund returns.
Elfakhani et al. (2005)	46 Islamic mutual funds	January 1, 1997, and ends on August 31, 2002	Mutual fund monthly returns from Failaka International and Standard & Poor's	Comparing the performance of Islamic mutual funds with conventional equity benchmarks also at market timing and selectivity issues	Sharpe, Treynor, Jensen ratios plus the Mazury (TM) model	There is no statistically significant risk-adjusted abnormal reward or penalty associated with investing in Sharia compliant mutual funds.
Hayat (2006)	59 (Malaysian and International)	August 2001 to August 2006	Fund weekly returns from Bloomberg	Comparing return/risk performance against conventional and Islamic benchmarks	Sharpe, CAPM Jensen Alpha, Timing and Mazury (TM) model	Islamic fund do not significantly under or outperform their Islamic as well as conventional benchmarks under normal market conditions. During the bear market of 2002 Islamic funds did however significantly outperform the Islamic and conventional market.

(continued)

Table 4. (*Continued*)

Authors	Sample	Period	Data Type	Research Focus	Methodology	Main Finding
Abdullah *et al.* (2007)	65 Malaysian funds, 14 of which are Islamic funds	January 1992 to December 2001	Mutual fund monthly returns from	Comparing the performance of Islamic mutual funds with conventional equity benchmarks	Sharpe, Jensen Alpha, Timing and selectivity ability	Islamic funds performed better than the conventional funds during bearish economic trends while, conventional funds showed better performance than Islamic funds during bullish economic conditions.
Ferdian and Dewi (2007)	20 Malaysia 5 Indonesian Islamic Funds	1 October 2005 to 30 April 2007	Monthly returns obtained from Bloomberg	Comparing returns with the market and Islamic indexes	Treynor, Sharpe and Jensen measures	Malaysian Islamic funds outperform Indonesian Islamic Funds. Islamic mutual funds relatively outperform the market.
Cakir and Raei (2007)	Sovereign and conventional bond issues in international markets by Malaysia, Pakistan, Qatar, and Bahrain.	Date of issue to end-June 2007	Daily and Weekly price data. DataStream for Malaysian, Pakistani, and Qatari bonds. Bloomberg for Bahrain	Assesses the impact of issuance of *Sukuk* on the cost and risk structure of investment portfolios	Value-at-Risk (VaR) measures. Delta-normal and Monte Carlo simulation	Correlations of *Sukuk* returns with returns on conventional bonds are much smaller than the correlations of returns on conventional bonds with each other. They can provide portfolio diversification benefits.
Abderrezak (2008)	46 International Islamic funds	January 1997 to August 2002	Monthly returns	Comparing returns with the market and Islamic indexes and conventional funds	Sharpe, Fama and 3-factor Fama and French model. Selectivity and timing	No significant performance difference between Islamic and conventional funds. Islamic and conventional funds did not outperform the SP500.

Study	Sample	Period	Data	Objective	Methodology	Findings
Derigs and Marzban (2008)	Assets included in the S&P 500 index	S&P500 index on the September 17, 2007 and company data from 2006	Monthly Index and company returns from Bloomberg	Simulating various types of *Shariá* compliant portfolios	Portfolio simulation	*Shariá*-compliant portfolios can be constructed that have return and risk profiles comparable to conventional non-constrained portfolios.
Haddad *et al.* (2009)	46 International Islamic funds	January 1997 to August 2002	Monthly returns	Examine systematic risk and fund returns relating to S&P500 and FT Global Islamic index	Single factor Schwert and Seguin model	Islamic mutual funds are similar to conventional funds. Volatility persistence is affected by the market proxy.
Saad *et al.* (2010)	27 Malaysian funds of which 5 are Islamic	2002–2005	Input and Output measures (returns are an output)	Examines the efficiency and productivity (Malmquist) of the funds industry in Malaysia	Data Envelopment Analysis (DEA)	Some of the Islamic funds are more efficient than their conventional counterparts.
Godlewski *et al.* (2010)	170 Malaysian bond issues of which 77 are *Sukuk* and 93 conventional bonds	2002–2009	Date of issuance and closing stock price of companies issuing debt (from Bloomberg)	Impact of conventional bonds and *Sukuk* announcements on market	Market model event study	No significant stock-market reaction to conventional bond announcements, a negative reaction to *Sukuk* issues and significant difference in stock market reactions to *Sukuk* and conventional bond issues.

(*continued*)

Table 4. (*Continued*)

Authors	Sample	Period	Data Type	Research Focus	Methodology	Main Finding
Mansor and Bhatti (2011)	128 Islamic and 350 conventional Malaysian funds	January 1995 to December 1998 and January 2005 to December 2008	Monthly returns of funds from Morningstar	Examines descriptive statistics on return and volatility comparing conventional and Islamic funds	Summary return and volatility statistics	Islamic and conventional funds outperform the market return Islamic funds are more risky than conventional Malaysian funds.
Hayat and Kräussl (2011)	145 Islamic equity funds	January 2000 to February 2009	Weekly returns	Comparing return/risk performance against conventional and Islamic benchmarks	CAPM and investigating market timing	Islamic equity funds underperform compared to conventional equity benchmarks. Underperformance seems to have increased during the 2007–2008 financial crisis.
Hoepner *et al.* (2011)	265 Islamic equity funds from 20 countries	September 1990 – April 2009	Mutual fund monthly returns and related data from Eureka hedge	Comparing Islamic fund performance and investment style with an array of conventional benchmarks	CAPM and Carhart models	No strong evidence that Islamic funds in general under- or outperform equity markets. National characteristics explain the heterogeneity in Islamic fund performance. Islamic funds from the GCC and Malaysia perform competitively or even outperform international equity market benchmarks.
Razzaq *et al.* (2012)	9 Pakistan Islamic funds	2009–2010	Daily returns	Case study on the performance of nine funds	Sharpe, Treynor, Jensens alpha	Returns on Islamic funds are risk related.

Study	Sample	Period	Data	Focus	Methodology	Findings
Białkowski *et al.* (2012)	Countries where the proportion of Muslim population exceeded 50% - 14 countries	1994–2006 (Various for different countries)	Stock market index data from Datastream	Event study on the impact of Ramadan	Market model, event study	Stock returns during Ramadan are significantly higher and less volatile than during the rest of the year. No declines in market liquidity are recorded.
Alam *et al.* (2013)	79 *Sukuks* and 87 conventional bonds from Malaysia, Indonesia, Singapore, Pakistan, UAE, Bahrain and Qatar	2004–2012	Closing stock prices for firms issuing debt from Bloomberg	Impact of conventional bonds and *Sukuk* announcements on shareholder wealth	Market model event study	Negative market reaction for the announcements of *Sukuk* issues before and during 2007 global financial crisis.
Abdelsalam *et al.* (2014a)	138 Islamic funds and 636 socially responsible funds	January, 1989 to March, 2011	Input and output fund measures	Efficiency analysis comparing Islamic with social responsible mutual funds	Non-parametric Free Disposable Hull (FDH) efficiency analysis and second stage quantile regression	The average efficiency of socially responsible (SRI) funds is slightly higher than that of Islamic funds.
Azmat *et al.* (2014)	Malaysian	2002–2010	Islamic bond issuers from the IFIS data base.	Evaluation of the credit risk of Islamic (*Sukuk*) bonds	Survival probability simulation	Traditional credit risk methodologies underestimate the survival risk of Islamic bonds, or to put another way, they rate them as higher credit risk.
Abdelsalam *et al.* (2014b)	138 Islamic funds and 636 socially responsible funds	December 2000 to March 2011	Input and output fund measures. Simulation to evaluate persistence	Analyses performance persistence using efficiency analysis	Non-parametric Free Disposable Hull (FDH) efficiency analysis with second and third stage analysis	Performance of Islamic and Socially Responsible funds persist but only for worst and best performing funds.

7.3 *Islamic Micro and Social Finance*

The current practice is to avoid subterfuges concealing interest bearing lending involving Murabaha facilities (see El-Gamal, 2005). This initiative stems from charitable organizations such as Akhuwat in Pakistan to help the poor and underprivileged (see http://www.akhuwat. org.pk/). This trend is supported by academic research espousing mutual savings banks or financial cooperatives to avoid subterfuges (see El-Gamal, 2007). The rationale behind this is elaborated in Salleh *et al.* (2014) as emanating from the Qur'anic contrast of *Riba* with charity (*sadaqah*) (Q 2: 276–277, 30:39). This implies incorporating the Qard Al-Hasan facility in mutual/financial cooperatives and employing the technology of Accumulating Savings and Credit Associations (ASCRAs): (i) to fund homes for the poor and underprivileged (Ebrahim, 2009); and (ii) offer inexpensive short-term credit facility as an alternative to usurious payday loans (Salleh *et al.*, 2014). The employment of Qard Al-Hasan is deemed charitable helping social cohesiveness in contrast to *ribawi* loans, which factionalizes society (see again Ibn Taymiyah, 1951).

8. Conclusion and Future Research

An extensive empirical literature has emerged over the last decade or so investigating Islamic banking and financial issues. The main finding from this body of works is that Islamic banks are at least as efficient and (particularly for smaller banks) have lower default/insolvency risk than their conventional counterparts. Islamic banks typically focus more on higher margin small business borrowers who are less likely to default. Evidence on market power issues is mixed although there is some evidence that Islamic banks can be more competitive than their conventional counterparts. Other (albeit somewhat limited evidence) suggest that the spread of Islamic banking can aid financial inclusion and economic development. Results from the empirical finance literature, dominated by studies that focus on the risk/return features of mutual funds, finds that Islamic funds generally perform the same or better than conventional funds – there is little evidence that they perform worse than standard industry benchmarks.

Nowadays a broader array of issues are being analysed, including the link between Islamic banking and financial and economic development, the diffusion of Islamic banking, the role of *Shariá* Supervisory Boards and governance issues, the impact of religious and financial screening on fund performance, and comparisons of *Shariá* screening with other types of investment filtering – like those for socially responsible or environment friendly investments. Much of the governance work is in its infancy, as is the analysis of *Sukuk* and related instruments. In the banking area there still needs to be work done on examining systemic risks and seeing how this links to Islamic and conventional banking. Also, (as in the conventional empirical banking literature) more work is needed on the features and links between liquidity and market funding risks. There is room for more work to be done on pricing too-big-to fail and other government safety net subsidies in Islamic banking systems, as well as (hypothetical) stress testing of banks in Muslim countries. Can one identify systemically important financial institutions and measure the risks they pose to the countries and regions in which they operate? Also, as many Islamic institutions are based in the GCC countries, and as their economies are mainly driven by energy prices, it would be interesting to investigate to what extent such factors influence bank performance and risk? Broader questions should focus on linking financial and social inclusion in the Islamic world and see how this is related to notions of poverty, equality and economic development. Is there a link between health and finance in the Islamic world (see Clayton *et al.*, 2015)? These and many more questions pertinent to both the conventional and Islamic banking and financial sectors are worthy (in our view at least) of future academic investigation.

Notes

1. In general, we have abstained from taking a partisan (for or against) approach to studies in the literature to avoid the accusation of being prejudiced. However, in specific cases we have been critical of the literal perspective adopted by Islamic scholars.
2. It should be noted that not all asset-backed *Sukuk* are financial obligations resembling bonds. There are, however, other *Sukuk* structures that are quasi-equity in nature resembling the classic *Mudharabah* or *Musharakah* vehicles in early Islam.
3. See also Cizakca (1996) for an economic history of the classic *Mudharabah* facility.
4. Please note that LembagaTabung Haji (Pilgrims Fund Board) of Malaysia was the first Islamic Investment Company established in 1962 to help fund pilgrimage activities of the Malaysian Muslim Community. We are grateful to an anonymous referee for pointing this out.
5. While promoted by government, as far as we are aware, Islamic banks operating in dual economies coexist with their conventional counterparts and operate under a level regulatory playing field/competitive environment with seemingly no obvious tax advantages or incentives. It is for the same reason that empirical research typically uses similar accounting benchmarks to compare their performance such as: ROE, ROA, cost of deposits, spreads, capital ratios and so on. The Islamic Financial Services Board has published standards to customize/tailor Basel II/III capital adequacy standards to fit to the Islamic banking model, where the deposit side contractually operates on a Profit and Loss sharing basis to highlight the quasi-equity nature of the liability side of the balance sheet. Despite the fact that the adoption of the aforementioned IFSB capital adequacy approach would ease pressure on Islamic bank capital requirements, in the major jurisdictions (Saudi Arabia, UAE, Pakistan, and Malaysia) regulators tend to operate and calculate their capital adequacy requirements based on standard/conventional Basel III regulation. Furthermore, industry databases like Bloomberg, Thomson Reuters and Bankscope report data on Islamic banks absolutely comparable to that of conventional banks.
6. This misunderstanding ensues from a literal Arabic translation of the word *Riba* implying an excess or an addition over the amount loaned (see al-Zuhayli, 2006). The Qur'an, in contrast to the majority of the religious scholars, describes *Riba* as an expropriation of a counterparty's assets whether it be on a spot-trade (*riba al-fadl*) or a deferred trade (*riba an-nasi'ah*) (see Q 4:161). This is reflected in the Sunnah, where the Prophet (PBUH) is reputed to have prohibited all kinds of market manipulations (see Thomas, 2005). This outlook of the Qur'an and the Sunnah is reflected in scholarly studies such as those of Ibn Taymiya (1951) as well as that of Ibn Qayyim (1973). Ebrahim *et al.* (2014a), thus rationalize this injunction as deterring the employment of financial facilities with endemic agency costs of debt as they lead to expropriation of the assets of either the lender (in case of risk shifting) or that of the borrower (in case of underinvestment). In the context of the recent subprime crisis, *Riba* can be construed as 'toxic' debt that can infect institutions thus impinging on both the real and financial sectors of the economy.
7. This legality or permissibility is deduced from the precedence of Prophet Muhammad and his companions. It is also rationalized by religious scholars as emanating from the

Qur'anic verse (2: 275): '*God has permitted trade* (implying credit sales) *and forbidden Riba* (implying financial facilities with embedded agency issues). The ramification of this precedence has not been understood from a financial economics perspective until recently. This is explicated by Sen (1998, p. 435) as follows: '*when financial markets are imperfect* (as in the medieval era of the Prophet and his companions), *a seller can find it optimal to offer a menu of deferred payment plans*".

8. From a financial economics perspective '*Gharar*' can be construed as the following. One, it involves market manipulation ensuing from asymmetric information (Thomas, 1995). This definition is consistent with the views of Greenbaum and Thakor (1987) and has credence in the light of the recent market manipulating scandals such as LIBOR fixing, gold price fixing etc. (http://www.ft.com/indepth/libor-scandal, http://online.wsj.com/news/articles/SB10001424127887324077704578358381575462340). Two, it involves 'trading in risk' (El-Gamal, 2009). This view is consistent with that of Claessens *et al.* (2012).

9. The AAOIFI Governance Standard on Shariá Supervisory Boards mandate the appointment, composition, and report of a Shariá Supervisory Board (SSB) comprising of three members of which one is an expert in accounting, economics etc. Members of executive management are not normally members of the SSB. We are grateful to an anonymous referee for this comment.

10. We are grateful to an anonymous referee, who has pointed out that these *Sukuk* are tradable denominated in U.S. Dollars and rated 'A-1' by the Standard and Poor's Rating Services. According to various press releases, the IILM has issued *Sukuk* amounting to 1.85 million U.S. Dollars during the period August 2013 to November 2014 (see www.iilm.com). These facilities were reissued ten times at maturity. The amount of *Sukuk* that were issued and reissued until January 2015 amounted to 7.64 U.S. billion.

11. This study measures macroeconomic efficiency as a form of technical efficiency, which measures how close a country's production is to what that country's optimal production would be for using the same bundle of inputs and outputs.

12. An interesting question asked by one referee is to what extent is the finding of less risky lending by Islamic financial institutions due to credit rationing? It could be that because of a limited supply of funds only the least risky Islamic investors are able to borrow? We have no hard empirical evidence on this although in our opinion this cannot be explained by credit rationing; because the interest (called mark-up in Islamic terminology) rate of Islamic finance is not significantly lower than conventional finance. Even some studies claim that Islamic finance is even more expensive (Baele *et al.*, 2014). Abedifar *et al.* (2013) suggest that the lower default rate could be attributed to religiosity of borrowers as for instance they are more risk averse.

13. The distance-to-default measure used in the study is based on the structural valuation model of corporate debt by Merton (1974) and was developed by Moody's KMV as a company default indicator. It includes information from both financial statements and equity market prices. Distance-to-default indicates the number of standard deviations from a default point at a fixed time horizon, so a decline in distance-to-default suggests greater insolvency risk.

14. Islamic banks are (to some extent) discouraged from equity/quasi-equity based lending due to the relatively high capital charges PLS based lending incurs. All forms of contractual lending can of course be collateralized as legitimized by the concepts '*Rahn*' (collateral) and '*Waad*' (promise), however equity based lending is usually a modest proportion in most Islamic bank's balance sheets.

15. As pointed out by a referee, as Islamic banks mainly use non-PLS instruments this may have implications for the types of investment project that they fund, e.g. less new start-ups. Although we do not have empirical evidence on this, there is anecdotal evidence that Islamic banks are more conservative in their lending approach and are more likely to extend credit to established business.

16. *Shariá* screening has been found to tilt a portfolio towards 'growth' stocks with the exclusion of value stocks. This leads to a style bias impacting on the long term performance of the portfolio (Hoepner *et al.*, 2011).

References

Abdelsalam, O., Duygun, M.F., Matallín-Sáez, J.C., and Tortosa-Ausina, E. (2014a) On the comparative performance of socially responsible and Islamic mutual funds. *Journal of Economic Behavior and Organization* 103(Supplement Special Issue on Islamic Finance, July): S108–S128.

Abdelsalam, O., Duygun, M.F., Matallín-Sáez, J.C., and Tortosa-Ausina, E. (2014b) Do ethics imply persistence? The case of Islamic and socially responsible funds. *Journal of Banking and Finance* 40(3): 182–194.

Abderrezak, F. (2008) *The Performance of Islamic Equity Funds: A Comparison to Conventional, Islamic and Ethical Benchmarks*. PhD Thesis, Netherlands: Department of Finance, University of Maastricht.

Abdul-Majid, M., Saal, D.S., and Battisti, G. (2010) Efficiency in Islamic and conventional banking: An international comparison, *Journal of Productivity Analysis* 34(1): 25–43.

Abdul-Majid, M., Saal, D.S., and Battisti, G. (2011a) Efficiency and total factor productivity change of Malaysian commercial banks. *Service Industries Journal* 31(13): 2117–2143.

Abdul-Majid, M., Saal, D.S., and Battisti, G. (2011b) The impact of Islamic banking on the cost efficiency and productivity change of Malaysian commercial banks. *Applied Economics* 43(16): 2033–3054.

Abdullah, F., Hassan, T., and Mohamad, S. (2007) Investigation of the performance of Malaysian Islamic unit trust funds. *Managerial Finance* 33(2): 142–153.

Abedifar, P., Molyneux, P., and Tarazi, A. (2013) Risk in Islamic banking, *Review of Finance* 17(6): 2035–2096.

Aggarwal, R.K. and Yousef, T. (2000) Islamic banks and investment financing, *Journal of Money, Credit and Banking* 32(1): 93–120.

Alam, N., Hassan, M.K., and Haque, M.A. (2013) Are Islamic bonds different from conventional bonds? International evidence from capital market tests. *Borsa Istanbul Review* 13(3): 22–29.

Al-Jarrah, I. and Molyneux, P. (2005) Efficiency in Arabian banking. In M. Iqbal and R. Wilson (eds.), *Islamic Perspectives on Wealth Creation*, Chapter 6, (pp. 97–117). Edinburgh: Edinburgh University Press.

Al-Zuhayli, W. (2006). The juridical meaning of *riba*. In A.S. Thomas (ed.), *Interest in Islamic economics: Understanding riba*, (pp. 26–54). London, New York: Routledge.

Archer, S. and Abdel Karim, R.A. (2009). Profit-sharing investment accounts in Islamic banks: Regulatory problems and possible solutions. *Journal of Banking Regulation* 10: 300–306.

Aysan, A.F., Disli, M., and Oztur, H. (2014) The impact of religious commitment on Islamic bank depositors: Does size matter? Paper presented at a seminar on *Finance and Development in Muslim Economies*, sponsored by Islamic Research Training Institute (IRTI), Islamic Development Bank and the Journal of Financial Services Research, 15 September, Bangor University, UK.

Azmat, S., Skully, M., and Brown, K (2014) Credit risk in Islamic joint venture bond. *Journal of Economic Behavior and Organization* 103(Supplement Special Issue on Islamic Finance, July): S129–S145

Bader, M.K.I., Mohamad, S., Ariff, M., and Hassan, T. (2008) Cost, revenue and profit efficiency of Islamic versus conventional banks: International evidence using Data Envelopment Analysis. *Islamic Economic Studies* 15(2): 23–76.

Baele, L., Farooq, M., and Ongena, S. (2014) Of religion and redemption: Evidence from default on Islamic loans. *Journal of Banking and Finance* 44(6):141–159.

Bank Indonesia Report (2009) *The Lack of Profit-and-Loss Sharing Financing in Indonesia's Islamic Banks: Revisited.* Jakarta, Indonesia: Center of Education and Central Banking Studies, Bank Indonesia.

Bashir, A. (1999) Risk and profitability measures in Islamic banks: The case of two Sudanese banks, *Islamic Economic Studies* 6(2): 1–24.

Beck, T., Demirgüç-Kunt, A. and Merrouche, O. (2013) Islamic vs. conventional banking: business model, efficiency and stability. *Journal of Banking and Finance* 37(2): 433–447.

Białkowski, J., Etebari, A., and Wisniewski, T.P (2012) Fast profits: Investor sentiment and stock returns during Ramadan'. *Journal of Banking and Finance* 36(3): 835–845.

Cakir, S and Raei, F. (2007) Sukuk vs. Eurobonds: Is there a difference in Value-at-Risk? *International Monetary Fund Working Paper*, WP/07/237, October, Washington, DC: IMF

Chong, B.S. and Liu, M.H. (2009) Islamic banking: Interest-free or interest-based? *Journal of Pacific-Basin Finance* 17(1): 125–144.

Čihák, M. and Hesse, H. (2010) Islamic banks and financial stability: An empirical analysis. *Journal of Financial Services Research* 38(2): 95–113.

Cizakca, M. (1996). *Comparative Evolution of Business Partnerships.* Leiden: E. J. Brill

Claessens, S., Pozsar Z., Ratnovski L., and Singh M. (2012) Shadow Banking: Economics and Policy. *International Monetary Fund Staff Discussion Note* SDN/12/12, Washington, DC: IMF

Clayton, M., Liñares-Zegarra, J., and Wilson, J.O. (2015) Does debt affect health? Cross country evidence on the debt-health nexus. *Social Science and Medicine* 130: 51–58.

Credit Suisse (2013) *Global Wealth Databook.* Zurich: Credit Suisse Research Institute. Available at: https://publications.credit-suisse.com/tasks/render/file/?fileID=1949208D-E59A-F2D9-6D0361266E44A2F8. (Last accessed March 3, 2015).

Dar, H. A. and Presley, J. R. (2000) Lack of profit loss sharing in Islamic banking: Management and control imbalances. Department of Economics, Loughborough University.

Derigs, U. and Marzban, S. (2008) Review and analysis of current Shariah-compliant equity screening practices. *International Journal of Islamic and Middle Eastern Finance and Management* 1(4): 285–303.

Ebrahim, M.S. (2009). Can an Islamic model of housing finance cooperative elevate the economic status of the underprivileged?" *Journal of Economic Behavior and Organization* 72(3): 864–883.

Ebrahim, M.S., Jaafar, A., Molyneux, P. and Salleh, M.O. (2014a). Agency costs, financial contracting and the Muslim world. Working Paper, UK: Durham University Business School, University of Durham.

Ebrahim, M.S., and Sheikh, M. (2014b). The *Muḍāraba* facility: Evolution, stasis and contemporary revival, Working Paper, England, UK: Durham University Business School.

Economist, The (2014) Islamic finance, Big interest, no interest, 412 (8904) September 13, 75–76.

Elfakhani, S., Hassan, M.K., and Sidani, Y. (2005) Comparative performance of Islamic versus secular mutual funds. Presentation at the *Economic Research Forum Conference* in Cairo, Egypt, May, 19–21.

El-Gamal, M.A. and Inanoglu, H. (2002) Efficiencies and unobserved heterogeneity in Turkish banking: 1990–2000, unpublished working paper, Rice University, Department of Economics.

El-Gamal, M.A. (2005). Limits and dangers of Shari'a arbitrage. In S. Ali (ed.), *Islamic Finance: Current Legal and Regulatory Issues.* Cambridge, MA: Islamic Finance Project, Harvard Law School.

El-Gamal, M.A. (2007) Mutuality as an Antidote to Rent-Seeking *Shariah* Arbitrage in Islamic Finance. *Thunderbird International Business Review* 49(2): 187–202.

El-Gamal, M.A. (2009) *Islamic Finance: Law, Economics and Practice*. NY: Cambridge University Press.

Elnahass, M, Izzeldin, M., and Abdelsalam, O. (2014) Loan loss provisions, bank valuations and discretion: A comparative study between conventional and Islamic banks. *Journal of Economic Behavior and Organization* 103(Supplement Special Issue on Islamic Finance, July): S160–S173.

Errico, L and Farahbaksh, M (1998) Islamic banking: Issues in prudential regulations and supervision, IMF Working Paper No 98/30, pp. 1–32.

Ferdian, I. and Dewi, M. (2007) The performance analysis of Islamic mutual funds – A comparative study between Indonesia and Malaysia. Presentation at the *International Conference on Islamic Capital Markets*, August 27–29, Jakarta, Indonesia.

Gheeraert, L. and Weill, L. (2014) Does Islamic banking development favour macroeconomic efficiency? Evidence on the Islamic finance-growth nexus. *Laboratoire de RechercheenGestion&Economie Working Paper* 2014-04. University of Strasbourg, Strasbourg: LaRGE.

Gheeraert, L. (2014) Does Islamic finance spur banking sector development? *Journal of Economic Behavior and Organization* 103(Supplement Special Issue on Islamic Finance, July): S4–S20.

Godlewski, C.J, Turk Ariss, R., and Weill, L. (2010) 'Are Islamic investment certificates special? Evidence on the post-announcement performance of Sukuk issues', *Laboratoire de RechercheenGestion et Economie Working Paper2010-05*, University of Strasbourg, Strasbourg: LaRGE.

Goitein, S.D. (1971) *A Mediterranean Society*. Berkeley and Los Angeles: University of California Press.

Haddad, M., Homaifar, G., Elfakhani, S., and Ahmedov, H. (2009) Intertemporal test of beta stationarity performance of Islamic sector structured mutual funds. *Journal for International Business and Entrepreneurship Development* 4(4): 275–285.

Hassan, M.K. and Bashir, A. (2003) Determinants of Islamic banking profitability, paper presented at the *Economic Research Forum (ERF) Tenth Annual Conference*, Marrakesh, Morocco, 16–18 December.

Hassan, M.K. and Dridi, J. (2010) The effects of the global crisis on Islamic and conventional banks: A comparative study. *International Monetary Fund Working Paper No. 10/201*, Washington, DC: IMF

Hassan, M.K, Yu, J-S, and Kim, D-W. (2014) Financial inclusion and economic growth in OIC countries. Paper presented at the seminar on *Finance and Development in Muslim Economies*, sponsored by Islamic Research Training Institute (IRTI), Islamic Development Bank and the Journal of Financial Services Research, 15 September, Bangor University, UK.

Hayat, R. (2006). An empirical assessment of Islamic equity fund returns. Failaka website: 1–69. Available at: http://www.kantakji.com/media/7134/70093.pdf. (Last accessed May 8, 2015).

Hayat, R. and Kräussl, R. (2011) Risk and return characteristics of Islamic equity funds. *Emerging Markets Review* 12(2): 189–203.

Hillebrand, H. J. (ed.) (2009). *The Protestant Reformation*, Revised Edition, NY: Harper Perennial.

Hoepner, A., Rammal, H., and Rezec, M. (2011) Islamic mutual funds' financial performance and international investment style: Evidence from 20 countries. *The European Journal of Finance* 17(9-10): 829–850.

Ibn Qayyim, al-JawziyyaShams al-Din Abu'Abd Allah Muhammad. (1973). *I'lam al-muwaqqa'in 'ala rabb 'al-'alamin*. In Taha'Abd Al-Ra'ufSa'd (Ed.), Vol. II, 153–164 and Vol. III, 4. Lebanon: Dar Al-Jil, Beirut.

Ibn Taymiyah, Taqi al-Din Ahmed bin 'Abd al-Halim. (1951) Al-Qawā'id al-Nūrāniyya al-fiqhiyya. In M.al-Fiqi (ed.) (pp. 112–113) Cairo, Egypt: Al-sunna al-muhammadiyya.

Imam, P. and Kpodar, K. (2010) Islamic banking: How has it diffused? *International Monetary Fund Working Paper No. 10/195*, Washington, DC: IMF.

Iqbal, M and Molyneux, P. (2005) *Thirty Years of Islamic Banking*. London: Palgrave Macmillan.

Islamic Financial Services Board (2013) *Islamic Financial Services Industry Stability Report*, IFSB Bank Negara Malaysia: Kuala Lumpur.

Ismail, A. and Shakrani, M.S. (2003) The conditional CAPM and cross-sectional evidence of return and beta for Islamic unit trusts in Malaysia. *Journal of Economics and Management* 11(1): 1–31.

Johnes, J., Izzeldin, M. and Pappas, V. (2009) The efficiency of Islamic and conventional banks in the Gulf Cooperation Council (GCC) countries: An analysis using financial ratios and Data Envelopment Analysis. Lancaster University Management School Working Paper 2009/023, Lancaster, UK. *Management School Working Paper* 2009/023. Lancaster UK: Lancaster University.

Johnes, J., Izzeldin, M., and Pappas, V. (2014) A comparison of performance of Islamic and conventional banks 2004–2009, *Journal of Economic Behavior and Organization* 103(Supplement Special Issue on Islamic Finance, July): S93–S107.

Kahf, M. and Khan, T. (1992). Principles of Islamic Financing: A Survey, Research paper No. 16.Jeddah, KSA: Islamic Research and Training Institute, Islamic Development Bank.

Khan, T. and Ahmed, H. (2001) Risk management: An analysis of issues in Islamic financial industry, *Islamic Development Bank Occasional Paper No. 5*, Islamic Research Training Institute, Jeddah: Islamic Development Bank.

Majid, A.M., Nor, N.G., and Said, F.F. (2003) Efficiency of Islamic banks in Malaysia, Paper presented to the *Fifth International Conference on Islamic Economics and Banking*, Bahrain, October, 7–9.

Mallin, C., Farag, H., and Ow-Yong, K. (2014) Corporate social responsibility and financial performance in Islamic banks. *Journal of Economic Behavior and Organization* 103(Supplement Special Issue on Islamic Finance, July): S21–S38.

Mansor, F. and Bhatti, M. (2011) Islamic mutual funds performance for emerging markets, during bullish and bearish periods: The case of Malaysia. Paper presented at the *2nd International Conference on Business and Economic Research*. 14–16 March, Langkawi, Kedah, Malaysia.

Merton, R.C., 1974. On the pricing of corporate debt: the risk structure of interest rates. *Journal of Finance* 29: 449–470.

Mohamad, S., Hassan, T., and Bader, M.K.I. (2008) Efficiency of conventional versus Islamic banks: International evidence using the stochastic frontier approach (SFA). *Journal of Islamic Economics, Banking and Finance* 4(2): 107–130.

Mollah, S., Hassan, M.K., and Al Farooque, O. (2014) Corporate governance, risk-taking and firm performance of Islamic banks during the global financial crisis, Paper presented at the seminar on *Finance and Development in Muslim Economies*, sponsored by Islamic Research Training Institute (IRTI), Islamic Development Bank and the Journal of Financial Services Research, 15 September, Bangor University, UK.

Molyneux, P. and Iqbal, M., (2005) *Arab Banking and Financial Systems*, London: Palgrave Macmillan.

Obaidullah, M. (2005) Islamic financial services, *Islamic Economics Research Center*, Occasional Paper 158, King Abdulaziz University, Jeddah, Saudi Arabia.

Ongena, S. and Şendeniz-Yüncü, I. (2011) Which firms engage small, foreign, or state banks? And who goes Islamic? Evidence from Turkey. *Journal of Banking and Finance* 35(12): 3213–3224.

Pappas, V., Ongena, S., Izzeldin, M. and Fuertes, A.-M. (2014) Do Islamic banks 'Live free and die harder'?, Paper presented at the seminar on *Finance and Development in Muslim Economies*, sponsored by Islamic Research Training Institute (IRTI), Islamic Development Bank and the Journal of Financial Services Research, 15 September, Bangor University, UK.

Pryor, F.L. (2007) The economic impact of Islam on developing countries. *World Development* 35(11): 1815–1835.

Rashwan, M. H. (2010) A comparison between Islamic and traditional banks: Pre and post the 2008 financial crisis, Available at SSRN: http://ssrn.com/abstract=1724451 or doi:10.2139/ssrn.1724451. (Last accessed May 8, 2015).

Razzaq, N., Gul, S., Sajid, M., and Mughal, S. (2012) Performance of Islamic mutual funds in Pakistan. *Economic and Finance Review* 2(3): 16–25.

Saad, N., Majid, M., Kassim, S., Hamid, Z., and Yusof, R. (2010) A comparative analysis of the performance of conventional and Islamic unit trust companies in Malaysia. *International Journal of Managerial Finance* 6(1): 24–47.

Saeed, M. and Izzeldin, M (2014) Examining the relationship between default risk and efficiency in Islamic and conventional banks. *Journal of Economic Behavior and Organization* (forthcoming).

Salleh, M.O., Jaafar, A., and Ebrahim, M.S. (2014). Can an interest-free credit facility be more efficient than a usurious payday loan? *Journal of Economic Behavior and Organization* 103: S74-S92.

Samad, A. (1999) Comparative efficiency of the Islamic bank vis-à-vis conventional banks in Malaysia. *IIUM Journal of Economics and Management* 7(1): 1–25.

Sen, A. (1998) Seller financing of consumer durables. *Journal of Economics and Management Strategy* 7(3): 435–460.

Shaban, M., Duygun, M., Anwar, M., and Akbar, B. (2014) Diversification and banks' willingness to lend to small businesses: Evidence from Islamic and conventional banks in Indonesia. *Journal of Economic Behavior and Organization* 103(Supplement Special Issue on Islamic Finance, July): S39–S55.

Sundararajan, V. and Errico, L. (2002) Islamic financial institutions and products in the global financial system: Key issues in risk management and challenges ahead. *International Monetary Fund Working Paper WP/02/192*. Washington, DC: IMF.

The City UK (2013) *Islamic Finance*. London: TheCityUK. Available at: http://www.thecityuk.com/research/our-work/reports-list/islamic-finance-2013/. (Last accessed May 8, 2015).

Turk Ariss, R. (2010) Competitive conditions in Islamic and conventional banking: A global perspective, *Review of Financial Economics* 19(3): 101–108.

Uzair, M. (1978). *Interest-Free Banking*. Karachi, Pakistan: Royal Book Company.

Weill, L. (2011) Do Islamic banks have greater market power? *Comparative Economic Studies* 53(2): 291–306.

World Bank (2013) *Economic Development and Islamic Finance*. In Z. Iqbal and A. Mirakhor (eds.), Washington, DC: World Bank. Available at: http://dx.doi.org/10.1596/978-0-8213-9953-8. (Last accessed May 8, 2015).

Yudistra, D. (2004) Efficiency in Islamic banking: An empirical analysis of eighteen banks. *Islamic Economic Studies* 12(1): 1–19.

5

WEALTH INEQUALITY: A SURVEY

Frank A. Cowell

STICERD, London School of Economics

PhilippeVan Kerm

Luxembourg Institute of Socio-Economic Research

1. Introduction

The distribution of wealth lies at the heart of the broad research field of economic inequality. It is a topic that has recently gained considerable attention in view of the widespread phenomenon of increasing wealth inequality and given the growing availability of suitable data for analysing wealth inequality.

A survey of wealth inequality properly deserves a good-sized book rather than a modest-sized survey article, so we have necessarily been selective. Here we concentrate on key aspects of the following problems:

The nature of wealth

What is the appropriate definition of wealth? Is there a single 'right' concept of wealth that should be used for empirical analysis?

Measurement issues

How does the measurement of the inequality of wealth differ from that of income or earnings?

Empirical implementation

Where do wealth data come from? What are the appropriate procedures for analysing wealth data and drawing inferences about changes in inequality?

So, in contrast with some other surveys,[1] we have deliberately kept the range of topics narrow and have focused our attention more on the measurement apparatus – inequality indicators, parametric functional forms, inference – and in particular point out what is different from the tools and procedures appropriate to income inequality measurement. We only briefly

A Collection of Surveys on Savings and Wealth Accumulation, First Edition. Edited by Edda Claus and Iris Claus.
Chapters © 2016 The Authors. Book compilation © 2016 John Wiley & Sons, Ltd. Published 2016 by John Wiley & Sons, Ltd.

discuss theoretical models of wealth accumulation and do not attempt to summarize the empirical evidence on wealth inequality internationally but instead provide some fresh empirical evidence drawn from recently collected survey data in Europe. We focus on the 'direct' issue of wealth inequality, rather than discussing aspects of inequality that are indirectly related to wealth holdings[2] or related issues such as poverty.[3]

Throughout the paper, we illustrate a number of concepts and methods discussed in this survey using data from the Eurosystem Household Finance and Consumption Survey (HFCS) initiated and coordinated by the European Central Bank (HFCS, 2014). We use the first wave of HFCS which collected household-level data on household finances and consumption in late 2010 or early 2011 in 15 Eurozone countries. The HFCS provides comparable data across Eurosystem countries using coordinated definitions of core target variables, harmonized questionnaire templates and survey design and processing. The HFCS was modelled on the US Survey of Consumer Finances, the 'gold standard' of household wealth surveys. See European Central Bank (2013) for details.

The paper is organized as follows. We begin with measurement issues: Section 2 examines the basic issues of the measurement of wealth and Section 3 focuses on the way in which wealth-inequality measurement differs from inequality measurement in other contexts. Section 4 discusses issues relating to parametric and non-parametric representations of wealth distributions, Section 5 discusses some of the key features of wealth distributions that require special care when making inequality comparisons. Section 6 deals with empirical issues from the way the underlying data are obtained through to some of the more recondite issues concerning estimation and inference.

2. Measuring Wealth

The right place to start is the meaning of wealth. It has variously been seen as a simple stock of assets, a measure of command over resources, or a key component of economic power (Vickrey, 1947, p. 340; Atkinson, 1975, p. 37; OECD, 2013).

A brief reflection on one's own circumstances will probably be enough to demonstrate that wealth is not a homogeneous entity and a moment's further reflection suggests that more than one concept of wealth may be relevant for the purposes of inequality comparisons. The nature of wealth inequality is clearly going to depend on the definition that is adopted.

Wealth could in principle be taken to refer to one specific type of asset or group of assets. However, for most purposes the standard wealth concept that is considered relevant for empirical analysis is current *net worth* which can be thought of as the following simple expression:

$$w = \sum_{j=1}^{m} \pi_j A_j - D \tag{1}$$

where $A_j \geq 0$ is the amount held of asset type j, π_j is its price and D represents the call on those assets represented by debt:[4] the key notion of 'net wealth' or 'net worth' is the difference between assets and debts. The expression (1) reveals three things that ought to be taken into account:

- The range of asset types to be included; depending on institutional arrangements in particular countries some individual assets, such as housing and pensions, may need to be treated with special care.[5]

- The valuation applied to the assets, which may have a huge impact on wealth inequality. Is the market price being used for each asset j, or is it rather some type of imputed price?[6]
- The possibility that the expression (1) may be negative for some households at a given moment.

Furthermore in practice we often want to focus on *household* wealth which is the sum of all assets minus debts for all the household members. We may also wish to distinguish between *real* and *financial* assets: real assets include the value of household's main residence, real estate property other than the main residence, self-employment businesses, vehicles, jewellery, etc.; financial assets include deposits on current or savings accounts, voluntary private pensions and life insurance, mutual funds, bonds, shares, and other financial assets. Debts include home-secured debts (principal residence mortgage primarily), vehicle loans, educational loans, lines of credit and credit card balance, and any other financial loans and informal debts. Typically one finds that assets are primarily composed of real rather than financial assets. In the Eurozone countries, real assets represent 85% of total gross assets (European Central Bank, 2013). And the household main residence is typically the lion's share of real assets (61% on average in the Eurozone). Financial assets are mostly composed of deposits and savings accounts. Debts largely consist of mortgage debt.

Clearly, wealth contributes to individual well-being over and above any income flows that may arise from the wealth-holding, including economic and financial security and some form of economic power. Accounting for such benefits is in itself an interesting exercise,[7] but for now it is sufficient to note that translating wealth into an equivalent income stream, or vice versa, is an exercise that may miss some of the personally beneficial aspects of wealth holding and that the study of wealth inequality is an exercise that merits separate investigation and study, distinct from the study of income inequality.

The precise definition is not a matter of purely technical interest. It is often the case that practical applications that appear conceptually straightforward prove to be considerably more complicated because of the ambiguity of the wealth concept or the different ways in which supposedly the same wealth concept is interpreted in different countries or at different times.

To fix ideas, Table 1 describes the size and composition of net worth as calculated in 15 countries from the Eurosystem Household Finance and Consumption Survey. In each country a (small) fraction of households – between 1% and 12% – report negative or zero net worth and mean net worth is generally large and positive. Mean net worth is also much higher than median net worth: net worth distributions are indeed strongly left-skewed. Inspection of the components of net worth illustrate how important is the value of the main residence in the net worth with between 44% (in Germany) and 90% (in Slovakia) of household having some wealth from this particular asset. Between 25% (in Italy) and 65% (in Cyprus) hold some debt. While the HFCS aims to collect fully comprehensive and detailed information on a wide array of asset sources (our estimates are aggregates of finer component details available in the source data), cross-country data collections remain inevitably imperfect. Some components were not fully systematically collected in all countries – Finland, for example, does not record a range of asset sources – while some differences in underlying survey design may lead to national peculiarities; see Tiefensee and Grabka (2014) for a detailed review of data quality and cross-country comparability of HFCS data. Note finally that one potentially crucial wealth component for cross-country comparisons that is not available from the HFCS are public pension entitlements.[8] It remains the case that the HFCS is probably the best quality survey data source on wealth available to date for cross-national comparisons.

Table 1. Household Net Worth and Its Components in 15 Countries.

| | Total net worth | | | | Real assets | | | | | | Financial assets | | | | Debts | |
| | < 0 (%) | = 0 (%) | Mean | Median | Main residence | | Self-emp bus. | | Other real | | Priv. bus. | | Other fin. | | Debts | |
					> 0 (%)	Mean	> 0 (%)	Mean	> 0 (%)	Mean	> 0 (%)	Mean	> 0 (%)	Mean	> 0 (%)	Mean
Austria (AT)	5	0	265,033	76,445	48	123,154	9	68,471	80	43,462	1	596	97	46,096	36	16,746
Belgium (BE)	3	1	338,647	206,249	70	190,173	6	15,942	82	55,488	1	1,770	96	105,500	45	30,226
Cyprus (CY)	3	3	670,910	266,888	77	243,461	19	159,472	91	278,755	1	4,502	86	55,824	65	71,104
Germany (DE)	7	2	195,170	51,358	44	90,961	7	28,972	74	55,144	1	376	96	46,752	47	27,035
Spain (ES)	3	1	291,352	182,725	83	174,586	12	29,135	83	86,766	1	2,613	93	30,872	50	32,621
Finland (FI)	11	0	161,534	85,750	68	108,126	14	6,508	72	53,628	0	0	100	29,623	60	36,351
France (FR)	4	0	233,399	115,804	55	122,840	9	21,799	100	63,717	2	2,410	99	47,532	47	24,898
Greece (GR)	3	3	147,757	101,934	72	89,333	10	7,602	80	51,670	0	57	74	11,042	37	11,948
Italy (IT)	1	1	275,205	173,500	69	174,524	12	23,780	95	59,974	1	1,145	84	27,565	25	11,784
Luxembourg (LU)	4	0	710,092	397,841	67	410,615	5	23,506	89	269,332	1	446	97	87,978	58	81,785
Malta (MT)	1	1	365,988	215,932	78	167,059	11	84,843	89	75,477	0	1,276	96	49,536	34	12,203
Netherlands (NL)	12	0	170,244	103,562	57	154,460	4	5,622	83	25,059	0	5	96	66,937	66	81,840
Portugal (PT)	3	2	152,920	75,209	71	81,360	8	20,275	78	47,479	0	32	94	21,185	38	17,410
Slovenia (SI)	2	2	148,736	100,659	82	103,543	11	14,357	83	27,520	0	63	82	8,550	44	5,297
Slovak Republic (SK)	1	0	79,656	61,182	90	61,724	9	3,746	71	10,596	0	350	90	6,572	27	3,332

Notes: Columns 1–2 show percentage of the population with negative and zero net worth. Columns 3–4 show mean and median net worth. Columns 5–16 show the percentage of the population with positive holdings and mean holdings for a range of net worth components, namely the value of the main residence, the value of self-employment business, the value of other real assets, the value of a privately owned business, the value of other financial assets, and the total value of liabilities. Estimates are from the Eurosystem Household Finance and Consumption Survey, averaged over five multiple imputation replications of the data. No equivalence scales are applied.

3. Inequality Measurement

A survey on the inequality of anything almost always raises measurement issues. Some conceptual and measurement issues make measurement of inequality of wealth somewhat more challenging than analysis of income or consumption – these include the presence of a substantial fraction of negative net worth in most sample data on wealth, and the skewness and fat tails of the wealth distributions resulting in sparse, extreme data in typical samples. These features make some traditional measures of relative inequality inadequate, in particular because of negative net worth (Jenkins and Jäntti, 2005). We illustrate in this section how these can be taken into account in our measurement apparatus. The presence of negative net worth also requires the design of different parametric models from those typically used for income distribution; we address this in Section 4. Finally, extreme data affect the performance of standard statistical inference apparatus (for point estimation, sampling variance estimation and testing) and call for robust estimation techniques to keep the impact of extreme data under control (Cowell and Victoria-Feser, 1996; Cowell and Flachaire, 2015). We address these additional issues in Section 6.3.

3.1 *Principles*

In principle the measurement of inequality of wealth should be just like the measurement of inequality of income – almost. There will be differences between the two areas of application because some of the issues that arose in Section 2 affect what one can logically do within the context of wealth inequality.

The equalisand

In the case of income inequality it is usually appropriate to assume that the equalisand (income, earnings) is something that is intrinsically non-negative. Of course, researchers with practical experience will quickly point out exceptions to this (for example, where an individual's business losses are sufficiently great to make annual income negative) but, in the main, they are just that, exceptions. However, the non-negativity assumption just will not do in the case of wealth. If we want to examine the inequality of net worth – which is for many researchers, the theoretically ideal wealth concept – then we have to accept that in many cases a substantial proportion of the population will have negative current wealth.

In the case of *income* inequality there are good arguments for using equivalized income as an appropriate indicator of current individual welfare within a household. Converting total household income y of a family consisting of n_A adults and n_C children into the 'single-adult equivalent income' of each household member is considered uncontroversial and indeed there is a broad consensus as to the precise equivalence scale to use: many studies use either the square-root scale (dividing y by $\sqrt{n_A + n_C}$) or the modified OECD scale (dividing y by $1 + 0.5(n_A - 1) + 0.3n_C$). The application of such scales is intended to account for economies of scale in household spending and the lower needs of children when evaluating the living standard attained with a given income level and household size. By contrast, application of equivalence scales to household *wealth* data is more controversial (Sierminska and Smeeding, 2005; Bover, 2010; Jäntti *et al.*, 2013; OECD, 2013). A key issue is that if wealth is interpreted as the value of potential *future* consumption (say after retirement), it is not current household composition that should matter, but *future* composition. In case wealth is assumed to be consumed after retirement, one would probably not want to account for the presence of children in the household (but bequest intentions and future inter-vivos transfers make this decision less than obvious). Of course, if instead one is willing to interpret wealth as the ability to finance *current* consumption, arguments for applying equivalence scales are strong. Along an entirely different line of reasoning, if one does not interpret wealth as potential consumption but instead interprets wealth as an indication of status or power, there is little reason to adjust wealth for household size at all. Practice therefore varies in empirical work and choices can legitimately differ according to the purpose of one's analysis.

Illustrative estimates from the HFCS reported in this review ignore economies of scales altogether. We take the household as unit of analysis and analyse the wealth (and income) distribution across households in each country (not across individuals). In doing so, we effectively ignore the potential connection between household size and wealth as well as issues related to the sharing of wealth across household members and potential economies of scale. That we make such particular choices is largely a convenience decision and should not be misinterpreted as a recommendation in general.

The unit of analysis

As with the case of income distribution there is a case for considering either the individual or the household as the basic unit of population in the distributions under consideration. Clearly the choice of unit is going to be largely influenced by laws regarding the ownership of wealth and the way the wealth data are collected.

The distribution

In many cases, all one needs to do is to take the current distribution of net worth (or other wealth concept) in order to examine inequality. However, in some cases it could be advisable to adjust the wealth distribution before carrying out the inequality analysis: for example, it may be appropriate to make some kind of age adjustment in order to filter out purely life-cycle effects (Almås and Mogstad, 2012) – see Section 5.2. Our basic concept for analysing inequality will be the standard (cumulative) distribution function of wealth F, where $F(w)$ means the proportion of the population that has wealth w or less: this function produces a number q that lies between 0 and 1 and that indicates the position in the wealth distribution.

3.2 Ranking Tools

Let us start by taking the basic tool, the distribution function F, and inverting it. If we pick a particular proportion of the population q, then the *qth wealth quantile* is:

$$Q(F; q) := \inf\{w|F(w) \geq q\} \tag{2}$$

The way to read the definition in (2) is this: for any distribution F find the smallest wealth value w such that $100q\%$ of the population have exactly that wealth or less. The graph $\{(q, Q(F; q)) : 0 \leq q \leq 1\}$ is *Pen's Parade,* a basic tool used in first-order dominance comparisons (Cowell, 2000, 2011, 2015). Figure 1 shows Pen's Parade (the quantile functions) for both net worth and income calculated on our illustrative HFCS data. Estimates are calculated for 19 equally spaced quantiles from 0.05 to 0.95 (that is 19 'vingtiles'). Net worth quantiles exhibit much

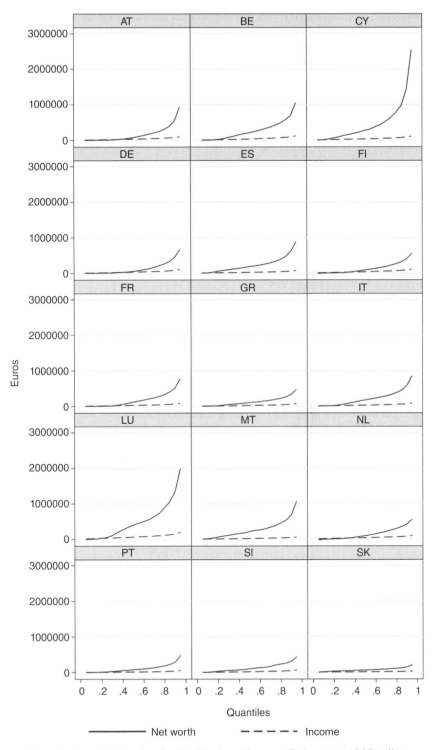

Figure 1. Quantile Function for Net Worth and Income (Estimates at 19 Vingtiles).

bigger disparities than income: they are both higher than income quantiles at the top and flatter in most of the quantile range.

We can build on the concept defined in (2) to give us some other useful tools. The *qth wealth cumulation* is defined as:

$$C(F; q) := \int_{\underline{w}}^{w_q} w \, dF(w) \qquad (3)$$

where $w_q = Q(F; q)$ and $\underline{w}$ is the lower bound of the support of F.[9] An important special case of this is found when $w_q = \overline{w}$, the upper bound of the support of F. The mean of the distribution F is defined as

$$\mu(F) := \int w dF(w) \qquad (4)$$

and equals $C(F, 1)$. The graph $\{(q, C(F; q)): \ 0 \leq q \leq 1\}$ is the *Generalized Lorenz curve* which plots the (normalized) cumulations of wealth against proportions of the population. It is a basic tool used in second-order dominance comparisons (Shorrocks, 1983). An additional tool – of tremendous importance – that can be derived from (3) is the wealth share (or Lorenz ordinate)

$$L(F; q) := \frac{C(F; q)}{\mu(F)} \qquad (5)$$

and the associated *(relative) Lorenz curve* (Lorenz, 1905) which is simply the graph[10]

$$\{(q, L(F; q)): \ 0 \leq q \leq 1\} \qquad (6)$$

It is clear from the definition in (5) that a word of caution is necessary. The wealth shares and Lorenz curve are well defined for negative wealth only as long as the mean is positive.[11] The Lorenz curve is undefined if the mean is zero and is unreliable if the mean is close to zero. In these cases it may be interesting to use the absolute Lorenz ordinates defined by

$$A(F; q) := C(F; q) - q\mu(F); \qquad (7)$$

the graph $\{(q, A(F; q)): \ 0 \leq q \leq 1\}$ is the *absolute Lorenz curve*, a convex curve running from (0,0) to (1,0) (Moyes, 1987).

The shape of some of these various graphical tools are illustrated in Figures 2–4. Figure 2 shows the share of total wealth (respectively income) held by each of the twenty 'vingtile groups' defined by the 19 quantiles shown in Figure 1. What most strikingly stands out from the figure is the large share of net worth held by the top vingtile group—that is the richest 5% of the population: it ranges between about 20–25% in Slovenia, Slovakia or Greece to up to about 45% in Austria, Cyprus or Germany. The concentration of wealth at the very top of the distribution is much larger than in the income distribution, where the share held by the richest 5% of households is between 15% and 25%.

Lorenz curves are shown in Figure 3. Remember that the more convex is the Lorenz curve, the greater is the concentration of wealth (or income) at the top. The Lorenz curves for wealth typically reveal much bigger concentration than for income, in almost all countries – Slovenia and Slovakia being exceptions.

Figure 4 shows absolute Lorenz curves. The shape of the absolute Lorenz curve is probably less familiar to most readers. It depicts the area between the Generalized Lorenz curve and a straight line joining its two end points at $(0, 0)$ and $(\mu(F), 1)$. It therefore represents the

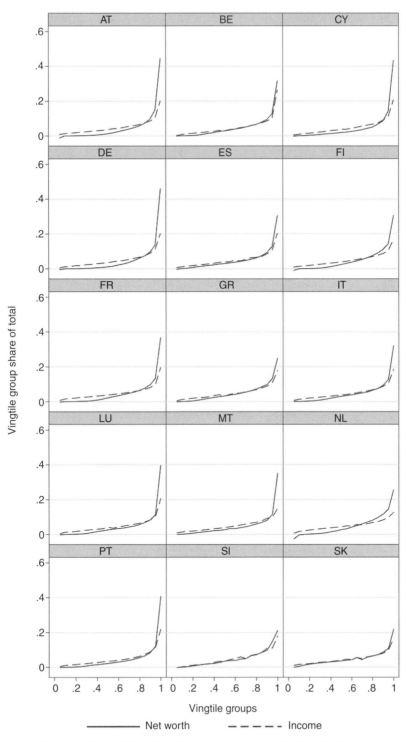

Figure 2. Share of Total Net Worth and Income for 20 Vingtile Groups.

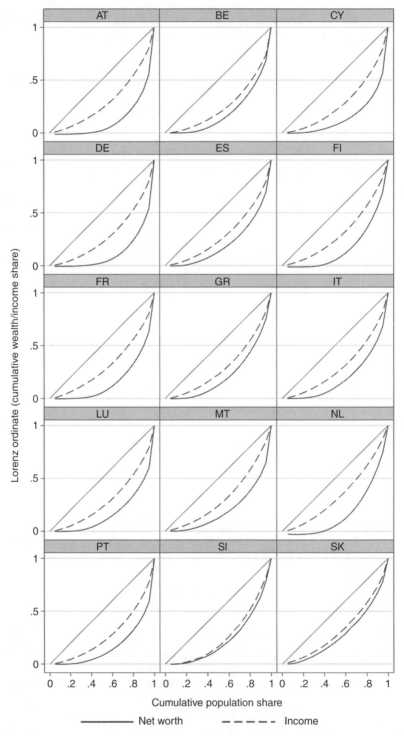

Figure 3. Lorenz Curve of Net Worth and Income.

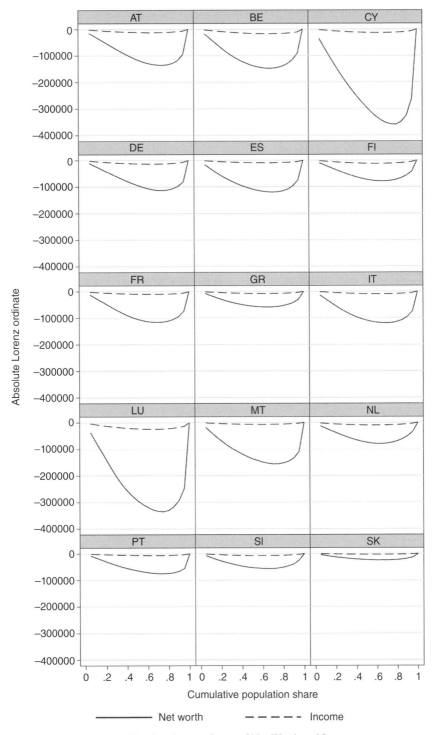

Figure 4. Absolute Lorenz Curve of Net Worth and Income.

cumulative wealth deficit in euros of the bottom $100q\%$ of households compared to what they would have held in an hypothetical equal distribution. Income differences are dwarfed by the size of wealth differences. Wealth differences in euros are clearly much larger in countries with higher levels of wealth (Luxembourg and Cyprus) and give a different picture of cross-national differences in wealth inequality. Note in passing how the shape of the absolute Lorenz curves signals the skewness of wealth distributions: the population share corresponding to minimum value of the curve is the share of the population with wealth below average. This share is well above one-half, between 0.6 in Greece and up to about 0.75 for many countries.

3.3 Measures

One could press into service the constituent parts of the ranking tools discussed in Section 3.2 to give us very simple inequality measures that just focus on one part of the distribution. Perhaps the most obvious of these is the Lorenz ordinate (5) which gives the share of wealth owned by the bottom $100q\%$ of the population. By simply writing $p = 1 - q$ and defining

$$S(F; p) := 1 - L(F; 1 - p)$$

we obtain the top $100p\%$ wealth share, a concept that is widely used in the empirical literature – see, for example, Edlund and Kopczuk (2009), Kopczuk and Saez (2004), Piketty (2014a) and Saez and Zucman (2014).

But what if we want an inequality measure that effectively summarizes the whole distribution, rather than just focusing on one location in the distribution? Here we encounter a difficulty. Because of the qualifications introduced in Section 3.1 we have to use tools that allow for negative values of wealth. This severely limits the choice of inequality indices: for example, it rules out measures that involve $\log(w)$ or w^c (except where c is a positive integer).

3.3.1 Scale-Independent Indices

Amongst the commonly used scale-independent inequality indices, only the coefficient of variation, the relative mean deviation and the Gini coefficient are available (Amiel *et al.*, 1996) given by:

$$I_{CV}(F) := \frac{1}{\mu(F)} \sqrt{\int [w - \mu(F)]^2 \, dF(w)} \tag{8}$$

$$I_{RMD}(F) := \int \left| \frac{w}{\mu(F)} - 1 \right| dF(w) \tag{9}$$

$$I_{Gini}(F) := \frac{1}{2\mu(F)} \int |w - w'| \, dF(w) \, dF(w') \tag{10}$$

respectively where, once again, $\mu(F)$ is the mean of F, defined in (4); clearly all of these measures remain invariant if the wealth distribution were to undergo a transformation of scale, where all the wealth values are multiplied by an arbitrary positive number. We are also able to rewrite (10) in terms of the Lorenz curve to obtain the equivalent expression

$$I_{Gini}(F) = 1 - 2 \int_0^1 L(F; q) \, dq \tag{11}$$

which gives the Gini coefficient as twice the area between the main diagonal and the Lorenz curve. Two qualifications should be added.

First, apart from (8–11) there are, of course, other less well-known indices that could be used in the presence of negative net worth. If we re-examine the structure of the Gini coefficient (11) we will see a way in which other similar inequality measures can be obtained. The integral expression in (11) can be seen as the limit of a weighted sum of rectangles with height $L(F; q)$ (the Lorenz ordinate) and base the interval $[q, q + dq]$: each rectangle is assigned the same weight, irrespective of q, the position in the distribution. Suppose we weight each of these rectangles by a position-dependent amount ω_q; if the weight is given by

$$\omega_q = 1/2k[k-1][1-q]^{k-2} \tag{12}$$

where $k > 1$ is a parameter,[12] then we obtain a family of inequality indices known as the Single-Parameter Gini, or 'S-Gini' (Donaldson and Weymark 1980, 1983; Yitzhaki, 1983) as follows:

$$I_{\text{SGini}}(F) := 1 - 2 \int_0^1 \omega_q L(F; q) \, dq \tag{13}$$

The members of the S-Gini family are indexed by the parameter k and all have the property of the regular Gini that they are well-defined for distributions that incorporate negative net worth, as long as the Lorenz ordinates $L(F; q)$ are well defined.[13] The parameter k acts as an inequality aversion parameter: the larger is k, the stronger is the weight associated to low wealth. In the limit as $k \to \infty$, the S-Gini coefficient is given by the relative difference between the lowest wealth $\underline{w}$ and the mean: $1 - \underline{w}/\mu(F)$.[14]

Second, as the previous sentence has just hinted, there is a problem if the Lorenz ordinates $L(F; q)$ are *not* well defined; this will happen if the mean of the distribution is zero. This affects all the scale-independent (relative) inequality indices that we have considered so far, including I_{CV} and I_{RMD}, not just those based directly on the Lorenz ordinates. For this reason it may make sense to consider using 'absolute' counterparts.

3.3.2 Translation-Independent Indices

The absolute counterparts of (8–10) are found just by multiplying each of the expressions by $\mu(F)$. So, instead of I_{CV} we have the standard deviation, or its square, the variance and instead of I_{RMD}, we have the mean deviation. The counterpart to (10) is the *Absolute Gini coefficient* (Cowell, 2007):

$$I_{\text{AGini}}(F) := \frac{1}{2} \iint |w - w'| \, dF(w) \, dF(w') \tag{14}$$

which is half the mean difference (see, for example, Zanardi, 1990). All of these indices are translation-independent in that, if any constant is added or subtracted to all the wealth values (the wealth-distribution is 'translated'), then the values of the inequality indices remain unchanged. One may also use the class of absolute decomposable inequality indices given by

$$I_{\text{AD}}^\beta(F) := \begin{cases} \int [e^{\beta[w-\mu(F)]} - 1] \, dF(w) & \text{if } \beta \neq 0 \\ \int [w - \mu(F)]^2 \, dF(w) & \text{if } \beta = 0 \end{cases} \tag{15}$$

Table 2. Household Net Worth and Income Inequality: Scale Invariant Measures.

	CoV		RMD		Gini		SGini(3)		SGini(4)	
Country	nw	y	nw	y	nw	y	nw	y	nw	y
Austria (AT)	2.945	1.079	0.572	0.300	0.762	0.420	0.902	0.546	0.960	0.612
Belgium (BE)	1.630	1.656	0.436	0.345	0.608	0.484	0.773	0.622	0.854	0.696
Cyprus (CY)	2.479	1.161	0.526	0.318	0.698	0.446	0.832	0.586	0.890	0.660
Germany (DE)	3.394	0.986	0.574	0.307	0.758	0.428	0.900	0.565	0.957	0.637
Spain (ES)	4.063	1.395	0.413	0.291	0.580	0.413	0.734	0.545	0.814	0.618
Finland (FI)	1.917	0.844	0.488	0.275	0.664	0.381	0.851	0.515	0.939	0.587
France (FR)	3.605	1.174	0.495	0.270	0.679	0.384	0.840	0.506	0.912	0.573
Greece (GR)	1.279	0.863	0.401	0.286	0.561	0.400	0.734	0.539	0.822	0.615
Italy (IT)	1.912	0.867	0.434	0.285	0.609	0.398	0.770	0.530	0.848	0.602
Luxembourg (LU)	2.575	1.071	0.474	0.298	0.661	0.420	0.808	0.552	0.880	0.623
Malta (MT)	3.496	0.720	0.428	0.268	0.600	0.367	0.739	0.503	0.810	0.576
Netherlands (NL)	1.398	0.599	0.476	0.225	0.654	0.319	0.876	0.448	0.994	0.524
Portugal (PT)	3.770	1.127	0.487	0.323	0.670	0.450	0.813	0.584	0.880	0.655
Slovenia (SI)	1.171	0.957	0.387	0.344	0.534	0.479	0.706	0.653	0.793	0.747
Slovak Republic (SK)	1.055	0.832	0.313	0.253	0.448	0.356	0.594	0.481	0.675	0.549

Notes: Columns 1–10 report estimates of scale invariant inequality indices: the coefficient of variation, the relative mean deviation, the Gini coefficient, the generalized Gini coefficient with inequality aversion parameters 3 and 4. Each index is reported for both total net worth (nw) and total household pre-tax income (y). Estimates are from the Eurosystem Household Finance and Consumption Survey, averaged over five multiple imputation replications of the data. No equivalence scales are applied.

where β is a sensitivity parameter that may take any real value. Clearly the case $\beta = 0$ is just the variance; if $\beta > 0$ then $I_{AD}^{\beta}(F)$ is ordinally equivalent to the Kolm indices given by

$$I_{\text{Kolm}}^{\beta}(F) = \frac{1}{\beta} \log \left(I_{AD}^{\beta}(F) + 1 \right)$$ (16)

– see Bosmans and Cowell (2010) and Kolm (1976).

3.3.3 *Examples*

Table 2 reports a range of scale-independent inequality measures estimated for both net worth and income. Here we confine ourselves to measures defined for negative and zero values. Table 3 does the corresponding job for translation-independent inequality measures. Unsurprisingly, inequality measures are (much) larger for wealth than for income, in particular for translation invariant measures. The net worth Gini coefficient ranges between 0.45 (Slovakia) and 0.76 (Austria and Germany) while it ranges between 0.32 (Netherlands) and 0.48 (Slovenia) for household pre-tax income. Equally unsurprisingly, different summary indices rank countries differently, although Luxembourg and Cyprus remain the most unequal according to any translation invariant measure and Austria and Germany are generally (but not always) the most unequal according to scale invariant measures. Slovakia is the least unequal according to both perspectives. Note how countries with most prevalent negative net worth

Table 3. Household Net Worth and Income Inequality: Translation Invariant Measures.

Country	$\sqrt{V}$ nw	$\sqrt{V}$ y	Gini nw	Gini y	SGini(3) nw	SGini(3) y	SGini(4) nw	SGini(4) y	Kolm(.125) nw	Kolm(.125) y	Kolm(1) nw	Kolm(1) y	Kolm(2) nw	Kolm(2) y
Austria (AT)	798,567	47,611	202,853	18,483	239,547	24,040	254,734	26,941	103,314	1,190	324,039	6,049	509,170	9,251
Belgium (BE)	551,986	82,062	206,002	23,989	261,792	30,837	289,091	34,458	86,802	2,623	224,246	9,783	329,452	14,062
Cyprus (CY)	1,662,701	50,251	468,141	19,291	558,434	25,330	597,507	28,558	318,510	1,284	589,222	6,378	915,030	9,790
Germany (DE)	662,517	42,937	147,913	18,621	175,677	24,576	186,873	27,714	63,935	979	133,969	5,649	166,502	9,092
Spain (ES)	1,184,078	43,721	169,128	12,953	213,922	17,088	237,245	19,348	66,914	728	195,288	3,334	735,039	5,173
Finland (FI)	309,656	38,101	107,292	17,212	137,416	23,261	151,642	26,509	28,360	769	96,999	4,636	255,527	7,781
France (FR)	841,349	43,329	158,484	14,176	196,057	18,680	212,798	21,163	62,350	836	151,268	4,243	195,982	19,834
Greece (GR)	189,026	23,864	82,855	11,070	108,438	14,918	121,495	17,017	16,171	312	63,987	2,083	87,318	3,632
Italy (IT)	526,060	29,787	167,714	13,670	211,822	18,218	233,418	20,666	64,618	489	166,215	3,178	203,397	5,365
Luxembourg (LU)	1,828,169	89,574	469,692	35,130	573,973	46,166	624,603	52,149	312,468	3,797	585,056	16,882	726,650	25,049
Malta (MT)	1,279,337	19,048	219,472	9,716	270,412	13,307	296,306	15,243	107,668	205	227,251	1,492	272,174	2,730
Netherlands (NL)	237,997	27,415	111,344	14,588	149,174	20,496	169,273	23,972	25,590	424	112,184	3,110	188,899	5,713
Portugal (PT)	576,481	22,895	102,466	9,130	124,287	11,871	134,598	13,293	36,776	283	82,516	1,722	101,289	2,864
Slovenia (SI)	174,509	21,368	79,526	10,707	104,984	14,593	118,026	16,683	14,501	256	60,472	1,839	83,530	3,322
Slovak Republic (SK)	84,026	11,206	35,706	4,800	47,291	6,475	53,805	7,393	3,563	70	17,294	479	25,997	849

Notes: Columns 1–14 report estimates of translation invariant inequality indices: the standard deviation, the absolute generalized S-Gini coefficient with inequality aversion parameters 3 and 4, the Kolm index with β parameter set to varying fractions of the reciprocal of median Eurozone-wide household net worth, namely 108,782 euros (see Atkinson and Brandolini, 2010). Each index is reported for both total net worth (nw) and total household pre-tax income (y). Estimates are from the Eurosystem Household Finance and Consumption Survey, averaged over five multiple imputation replications of the data. No equivalence scales are applied.

(Finland and the Netherlands) exhibit high inequality according to S-Gini measures with large inequality aversion parameters.

3.3.4 *Decomposition by Subgroups*

In many applications, it is convenient to decompose measures of wealth inequality by subgroups of the population. Obviously one could use the indices I^β_{Kolm} – although this is surprisingly rare in empirical work – or the variance, which tends to be very sensitive to outliers in the upper tail. One other tool is available for certain types of decomposition.

Although the Gini coefficient is not generally decomposable by population subgroups – see the discussion of the age adjustment in Section 5.2 – it can be decomposed into subgroups that do not 'overlap', i.e. subgroups that can be unambiguously ordered by the wealth of their members.[15] The simplest version of this 'non-overlapping' case is where we partition the population into the 'poor' P and the 'rich' R: the wealth of anyone in P is less than the wealth of anyone in R. Denote the wealth distribution of the whole population by the function F and that of the poor group and the rich group by F_P and F_R, respectively; the population share and the income share of the poor are denoted by π_P and s_P, with the corresponding shares for the rich being written as π_R and s_R; also let F_{Betw} be the wealth distribution if everyone in group P had the mean wealth of group P and everyone in group R had the mean wealth of group R. We then have the following formula (Radaelli, 2010; Cowell, 2013)

$$I_{\text{Gini}}(F) = \pi_P s_P I_{\text{Gini}}(F_P) + \pi_R s_R I_{\text{Gini}}(F_R) + I_{\text{Gini}}(F_{\text{Betw}}) \tag{17}$$

which gives an exact formula for decomposing the Gini coefficient into the non-overlapping subgroups P and R.

4. Representing Wealth Distributions

Apart from the technical issues involved in measuring the inequality of wealth (discussed in Section 3), there is a second issue to be considered before undertaking empirical work: whether inequality comparisons are to be made indirectly through a statistical 'model' of the wealth distribution or directly from the observations on households or individuals. What we mean by a 'model' in this context is a particular functional form that is used to characterize all or part of the wealth distribution. Typically such a functional form can be expressed as $F(w) = \Phi(w; \theta_1, \dots, \theta_k)$ where Φ is a general class of functions, with an individual member of the class being specified by parameters $\theta_1, \dots, \theta_k$ that are typically to be estimated from the data. In effect we have three possible approaches:[16]

- *Non-parametric approach*: make inequality comparisons using the wealth observations directly;
- *Semi-parametric approach*: model a part of the distribution (typically the upper tail) using a functional form and use the wealth observations directly for the remainder of the distribution, a procedure that is commonly used if data are sparse or unreliable in the upper tail;
- *Parametric approach*: use a model for all of the distribution.

The second and third approaches require the specification of a functional form Φ, which immediately raises the question: what makes a 'good' functional form? There are two types of answer. First, how well the models appear to work in representing real-world distributions – this issue is discussed in the remainder of this section. Second, whether there is reason to suppose that a particular functional form is linked with a suitable *economic* model of wealth distribution – this is considered briefly in Section 5.1.

4.1 Describing Wealth at the Top: The Pareto Distribution

The upper tail of income and wealth distributions are commonly described by the Pareto Type I (or 'power law') distribution (Arnold, 2008; Maccabelli, 2009). The key characteristic of the distribution introduced by Pareto (1895) is the linear relationship between the logarithm of the proportion p_w of individuals with wealth greater than w and the logarithm of w itself. This observation describes a distribution that is said to decay like a power function, a behaviour that characterizes 'heavy-tailed' distributions.[17] In the context of income or wealth, this relationship is expected to hold only in the upper tail of the distribution, that is, above a certain minimum level of wealth w_0: the Pareto distribution is a model for describing top wealth distributions. It has been used, for example, to model wealth in the Forbes 'rich lists' (see, e.g., Levy and Solomon, 1997; Klass *et al.*, 2006).[18]

The Pareto Type I distribution is characterized by the distribution function

$$F(w) = 1 - [\underline{w}/w]^\alpha, \ w > \underline{w} \tag{18}$$

and so has density

$$f(w) = \alpha \underline{w}^\alpha w^{-1-\alpha}$$

where α is a parameter that captures the 'weight' of the upper tail of the distribution and $\underline{w}$ is a parameter that 'locates' the distribution. The proportion of the population with wealth greater than or equal to w (for $w > \underline{w}$) is $p_w = 1 - F(w)$ and the linearity of the Pareto plot follows from

$$\log p_w = \log \underline{w}^\alpha - \alpha \log w \tag{19}$$

The value of α (also called the Pareto index) is related to the inequality associated with the Pareto distribution: but note that inequality *decreases* with α. So, for example in this case the Gini coefficient is given by $\frac{1}{2\alpha-1}$ (Kleiber and Kotz, 2003). Another useful property of the Pareto distribution is that if one considers any wealth level w, then the average wealth of those with wealth greater than w is given by $\frac{\alpha}{\alpha-1}w$, a relationship known as 'van der Wijk's law' (Cowell, 2011); so in the case of the Pareto distribution another intuitive inequality concept can be easily defined as the ratio

$$\frac{\text{average}}{\text{base}} = \frac{\alpha}{1-\alpha};$$

which describes, for any base wealth level, how much richer on average are all those with wealth at or above the base wealth level (Atkinson *et al.*, 2011).

Figure 5 shows 'Pareto diagrams' for our illustrative HFCS data.[19] Each diagram shows the logarithm of net worth plotted against $\log p_w$ for all sample data. According to (19), all points should be aligned on a straight line with slope $-\alpha$ for Pareto-distributed data. The Pareto diagrams indicate a broadly linear relationship for the upper quarter of the data in most countries, that is beyond $p_w = 0.25$. The fit to the Pareto assumption is however not entirely satisfactory throughout the whole range of net worth: linearity disappears or the slope changes

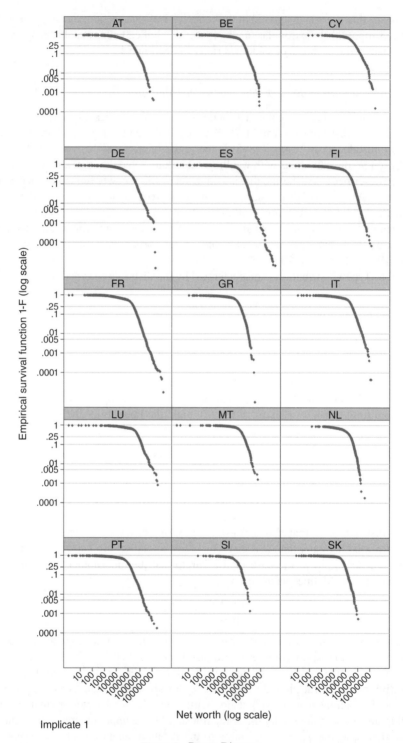

Implicate 1

Figure 5. Pareto Diagram.

at the very top, say above $p_w = 0.99$ or even $p_w = 0.999$ or so, that is above the top 1% of the samples. We return to this issue in Section 6.3 when discussing data contamination and robustness.

4.2 Overall Wealth Distributions

The Pareto distribution just described is a simple, convenient model for summarizing the upper tail of a wealth distribution. It is however inappropriate as a model for the overall wealth distribution. A comprehensive functional form obviously requires adequate modelling of the lower part of the distribution too.

Typical options for income distribution analysis include the log-normal, the gamma distribution (Chakraborti and Patriarca, 2008), the Singh-Maddala (Singh and Maddala, 1976), the Dagum Type I (Dagum, 1977; Kleiber, 2008) or the more flexible Generalized Beta distribution of the Second Kind (McDonald and Ransom, 2008; Jenkins, 2009); see Kleiber and Kotz (2003) for a detailed description of all these distributions, Bandourian *et al.* (2003) for a comparison and Clementi and Gallegati (2005), Dagsvik *et al.* (2013), Reed and Fan (2008) or Sarabia *et al.* (2002) for yet other possibilities. All of these models have however been developed for 'size distributions' and are defined for random variables that take on strictly positive values. None of these models is therefore useful for wealth distributions that involve zero or negative observations.

A practical approach to address this singularity of wealth distributions may be to work with 'shifted' or 'displaced' distributions. This involves adding a shift parameter and specifying the wealth distribution as $F^s(w) = F(w + c)$ where F is a conventional size distribution defined on the positive halfline (say a log-normal) and $c > 0$ is an additional shifting parameter that slides the distribution into the negative halfline. For the log-normal, this model is referred to as the displaced log-normal; see Gottschalk and Danziger (1985) for an application. While simple, this strategy has key drawbacks. First, estimation of the c parameter can be problematic (see the discussion in Aitchison and Brown (1957) or Kleiber and Kotz (2003)). Second, such a specification assumes continuity at zero that is potentially problematic in applications to net worth distributions.

A more elaborate approach is developed in Dagum (1990, 1999) who suggested combining three separate models: an exponential distribution for negative data, a point-mass at zero and a Dagum Type I distribution for positive data

$$F^D(w) = \begin{cases} \pi_1 \, \exp(\theta w) & \text{if } w < 0 \\ \pi_1 + \pi_2 & \text{if } w = 0 \\ \pi_1 + \pi_2 + (1 - \pi_1 - \pi_2)\left(1 + \left(\frac{\beta}{w}\right)^\alpha\right)^{-\gamma} & \text{if } w > 0 \end{cases} \tag{20}$$

where π_1 and π_2 are the shares of negatives and zeros, α, β and γ are the parameters of a Dagum Type I distribution for positive data (Dagum, 1977) and $\theta > 0$ is the shape parameter for the negative distribution. Lower values of θ lead to a longer left tail in the negative halfline but the exponential distribution specification maintains a relatively fast convergence to zero (unlike in the upper tail) 'because of institutional and biological bounds to an unlimited increase of economic agent's liability' (Dagum, 1999, p. 248). A more restricted model combining the Dagum Type I on the positive halfline and the mass at zero was presented as the Dagum Type II distribution in Dagum (1977); see also Kleiber and Kotz (2003). Jenkins and Jäntti (2005) provide an application of this model; Jäntti *et al.* (2012) replace the Dagum specification with a Singh-Maddala model in a parametric model for the joint distribution of income and wealth.

The mixture distribution just described allows comprehensive description of the overall wealth distribution, allowing for negative net worth and a spike at zero that is often observed in sample data. Figure 6 shows the empirical CDF of net worth F overlaid over the CDF predicted from estimation of a Dagum Type 3 model F^D in our HFCS data. The empirical and predicted CDFs turn out to be close to each other, with noticeable differences only in Belgium and Luxembourg (in the middle) and France or Slovakia (in the bottom). The fit in the negatives reveal satisfactory (see Finland and the Netherlands where more than 10% of net worth observations are below zero).

However, the flexibility of the model comes at the cost of significantly increased complexity since the specification now requires 6 parameters. In the end, this may somewhat reduce the attractiveness of estimating a parametric model, compared to calculating fully non-parametric estimation of the distribution function by, say, kernel or related methods.

5. Wealth Inequality and the Structure of Wealth Distributions

As we noted in Section 4, wealth inequality presents special problems in the way that data are to be presented and modelled statistically. Wealth inequality also presents special problems in terms of the economic rationale for the type of distribution used to evaluate inequality.

The key issue has to do with the time frame that is implicit in the inequality comparisons. Although we do not pretend to cover the large field of economic models of the generation of wealth distribution, a few points from that literature are needed to clarify the distinction between different factors that determine the wealth distribution and indeed different types of wealth distribution. This clarification helps one understand what wealth differences are to be considered as 'genuine' wealth inequality.

Wealth inequality and the life cycle issue. Simple life-cycle accumulation models predict wealth to be hump shaped over a person's lifetime (Davies and Shorrocks, 2000). Empirical evidence shows that assets are typically accumulated over the working age and decline after retirement age, in response to changing needs and circumstances; debts tend to peak at younger adult age and decline drastically in old age (see, for example, OECD, 2008; European Central Bank, 2013). Some households may have negative net worth at certain points in the life cycle (for example, during a period when they incur mortgage debt that they expect to pay off during the time that they are employed). If we take a snapshot of the economy at a particular moment in history the data will typically pick up individuals at every stage of the adult life cycle. As a consequence even if one were to imagine an economy in which individuals were identical in every respect, other than their date of birth, one would observe substantial wealth inequality that arose purely from this life-cycle process: the extent of this apparent inequality would depend on the age distribution. An uncritical look at the current wealth distribution can therefore pick up wealth differences between persons and between households that have arguably, not much to do with underlying inequality of circumstances. This issue also arises in the analysis of income distributions, but is more problematic in the case of wealth inequality.

Wealth inequality in the long run. Following this line of reasoning it might be thought that all the short-term influences on the wealth distribution should effectively be netted out so as to leave only a wealth distribution that somehow captures inequality in the long run. This may be attractive in principle, but presents a number of important difficulties in practice.

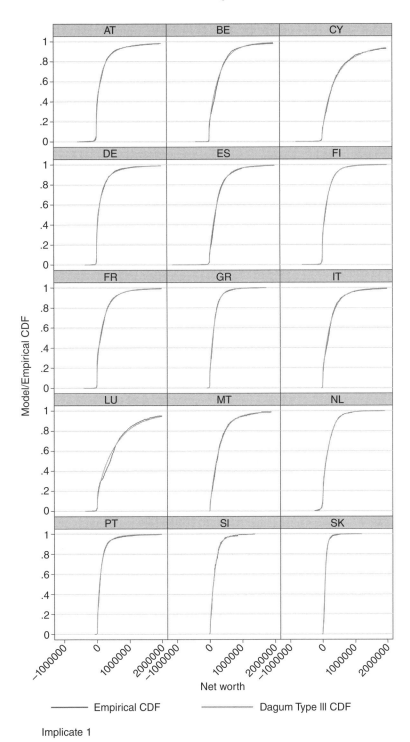

Implicate 1

Figure 6. Empirical and Dagum Type 3 CDFs for Net Worth.

In Section 5.1 we consider briefly the issue of long-run modelling and then in Section 5.2 we tackle the more modest task of making age adjustments to allow for the life-cycle effect on wealth dispersion.

5.1 *Long-Run Inequality Modelling*

If we want to take a truly long-term view of wealth inequality then perhaps we could proceed as follows. Imagine society as a sequence of generations $\ldots, n - 1, n, n + 1, \ldots$ and consider each person alive at a given moment as the representative in generation n of a particular family line or dynasty. Then attribute to that representative of generation n a wealth value that represents his or her lifetime economic position – for example, inherited assets plus a computation of lifetime earnings. Letting F_n denote the distribution function of this concept of wealth in generation n, the precise distribution of wealth at a given calendar time t will be derived from the relevant F_n and information about within-lifetime wealth profiles and the age structure. The dispersion of wealth implied by F_n could be taken as a first cut at long-run inequality, purged of all the short-run – i.e. within lifetime – effects. This 'generation-n' distribution would yield an interpretation of a long-run wealth distribution that gradually evolves through time as one progresses through the generations n.

One might want to go further. To do this, introduce the concept of an *equilibrium distribution* which can be explained as follows. Represent all the economic and social forces that operate on the wealth distribution from generation n to generation $n + 1$ by a single process P; the generation-to-generation development of the wealth distribution is then written as

$$F_n \overset{P}{\longmapsto} F_{n+1} \tag{21}$$

As a simplified version of this one could imagine that F_n is discrete and gives the cumulative proportions in each of K wealth categories. Then the process P is simply a transition matrix. It is easy to characterize equilibrium using equation (21). If there is a distribution F^* such that

$$F^* \overset{P}{\longmapsto} F^* \tag{22}$$

then the self-reproducing F^* is the equilibrium distribution for P: if the process P remains unchanged then F^* remains unchanged (Cowell, 2014). Notice that this concept is consistent with long-run wealth mobility within the equilibrium distribution – it is just the (marginal) distribution of wealth that remains unchanged through the generations.

This equilibrium distribution is the concept underlying many recent approaches to long-run inequality and can also be understood as a way of rationalizing some of the very early contributions to the literature that used terms such as 'Laws of Distribution'.[20] Of course, in some cases there exist no F^* at all for a given P and, where such a F^* does exist, there is no reason to suppose that it will be representable in a convenient functional form. But for models of P that yield a tractable closed-form solution for the equilibrium distribution, F^* very often turns out to be of the Pareto (type 1) form discussed in Section 4.1 above. Characterizing long-run wealth inequality then becomes a matter of appropriately modelling P and of estimating the parameter(s) of the equilibrium distribution F^*.

However, the above account is just a sketch, even if it is an attractive sketch. Once one tries to sort out the components of a serious model of wealth inequality it is clear that the story is inevitably complicated. Sometimes the many forces that determine the development of the wealth distribution are summarized in the form of a two-chapter story, the first chapter

concentrating on within-lifetime decisions (savings for retirement, labour supply, the acquisition of human capital) and the second consisting of decisions and circumstances relating
to connections between the generations (bequest planning) – see Champernowne and Cowell
(1998). But the two-chapter approach is for methodological convenience only: in practice the
divide between the two is blurred and one cannot assume that the wealth adjustments arising
from 'Chapter 1 decisions' can be separated out neatly from those that are conventionally
considered as 'Chapter 2 issues'; for example, it is argued that the observed inequality and
heterogeneity of wealth in retirement years is attributable to interaction of decisions from
each of the two chapters (Hendricks, 2007; Yang, 2008; De Nardi and Yang, 2014); again
the anticipation of a wealth transfers may affect within-lifetime decisions. This suggests that
trying to examine long-run wealth inequality by filtering out the within-lifetime component is
a daunting task.

5.2 Age-Adjusted Wealth Inequality Measures

However, a less daunting task is worth considering: making adjustments to measured wealth
inequality to take account of the distinctive lifetime pattern of personal wealth holding. The
implication of this pattern is that cross-section measures of wealth inequality at a point in
time in a population are shaped by a society's age structure. Even if everyone had common
wealth accumulation paths over the life-cycle, wealth at any point in time would turn out to be
unequally distributed when pooling observations of individuals of different age. In practice,
there is also much within-cohort heterogeneity in wealth holdings between individuals and
heterogeneity in wealth trajectories. Since wealth-inequality indicators conflate demographic
influences of the age structure as well as inequality in life-cycle wealth accumulation, the
relevance of differences in cross-section wealth inequality measures across countries or over
time may be questioned (Atkinson, 1971; Davies and Shorrocks, 2000).

The Gini coefficient within age groups can be connected to the overall Gini coefficient by
the relation

$$I_{\text{Gini}}(F) = \sum_{a=1}^{A} s_a \pi_a I_{\text{Gini}}(F_a) + I_{\text{Gini}}(F_{\text{Betw}}) + R \tag{23}$$

where F_a is the wealth distribution within age group a, s_a and π_a are, respectively, the
population share and the total wealth share of age group a, F_{Betw} is the 'between-group'
distribution (see Section 3.3.4) which in this case is derived by assigning to each individual the
mean wealth within their age group, and finally R captures the degree of overlap between the
wealth distributions of the different age groups. The last term disappears only in the unrealistic
case of wealth in each subgroup having strictly non-overlapping support. The decomposition
makes it clear that the overall Gini can be influenced by inequality within age groups – that may
be considered of genuine interest – but also by the distribution of population over different age
groups, as well as by the differences in mean wealth between age groups which are driven by
life-cycle accumulation patterns and changes in wealth holdings over successive birth cohorts.

Variation in inequality within and between age groups is documented in Figure 7. The
diagram shows the Gini coefficient calculated within each age group $I_{\text{Gini}}(F_a)$ (the solid
lines), along with the population share in each group s_a (the vertical dark grey bars) and the
share of total wealth held by each age group π_a (the vertical light grey bars). The overall
Gini coefficient $I_{\text{Gini}}(F)$ is given by the upper horizontal reference line (dot-dashed) and

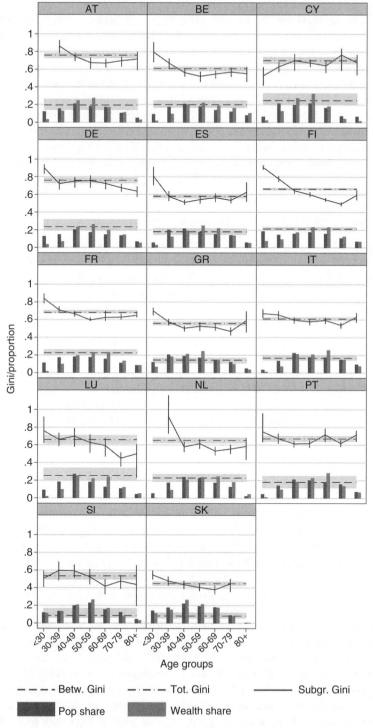

Figure 7. Population and Wealth Shares and Gini Coefficient by Age Group.

the between-group Gini $I_{\text{Gini}}(F_{\text{Betw}})$ is given by the lower reference line (dashed). The Gini coefficient calculated within groups generally declines with age although the decline is not monotone in most countries and in a country like Cyprus it actually increases across age groups. In all countries (except Slovenia) the wealth share of the younger age groups is (substantially) below their population shares, and the reverse holds for the middle age groups: the extent of those deviations is reflected in the level of the between group Gini. Note that the within group Gini coefficients are estimated on relatively small samples and are relatively imprecisely estimated: 95% confidence intervals are shown by the vertical segments and the shaded area behind total and between group Ginis.[21] Perhaps surprisingly, population shares across the different age groups do indeed vary across European countries. For example, the share of households with reference aged less than 30 ranges from almost 20% in Finland to less than 5% in Italy.

Various authors have proposed age-adjusted inequality measures to address this concern. The idea is simply to derive summary indices purged from the effect of age. For example, Paglin (1975) proposed a simple age-adjusted Gini index of the form

$$I_{\text{PaglinGini}}(F) = I_{\text{Gini}}(F) - I_{\text{Gini}}(F_{\text{Betw}}) \tag{24}$$

where F is the overall distribution and F_{Betw} is the 'between-group' distribution. So $I_{\text{PaglinGini}}$ is given by the vertical distance between the two horizontal reference lines in Figure 7. $I_{\text{PaglinGini}}$ turns out to be approximately one-third smaller than I_{Gini} – more so in Luxembourg and less so in Slovenia. Paglin essentially argues that instead of assessing inequality by the area between the Lorenz curve and a 45 degree line of perfect equality (a Lorenz curve where everyone has the same wealth), one should calculate the area between the Lorenz curve and a Lorenz curve calculated after assigning each individuals the mean wealth in his age group. Paglin's simple proposal turned out to be controversial. A string of comments and replies followed in the American Economic Review in 1977, 1979 and 1989 (Danziger et al., 1977; Johnson, 1977; Kurien, 1977; Minarik, 1977; Nelson, 1977; Paglin, 1977; Paglin, 1979; Wertz, 1979; Formby et al., 1989; Paglin, 1989). Without fundamentally disagreeing on the basic idea of age-adjustment, later papers pointed out various weaknesses of $I_{\text{PaglinGini}}$ and proposed various corrections or alternatives.

In particular, Wertz (1979) proposed an alternative index defined as

$$I_{\text{WertzGini}}(F) = \frac{1}{2\mu(F)} \iint |[w - \mu(a(w))] - [w' - \mu(a(w'))]| \, dF(w) \, dF(w') \tag{25}$$

where $\mu(a)$ is the mean wealth among individuals of age a. $I_{\text{WertzGini}}$ can be contrasted to the similar formulation of the standard Gini coefficient (10) which can be rewritten as

$$I_{\text{Gini}}(F) = \frac{1}{2\mu(F)} \iint |[w - \mu(F)] - [w' - \mu(F)]| \, dF(w) \, dF(w') \tag{26}$$

where, again, μ is the overall mean wealth (see, e.g., Yitzhaki and Schechtman (2013) on alternative formulations of the Gini coefficient). The distinction between $I_{\text{WertzGini}}$ and I_{Gini} is the reference against which individual wealth deviations are measured. By taking within age group means as reference, $I_{\text{WertzGini}}$ captures inequality driven by within age group deviations only.

Pudney (1993) suggests a similar approach based on calculations of functions of mean wealth conditional on individual age but for other inequality functionals (Atkinson indices). More immediately perhaps, one could think of additively decomposable inequality measures such as the Generalized Entropy measures – decomposed as in (23) but without the problematic R term. They could be used to sort out 'within' from 'between' age-group factors and composition effects across age groups in comparisons of wealth inequality over time or across countries. However the limitations due to the presence of zero and negative net worth data restricts the applicability of these alternatives to a fairly small subclass of inequality measures;[22] within the Generalized-Entropy class only a measure related to the coefficient of variation is likely to be of practical use and even that may be considered to be too sensitive to outliers in the upper tail. This is one reason for the focus on the Gini coefficient in this literature.

A key limitation of the simple Paglin- or Wertz-type of age-adjustment just described is that additional factors that determine wealth are ignored. This is unproblematic to the extent that these factors are independent of age. However, take the effect of education for example: this is both a determinant of earnings and wealth accumulation and is strongly correlated with age in a typical cross-section of the population. To address this, Almås and Mogstad (2012) propose a measure similar to (25) and (26) but where the reference level of wealth for observation i, instead of $\mu(a_i)$ or μ, is a counterfactual value given by the average wealth that would be observed if all the population had age a_i but otherwise kept their other characteristics at the observed values. This counterfactual reference captures differences in wealth by age netted out of the composition effect implied by the association between age and other factors. Almås and Mogstad (2012) show how the counterfactual can be estimated from predictions based on a multivariate regression model relating wealth to age and other factors.

It turns out that methods for purging inequality from the effects of a factor while holding others constant as in Almås and Mogstad (2012) have been the focus of the literature on responsibility and compensation (Fleurbaey and Maniquet, 2010). Indeed, technically and conceptually, the age-adjustment procedures in wealth inequality bear resemblance to the measures of (in-)equality of opportunity that attempt to disentangle 'fair' and 'unfair' inequalities attributable to effort, luck or individual *a priori* circumstances (Almås *et al.*, 2011; Roemer and Trannoy, 2015).

To conclude, one qualification about age-adjustments of this sort must be made. In a cross-section, differences in wealth across age do not necessarily reflect movements along individual life-cycles alone, but also secular shifts of the life-cycle patterns across cohorts. So, adjusting inequality for age does not just wipe out differences due to life-cycle positions but also changes in the life-cycle patterns across cohorts. With cross-section data, nothing much can be done to address this. For example, Almås and Mogstad (2012) adjust wealth holdings of different cohorts of individuals in their cross-section data based on specific, but very strong assumptions about the evolution of life-cycle accumulation patterns across cohorts (which is assumed multiplicative, constant over time and homogenous across individual types).

6. Empirical Implementation

Rather than trying to provide an extensive empirical review,[23] here we deal with a more narrowly focused pair of questions: (1) How are the raw materials for wealth-inequality comparisons obtained? (2) Given household or individual-level data on wealth, how can analysts make inference about inequality in the distribution of wealth?

In this section, we succinctly summarize issues concerning data, estimation and inference and describe standard methods, workarounds and convenient remedies for potential problems; a more detailed review is available in Cowell and Flachaire (2015).

6.1 *Data: Sources and Methods*

Official sources such as government statistical bureaux and tax authorities are still the main source of information about individual wealth holdings, although their output comes in a variety of forms.

Administrative data. Perhaps the most obvious data source is where there is a comprehensive wealth tax, as used to be the case in Sweden – see Sweden: Ministry of Finance (2006) on the HINK database. However, other forms of wealth taxation also yield valuable data, in particular taxes on the *transfer* of wealth (inheritance tax/estate tax): an excellent example is the construction by the UK's HM Revenue and Customs of a Personal Wealth Survey (HM Revenue and Customs, 2012). This type of data typically requires the application of mortality multipliers, where one treats those dying in a given year as a weighted sample of the current population the weights being determined by estimates of the probability of death for various groups in the population (Lampman, 1962; Atkinson and Harrison, 1978, Chapter 3; Kopczuk and Saez, 2004). However, for administrative data derived from taxation there may be limitations imposed by the nature of the tax law: what proportion of wealth and what proportion of the population of interest is effectively 'missing' because of tax exemptions; how the tax law values specific assets in the compilation of taxable wealth.

Survey data. Several sample surveys focusing on wealth have semi-official or official status, such as the US Survey of Consumer Finances (Bover, 2010; Cowell *et al.*, 2012), Italy's Survey of Household Income and Wealth (Jappelli and Pistaferri, 2000), and the Eurozone Household Finance and Consumption Survey used in this paper; standard problems of non-response and under-reporting are to some extent addressed by techniques such as oversampling. Incorporating a longitudinal element in the manner of the UK's Wealth and Assets Survey (Department of Work and Pensions, 2014; Office for National Statistics, 2014) or extracting data from more general panel studies such as the British Household Panel Survey or the Panel Study of Income Dynamics (Banks *et al.*, 2002; Hills *et al.*, 2013) can be useful in ensuring that some types of asset-holding are more thoroughly and consistently covered. In some cases statistical matching is carried out to complement survey information with information from administrative records (Rasner *et al.*, 2014).

Indirect approaches. Where wealth cannot be directly observed, one might try to rely on observing the traces that wealth leaves. Standard sampling techniques tend to miss out some of the most interesting wealth holders, the tiny minority of the very, very rich (Kennickell, 2006) and some types of asset are difficult to identify or to value. Capitalization, the technique of inferring the value of assets held from the flow of income observed, can be used as a forensic device for these types of cases.[24] In order to infer the value of the assets by working backwards from the income generated by the assets clearly, one needs reliable microdata on incomes and reliable estimates of the rates of return on different types of asset (King, 1927; Stewart, 1939; Greenwood, 1983; Saez and Zucman, 2014). Even when those conditions are met, capitalization works under the assumption of uniform rates of return on assets for different wealth groups. Such an assumption is problematic if, say, the wealthy are able to obtain higher returns on their investments, e.g. though more sophisticated fund management.

Cross-country comparisons. Many of the problems that we have mentioned in connection with the standard methods of extracting wealth data apply with extra force when one attempts to investigate wealth inequality that involves international comparisons or international aggregation. A particularly challenging example of this is the problem of providing estimates of the global distribution of wealth (Davies *et al.*, 2010; Davies *et al.*, 2014): how does one cover the missing population in countries where the data are sparse? In valuing assets in different countries should one use official exchange rate or purchasing-power parity? However some problems of comparability of definitions can be addressed by using a purpose-built study such as the HFCS used to provide illustrations here (HFCS, 2014), or a secondary source of micro-data harmonized ex post such as the Luxembourg Wealth Study (LWS, 1994; Sierminska et al., 2006).[25]

6.2 Statistical Inference with Survey Data on Wealth

Numerous surveys and textbooks have discussed the estimation of income inequality from micro-data (Cowell, 2011) and, of course, many of the concepts and methods carry over to the measurement of wealth inequality. Yet, empirical analysis of wealth distributions is not just quite the same as the analysis of income distributions, and comes with a number of special features (for example, the presence of zero or negative values in net worth) and compounded inferential problems (related to the typical heavy tail of wealth distributions).

6.2.1 Inequality Statistics: Estimation Problems

Wealth inequality inference from survey data involves estimation of summary measures of inequality, cumulative income functionals, Lorenz ordinates and/or parameters of functional models from representative household or individual-level micro-data. The shape of wealth distributions with their typically long, heavy right tails challenges standard statistical inference mechanics. Most inequality functionals of interest are known to be sensitive to extreme values (Cowell and Flachaire, 2007; Van Kerm, 2007), much more so than quantiles or indicators of central tendency. This has two main consequences.

First, sensitivity to extreme data makes inequality estimates vulnerable to data contamination and measurement error in the tails of the distribution (Cowell and Victoria-Feser, 1996). Most inequality indicators can in principle be driven arbitrarily large by a single extreme data point.

Second, simple 'plug in' estimators of inequality functionals exhibit finite sample bias and their sampling error remains large and difficult to estimate reliably even in large samples (Cowell and Flachaire, 2007; Schluter and van Garderen, 2009; Schluter, 2012).

6.2.2 Parametric Modelling

The issues just outlined arise in the context of a non-parametric approach to estimation and inference. What if we used instead a parametric-modelling approach, as discussed in Section 4?

Estimation of parametric model parameters can usually be undertaken by standard maximum likelihood methods. However, maximum likelihood estimators are known not to be robust to data contamination: parameter estimates can often be driven arbitrarily large by infinitesimal data contamination, provided this is located at sensitive values of income or net wealth (Hampel et al., 1986; Victoria-Feser and Ronchetti, 1994). It is therefore desirable to implement estimators robust to the presence of extreme data. One commonly-used option is the optimal B-robust estimator (OBRE) described by Hampel et al. (1986) and applied to income distribution models by Victoria-Feser and Ronchetti (1994), Victoria-Feser (2000) and Cowell and Victoria-Feser (2008). More recent approaches are based on Robust Indirect Inference (Genton and Ronchetti, 2003). Various robust estimators for the Pareto distribution parameters are reviewed and compared in Brzezinski (2013). Robust estimators of functional form parameters generally require determining a tuning constant for the tradeoff between efficient estimation of the unknown parameters and robustness of the estimator, that is protection of the estimator against extreme data contamination. More of this in Section 6.3.2 below.

6.2.3 A General Modelling Strategy?

Cowell and Victoria-Feser (1996) and Cowell and Victoria-Feser (2002) demonstrate the non-robustness of relative inequality measures and of Lorenz dominance comparisons. Using the influence function of appropriate inequality functionals (see below), they show how small data contamination in the tails of an income distribution can ruin inequality inference. Cowell and Flachaire (2007) further illustrate the sensitivity of inequality measures to extreme data and illustrate the relative sensitivity of different inequality measures (also see Van Kerm, 2007). Cowell and Flachaire (2007) recommend addressing this concern with a semi-parametric estimation based on parametric modelling of the upper tail of the income distribution, an approach adopted in Schluter and Trede (2002) too. The idea of a semi-parametric model combining empirical data for the lower tail and a parametric Pareto distribution model for the upper tail is developed in Cowell and Victoria-Feser (2007) to deal with data contamination in point estimation and in Davidson and Flachaire (2007) for confidence interval estimation and hypothesis testing using bootstrap methods. Davidson and Flachaire (2007) discuss asymptotic and several standard and non-standard bootstrap methods for inference on inequality measures. They show how asymptotic and standard bootstrap methods perform poorly and how semi-parametric bootstrap resampling from a semi-parametric model just described can significantly improve inference in large samples. Brzezinski (2013) obtain similar results for estimation of 'top income shares'. In the semi-parametric bootstrap, resamples are created by drawing with replacement from the observed data with given probability β and simulated from a Pareto model fitted to the upper tail of the data with probability $1 - \beta$.[26]

Note that all of these papers are framed in terms of inference on *income* inequality because, it is argued, income often follows heavy tailed distributions. Clearly, the problems are compounded with *wealth* distributions that typically exhibit heavier upper (and possibly lower) tails than income distributions.

A key tool to study these issues is the influence function. The *influence function (IF)* of a distribution statistic calculated on distribution F, $I(F)$, captures the impact of a marginal increase in the density of the distribution function at income z on the value of the statistic. To see this formally, denote $F \in \mathbb{F}$ the distribution function of interest and assume that $H^{(z)} \in \mathbb{F}$ is another distribution that consists just of a single point mass at z. The mixture distribution

$$G := [1 - \delta]F + \delta H^{(z)}, \ 0 \le \delta \le 1 \tag{27}$$

is a representation of a perturbation of the distribution F by a point mass at z. Then the *IF* measures the impact of the perturbation at income/wealth z on the statistic I for an infinitesimal δ

$$IF(z; I, F) := \lim_{\delta \downarrow 0} \left[\frac{I(G) - I(F)}{\delta} \right] \tag{28}$$

The IF therefore captures the sensitivity of the functional I to variations in the data at different z and interest lies in assessing how the IF evolves when z becomes large (or small), that is, when the contamination is in the upper (or lower) tail. Furthermore, Hampel *et al.*

(1986) show that, asymptotically, the sampling variance of the distribution functional $I(F)$ is related to the IF by the relation

$$AV(I(F)) = \int IF(y; I, F) IF^T(y; I, F) \, dF(y) \qquad (29)$$

(see also Deville, 1999; Osier, 2009). So, if the IF of $I(F)$ increases rapidly for high or low z, it will exhibit large sampling variance. Indeed, IF for inequality measures can grow large at the upper tail where data are typically sparse (Cowell and Flachaire, 2007). This implies large and imprecisely estimated standard errors for inequality measures from survey data. This is an issue in income inequality estimation, and this is compounded with the heavy tail of wealth distributions.

To help appreciate the relative influence of income and net worth observations in the tails of the samples, Figure 8 shows the relative influence function $(IF(I(F))/I(F))$ for two inequality measures: the Gini coefficient (left) and the share of total income or wealth held by the richest 5% (right) calculated from HFCS data. To help comparison of the curves for income and

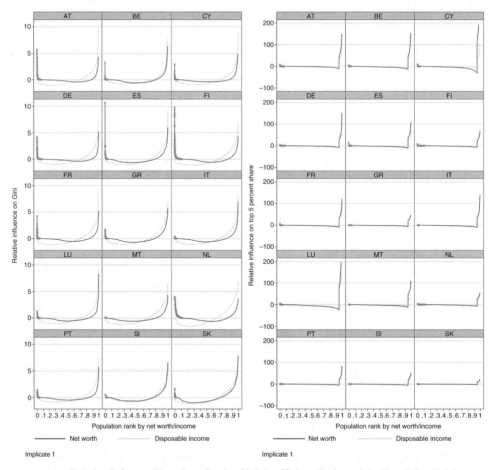

Figure 8. Relative Influence Functions for the Gini Coefficient (Left) and the Top 'Vingtile' share (Right). Crosses Indicate Negative Net Worth.

wealth, the x axis is transformed into fractional ranks: the value of the curves at, say, rank 0.50 shows how much the inequality index would be influenced by an infinitesimal perturbation at the median of the net worth (respectively income) distribution. The sensitivity of the measures to the extreme high values is well-known. What is not so well appreciated, is the sensitivity of the Gini coefficient to the very small, negative net worth data (marked with crosses on the figure): net worth Gini coefficients are not just driven by the very top, but also by the net worth of households with negative wealth. Unsurprisingly, this sensitivity to the bottom is absent for the 'top 5% share'.

6.3 Inference Based on Semi-Parametric Modelling of the Wealth Distributions

One convenient approach to address inferential issues is to substitute the standard fully non-parametric analysis of sample data by a semi-parametric analysis combining a parametric model for top wealth and observed sample data for the lower part of the distribution. This approach allows addressing several issues at relatively low computational cost: (i) attenuating the impact of outliers and data contamination, (ii) improving sampling variance calculation, both analytical and bootstrap-based and (iii) an issue we have not yet discussed so far, top-coding of data.

6.3.1 The Model

A parametric model is used for modelling a proportion β of upper wealth data while the empirical distribution function is used directly for the rest of the distribution (the remaining proportion $1 - \beta$ of lower wealth). The parametric model most commonly used for the upper tail is the Pareto distribution—see Section 4.1. The *semi-parametric distribution* is then

$$\widetilde{F}(y) = \begin{cases} F(y) & y \leq Q(F; 1 - \beta) \\ 1 - \beta \left(\frac{y}{Q(F; 1-\beta)} \right)^{-\alpha} & y > Q(F; 1 - \beta) \end{cases} \tag{30}$$

6.3.2 Estimation of α

Of course the α parameter for the upper tail needs to be estimated from the sample.[27] At this stage, issues of the sensitivity of the estimator to data contamination come into play. As mentioned in Section 6.2.2, standard maximum likelihood estimation of the parameter is not 'robust' in the sense that parameter estimates can be driven arbitrarily large by data contamination (Victoria-Feser and Ronchetti, 1994). Formally, the influence function of the maximum likelihood estimator of the Pareto index is unbounded, that is, it can be driven arbitrarily large by data contamination. Several 'robust' alternative estimators of the Pareto index have been proposed. From detailed comparison of the performance of five robust estimators of the Pareto distribution parameter in small samples, Brzezinski (2013) recommends use of the 'probability integral transform statistic estimator' of Finkelstein et al. (2006) which performs as well as the generic and more commonly used OBRE (Victoria-Feser and Ronchetti, 1994) at lower computational cost. In any case, Cowell and Flachaire (2007) find that even with a standard non-robust estimator of α, the semi-parametric model provides significant improvement on inference compared to the fully non-parametric approach.

6.3.3 *Choice of β*

The second key issue is to identify the proportion of the data that ought to be modelled parametrically, that is, selection of β. Systematic approaches can be adopted to identify the value of β beyond which wealth are effectively Pareto distributed. The Hill plot, for example, involves estimating the α parameter for all candidate values of β and to select the smallest value of β beyond which the estimated parameter stabilizes to a constant (Beirlant *et al.*, 1996). Sophisticated approaches account for potential data contamination in this procedure and rely on robust techniques; see, for example, Dupuis and Victoria-Feser (2006). In practice, however, β is generally determined heuristically, selecting by eye the amount of the upper tail that needs to be replaced by inspecting a Pareto diagram showing the linear relationship between the log of wealth and the log of the inverse cumulative distribution function (see Section 4.1).

6.3.4 *Calculation of Inequality Measures*

The full, semi-parametric estimate of the distribution function is recovered from the parameter estimate for the Pareto tail model and sample data for the lower part of the distribution using (30). Functionals of interest defined on the semi-parametric distribution $\widetilde{F}(y)$ can generally be recovered easily from closed-form expressions, e.g. the quantile functional is given by Cowell and Victoria-Feser (2007)

$$
Q(\widetilde{F}, q) = \begin{cases} Q(F, q) & q \leq 1 - \beta \\ Q(F; 1 - \beta) \left(\frac{1-q}{\beta}\right)^{-1/\hat{\alpha}(\widetilde{F})} & q > 1 - \beta \end{cases} \tag{31}
$$

(See Cowell and Flachaire (2015) for additional functionals.) Alternatively, and if no closed form expression is available or tractable, inequality functionals can be recovered from standard expressions for sample data based on a pseudo-sample composed of (i) the observed data in the lower tail and (ii) random draws from the Pareto distribution for the upper tail (Van Kerm, 2007). The number of random draws should be sufficiently large to guarantee precision of the simulation in the upper tail (it is not limited to the number of sample data in the upper tail) and the randomly drawn observations must be weighted so that their share in the full pseudo-sample is equal to β. Alternatively, Alfons *et al.* (2013) use the Pareto model only to identify outlying observations and use either calibration or single-draw replacement from the Pareto distribution to deal with the few extreme observations identified as outliers.

6.3.5 *Semi-Parametric Bootstrap*

Davidson and Flachaire (2007) show that the semi-parametric model helps addressing inference. Constructing bootstrap inference on the basis of the semi-parametric model enhances precision of confidence intervals and tests. The idea is to build bootstrap samples by resampling from $\widetilde{F}$, that is by drawing observations with replacement from the bottom of the sample with probability $1 - \beta$ and taking observations simulated from the Pareto distribution with probability β. Note that in this procedure, point estimates are still calculated on the basis of the full non-parametric sample (both in the full sample and in the resamples) and the semi-parametric bootstrap does not involve re-estimation of the α parameter in each bootstrap sample.

6.3.6 *Top-Coding*

Parametric estimation of the upper tail can finally help addressing top-coding issues. Some micro-data providers do not release income or wealth data in full, but rather top-code data beyond a certain threshold in order to protect the confidentiality of respondents. This strategy is also a drastic way to prevent contamination of extreme outliers. Such form of censoring can take various forms (Cowell and Flachaire, 2015) but the top-coding just described can be easily addressed with a parametric model. Jenkins *et al.* (2011) show how maximum likelihood estimation of the distribution parameters can be adjusted to account for top-coding and then be used to recover uncensored observations by simulation. See Sologon and Van Kerm (2014) for an application with a Pareto upper tail model.

7. Conclusion

Wealth inequality is a key component of the broad picture of socio-economic inequalities and one that has recently received much attention. A lot of this attention has been fuelled by the accumulation of evidence on an upward trend in the concentration of wealth among the extremely wealthy (Piketty, 2014b; Saez and Zucman, 2014).

However, measuring inequality in wealth is not only a matter of estimating the size of top shares. With this in mind, our paper has covered a broader set of concepts and tools available for the analysis of wealth inequality. So, rather than just dealing with inequality in respect of the extremely rich we have focused on the case of typical survey data where an analyst has access to data on wealth and its components for a large number of households or individuals. Analysing wealth inequality is in many ways similar to analysing income inequality, but it is not an identical exercise. While income inequality measurement methods are now well grounded, some issues specific to empirical wealth inequality measurement remain problematic.

These issues include (1) the problems of dealing with the presence of a substantial number of negative observations in the wealth distribution, where liabilities exceed the value of assets (2) the importance of life cycle accumulation dynamics (3) inferential difficulties that arise from the heavy tail of wealth distributions. The tools that are used to address these issues are not new: they include standard inequality measures, adjustments to empirical wealth distributions and modelling parts of the distribution using functional forms. However, the application of these tools needs perhaps to be better understood in order to throw light on this important aspect of inequality.

Acknowledgements

We thank Xuezhu Shi and Julia Philipp for excellent research assistance. This paper uses data from the Eurosystem Household Finance and Consumption Survey distributed by the European Central Bank. The survey was initiated when Van Kerm visited the London School of Economics with the support of the Luxembourg Fonds National de la Recherche (INTER/Mobility/13/5456106).

Notes

1. Detailed surveys of the literature on wealth inequality are available in Jenkins (1990), Davies and Shorrocks (2000) or Davies (2009).

2. For example, we exclude discussion of debt constraints and incomplete asset markets (Cordoba, 2008) or the role of capital gains from asset holdings on the distribution of income (Roine and Waldenström, 2012; Alvaredo et al., 2013).

3. On the important related issue of asset-based *poverty*, see Azpitarte (2011), Fisher and Weber (2004), Brandolini et al. (2010), Carter and Barrett (2006), Carney and Gale (2001), Caner and Wolff (2004), Haveman and Wolff (2004) and Rank and Hirschl (2010).

4. Clearly one may also usefully break down the debt into different components.

5. For example, although housing is usually very important for many households as a means of asset accumulation (Denton, 2001; Silos, 2007) it is sometimes difficult to disentangle housing wealth and housing debt – see the case of Sweden discussed in Cowell et al. (2012). Sometimes it is not clear which forms of pension wealth should be included in wealth computations, but the inclusion or exclusion of this form of wealth can make a huge difference to measured wealth inequality. In the UK, this used to be dramatically illustrated by the HMRC series C, series D and series E definitions of wealth inequality (Hills et al., 2013, p. 32): augmenting net worth with private pension wealth typically reduced inequality unambiguously and further augmenting it with the wealth attributable to the state-provided retirement pension reduced inequality still more. However, those data largely applied to an era of traditional defined-benefit (DB) pensions; the switch to defined-*contribution* (DC) pensions that has occurred in many countries in recent years is unlikely to have been inequality-neutral, because DC pensions are unequal compared to DB pensions and are likely to be positively correlated with net worth. As a result the DB-to-DC switch is likely to have increased inequality when net worth is augmented by pension wealth (Wolff, 2014).

6. For an interesting practical analysis of how sharp changes in asset prices affect the wealth distribution, see Wolff (2012). For a careful analysis of the dramatic effect of house prices on wealth inequality in the UK, see Bastagli and Hills (2013).

7. Appropriately accounting for wealth in this way substantially changes the structure of the distribution of economic well-being (Wolff and Zacharias, 2009).

8. Including public pension entitlements would normally reduce wealth inequality – see note 5.

9. Note that the cumulations are 'normalized' by dividing through by the size of the population (the number of households or individuals depending on the unit of observation adopted).

10. A further development of the approach is as follows. Consider some other attribute of the individual or household that may be considered relevant in the discussion of wealth distribution; let the position in the distribution of this other attribute be denoted θ: then $\theta(q)$ gives the position in the 'other-attribute' distribution of someone located at the qth wealth quantile, and if this other attribute were perfectly correlated with wealth, the function $\theta(\cdot)$ would be a straight line from (0,0) to (1,1). If we modify (6) and plot the graph $\{(\theta(q), L(F; q)) : 0 \leq q \leq 1\}$ we obtain the *concentration curve* (Salvaterra, 1989; Dancelli, 1990; Yitzhaki and Olkin, 1991); we shall not pursue this approach further here.

11. If the mean is positive then the Lorenz curve is decreasing throughout the part of the distribution where wealth is negative and has a turning point where $w = 0$; it is still a convex curve joining (0,0) and (1,1). The Lorenz curve is also defined in the case where the mean is strictly negative; however, the shape is dramatically different: the curve lies everywhere *above* the perfect equality line and is concave rather than convex (Amiel et al., 1996).

12. If $k = 2$ then $\omega_q = 1$ and we have the regular Gini (11) as a special case.

13. However, there is a further technical detail that has attracted some attention in the literature. If there are negative values in the distribution (but the mean is positive) the Gini coefficient still has a lower bound of zero, attained when all households have identical net worth, but it is not bounded above by 1; the reason for this is clear when one considers the behaviour of the Lorenz curve in the presence of negative data (see note 11) which is initially downward sloping and drops below zero before sloping upwards when positive wealth are cumulated. It should be clear from the definition of the Gini in (11) that it can take on values greater than 1 if the Lorenz curve turns negative. Some authors have proposed rescaled versions of the Gini coefficient to ensure it is bounded between 0 and 1 (Chen *et al.*, 1982; Berrebi and Silber, 1985; van de Ven, 2001). The rationale for imposing an upper bound for the inequality index is however debatable. Notionally, if all but one households could enter into debt without limits to transfer wealth to the one household accumulating all positive wealth, there is no reason to consider that a 'maximum' level of inequality exists. That is, it would always be possible to make a regressive transfer from a poor to a rich household to increase inequality, by further indebting the poor household.

14. As with the regular Gini, note how the S-Gini can exceed 1 if $\underline{w} < 0$.

15. Note that this cannot be done for the S-Gini if $k \neq 2$ in (12).

16. For overviews of parametric models of income distributions, see Bordley *et al.* (1996), Chotikapanich (2008), Chotikapanich *et al.* (2012), Kleiber and Kotz (2003) and Sarabia (2008).

17. A distribution F is considered 'heavy-tailed' if the tail is heavier than the exponential: for all $\lambda > 0$ $\lim_{y \to \infty} e^{\lambda y}[1 - F(y)] = \infty$.

18. Whether the Pareto Type 1 distribution provides satisfactory fit to wealth recorded in the Forbes rich lists is somewhat controversial; see Ogwang (2013), Brzezinski (2014) and Capehart (2014). The debate revolves around the reliability of Kolmogorov–Smirnov type of goodness-of-fit tests when data are measured with error.

19. Missing wealth components in HFCS data have been multiply imputed. Figure 5 shows data from the 'implicate' no. 1.

20. See, for example, Pareto (1896, 1965, 2001), Davis (1941), Bernadelli (1944), Wold and Whittle (1957), Champernowne (1973), Champernowne and Cowell (1998), Cowell (1998), Piketty and Zucman (2015) and the on-line Appendix to Piketty (2014a).

21. Confidence intervals are calculated from 499 bootstrap replications of all estimates on the basis of the replication weights provided with the HFCS data. Estimates shown in Figure 7 are based on the first 'implicate' of the multiply imputed HFCS data. Within-group Gini estimates are not reported in the figure if the range of the confidence interval is greater than 0.5.

22. See Section 3.3 above for a general discussion. The Generalized-Entropy (GE) index of inequality for a wealth distribution F would be written as

$$\frac{1}{\theta[\theta - 1]} \int \left[\left[\frac{w}{\mu(F)} \right]^\theta - 1 \right] \, dF(w)$$

where θ is a parameter that may be assigned any real value: higher values of θ make the index more sensitive to perturbations at the top of the distribution. It is clear that a GE index will only be well defined for negative values of w in the special cases where θ is an integer greater than 1; the case $\theta = 2$ gives a GE index that is ordinally equivalent to

128 COWELL AND VAN KERM

$I_{\mathrm{CV}}(F)$ in equation (8) above. GE indices with $\theta > 2$ are likely to be so over-sensitive to extremely high values of w as to limit their practical applicability (Cowell and Flachaire, 2007).

23. For some recent country studies on wealth inequality, see the following: Canada (Brzozowski *et al.*, 2010), China (Li and Zhao, 2008; He and Huang, 2012; Ward, 2013), Egypt (Alvaredo and Piketty, 2014), France (Piketty 2003, 2007a, 2011; Piketty *et al.*, 2006; Frémeaux and Piketty, 2013), Germany (Fuchs-Schündeln *et al.*, 2009), India (Banerjee and Piketty 2004, 2005; Subramanian and Jayaraj, 2008), Ireland (Turner, 2010), Italy (Brandolini *et al.*, 2004; Mazzaferro and Toso, 2009), Japan (Bauer and Mason, 1992), Spain (Alvaredo and Saez, 2006, 2009), Sweden (Bager-Sjogren and Klevmarken, 1997), Switzerland (Saez *et al.*, 2007), the UK (Oldfield and Sierminska, 2009; Hills *et al.*, 2013), the US (Juster and Kuester, 1991; Wolff, 1995, 2014; Díaz-Giménez *et al.*, 1997; Piketty and Saez, 2003; Piketty and Saez, 2007; Cagetti and De Nardi, 2008; Kopczuk, 2014).

24. This technique requires some heroic assumptions: for example, it is common to assume a uniform rate of return across wealth groups, which clearly may be unsatisfactory.

25. Examples of wealth comparisons using LWS include Jäntti *et al.* (2008) and Sierminska *et al.* (2008) but, of course, there is a large number of recent studies that have addressed the issues of international comparability directly (Banks *et al.*, 2000; Piketty, 2005, 2007b, 2014a; Atkinson and Piketty, 2007; Ohlsson *et al.*, 2008; Bover, 2010; Alvaredo *et al.*, 2013; Piketty and Saez, 2013; Piketty and Saez, 2014; Piketty and Zucman, 2014, 2015). Many of these studies draw on the Top Incomes Database http://topincomes.g-mond.parisschoolofeconomics.eu/

26. A different strategy for inference is developed in Schluter and van Garderen (2009) and Schluter (2012) who propose normalizing transformation of the index before application of the bootstrap.

27. Note that α must be assumed to be greater than 2 for the Pareto distribution to have finite variance.

References

Aitchison, J. and Brown, J.A.C. (1957) *The Lognormal Distribution*. London: Cambridge University Press.

Alfons, A., Templ, M. and Filzmoser, P. (2013) Robust estimation of economic indicators from survey samples based on Pareto tail modelling. *Journal of the Royal Statistical Society: Series C (Applied Statistics)* 62: 271–286.

Almås, I. and Mogstad, M. (2012) Older or wealthier? The impact of age adjustment on wealth inequality. *Scandinavian Journal of Economics* 114: 24–54.

Almås, I., Cappelen, A.W., Lind, J.T., Sørensen, E.Ø. and Tungodden, B. (2011) Measuring unfair (in)equality. *Journal of Public Economics* 95(7): 488–499.

Alvaredo, F. and Piketty, T. (2014) Measuring top incomes and inequality in the Middle East: Data limitations and illustration with the case of Egypt. Working Paper, EMOD/Oxford, Paris School of Economics, and Conicet.

Alvaredo, F. and Saez, E. (2006) Income and wealth concentration in Spain in a historical and fiscal perspective. Discussion Paper 5836, CEPR.

Alvaredo, F. and Saez, E. (2009) Income and wealth concentration in Spain from a historical and fiscal perspective. *Journal of the European Economic Association* 7(5): 1140–1167.

Alvaredo, F., Atkinson, A.B., Piketty, T. and Saez, E. (2013) The Top 1 Percent in international and historical perspective. *Journal of Economic Perspectives* 27: 3–20.

Amiel, Y., Cowell, F.A. and Polovin, A. (1996) Inequality amongst the kibbutzim. *Economica* 63: S63–S85.

Arnold, B.C. (2008) Pareto and generalized Pareto distributions. In D. Chotikapanich (ed.), *Modeling Income Distributions and Lorenz Curves*, Chapter 7 (pp. 119–146). Springer-Verlag, New York, USA.

Atkinson, A.B. (1971) The distribution of wealth and the individual life cycle. *Oxford Economic Papers* 23: 239–254.

Atkinson, A.B. (1975) *The Economics of Inequality* (First ed.). Oxford: Clarendon Press.

Atkinson, A.B. and Brandolini, A. (2010) On analyzing the world distribution of income. *The World Bank Economic Review* 24: 1–37.

Atkinson, A.B. and Harrison, A.J. (1978) *Distribution of Personal Wealth in Britain*. Cambridge University Press.

Atkinson, A.B. and Piketty, T. (Eds.) (2007) *Top Incomes over the 20th Century: A Contrast between Continental European and English-Speaking Countries*. Oxford: Oxford University Press.

Atkinson, A.B., Piketty, T. and Saez, E. (2011) Top incomes in the long run of history. *Journal of Economic Literature* 49(1): 3–71.

Azpitarte, F. (2011) Measurement and identification of asset-poor households: A cross-national comparison of Spain and the United Kingdom. *Journal of Economic Inequality* 9: 87–110.

Bager-Sjogren, L. and Klevmarken, N.A. (1997) Inequality and mobility of wealth in Sweden 1983/84–1992/93. Working Paper 1997:7, Department of Economics, Uppsala University.

Bandourian, R., McDonald, J.B. and Turley, R.S. (2003) A comparison of parametric models of income distribution across countries and over time. *Estadística* 55: 135–152.

Banerjee, A. and Piketty, T. (2004) Are the rich growing richer? Evidence from Indian tax data. In A. Deaton and V. Kozel (eds.), *Data and Dogma: The Great Indian Poverty Debate* (pp. 598–611). New Delhi: McMillan Press.

Banerjee, A. and Piketty, T. (2005) Top Indian incomes, 1922–2000. *World Bank Economic Review* 19: 1–20.

Banks, J., Blundell, R. and Smith, J.P. (2000) Wealth inequality in the United States and Great Britain. Working Paper WP00/20, The Institute For Fiscal Studies, Ridgmount St., London.

Banks, J., Smith, Z. and Wakefield, M. (2002) The distribution of financial wealth in the UK: Evidence from 2000 BHPS data. Working paper W02/21, Institute for Fiscal Studies.

Bastagli, F. and Hills, J. (2013) Wealth accumulation, ageing and house prices. In J. Hills, F. Bastagli, F. Cowell, H. Glennerster, E. Karagiannaki and A. McKnight (eds.), *Wealth in the UK: Distribution, Accumulation, and Policy*. Oxford: Oxford University Press.

Bauer, J. and Mason, A. (1992) The distribution of income and wealth in Japan. *Review of Income and Wealth* 38: 403–428.

Beirlant, J., Vynckier, P. and Teugels, J.L. (1996) Tail index estimation, Pareto quantile plots, and regression diagnostics. *Journal of the American Statistical Association* 91: 1651–1667.

Bernadelli, H. (1944) The stability of the income distribution. *Sankhya* 6: 351–362.

Berrebi, Z.M. and Silber, J. (1985) The Gini coefficient and negative income: a comment. *Oxford Economic Papers* 37: 525–526.

Bordley, R.F., McDonald, J.B. and Mantrala, A. (1996) Something new, something old: Parametric models for the size distribution of income. *Journal of Income Distribution* 6: 91–103.

Bosmans, K. and Cowell, F.A. (2010) The class of absolute decomposable inequality measures. *Economics Letters* 109: 154–156.

Bover, O. (2010) Wealth inequality and household structure: U.S. versus Spain. *Review of Income and Wealth* 56(2): 259–290.

Brandolini, A., Cannari, L., D'Alessio, G. and Faiella, I. (2004) Household wealth distribution in Italy in the 1990s. Working paper 414, Bank of Italy, Economic Research Department.

Brandolini, A., Magri, S. and Smeeding, T.M. (2010) Asset-based measurement of poverty. *Journal of Policy Analysis and Management* 29(2): 267–284.

Brzezinski, M. (2013) Asymptotic and bootstrap inference for top income shares. *Economics Letters* 120: 10–13.

Brzezinski, M. (2014) Do wealth distributions follow power laws? Evidence from 'rich lists'. *Physica A: Statistical Mechanics and its Applications* 406, 155–162.

Brzozowski, M., Gervais, M., Klein, P. and Suzuki, M. (2010) Consumption, income, and wealth inequality in Canada. *Review of Economic Dynamics* 13(1): 52–75.

Cagetti, M. and De Nardi, M. (2008) Wealth inequality: Data and models. *Macroeconomic Dynamics* 12: 285–313.

Caner, A. and Wolff, E.N. (2004) Asset poverty in the United States, 1984–99: Evidence from the panel study of income dynamics. *Review of Income and Wealth* 50(4): 493–518.

Capehart, K.W. (2014) Is the wealth of the world's billionaires not Paretian? *Physica A: Statistical Mechanics and its Applications* 395, 255–260.

Carney, S. and Gale, W.G. (2001) Asset accumulation among low-income households. In T.A. Shapiro and E.N. Wolff (eds.), *Assets for the Poor: The Benefits of Spreading Asset Ownership*, Chapter 5. New York: Russell Sage Foundation.

Carter, M.R., and Barrett, C.B. (2006) The economics of poverty traps and persistent poverty: An asset-based approach. *Journal of Development Studies* 42(2): 178–199.

Chakraborti, A. and Patriarca, M. (2008) Gamma-distribution and wealth inequality. *Pramana* 71(2): 233–243.

Champernowne, D.G. (1973) *The Distribution of Income Between Persons*. Cambridge University Press.

Champernowne, D.G. and Cowell, F.A. (1998) *Economic Inequality and Income Distribution*, Chapter 10: Fantastic models of wealth and income distribution (pp. 218–249). Cambridge University Press.

Chen, C.-N., Tsaur, T.-W. and Rhai, T.-S. (1982) The Gini coefficient and negative income. *Oxford Economic Papers* 34(11): 473–476.

Chotikapanich, D. (Ed.) (2008) *Modeling Income Distributions and Lorenz Curves*. Springer-Verlag, New York, USA.

Chotikapanich, D., Griffiths, W.E., Prasada Rao, D. and Valencia, V. (2012) Global income distributions and inequality, 1993 and 2000: Incorporating country-level inequality modeled with Beta distributions. *Review of Economics and Statistics* 94(1): 52–73.

Clementi, F. and Gallegati, M. (2005) Pareto's law of income distribution: evidence for Germany, the United Kingdom, and the United States. In A. Chatterjee, S. Yarlagadda and B.K. Chakrabarti (eds.), *Econophysics of Wealth Distributions*. Berlin: Springer.

Cordoba, J.-C. (2008) U.S. inequality: Debt constraints or incomplete asset markets? *Journal of Monetary Economics* 55: 350–364.

Cowell, F.A. (1998) Inheritance and the distribution of wealth. Distributional Analysis Discussion Paper 34, STICERD, London School of Economics, London WC2A 2AE.

Cowell, F.A. (2000) Measurement of inequality. In A.B. Atkinson and F. Bourguignon (eds.), *Handbook of Income Distribution*, Chapter 2 (pp. 87–166). New York: Elsevier Science B. V.

Cowell, F.A. (2007) Gini, deprivation and complaints. In G. Betti and A. Lemmi (eds.), *Advances in Income Inequality and Concentration Measures*, Chapter 3. London: Routledge.

Cowell, F.A. (2011) *Measuring Inequality* (3rd ed.). Oxford: Oxford University Press.

Cowell, F.A. (2013) UK wealth inequality in international context. In J.R. Hills (ed.), *Wealth in the UK*, Chapter 3. Oxford: Oxford University Press.

Cowell, F.A. (2014) Piketty in the long run. *British Journal of Sociology* 65: 708–720.

Cowell, F.A. (2015) Inequality and poverty measures. In M.D. Adler and M. Fleurbaey (eds.), *Oxford: Oxford Handbook of Well-Being And Public Policy*, Chapter 4. Oxford: Oxford University Press.

Cowell, F.A., Karagiannaki, E. and McKnight, A. (2012) Accounting for cross-country differences in wealth inequality. LWS Working Paper Series 13, LIS Data Centre.

Cowell, F.A. and Flachaire, E. (2007) Income distribution and inequality measurement: The problem of extreme values. *Journal of Econometrics* 141: 1044–1072.

Cowell, F.A. and Flachaire, E. (2015) Statistical methods for distributional analysis. In A.B. Atkinson and F. Bourguignon (eds.), *Handbook of Income Distribution*, Volume 2. Amsterdam: Elsevier.

Cowell, F.A. and Victoria-Feser, M.-P. (1996) Robustness properties of inequality measures. *Econometrica* 64: 77–101.

Cowell, F.A. and Victoria-Feser, M.-P. (2002) Welfare rankings in the presence of contaminated data. *Econometrica* 70: 1221–1233.

Cowell, F.A. and Victoria-Feser, M.-P. (2007) Robust stochastic dominance: A semi-parametric approach. *Journal of Economic Inequality* 5: 21–37.

Cowell, F.A. and Victoria-Feser, M.-P. (2008) Modelling Lorenz curves: Robust and semi-parametric issues. In D. Chotikapanich (ed.), *Modeling Income Distributions and Lorenz Curves*, Chapter 13 (pp. 241–255). Springer-Verlag, New York, USA.

Dagsvik, J., Jia, Z., Vatne, B.H. and Zhu, W. (2013) Is the Pareto-Lévy law a good representation of income distributions? *Empirical Economics* 44: 719–737.

Dagum, C. (1977) A new model of personal income distribution: Specification and estimation. *Economie Appliquée* 30: 413–436.

Dagum, C. (1990) A model of net wealth distribution specified for negative, null and positive wealth. A case study: Italy. In C. Dagum and M. Zenga (eds.), *Income and Wealth Distribution, Inequality and Poverty* (pp. 42–56). Berlin and Heidelberg: Springer.

Dagum, C. (1999) A study of the distributions of income, wealth and human capital. *Revue Européenne des Sciences Sociales* 37(113): 231–268.

Dancelli, L. (1990) On the behaviour of the Zp concentration curve. In C. Dagum and M. Zenga (eds.), *Income and Wealth Distribution, Inequality and Poverty* (pp. 111–127). Heidelberg: Springer-Verlag.

Danziger, S., Haveman, R. and Smolensky, E. (1977) Comment on Paglin 1975. *American Economic Review* 67: 505–512.

Davidson, R. and Flachaire, E. (2007) Asymptotic and bootstrap inference for inequality and poverty measures. *Journal of Econometrics* 141: 141–166.

Davies, J.B. (2009) Wealth and economic inequality. In W. Salverda, B. Nolan and T.M. Smeeding (eds.), *The Oxford Handbook of Economic Inequality*, Chapter 6. Oxford University Press.

Davies, J.B. and Shorrocks, A.F. (2000) The distribution of wealth and its evolution. In A.B. Atkinson and F. Bourguignon (eds.) *Handbook of Income Distribution* (pp. 607–675). Elsevier B.V. North Holland, Amsterdam.

Davies, J.B., Sandström, S., Shorrocks, A. and Wolff, E.N. (2010) The level and distribution of global household wealth. *The Economic Journal* 121: 223–254.

Davies, J.B., Lluberas, R. and Shorrocks, A.F. (2014) Global wealth report 2014. The year in review, Credit Suisse Research Institute.

Davis, H.T. (1941) *The Analysis of Economic Time Series*. Bloomington, IN: the Principia Press.

De Nardi, M. and Yang, F. (2014) Bequests and heterogeneity in retirement wealth. *European Economic Review* 72: 182–196.

Denton, N.A. (2001) Housing as a means of asset accumulation: A good strategy for the poor? In T.A. Shapiro and E.N. Wolff (eds.), *Assets for the Poor: The Benefits of Spreading Asset Ownership*, Chapter 7. Russell Sage Foundation.

Department of Work and Pensions (2014) *Statistics on Household Wealth*. London: Department of Work and Pensions.

Deville, J.-C. (1999) Variance estimation for complex statistics and estimators: Linearization and residual techniques. *Statistics Canada: Survey Methodology* 25: 193–203.

Díaz-Giménez, J., Quadrini, V. and Rios-Rull, J.-V. (1997) Dimensions of inequality: Facts on the U.S. distribution of earnings, income and wealth. *Federal Reserve Bank of Minneapolis Quarterly Review* 21: 3–21.

Donaldson, D. and Weymark, J.A. (1980) A single parameter generalization of the Gini indices of inequality. *Journal of Economic Theory* 22: 67–68.

Donaldson, D. and Weymark, J.A. (1983) Ethically flexible Gini indices for income distribution in the continuum. *Journal of Economic Theory* 29(4): 353–358.

Dupuis, D.J. and Victoria-Feser, M.-P. (2006) A robust prediction error criterion for Pareto modeling of upper tails. *Canadian Journal of Statistics* 34(4): 639–658.

Edlund, L. and Kopczuk, W. (2009) Women, wealth, and mobility. *American Economic Review* 99: 146–178.

European Central Bank (2013) The eurosystem household finance and consumption survey: Results from the first wave. Statistics Paper Series 2, European Central Bank, Frankfurt am Main, Germany.

Finkelstein, M., Tucker, H.G. and Veeh, J.A. (2006) Pareto tail index estimation revisited. *North American Actuarial Journal* 10(1): 1–10.

Fisher, M.G. and Weber, B.A. (2004) Does economic vulnerability depend on place of residence? Asset poverty across the rural-urban continuum. Rprc working paper no. 04-01, Rural Poverty Research Center.

Fleurbaey, M. and Maniquet, F. (2010) Compensation and responsibility. In K. Arrow, A. Sen and K. Suzumura (eds.), *Handbook of Social Choice and Welfare*, Volume 2, Chapter 22. North Holland.

Formby, J.P., Seaks, T.G. and Smith, W.J. (1989) On the measurement and trend of inequality: A reconsideration. *American Economic Review* 79(1): 256–264.

Frémeaux, N. and Piketty, T. (2013) GINI country report: Growing inequalities and their impacts in France. Working paper, AIAS, Amsterdam Institute for Advanced Labour Studies.

Fuchs-Schündeln, N., Krueger, D. and Sommer, M. (2009) Inequality trends for Germany in the last two decades: A tale of two countries. NBER Working Paper 15059, National Bureau of Economic Research.

Genton, M. and Ronchetti, E. (2003) Robust indirect inference. *Journal of the American Statistical Association* 98: 67–76.

Gottschalk, P. and Danziger, S. (1985) A framework for evaluating the effects of economic growth and transfers on poverty. *American Economic Review* 75(1): 153–161.

Greenwood, D. (1983) An estimation of U.S. family wealth and its distribution from microdata, 1973. *Review of Income and Wealth* 29: 23–43.

Hampel, F.R., Ronchetti, E.M., Rousseeuw, P.J. and Stahel, W.A. (1986) *Robust Statistics: The Approach Based on Influence Functions*. New York: John Wiley.

Haveman, R. and Wolff, E.N. (2004) The concept and measurement of asset poverty: Levels, trends and composition for the U.S., 1983–2001. *Journal of Economic Inequality* 2: 145–169.

He, X. and Huang, Z. (2012) Ownership restructuring, marketization and wealth inequality in urban China: 1995 and 2002. *China & World Economy* 20(5): 37–62.

Hendricks, L. (2007) Retirement wealth and lifetime earnings. *International Economic Review* 48: 421–456.

HFCS (2014) Household finance and consumption survey. Statistical micro-level database, European Central Bank, Frankfurt am Main, Germany, https://www.ecb.europa.eu/home/html/researcher_hfcn.en.html. Accessed June 2, 2015.

Hills, J., Bastagli, F., Cowell, F., Glennerster, H., Karagiannaki, E. and McKnight, A. (2013) *Wealth in the UK: Distribution, Accumulation, and Policy*. Oxford University Press.

HM Revenue and Customs (2012) *UK Personal Wealth Statistics. 2008 to 2010*. London: HMRC.

Jäntti, M., Sierminska, E. and Smeeding, T. (2008) The joint distribution of household income and wealth: Evidence from the Luxembourg Wealth Study. OECD Social, Employment and Migration Working Paper 65, OECD, Paris.

Jäntti, M., Sierminska, E. and Van Kerm, P. (2012) Modelling the joint distribution of income and wealth. Paper Prepared for the 32nd General Conference of The International Association for Research in Income and Wealth, Boston, USA.

Jäntti, M., Sierminska, E. and Van Kerm, P. (2013) The joint distribution of income and wealth. In J.C. Gornick and M. Jäntti (eds.), *Income Inequality: Economic Disparities and the Middle Class in Affluent Countries*, Chapter 11. Palo Alto, CA: Stanford University Press.

Jappelli, T. and Pistaferri, L. (2000) The dynamics of household wealth accumulation in Italy. *Fiscal Studies* 21: 269–295.

Jenkins, S.P. (1990) The distribution of wealth: Measurement and models. *Journal of Economic Surveys* 4: 329–360.

Jenkins, S.P. (2009) Distributionally-sensitive inequality indices and the GB2 income distribution. *Review of Income and Wealth* 55: 392–398.

Jenkins, S.P. and Jäntti, M. (2005) Methods for summarizing and comparing wealth distributions. ISER Working Paper 2005-05, Institute for Social and Economic Research, University of Essex, Colchester, UK.

Jenkins, S.P., Burkhauser, R.V., Feng, S. and Larrimore, J. (2011) Measuring inequality using censored data: A multiple imputation approach. *Journal of the Royal Statistical Society, Series A* 174(866): 63–81.

Johnson, W.R. (1977) The measurement and trend of inequality: Comment. *American Economic Review* 67: 502–504.

Juster, F.T. and Kuester, K.A. (1991) Differences in the measurement of wealth, wealth inequality and wealth composition obtained from alternative U.S. wealth surveys. *Review of Income and Wealth* 37: 33–62.

Kennickell, A.B. (2006) A rolling tide: Changes in the distribution of wealth in the US, 1989–2001. In E.N. Wolff (ed.), *International Perspectives on Household Wealth*, Chapter 2, pp. 19–88. Cheltenham, UK: Edward Elgar in Association with the Levy Economics Institute.

King, W.I. (1927) Wealth distribution in the continental United States at the close of 1921. *Journal of the American Statistical Association* 22: 135–153.

Klass, O.S., Biham, O., Levy, M., Malcai, O. and Solomon, S. (2006) The Forbes 400 and the Pareto wealth distribution. *Economics Letters* 90: 290–295.

Kleiber, C. (2008) A guide to the Dagum distributions. In D. Chotikapanich (ed.), *Modeling Income Distributions and Lorenz Curves*, Chapter 6, pp. 97–118. Springer-Verlag, New York, USA.

Kleiber, C. and Kotz, S. (2003) *Statistical Size Distributions in Economics and Actuarial Sciences*. Hoboken. NJ: John Wiley.

Kolm, S.-C. (1976) Unequal inequalities I. *Journal of Economic Theory* 12: 416–442.

Kopczuk, W. (2014) What do we know about evolution of top wealth shares in the United States? NBER Working Paper 20734, National Bureau of Economic Research.

Kopczuk, W. and Saez, E. (2004) Top wealth shares in the United States, 1916–2000: Evidence from estate tax returns. *National Tax Journal* 57: 445–487.

Kurien, C.J. (1977) The measurement and trends of inequality: Comment. *American Economic Review* 67: 512–519. Comment on Paglin 1975.

Lampman, R.J. (1962) *The Share of Top Wealth-Holders in National Wealth 1922–1956*. Princeton, New Jersey: Princeton University Press.

Levy, M. and Solomon, S. (1997) New evidence for the power-law distribution of wealth. *Physica A: Statistical Mechanics and its Applications* 242(1–2): 90–94.

Li, S. and Zhao, R. (2008) Changes in the distribution of wealth in China 1995–2002. In J.B. Davies (ed.), *Personal Wealth From A Global Perspective*, Chapter 5, pp. 42–63. Oxford: Oxford University Press.

Lorenz, M.O. (1905) Methods for measuring concentration of wealth. *Journal of the American Statistical Association* 9: 209–219.

LWS (1994) Luxembourg Wealth Study. Database, LIS, Luxembourg.

Maccabelli, T. (2009) Measuring inequality: Pareto's ambiguous contribution. *History of Political Economy* 41: 183–208.

Mazzaferro, C. and Toso, S. (2009) The distribution of total wealth in Italy: 1991–2002. *Review of Income and Wealth* 55(3): 779–802.

McDonald, J.B. and Ransom, M. (2008) The generalized beta distribution as a model for the distribution of income: Estimation of related measures of inequality. In D. Chotikapanich (ed.), *Modeling*

Income Distributions and Lorenz Curves, Chapter 8 (pp. 147–166). Springer-Verlag, New York, USA.

Minarik, J. (1977) The measurement and trend of inequality: Comment and reply. *American Economic Review* 67(6): 513–516.

Moyes, P. (1987) A new concept of Lorenz domination. *Economics Letters* 23: 203–207.

Nelson, E.R. (1977) The measurement and trend of inequality: Comment. *American Economic Review* 67: 497–501.

OECD (2008) *Growing Unequal? Income Distribution And Poverty In OECD Countries*. Paris: Organisation for Economic Co-Operation and Development.

OECD (2013) OECD Framework for Statistics on the Distribution of Household Income, Consumption and Wealth. Paris: OECD publishing, Organisation for Economic Cooperation and Development, http://www.oecd.org/statistics/302013041e.pdf. Accessed June 2, 2015.

Office for National Statistics (2014) *Wealth in Great Britain: Wave 3, 2010–2012*. ONS.

Ogwang, T. (2013) Is the wealth of the world's billionaires Paretian? *Physica A: Statistical Mechanics and its Applications* 392(4): 757–762.

Ohlsson, H., Roine, J. and Waldenström, D. (2008) Long-run changes in the concentration of wealth: An overview of recent findings. In J.B. Davies (ed.), *Personal Wealth From A Global Perspective*, Chapter 2 (pp. 42–63). Oxford: Oxford University Press.

Oldfield, Z. and Sierminska, E. (2009) Differences in the measurement and structure of wealth using alternative data sources: The case of the UK. *Journal of Financial Transformation* 26: 42–50.

Osier, G. (2009) Variance estimation for complex indicators of poverty and inequality using linearization techniques. *Survey Research Methods* 3(3): 167–195.

Paglin, M. (1975) The measurement and trend of inequality: A basic revision. *American Economic Review* 65: 598–609.

Paglin, M. (1977) The measurement and trend of inequality: Reply. *American Economic Review* 67(3): 520–531.

Paglin, M. (1979) Reply to Wertz. *American Economic Review* 79: 663–677.

Paglin, M. (1989) On the measurement and trend of inequality: Reply. *American Economic Review* 79(1): 265–266.

Pareto, V. (1895) La legge della domanda. *Giornale degli Economisti* (10): 59–68.

Pareto, V. (1896) La courbe de la répartition de la richesse. In C. Viret-Genton (ed.), *Recueil publié par la Faculté de Droit à l'occasion de l'exposition nationale suisse, Geneva 1896* (pp. 373–387). Lausanne: Université de Lausanne.

Pareto, V. (1965) *Écrits sur La Courbe de la Repartition de la Richesse*, Volume 3 of *Oeuvres Complètes*. Geneva: Librairie Droz. Edited by Busino, G.

Pareto, V. (2001) On the distribution of wealth and income. In M. Baldassarri and P. Ciocca (eds.), *Roots of the Italian School of Economics and Finance: From Ferrara (1857) to Einaudi (1944)*, Volume 2 (pp. 231–276). Houndmills: Palgrave.

Piketty, T. (2003) Income inequality in France, 1901–1998. *Journal of Political Economy* 111: 1004–1042.

Piketty, T. (2005) Top income shares in the long run: An overview. *Journal of the European Economic Association* 3(2–3): 1–11.

Piketty, T. (2007a) Income, wage and wealth inequality in France, 1901–98. In A.B. Atkinson and T. Piketty (eds.), *Top Incomes over the 20th Century: A Contrast between Continental European and English-Speaking Countries*, Chapter 1 (pp. 43–81). Oxford: Oxford University Press.

Piketty, T. (2007b) Top incomes over the 20th century: A summary of main findings. In A.B. Atkinson and T. Piketty (eds.), *Top Incomes over the 20th Century: A Contrast between Continental European and English-Speaking Countries*, Chapter 1 (pp. 1–17). Oxford: Oxford University Press.

Piketty, T. (2011) On the long-run evolution of inheritance: France 1820–2050. *Quarterly Journal of Economics* 126: 1071–1132.

Piketty, T. (2014a) *Capital in the 21st Century*. Harvard University Press.

Piketty, T. (2014b) Dynamics of inequality. *New Left View* 85: 103–116.

Piketty, T. and Saez, E. (2003) Income inequality in the United States, 1913–1998. *Quarterly Journal of Economics* 118: 1–39.

Piketty, T. and Saez, E. (2007) Income and wage inequality in the United States, 1913–2002. In A.B. Atkinson and T. Piketty (eds.), *Top Incomes Over the Twentieth Century*. Oxford University Press.

Piketty, T. and Saez, E. (2013) Top incomes and the Great Recession: Recent evolutions and policy implications. *IMF Economic Review* 61(3): 456–478.

Piketty, T. and Saez, E. (2014) Inequality in the long run. *Science* 344(6186): 838–843.

Piketty, T. and Zucman, G. (2014) Capital is back: Wealth-income ratios in rich countries 1700–2010. Working paper, Paris School of Economics.

Piketty, T. and Zucman, G. (2015) Wealth and inheritance in the long run. In A.B. Atkinson and F. Bourguignon (eds.) *Handbook of Income Distribution*, Volume 2, Chapter 15 (pp. 1303–1368). North Holland, Amsterdam.

Piketty, T., Postel-Vinay, G. and Rosenthal, J.-L. (2006) Wealth concentration in a developing economy: Paris and France, 1807–1994. *American Economic Review* 96(1): 236–256.

Pudney, S. (1993) Income and wealth inequality and the life-cycle. *Journal of Applied Econometrics* 8: 249–276.

Radaelli, P. (2010) On the decomposition by subgroups of the Gini index and Zenga's uniformity and inequality indexes. *International Statistical Review* 78(1): 81–101.

Rank, M.R. and Hirschl, T.A. (2010) Estimating the life course dynamics of asset poverty. Csd working papers no. 10–25, Washington University in St. Louis.

Rasner, A., Frick, J.R. and Grabka, M.M. (2014) Statistical matching of administrative and survey data: An application to wealth inequality analysis. *Sociological Methods & Research* 43: 192–224.

Reed, W.J. and Fan, W. (2008) New four- and five-parameter models for income distributions. In D. Chotikapanich (ed.), *Modeling Income Distributions and Lorenz Curves*, Chapter 13 (pp. 211–224). Springer-Verlag, New York, USA.

Roemer, J.E. and Trannoy, A. (2015) Equality of opportunity. In A.B. Atkinson and F. Bourguignon (eds.), *Handbook of Income Distribution*, Volume 2. Elsevier.

Roine, J. and Waldenström, D. (2012) On the role of capital gains in Swedish income inequality. *Review of Income and Wealth* 58: 569–587.

Saez, E. and Zucman, G. (2014) Wealth inequality in the United States since 1913: Evidence from capitalized income tax data. NBER Working Paper 20625, National Bureau of Economic Research.

Saez, E., Piketty, T. and Dell, T. (2007) Income and wealth concentration in Switzerland over the twentieth century. In A.B. Atkinson and T. Piketty (eds.), *Top Incomes Over the Twentieth Century*, Chapter 11 (pp. 472–500). Oxford: Oxford University Press.

Salvaterra, T. (1989) Comparison among concentration curves and indexes in some empirical distributions. In C. Dagum and M. Zenga (eds.), *Income and Wealth Distribution, Inequality and Poverty* (pp. 194–214). New York: Springer-Verlag.

Sarabia, J.M. (2008) Parametric Lorenz curves: Models and applications. In D. Chotikapanich (ed.), *Modeling Income Distributions and Lorenz Curves*, Chapter 9 (pp. 167–190). Springer-Verlag, New York, USA.

Sarabia, J.M., Castillo, E. and Slottje, D.J. (2002) Lorenz ordering between McDonald's generalized functions of the income size distribution. *Economics Letters* 75: 265–270.

Schluter, C. (2012) On the problem of inference for inequality measures for heavy-tailed distributions. *The Econometrics Journal* 15: 125–153.

Schluter, C. and Trede, M. (2002) Tails of Lorenz curves. *Journal of Econometrics* 109: 151–166.

Schluter, C. and van Garderen, K. (2009) Edgeworth expansions and normalizing transforms for inequality measures. *Journal of Econometrics* 150: 16–29.

Shorrocks, A.F. (1983) Ranking income distributions. *Economica* 50: 3–17.

Sierminska, E. and Smeeding, T. (2005) Measurement issues in wealth: Equivalence scales, accounting framework, and reference unit. "Construction and usage of comparable microdata on wealth: the LWS" workshop paper, LWS, Perugia, Italy.

Sierminska, E., Brandolini, A. and Smeeding, T.M. (2006) The Luxembourg Wealth Study - a cross-country comparable database for household wealth research. *Journal of Economic Inequality* 4: 375–383.

Sierminska, E., Brandolini, A. and Smeeding, T.M. (2008) Comparing wealth distribution accross rich countries: First results from the Luxembourg Wealth Study. In *Household Wealth in Italy*. Rome: Banca d'Italia.

Silos, P. (2007) Housing tenure and wealth distribution in life cycle economies. *The B.E. Journal of Macroeconomics* 7: 1–22.

Singh, S.K. and Maddala, G.S. (1976) A function for the size distribution of income. *Econometrica* 44: 963–970.

Sologon, D.M. and Van Kerm, P. (2014) Earnings dynamics and inequality trends in Luxembourg 1988–2009. CEPS/INSTEAD Working Paper 2014-03, CEPS/INSTEAD, Esch/Alzette, Luxembourg.

Stewart, C. (1939) *Income Capitalization as a Method of Estimating the Distribution of Wealth by Size Group*, Volume 3 of *Studies in Income and Wealth*. New York: National Bureau of Economic Research.

Subramanian, S. and Jayaraj, D. (2008) The distribution of household wealth in India. In J.B. Davies (ed.), *Personal Wealth From A Global Perspective*, Chapter 6 (pp. 112–133). Oxford: Oxford University Press.

Sweden: Ministry of Finance (2006) Facts about wealth statistics.

Tiefensee, A. and Grabka, M.M. (2014) Comparing wealth - data quality of the HFCS. Discussion Paper 1427, DIW Berlin, German Institute for Economic Research.

Turner, J.D. (2010) Wealth concentration in the European periphery: Ireland, 1858–2001. *Oxford Economic Papers* 62(1): 1–22.

van de Ven, J. (2001) Distributional limits and the Gini coefficient. Research Paper 776, Department of economics, University of Melbourne, Melbourne, Australia.

Van Kerm, P. (2007) Extreme incomes and the estimation of poverty and inequality indicators from EU-SILC. IRISS Working Paper 2007-01, CEPS/INSTEAD, Differdange, Luxembourg.

Vickrey, W.S. (1947) *Agenda for Progressive Taxation*. Ronald Press.

Victoria-Feser, M.-P. (2000) Robust methods for the analysis of income distribution, inequality and poverty. *International Statistical Review* 68: 277–293.

Victoria-Feser, M.-P. and Ronchetti, E. (1994) Robust methods for personal income distribution models. *Canadian Journal of Statistics* 22: 247–258.

Ward, P. (2013) Measuring the level and inequality of wealth: An application to China. *Review of Income and Wealth*, DOI: 10.1111/roiw.12063.

Wertz, K. (1979) The measurement of inequality: comment. *American Economic Review* 79: 670–72.

Wold, H.O.A. and Whittle, P. (1957) A model explaining the Pareto distribution of wealth. *Econometrica* 25: 591–595.

Wolff, E.N. (1995) *Top Heavy: A Study of the Increasing Inequality of Wealth in America*. New York: 20th Century Fund Press.

Wolff, E.N. (2012) The asset price meltdown and the wealth of the middle class. Working Paper 18559, National Bureau of Economic Research.

Wolff, E.N. (2014) Household wealth trends in the United States, 1983–2010. *Oxford Review of Economic Policy* 30: 21–43.

Wolff, E.N. (2014) U.S. pensions in the 2000s: The lost decade? *The Review of Income and Wealth*, forthcoming.

Wolff, E.N. and Zacharias, A. (2009) Household wealth and the measurement of economic well-being in the United States. *Journal of Economic Inequality* 7: 83–115.

Yang, F. (2008) Accounting for the heterogeneity in retirement wealth. Federal Reserve Bank of Minneapolis Working Paper Series 638, Federal Reserve Bank of Minneapolis.

Yitzhaki, S. (1983) On an extension of the Gini inequality index. *International Economic Review* 24(10): 617–628.

Yitzhaki, S. and Olkin, I. (1991) Concentration indices and concentration curves. In K. Mosler and M. Scarsini (eds.), *Stochastic Orders and Decisions under Risk*, Volume 19 (pp. 380–392). Institute of Mathematical Statistics: Lecture-Notes Monograph Series.

Yitzhaki, S. and Schechtman, E. (2013) *The Gini Methodology: A Statistical Primer*. Springer Series in Statistics. Springer. Heidelberg: Springer-Verlag.

Zanardi, G. (1990) Constituent of the mean deviations and of the mean difference and concentration scheme. In C. Dagum and, M. Zenga (eds.), *Income and Wealth Distribution, Inequality and Poverty* (pp. 128–148). Heidelberg: Springer-Verlag.

6

DEFINING THE GOVERNMENT'S DEBT AND DEFICIT

Timothy C. Irwin

International Monetary Fund, Fiscal Affairs Department

1. Introduction

One might think that defining the government's debt and deficit debt was easy, but it turns out to raise difficult questions whose answers matter for the numbers. Canadian government debt in 2010, for instance, could plausibly be said to be as little as 38% of GDP and as much as 104%, depending on how *government* and *debt* were defined (Dippelsman *et al.*, 2012). The U.S. federal government's deficit in fiscal year 2010/2011 was either 8% of GDP or 14% depending on whether the source of the estimate was the government's mainly cash-based budget or its accrual-based financial statements (U.S. Treasury, 2011, p. vi), while Kotlikoff and Burns (2012, pp. 37–38) say the "true deficit"—the change in the fiscal gap—was actually 39% of GDP.[1]

Such uncertainties create problems for policymaking and economic research. Measures of debts and deficits are widely used to estimate the risks of fiscal crises. They also enter into assessments of the sustainability of the government's tax and spending policies and thus judgments about intergenerational equity. Deficits are used to estimate whether the government's fiscal policy is stimulating or constraining the rest of the economy. Debt must be measured to determine whether high levels inhibit economic growth. And estimates of spending and revenue must be made to assess the impact of the size of government on economic growth and other variables. If it is not possible to say how large are debt and deficits even for Canada and the United States, how useful can empirical research on these issues be?

The choices that arise in defining the deficit were reviewed by Blejer and Cheasty (1991a), but since then there has been a revolution in the practice of government accounting. In 1991, almost all central governments measured the deficit on a cash basis. Since then, many have started to publish accrual accounts—that is, accounts that record revenue and spending when economic value is deemed to have been transferred, not when cash changes hands, and that include balance sheets that are arithmetically linked to the measures of revenue and spending.

The views expressed in this paper are those of the author and do not necessarily represent the views of the IMF, its Executive Board, or IMF management.

New national and international standards calling for the preparation of such accounts by government have also been published. And a revival of interest in budget transparency and the proliferation of fiscal rules have both put government accounts under a spotlight.

Precisely how many governments now produce accrual accounts depends on how such accounts are defined. In a review that isn't exhaustive, Blondy et al. (2013) identify 13 central governments worldwide that produce accrual accounts that meet four relatively demanding criteria: that is, are audited; recognize real as well as financial assets; are for the government as a whole, not just individual ministries and agencies; and include a cash-flow statement as well as a balance sheet and an accrual operating statement. Many other governments produce accounts that do not meet all these criteria, but are still recognizably accrual based, and many more have plans to produce them. Looking at just the European Union, Ernst and Young (2012, p. 21) report that 22 out of 26 central governments say that they use some form of accrual accounting, sometimes alongside cash data.

Early adopters of accrual accounting, including most governments in Australasia, Scandinavia, and North America, followed standards based on those used by local firms. Starting in 2002, however, the International Federation of Accountants began to publish International Public Sector Accounting Standards (Chan and Zhang, 2013; IPSASB, 2014). These standards are derived from International Financial Reporting Standards—the standards used by large companies in much of the world—but have been adapted to some of the special characteristics of governments. Although IPSAS are promulgated by a private body, some governments have adopted them in whole or part (e.g., Government of Switzerland, 2014) and others have referred to them as a source of accounting doctrine (e.g., Government of France, 2014). In the United States, a radical change occurred in 1999, when the Governmental Accounting Standards Board issued a standard requiring all state and local governments to prepare accrual accounts (GASB, 1999). The European Union may create its own standards for accrual accounts (European Commission, 2013), which would be very influential.

The accounts produced by accountants, however, are not the only fiscal data produced by governments. There are also statistics on government finances. These have their origin in national accounts and thus complement data on other sectors of the economy. Whereas accounts are prepared for particular governments or government agencies, statistics may be prepared for collections of governments, like all governments in the United States or the European Union. Yet accounts and statistics may present very similar information, and both may be prepared for the central government of a given country.

The International Monetary Fund's first manual on government-finance statistics (IMF, 1986) recommended that such statistics be prepared on a cash basis. The 2001 manual (IMF, 2001), however, prescribed an accrual basis in which measures of the government's spending and revenue were linked to its opening and closing balance sheets. With IMF (2001), the guidelines for preparing government-finance statistics became more like accounting standards for businesses and very similar to the manuals for preparing national accounts, which had provided for accrual reporting and balance sheets since United Nations (1968) (see also European Commission et al., 2009). Data presented later in this paper show that at least 57 countries around the world now report fiscal statistics on some kind of accrual basis.

Accompanying these changes in accounting, there have been calls for greater budgetary transparency, by the IMF (Kopits and Craig, 1998; IMF, 2014a), the Organisation for Economic Cooperation and Development (OECD, 2002), and the United Nations (2012). The demands include good measurement of the government's debt and deficit, as well as regular publication of budgets and accounts, credible fiscal forecasts, and opportunities for citizens to participate in budget decisions. Various indices of transparency have been developed, including by Alt *et al.* (2002), Hameed (2005), and the International Budget Partnership (IBP, 2012), and these indices have been used by researchers trying to identify the causes of fiscal transparency (e.g., Alt *et al.*, 2006; Khagram *et al.*, 2013) and its consequences (e.g., Alt and Lassen, 2006). All this has drawn attention to the reliability of fiscal data.

Finally, government accounting has taken on a new prominence because of the proliferation of fiscal rules. According to research reported by Budina *et al.* (2013), only five central governments were subject to a fiscal rule in 1991 but, by 2014, 78 were.[2] Most such rules cap the debt or deficit; some cap spending or revenue. Writing about U.S. municipal accounting, Greene (1980, p. 59) joked that the "basic drives of man are few: to get enough food, to find shelter, and to keep debt off the balance sheet." Certainly, the spread of debt limits has encouraged governments to look for forms of financing that need not be counted as debt. This in turn has prompted accountants and statisticians to think harder about how to define debt. Deficit rules have done the same for the definitions of revenue and spending. Eurostat, which supervises the measurement of the debts and deficits subject to the European Union's fiscal rules, publishes not only the national-accounts manuals that underpin the measurements (Eurostat, 1996, 2013b), but also an annual volume on problems that arise in measuring debts and deficits specifically (e.g., Eurostat, 2013c).

Notwithstanding the international standards, there are still many differences in how debts and deficits are actually measured. Although many governments now produce some form of accrual data, the great majority of central governments still use cash accounting where it matters most—in the budget (Blöndal, 2004; Kahn, 2013). Among followers of the accrual principle, some prefer to treat the acquisition of real assets as an investment that leaves the deficit unchanged, while others prefer to treat it as deficit-increasing. Some think that governments should concentrate on government-finance statistics (Barton, 2011) while others say that accounts are more useful (Ball and Pflugrath, 2012). Partly because of the disagreements and partly because of enduring historical differences, cross-country fiscal data are not fully standardized, while time series for a single country are muddied by changes in definitions over time. Even in a single country in a single year, different measures are used in different contexts. In the European Union, a government may budget on a cash basis, prepare end-of-year accounts on an accrual basis, and strive to comply with fiscal rules that refer to fiscal statistics prepared on an accrual basis somewhat different from that of the accounts.

This paper surveys developments in practice and research related to government accounting and specifically the measurement of debts and deficits. It concentrates on developments after 1991 and, in keeping with the theme of this volume, on the use of debts and deficits in assessing governments' savings and solvency and the sustainability of their tax and spending policies. It touches on the accounting for several of the things discussed by other papers in this volume, including pensions, Islamic financing, and sovereign wealth funds. It does not address other questions, such as which deficit best shows the effect of fiscal policy on aggregate demand (the best measure might give different weights to different types of spending and revenue), how the deficit should be adjusted for the effects of inflation (which can cause government spending to be overstated since a portion of interest expense is really the repayment of principal), or how the deficit can be adjusted to isolate the effects of changes in government policy from those of the business cycle. (On these questions, see Blejer and Cheasty, 1991a, 1991b; for recent reviews of the political economy of deficits and the differences between forecast and actual deficits, among other things, see Eslava, 2011, and Cimadomo, 2014, respectively).

Although the paper surveys the research of economists, it also pays attention to the work of accountants and political scientists and to that of practitioners whose job it is to define, measure, and analyze debts and deficits. Economists have made major contributions to the theory and practice of government accounting and their empirical analyses of fiscal rules have helped clarify the effects of accounting choices, but the field would benefit from further theoretical clarification and more-convincing empirical evidence of the kind that economists might be able to bring to bear. For example, there is a large literature on the relative merits of cash and accrual measures of the surpluses of firms (e.g., Dechow, 1994; Sloan, 1996; Penman and Yehuda, 2009) but nothing comparable for governments. Part of the reason is no doubt the lack of large databases and natural experiments (Poterba, 1995). Yet the mathematical nature of accounting makes the subject amenable to theorizing, while the increasing number of governments reporting noncash accounts may create opportunities for new research. By setting out some current controversies in the field, the paper may encourage further research along these or other lines. Although it is by no means a guide to fiscal data, it may also alert researchers to questions they should ask when using estimates of debts and deficits.

The paper is organized around two aspects of the measurement of government debt and deficit: the definition of *government* and the definitions of *debt* and *deficit*. Some of the literature it reviews explicitly examines the possible choices. Other work sheds light on the choices indirectly by investigating how governments react to fiscal rules. A theme of the paper is that there are narrow and broad ways of defining both government and debt and deficit. Narrow definitions invite what could be called *window dressing*, or operations that, exploiting a weakness in accounting, reduce the reported debt or deficit without substantially changing public finances. For instance, a government using cash accounting may delay the payment of a bill from the end of one budget year to the beginning of the next. Broader definitions mitigate this problem, but create new ones, including what might be called *creative accounting*, which need not involve any new operations, just the convenient but misleading measurement of the state of public finances. A government using accrual accounting, for example, might improve its apparent fiscal position by choosing to measure its pension liability at a discount rate that is unreasonably high given the nature of the payments. (This distinction between two kinds of manipulation is made by Tirole (2006), who refers to "operating methods" and "accounting methods.")

2. Defining the Government

The first issue that arises in measuring government debt and deficit is the definition of government. Although distinctions are sometime drawn between different government *funds*, the dominant international approach to delimiting government is to specify the entities that lie within its perimeter. Some of the main options can be represented by nested sets (Figure 1). At the narrow end of the spectrum, the government can be defined as the state as a legal entity, and the state's spending and revenue as the flows shown in its budget. This entity can be called *budgetary central government* (IMF, 2014b, chap. 2). This definition is too narrow for many purposes, however, since governments create legally distinct, but government-controlled, tax-funded agencies to carry out their policies. Including such agencies gives *central government*, while adding subnational governments and their agencies gives *general government*. (About half the abovementioned difference between the high and low estimates of Canadian debt is the difference between budgetary central government and general government.[3]) Some definitions of government also include government-owned corporations. Adding the nonfinancial ones

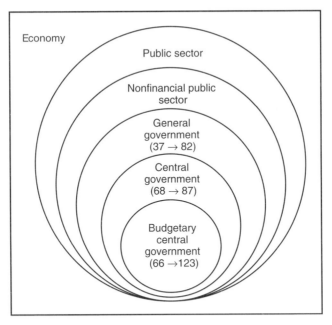

Figure 1. Five Definitions of Government.
The figure shows five increasingly broad sets of public institutions, each of which can be considered a definition of government. The first and second numbers in parentheses in the three smaller sets show how many countries reported data for the relevant definition of government in the 2003 and 2013 *Government Finance Statistics Yearbooks*, respectively. Countries are counted as providing data for a given definition of government if the most recent data reported in the 2003 *Yearbook* are for the year 2001 or later and for the 2013 *Yearbook* if they are for the year 2011 or later.
Source: Data are from the IMF's *Government Finance Statistics Yearbooks 2003* (pp. xix–xxii) and *2013* (pp. xxi–xxv).

gives the *nonfinancial public sector*; adding all of them, including the central bank, the *public sector*.

A lower bound on the availability of fiscal data for the three smallest sets can be gleaned from *Government Finance Statistics Yearbooks*. The first and second numbers in the parentheses in Figure 1 show how many countries reported data for the relevant definition of government in the 2003 and 2013 *Yearbooks*, respectively. They reveal both an increase in the reporting of fiscal data to the IMF and a large increase in reporting for general government. Only a few countries prepare fiscal data for the nonfinancial public sector or the public sector (IMF, 2012), and such data were not reported in the *Yearbooks*. Perhaps surprisingly, if "public" means the public sector of Figure 1, few governments publish information on public debt.

Definitions used in macroeconomic statistics are influenced by national accounting's division of the domestic economy into five sectors, one of which is general government. The others are households, nonprofit institutions serving households, financial corporations, and nonfinancial corporations (European Commission *et al.*, 2009, chap. 4). A tricky aspect of delimiting general government is distinguishing public enterprises that operate commercially and are properly considered corporations from those that have the legal form of a company but do not really operate commercially and should be included in general government. The classification of sovereign wealth funds (Megginson and Fotak, forthcoming) can also be difficult (IMF, 2014b).

Definitions used in accounting stress accountability and hence the scope of the government's ownership-like control. A business's accounts typically consolidate all the entities it controls, including majority-owned subsidiaries. In government accounting, the application of the same idea has led to a definition of government that includes not only the government and budget-funded agencies carrying out government policy but also any companies that the government owns or controls, and whose finances the government can thus ultimately be held accountable for. Determining what a government controls is of course tricky, since its coercive powers give it an influence quite unlike that of any company. International Public Sector Accounting Standards define control as "the power to govern the financial and operating policies of another entity so as to benefit from its activities" (IPSASB, 2014, vol. 2, p. 1633). Local governments are consolidated if they are deemed to be controlled by the central government, but not otherwise.

In the United States, narrow definitions of city and state governments can make debt and deficit rules easy to circumvent. Debt rules applying only to the borrowing of the government as a legal entity, for example, can be evaded by establishing a public authority and having it borrow. The revenue used to repay the borrowing may come from user fees, such as tolls on a highway, or from the government itself, in the form of payments for buildings leased from the authority. Kiewiet and Szakaly (1996) explain how state governments can circumvent debt rules in this way, and Sbragia (1996, chap. 7) explains how city governments can do the same thing to circumvent the debt rules imposed on them by states. In addition, most states have balanced-budget rules that apply to the government's general fund, but not to other government funds, such as those for capital projects and employee pensions. The rules thus constrain only a narrow definition of government. Peterson (2003) explains that state governments can eliminate a deficit in the general fund simply by transferring in money from one of the other funds.

Bunch (1991) was one of the first to systematically examine the effects of fiscal rules based on narrow definitions of government and the extent to which they lead to the creation of new public agencies outside government as defined. She considers a cross section of U.S. states in the 1980s, most of which have constitutions that limit state debt. All the rules limit general-obligation debt and some also limit revenue bonds, which are secured by a specified revenue stream and not the "full faith and credit" of the government. Some of the constitutional debt rules were set in nominal terms and have become very restrictive—limiting debt to $1 million or less. She finds that state governments subject to a constitutional debt rule that limits both general-obligation and revenue debt have on average more than six times as many public authorities as those subject to no constitutional debt restriction and that their authorities undertake a wider range of functions. These governments are also more likely to create a public building authority (that is, one that borrows money to build facilities that are then leased to the government) and more of their debt is issued by public authorities.

Kiewiet and Szakaly (1996) take a somewhat different approach to the issue. They investigate the effect of debt rules embedded in state constitutions on three kinds of debt: the generally guaranteed state debt that is the subject of the debt rules, the generally unguaranteed state debt that is not restricted by the rule, and the debt of cities and counties within the state. They analyze data on all 50 U.S. states over the 30-year period 1961–1990 and exploit both cross-state differences in debt rules and the fact that 12 states changed their debt rules during the period. They find that rules restricting state debt shift debt to cities and counties and do not "meaningfully" reduce the total debt issued by public authorities in the state (p. 91). They find no evidence, however, that restrictions on guaranteed state debt are circumvented by the issuance at the state level of unrestricted unguaranteed state debt. They find this result "more than a bit surprising" (p. 91) and conjecture that there is a (small) effect that they are unable to detect given the data they have, namely that restrictions on guaranteed state debt result in the issuance of lease-revenue bonds by the public building authorities mentioned above, but that these bonds make up a small part of total unguaranteed debt.

These results could of course be affected by the endogeneity of fiscal rules. States with fiscally conservative voters may elect governments that choose both to have little government debt and to enact tough rules. Yet governments could also be more likely to adopt fiscal rules when they know they can circumvent them. So the effect of endogeneity on circumvention is not clear. Kiewiet and Szakaly note that constitutional rules tend to change only slowly and that their data on fiscal rules are not strongly correlated with their data on state ideology or with their other explanatory variables. The investigations discussed in Section 3 of the effects of the fiscal rules of the European Union—which though not truly exogenous are accepted by governments as part of a much larger package of rights and obligations—may be less vulnerable to this problem.

A different kind of evidence on circumvention comes from the General Accounting Office (1993), which examined the extent to which U.S. states balanced their budgets with genuine spending cuts and tax increases. Its method was to ask budget officials how they closed gaps in the budget that was most recently completed and the one that was most recently enacted. For the most recently completed budget, 36% of the reported deficit gap was said to have been closed by means of actions other than cutting spending or raising revenue. Of this 36%, 22% came from transfers to the general fund from other government funds. Thus at least 8% of the total deficit reduction came from devices that exploited the narrow definition of government underlying the rule ("at least" because the nature of some of the "other" actions is unclear and because officials may have preferred not to disclose dubious measures). For the most recently enacted budget, a similar calculation shows that 10% of the total deficit reduction came from transfers from other funds, reduced contributions to pension funds, and the shifting of spending to cities and counties.[4] As Porterba (1996) notes, the results suggest that most apparent fiscal adjustment is real. Yet they also confirm that narrow definitions of government encourage the shifting of spending and debt to other public entities.

The European Union's debt and deficit rules, based on statistical standards, apply to general government, a broad and less easily manipulated definition of government. This definition also allows fair comparisons despite differences among countries in the way responsibilities for public services are divided between central and subnational governments. It also ensures that the debt and deficit rules affect the core, primarily tax-funded activities of government, without constraining those of the central bank or commercial government-owned companies. Faced with a gross-debt rule applying to even this fairly broad definition of government, however, a government can reduce its debt by selling assets to a public corporation that it owns and controls. To facilitate the operation, the government may even guarantee the corporation's borrowing. Examples of the use of public corporations to circumvent debt and deficit rules have been identified by Blanchard and Giavazzi (2008), Dafflon and Rossi (1999), and Prammer (2009), among others. The empirical research discussed in Section 3 on differences between deficits and the growth of debt in the European Union also provides indirect evidence of the shifting of spending and debt to public enterprises.

So should the broadest definition of government always be preferred? The United Kingdom tracks the finances of the entire public sector in both its accounts and its statistics (HM Treasury, 2014; ONS, 2014), thus minimizing the problem that arises with narrower definitions of government. Yet its experience suggests that the broadest measure is not always the most useful. When the government nationalized several banks during the financial crisis of 2008, its balance sheet grew enormously. In June 2009, the debt of the public sector including the banks (but excluding the Bank of England) was 198% of GDP, while the debt of general government was 58% (ONS, 2014, table PSA8B).[5] To have reported only the finances of the entire public sector would have frustrated attempts to monitor the government's core operations, and government statisticians chose to report measures of public finances that excluded the banks as well as measures that included them. Nor does defining the government as the public sector prevent all shifting of deficits or debts. There has been a long-running controversy over whether Network Rail, a company without shareholders, is part of the public sector or the private sector (Eurostat, 2013a; Joloza, 2013). And more generally governments can often achieve spending goals by means of regulation—that is, by requiring private firms to supply or subsidize services like electricity and health insurance and allowing the costs to be recouped from implicit taxes on the firms' employees, customers, or shareholders. Drawing a sharp line between fiscal and economic analysis may never be possible.

3. Defining the Debt and Deficit

Given a definition of *government*, the next issue is defining *debt* and *deficit*. There are a myriad of ways of doing so. Practice varies from country to country and, within a given country, central and local governments may follow different rules. To make analytical progress, it is necessary to abstract from much of this variation.

We can start with the deficit. It is natural to think of it as the difference between spending and revenue, without reference to the government's balance sheet. Yet it can also be defined in terms of changes in the balance sheet, and it often is because spending and revenue are themselves defined in this way (e.g., IMF, 2014b; IPSAB, 2014). The simplest measure of the deficit is the decline in the value of the government's net assets. Such a deficit is said to be *clean*, while one that excludes certain changes is said to be *dirty* (Nobes, 2006, pp. 66, 111). Although dirty deficits can be used to exclude losses for purely cosmetic reasons, certain dirty deficits are important. In particular, excluding capital gains and losses caused by changes in market prices generates a deficit that is more stable and more easily controlled by the government than the clean deficit. In government-finance statistics, the clean deficit is usefully split into a part arising from transactions and a part related to "other economic flows," and it is the deficit on transactions that gets most attention.

Different measures of the clean deficit arise from differences in the assets and liabilities that are recognized in the government's accounting. (To *recognize* an asset or liability is to record it on the balance sheet.) Four nested sets of assets and liabilities can be highlighted (Figure 2), each of which generates its own measure of net assets and hence its own clean deficit. Each set also tends to be associated with certain dirty deficits, as well as certain measures of the debt. The smallest set, *C*, contains cash and nothing else. The clean cash deficit is just the change in the government's cash balance, which is crucial when the government's liquidity is in doubt, but not very informative otherwise. When cash accounting is used, attention is paid to a dirty deficit that is derived by classifying transactions into groups. Often, financing cash flows are distinguished from operating and investing cash flows, and the deficit is taken to be the sum of

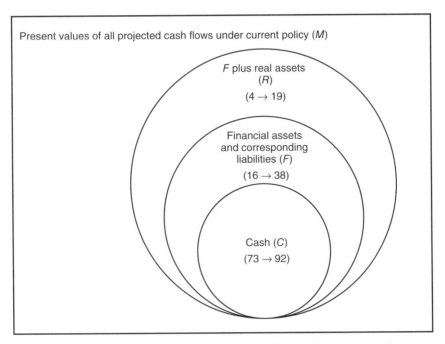

Figure 2. Four sets of Assets and Liabilities.
The figure shows four increasingly broad sets of assets and liabilities, each of which is associated with a type of accounts. The first and second numbers in parentheses in the three smaller sets show how many countries reported accounts of a given type in the *2003* and *2013 Government Finance Statistics Yearbooks*, respectively. Countries are classified as reporting cash-based accounts if they present a statement of sources and uses of cash, financial accounts if they report a financial balance sheet and net lending/borrowing, and full-accrual accounts if they report a full balance sheet and the net operating balance. Some countries report two or three kinds of accounts; other are not counted as producing any, even though they report some fiscal data. Countries are counted as providing data for a given definition of government if the most recent data reported in the 2003 *Yearbook* are for the year 2001 or later and for the 2013 *Yearbook* if they are for the year 2011 or later.
Source: Data are from the IMF's *Government Finance Statistics Yearbooks* 2003 and 2013.

operating and investing cash flows. The next set, *F*, contains cash and other financial assets, like loans, shares, and accounts receivable, as well as the liabilities that correspond to these assets. This set generates what could be called *financial accounting* and a clean deficit equal to the decline in the government's net financial worth. The part of this decline that arises from transactions is the deficit subject to the European Union's fiscal rule. The third set, *R*, also includes real assets, like land and buildings, and generates the kind of accounting that is used by businesses and required by IPSASB (2014). For convenience, *R*-based accounts can be called *full-accrual* (recognizing that financial accounting as defined above is also a form of accrual accounting). The clean deficit of full-accrual accounting is the decline in the government's *net worth*, and the change in net worth arising from transactions is the *net operating balance* (IMF, 2014b, chap. 4). The universal set, *M*, in Figure 2 includes assets and liabilities in respect of all the government's projected spending and revenue under current policy. It generates what can be called *comprehensive* accounting (Buiter, 1983) and a measure of the deficit equal to the decline in the government's comprehensive net worth, including the net present value of its projected spending and revenue under current policy.

A lower bound on the availability of fiscal accounts derived from the three smallest sets can be gleaned from *Government Finance Statistics Yearbooks*. The first and second numbers in the parentheses in Figure 2 show how many countries reported the corresponding accounts in the 2003 and 2013 *Yearbooks*, respectively. As well as revealing an increase in the reporting of fiscal data to the IMF, the numbers show that cash accounting remains by far the most common kind, but that financial and full-accrual accounting are becoming much more common. Many countries report just one kind of data, but some report two or three. Australia, for instance, reports cash, financial, and full-accrual accounts—and each for several definitions of government.[6]

Each set can be associated with a measure of debt. In a pure system of cash accounting, the natural measure of debt is the government's overdraft. In practice, governments that use cash-based accounting also record the loans they have taken out and the bonds they have issued, even if this measure is not produced by the accounting system that measures the deficit. In financial and full-accrual accounting, the range of possible liabilities is larger. The difference between the high and low estimates of Canadian government debt not explained by differing definitions of government comes from adding accounts payable, employee pensions, and other liabilities. Even when these measures are available, however, they are not always included in the most salient measures of debt. Finally, comprehensive accounting generates a measure of liabilities that includes the present value of all projected payments under current policy.

Debt may also be defined in net terms by deducting certain assets from gross debt. Taking account of a government's assets clearly provides a fuller picture of government finances than does considering only its liabilities. In assessing the risk that the government will fail to repay its debt, however, analysts may attach little weight to some assets. A strong case can be made for taking account of creditworthy government bonds denominated in the same currencies and with the same maturities as the government's debt. Indeed, if the assets and liabilities are identical—with one part of the government holding notes and bonds issued by another part—they are eliminated in the measurement of the government's gross debt. But assets like roads or shares in state-owned enterprises might be hard to sell, especially when the government was most in danger of not being able to repay its debt. And bonds denominated in different currencies from the government's debt might have depreciated when the government needed to sell them.

Narrow and broad definitions of deficits and debts have their own advantages and disadvantages. Narrow ones can be measured more reliably than broad ones and provide useful information on certain changes of public finances, such as in the government's ability to meet its obligations in the short term. Yet narrow definitions are poor indicators of the government's savings and of the sustainability of its policies, and they can be window-dressed by operations in off-balance-sheet assets and liabilities (Irwin, 2012). For instance, because cash accounting does not recognize accounts payable as a liability, a cash deficit can be reduced simply by deferring the payment of bills. Broad definitions are better indicators of the government's savings and the sustainability of its policies, and the corresponding deficits are less vulnerable to manipulation involving off-balance-sheet assets and liabilities. But the assets and liabilities on broader balance sheets can be hard to measure reliably—it is said that everything on a modern balance sheet is an estimate, with the possible exception of the date. The corresponding deficit measures are thus vulnerable to manipulation by mismeasurement (creative accounting). The comprehensive deficit, for instance, can be varied enormously by altering the rate at which tax revenues are forecast to grow or at which future cash flows are discounted.

3.1 *Cash and Accrual*

Because cash accounting is the traditional form of government accounting, its defense often takes the form of a rejection of a proposal to adopt business-like accrual accounting. Writing in about 1830, Bentham (1993) objected to a proposal that the U.K. government adopt the kind of accounting then used by merchants, on the grounds that its obscure terminology would prevent the public from understanding the government's finances. More recently, Ward (2004) questions the suitability of business-like accrual statistics and worries about their political implications. IMF (1986), the manual prescribing cash accounting, advances both practical and conceptual arguments against accrual accounts. It contends that a government cannot actually keep them because it is not a party to the transactions that give rise to its assets and liabilities. For instance, a sale may generate a sales-tax receivable, but the government isn't a party to the sale and therefore doesn't know when the receivable arises. Moreover, it argues, net worth is not even "meaningful" for government (p. 34). Levin (1991) acknowledges that other deficit measures may have their uses, but contends that the cash deficit is "probably the best single measure of the impact of government finances on the behavior of the rest of the economy" (p. 107). Even among those who accept the usefulness of accrual data, there are doubts about whether budgets in particular should be formulated on such a basis (Schick, 2007; see also Blöndal, 2004). Finally, the benefits of fuller information need to be weighed against the costs of collecting it (e.g., Blondy *et al.*, 2013; European Commission, 2013).

The arguments against cash accounting usually involve the desirability of recording transactions not when cash changes hands, but when value is "created, transformed, exchanged, transferred, or extinguished" (IMF, 2014b, p. 50). This reduces window-dressing and leads naturally to preparation of a balance sheet that includes accounts payable and receivable, among other items. IMF (2001) argues that accrual accounting for governments is both possible and desirable. It allows that governments may not know when tax-generating events like sales occur, but says that they can record a tax receivable when they have enough information to be reasonably confident of receiving payment (IMF, 2001, chap. 3). It also argues that accrual data are the most relevant for economic analysis, as do manuals for national accounts (e.g., European Commission *et al.*, 2009; see also Efford, 1996). A recent and influential defense of accrual accounting has been made by the European Commission (2013), which says it is "the only generally accepted information system that provides a complete and reliable picture of the financial and economic position and performance of a government" (p. 3).

Research on the effects of fiscal rules and targets has cast some light on the effects of different kinds of accounting, even if it cannot settle the debate about which is best. One line of research has shown how cash-deficit rules are partly circumvented by transactions in off-balance-sheet assets, though the size of the effect remains unclear. The survey of U.S. state budget officials referred to in Section 2 found that states defer payments to fill 13–16% of the budget gap not filled by genuine spending cuts or revenue increases (GAO, 1993). In a systematic empirical examination of U.S. states, Costello *et al.* (2012) find indirect evidence that governments meet stringent cash-based balanced-budget rules by deferring payments and direct evidence that they do so by selling assets (see also Block, 2008, and Bifulco *et al.*, 2012). Examining governments subject to IMF- and World Bank-supported adjustment programs in the 1980s and 1990s (which set targets for cash deficits) Easterly (1999) finds suggestive evidence of the deferral of deficits rather than sustained reductions.

Evidence on the effects of the European Union's gross-debt and financial-deficit rules also reveals partial circumvention by operations involving assets and liabilities not recognized in the financial accounts underlying the respective rules. Easterly (1999) shows that European governments wanting to join the euro privatized public enterprises after the signing of the Maastricht treaty—and also that three EU members not seeking to adopt the euro did not behave in this way. Similarly, Milesi-Ferretti and Moriyama (2006) find that reductions in the gross debt of EU members were strongly and positively correlated with reductions in their assets in the period 1992–1997, when governments were trying to meet the Maastricht debt criterion, but much less so in the period 1997–2002. They also show that the 1992–1997 reductions in assets were greater in countries with higher initial levels of debt and higher in member of the European Union than in other OECD countries. Looking at the period 1993–2003, Koen and van den Noord (2005) identify many transactions involving off-balance-sheet assets that reduced the reported deficit but did not improve public finances in a broader sense. In three countries, the dubious transactions they identify (they do not attempt to specify which involve off-balance-sheet assets and liabilities) averaged more than half a percent of GDP. The transactions were more likely to occur when the deficit rule was in danger of being breached. There is also some suggestive evidence of a different kind of problem. Auditors looking for made-up numbers in company accounts assess the extent to which the numbers in the accounts deviate from Benford's law—a distribution that describes the frequency of digits in many naturally generated data sets. Rauch *et al.* (2011) examine the extent to which fiscal data reported by 27 EU countries in the period 1999–2009 conform to Benford's law and find the largest deviations in Greece's numbers. Eurostat (2004) finds that Greece simply did not report some spending.

3.2 *Debt-Deficit Residuals and the Importance of Reconciling Stocks and Flows*

Evidence of the value of linking stocks and flows in the style of accrual accounts comes from research on the differences between deficits and the growth of debt. In simple models of public finance, the increase in the government's debt from one period to the next equals the deficit for that period:

$$debt_t - debt_{t-1} = deficit_t.$$

If the deficit were clean and debt were net liabilities, this equation would hold as an identity. Usually, however, the deficit is dirty and debt is gross, so the equation does not hold. The difference between the deficit and the increase in debt is often called the "stock-flow adjustment," but it could more precisely be called the *debt-deficit residual*. In any case, the relevant equation is

$$debt_t - debt_{t-1} = deficit_t + residual_t.$$

The existence of even a large residual is not necessarily a sign of a problem in the government's accounting. Large and consistently *negative* residuals, however, could suggest an attempt to contain debt without reducing spending. Likewise, large and consistently *positive* residuals might hint at efforts to hide spending. For instance, a government may choose to borrow in a low-interest-rate foreign currency to reduce a dirty deficit that excludes local-currency appreciation of foreign-currency debt. If interest-rate parity holds, the lower interest rate implies an expected appreciation of the foreign currency against the local currency, so borrowing in the foreign currency is not cheaper. Yet increases in the local-currency value of the debt show up only in the residual, and the reported deficit is misleading.

Several studies have found large positive residuals that raise suspicions. Kharas and Mishra (2005) examine the difference between reported deficits and increases in debt in 29 countries during the period 1980–1997. They find that on average debt increases more rapidly than can be explained by cumulative deficits. In the seven developed countries in their sample, however, reported deficits give "a fairly accurate picture" of the evolution of public debt (p. 160), while in the developing countries reported deficits are on average much less than the increases in debt. They argue that the unexplained increase is likely to have been caused by currency depreciations and bank rescues in which a government assumes liabilities without this affecting the deficit. They conclude with an appeal for better government accounting. Campos *et al.* (2006) find similar results in an investigation of 117 countries in the period 1972–2003, with 1900 country-year observations in all. In their sample, the average annual residual is 5% of GDP. It is less than 1% of GDP in high-income countries, however, and as much as 9% in Sub-Saharan Africa. Weber (2012), examining 163 countries in the period 1980–2010, also finds large residuals, but in a new twist discovers that the component of the residual that cannot be explained by her data on inflation, exchange rates, banking crises, and debt forgiveness is greater in countries that score less well on an index of fiscal transparency, lending some support to the view that debt-deficit residuals may reflect attempts to hide spending.

A limitation of these large-sample studies is that for many of the country-year observations little or no accounting information is available. Campos *et al.* and Weber therefore have to explain the residual by regression. For a smaller sample of mainly developed countries in recent years, it is possible to see how the residual arises simply by examining the accounts. Seiferling (2013) explains how the debt-deficit residual that arises from common statistical measures of the debt and the deficit is made up of (i) transactions in financial assets, (ii) transactions in liabilities that don't count as debt (e.g., liabilities from financial derivatives); and (iii) changes in the value of debt not caused by transactions (e.g., changes in the local-currency value of foreign-currency debt). Using data for 22 countries in the period 1996–2011, he shows that the part of the residual not explained by accounting data on items (i), (ii), and (iii) is very small. In principle, it should be zero, but small statistical discrepancies arise.

3.3 Debt-Deficit Residuals and the Valuation of Assets and Liabilities

Nevertheless, even a fully explained residual may reflect an attempt to hide a deficit, and studies of debt-deficit residuals can tell us something about the measurement problems that arise in financial accounting. For example, when the relevant deficit excludes both the spending of public enterprises and the government's acquisition of financial assets, a government can shift spending into the residual by transferring funds to public enterprises and having them spend the money, as long as it can describe the transfer to the enterprise as a loan or equity investment. The potential problem here is the mismeasurement of financial assets. If the public enterprise is profitable and the government can expect a market rate of return on its loan or investment, there is nothing amiss. But public enterprises often lose money, and the government's loan or equity investment may be made at an expected loss. Then some or all of the transfer is spending, not genuine investment. In principle, the part that is spending should be recorded as such. In practice, given the difficulty of estimating expected returns, the government may have some leeway to shift spending into the residual. To take a second example, if the deficit is measured on an accrual basis, spending includes increases in accounts payable and revenue includes increases in accounts receivable. If debt is gross and excludes accounts payable (as in the European Union), these components of the deficit do not affect the debt and are therefore part of the debt-deficit residual. Though not inherently suspicious, the components can arise from creative accounting that underestimates increases in payables or overestimates increases in receivables.

While European fiscal rules limit both debts and deficits, von Hagen and Wolff (2006) point out that that breaches of the deficit rule have often created more political problems than breaches of the debt rule. Governments are often well under or well over the debt limit of 60% of GDP, and in the short term nothing they can reasonably do is likely to change this. By contrast, whether or not the deficit target will be met is often an open question. Von Hagen and Wolff therefore argue that governments in danger of breaching the deficit rule will seek to shift increases in debt from the deficit to the residual, and point to the possibility of doing this by shifting spending to public enterprises. To test their hypothesis, they examine debt and deficit data for EU member states in the period 1980–2003. They find first that debt-deficit residuals tend to be positive, though they fall in the period leading up to the adoption of the euro (when the debt rule was more salient and governments sold financial assets to reduce gross debt) and increase thereafter. Second, they find that, after the Stability and Growth Pact came into force, the debt-deficit residual tends to increase when deficits are higher, especially when the 3% deficit rule is in danger of being breached, and especially during cyclical downturns when genuine spending reductions are likely to be more difficult.

Buti *et al.* (2007) find further evidence by analyzing not just the whole residual but also certain of its components. They first consider changes in accounts payable and receivable. Looking at 25 EU countries in the period 1994–2004 (with shorter periods for some countries), they find that this component of the residual increases with the deficit and increases by about 0.5% of GDP after the Stability and Growth Pact comes into force. They also find evidence that it increases during cyclical downturns and in election years. Next, they add the part of the residual most likely to be associated with the shifting of spending to public enterprises. They point out that the purchase of securities by a social-security institution that is investing surpluses may be commercially motivated even if other government investments are not. Given the available data, they single out as most likely to be suspicious lending and the purchase of securities by government entities other than social-security organizations. Examining a slightly smaller sample of observations for which these data are available, they find evidence that the sum of the two above components of the residual increases significantly after the introduction of the Stability and Growth Pact.

Alt *et al.* (2014) get similar results, but also show that the effects are smaller in countries that have greater budgetary transparency. Their primary source of data on transparency is the Open Budget Index (IBP, 2012), which they supplement, for countries not included in the OBI, with data from the IMF and Alt and Lassen (2006). Following the same logic as Buti *et al.* (2007), they look especially closely at the parts of the debt-deficit residual related to the acquisition of shares and other equities and decreases in accounts payable. Motivated by theoretical work on fiscal rules, accounting, and transparency by Milesi-Ferretti (2004) and Alt and Lassen (2006), they examine 14 EU countries in the period 1990–2007 and find that debt-deficit residuals increase (i) after the EU's fiscal rules came into force, (ii) as elections draw near, and (iii) when the economy goes into a slump. Most interesting, however, they find that the effect of fiscal rules, elections, and slumps on the residual is lower in countries where budgetary transparency is higher. They argue that governments with greater budgetary transparency are less likely to engage in budgetary gimmicks because such gimmicks are more likely to be discovered and publicized.

3.4 *Real Assets and Full-Accrual Accounting*

The assumption that debt-deficit residuals reflect attempts to hide the true deficit can be questioned when the issue is public investment in infrastructure and other real assets. Such investments increase the financial deficit, the one used in the European Union, even if the government gets a durable asset that, through user fees or growth-induced increases in tax revenue, ultimately pays for itself. If a government funds such an investment by borrowing, its financial net worth declines, but its net worth does not. By lending money to an enterprise outside the perimeter of government and having the enterprise invest, the government ensures that the investment takes place without any arguably misleading deterioration in its accounts.

Several studies have drawn attention to declines in net public investment encouraged by rules for gross debt and cash or financial deficits. Easterly (1999) finds that European governments cut back public investment in the run-up to the adoption of the euro. Easterly and Serven (2003) and Perry *et al.* (2008) collect papers that provide evidence that fiscal discipline in Latin America has an anti-investment bias and discuss accounting changes that would reduce this bias. (In Latin America, the constraints created by gross-debt targets and cash- or financial-deficit targets may be greater than elsewhere because government is more likely to be defined broadly to include public corporations). Also relevant is Poterba's (1995) finding that U.S. states that have separate capital budgets have higher capital spending than do other states.

These concerns have led to proposals that governments emphasize full-accrual measures of the deficit, counting depreciation but not investment as a cost. Blanchard and Giavazzi (2008) argue that the Stability and Growth Pact errs in treating public investment as spending that increases the deficit and that it is the full-accrual deficit that should be subject to the fiscal rule. Many others have argued in favor of full-accrual accounting on similar grounds (e.g., Eisner, 1984; Stiglitz, 1989; Bohn, 1992; Easterly *et al.*, 2008). But proposals to stress the full-accrual deficit have not been widely adopted, at least by central governments, perhaps partly because full-accrual accounts are relatively new, but also because governments' real investments do not necessarily pay for themselves and even a balanced accrual deficit can allow an excessive build-up of debt (Balassone and Franco, 2000).

3.5 *Off-Balance-Sheet Financing*

There are also debates about whether particular rights and obligations should be recognized as assets and liabilities. In the framework of this paper, these can be viewed as debates not about the relative merits of accounts based on sets C, F, and R, but about the boundaries of F and R. For instance, should these sets include liabilities related to government guarantees or employee pensions? Should R include assets and liabilities related to leases and public-private partnerships? The sometimes uncertain or contingent nature of such rights and obligations makes them fit uneasily on a balance sheet otherwise made up of clear-cut assets and hard-and-fast liabilities, but not putting them there invites window-dressing. In the United States, some subnational governments can circumvent debt rules, even without taking advantage of a narrow definition of government, by issuing revenue bonds—because such bonds are not recognized on the implicit balance sheet underlying the fiscal rule. Examining the effect of U.S. states' debt and deficit rules in the period 1975–1985, Von Hagen (1991) finds that the rules (along with narrow definitions of government) lead governments to "substitute nonrestricted for restricted debt instruments, thereby reducing the relevance and informativeness of data on government debt" (p. 209). Sbragia (2006, chap. 6) explains that one of the ways that cities respond to debt rules imposed on them by state governments is issuing revenue bonds. One might expect Islamic financing (Abedifar *et al.*, forthcoming) to create the same opportunities, though so far the governments that have issued Islamic bonds have treated them as debt in their accounts.[7]

Governments seldom have to recognize a liability when they issue a guarantee. By charging a guarantee fee, they may actually reduce their debt and deficit (Brixi and Mody, 2002). A few governments, however, follow debt rules that count guaranteed as well as direct debt. In the United States, the Federal Credit Reform Act of 1990 requires the government to recognize the estimated net present cost of certain guarantees in the budget in the year of issuance (Phaup, 1993). International accounting and statistical standards also require governments to recognize liabilities in relation to certain guarantees and similar instruments, like derivatives, financial guarantees, or groups of standardized guarantees (IMF, 2014b, chap. 7; IPSASB, 2014; see also Heald and Hodges, 2014). Yet guarantees are hard to value and most remain off balance sheet.

Likewise, governments can often acquire assets by means of leases and public-private partnerships without recording any debt. Greene's (1980) quip about the "basic drives of man" was made in a piece entitled "the joys of leasing." Nowadays, government accounting often treats a long-term lease as a liability, but assets can be acquired without recognizing debt by entering into a public-private partnership, in which a company builds and maintains an asset that provides a service that the government agrees to pay for over the life of a long-term contract. The government's obligations are not identical to those of debt; what it pays depends on whether the service is provided. But the expected fiscal effects are typically similar. The case for recognizing assets and liabilities related to public-private partnerships on the government's balance sheet has been made by Quiggin (2004) and Heald and Georgiou (2011)—and is reflected in IPSAB (2014, §32).

To take a final example, although some standards require the recognition of liabilities for employee pensions (e.g., IMF, 2014b; IPSASB, 2014), only a few governments recognize such liabilities. Except in these countries, budget deficits therefore include the cost of paying current retirees, rather than the cost associated with current employees' increasing entitlements. This is one reason that the U.S. federal government's accrual-based accounts, which recognize employee pensions as a liability, have generally shown a higher deficit than the budget has (CBO, 2006). Similarly, the post-employment costs of war veterans' health care and disability compensation are one of the reasons that Stiglitz and Bilmes (2008, chap. 2) conclude that the federal budget greatly understated the true fiscal costs of the war in Iraq. When employee-pension liabilities are estimated, they can turn out to be about as large as ordinary debt (e.g., U.S. Treasury, 2011; HM Treasury, 2014). The problem of not recognizing liabilities for employee pensions is starkly illustrated by transactions in the European Union in which governments have assumed the pension liabilities of public enterprises in return for cash or other financial assets. If the price is fair, the transaction leaves the government's true net worth unchanged, but, because employee pensions are not recognized as liabilities in the accounts, the transactions reduce the reported debt and deficit (Savage, 2005, chap. 4; Koen and van den Noord, 2005).

Even if employee-pension liabilities are recognized, their amount may be understated. Noting that the relevant accounting rules allow employers to discount future pension payments at the expected rate of return on pension-fund *assets*, rather than at a rate that reflects the low-risk nature of pension *payments*, Novy-Marx and Rauh (2011) show that U.S. state pension obligations are actually worth at least $3.2 trillion, an amount "clearly higher" than the liabilities reported in the states' accounts (p. 1246) and much higher than the states' ordinary debt of $1.0 trillion (see also Novy-Marx and Rauh, 2009; Munnell, 2012, chap. 3). Chaney *et al.* (2002) find that U.S. states subject to stringent balanced-budget rules make more optimistic assumptions about the discount rate when they are under fiscal stress, and Mohan and Zhang (2014) find that U.S. subnational governments' pension plans choose to invest in risky assets in order to exploit the accounting rule.

3.6 *Comprehensive Accounting*

For some, questions about guarantees, public-private partnerships, and employee pensions are details. While employee pensions may be costly, much more costly are the pensions governments provide to all retired employees or to all citizens above a certain age. The future cost of such pensions is not recognized as a liability on any conventional balance sheet, so a government can reduce this year's deficit by increasing taxes now and promising higher pensions (or lower taxes) in the future (Gokhale and Smetters, 2003). Preventing such effects requires comprehensive accounts that recognize assets and liabilities for all projected future revenue and spending. Buiter (1983) proposes the estimation of a comprehensive balance sheet and shows how it is related to the government's intertemporal budget constraint and also how macroeconomic stabilization can be viewed as a restructuring of the comprehensive balance sheet (e.g., more debt, but a higher present value of future primary surpluses). He recognizes the value of conventional accounts, but wants to supplement them with comprehensive accounts to ensure the government also keeps the long term in view. Kotlikoff (1986, 1998), by contrast, argues that conventional accounts are meaningless. His target is cash accounting, but his argument applies to financial and full-accrual accounting as well, irrespective of the treatment of guarantees, employee pensions, and the like. There is no difference in economic theory, he argues, between different kinds of cash inflow (e.g., taxes and the proceeds of borrowing) or between different kinds of cash outflow (e.g., payment of social security and repayment of debt). Or, to couch the claim in the framework of this paper, the boundaries of sets C, F, and R in Figure 2 are arbitrary.

The claim that conventional accounting is meaningless has not gained widespread acceptance. No government has replaced accounts based on C, F, or R with accounts based on M. Nor have international organizations and credit-rating agencies rejected conventional measures in their analyses. Gokhale and Smetters (2007) note that financial markets pay more attention to conventional than to comprehensive measures of debt—while arguing that they are mistaken to do so. The argument against distinguishing types of cash flows is quite persuasive when applied to the treatment of social security in the budget of the federal government of the United States, where people pay earmarked social-security taxes during their working lives and later receive social-security benefits whose amount depends on their prior contributions: it is easy to see the similarity between borrowing and collecting social-security taxes and between paying social-security benefits and repaying money previously borrowed. Less persuasive is the claim that there is no economically meaningful distinction between the repayment of debt and spending, say, to improve a road. The one extinguishes an economically meaningful legal obligation; the other at most fulfills a plan. Likewise, there is an economic difference for a developing country between receiving a grant and borrowing on commercial terms.

The value of comprehensive accounts has, however, been recognized by many, including Easterly (1999), Bradbury *et al.* (1999), Boskin (2008), Jackson (2008), and Blondy *et al.* (2013). Comprehensive measures of public finances have been estimated for New Zealand

(Huther, 1998), for the countries of the European Union (Velculescu, 2010), and for the U.S. federal government on many occasions (Auerbach, 1994; Gokhale and Smetters, 2003, 2006; Kotlikoff and Burns, 2012, chap. 3; and Auerbach and Gale, 2014). The upshot of all these estimates is that aging and the rising cost of health care pose fiscal problems that are hidden by conventional measures of the debt and deficit. Moreover, governments in most developed countries produce long-term fiscal projections, which allow the calculation of a comprehensive balance sheet, even if the present values of the projections are not calculated. The U.S. federal government, following FASAB (2009), is an exception in that its accounts include a kind of comprehensive balance sheet (e.g., U.S. Treasury, 2011). Generational accounts (Auerbach *et al.*, 1991, 1994), a relative of comprehensive accounts, have also been prepared for several countries (Kotlikoff and Raffelhüschen, 1999). These look through the government, as it were, and show for each age cohort the present values of its expected payments to and receipts from the government.

Of course, comprehensive accounts are enormously uncertain. They are not vulnerable to the kind of manipulation that works by trading in off-balance-sheet assets and liabilities, because all possible assets and liabilities are on balance sheet, but they are extremely sensitive to assumptions about growth rates and discount rates. Reasonable people can disagree about which assumptions are best, so there is much room for creative accounting (see Haveman, 1994, in relation to generational accounts). Comprehensive accounts also require current government policy to be specified (see, e.g., FASAB, 2009). For some items, this might seem straightforward: tax revenue, for instance, can be projected using the tax rates in the current tax code. But what is current policy regarding future spending on roads or defence? And what if the government passes a law that says that tax rates will rise in twenty years, simply in order to reduce the comprehensive deficit? Such questions leave room for much uncertainty about comprehensive accounts. While Kotlikoff and Burns (2012) conclude that the U.S. federal government ran a large comprehensive deficit in the year to June 2011, the U.S. Treasury reports a large surplus in the year to September 2011 (U.S. Treasury, 2011, p. 148).

4. Conclusions

Twenty-five years ago, when Blejer and Cheasty reviewed the measurement of deficits, there had been many proposals that governments adopt some form of accrual accounting or, more radically, measure the net present values of all their projected cash flows. In the following years, many governments did publish accrual accounts or statistics of some form. In a few countries, comprehensive accounts were also prepared by researchers or the government itself; in others, governments produced the long-term fiscal projections that underlie these accounts, even if they didn't calculate present values. There has been no comparably radical change in the definitions of government that have been employed, but data are now available for broader definitions of government in many countries. In the European Union, in particular, the new fiscal rules have ensured that financial accounts are available for the whole of general government.

Research since 1991 has confirmed that accounting matters—that it is not a veil that is pierced by decision makers (Poterba and von Hagen, 1999)—at least if it underlies a fiscal rule or salient budget target. There is little doubt that stringent rules succeed in constraining government debts or deficits as defined (see also Bohn and Inman, 1996; Poterba, 1994). Some of the effect, however, is achieved by window-dressing and creative accounting. Debt and deficits may be transferred to public entities that lie outside the defined perimeter of government. Depending on the accounting rules, governments may defer payments, sell real assets and acquire new ones by means of leases or public-private partnerships, issue guarantees instead of granting subsidies, and increase taxes this year while promising to reduce them next year. Such window-dressing can be eliminated by recognizing more assets and liabilities on the balance sheet, but only at the cost of requiring accountants and statisticians to make difficult judgments about the values of those assets and liabilities, which creates opportunities for creative accounting. Although the research surveyed here does not show that rule-governed debts and deficits lose their informative value, it is consistent with Campbell's (1976) law: "[t]he more any quantitative social indicator is used for social decision-making, the more subject it will be to corruption pressures and the more apt it will be to distort and corrupt the social processes it is intended to monitor" (p. 49).

What are the lessons for accountants, statisticians, and budget officials? One is that debt and deficit measures need protection from manipulation, such as independent measurement, independent auditing, the use of standards set by independent bodies, and the publication of the assumptions underlying the measurements so that calculations can be checked. Such measures are especially important for the particular measures of the debt and deficit that are subject to fiscal targets. A second lesson is that several measures of the deficit and debt should be produced, and reconciled, not only to paint a full picture of public finances but also to help reveal manipulation in targeted measures (Balassone *et al.*, 2006). To some extent, this is already happening. In the European Union, the United States, and other developed countries, several measures of the government's debt and deficit are available. In some cases, as in the Australian statistics mentioned above, many different measures are available in a single framework that makes them relatively easy to reconcile. Often, however, the many measures come from different systems and cannot easily be reconciled. It's good to have several maps of the terrain; it would be better to know more about why the maps differ.

Acknowledgments

Thanks for advice and comments to Richard Allen, Jim Alt, Alan Auerbach, Ian Ball, Jim Chan, Csaba Feher, Vítor Gaspar, David Heald, David Dreyer Lassen, Marvin Phaup, Mike Seiferling, Luis Servén, Alessandro Turrini, Joachim Wehner, Anke Weber, Frans van Schaik, and three anonymous referees.

Notes

1. The first two estimates of the U.S. government's deficit are for the year ending September 2011. The third is for the year ending June 2011. The dollar values reported in the sources have been divided by the average of the GDP estimates for 2010 and 2011 in the IMF's April 2014 World Economic Outlook database ($15.2 trillion).
2. Data provided by Tidiane Kinda.
3. Increasing the perimeter of government from budgetary central government to general government increases the estimate of debt by 74–109%, depending on the definition of debt.
4. 19% of the reduction comes from "other actions" (p. 27), of which 20% comes from "interfund transfers" and 25% from an action by the state of California, which reduced the forecast gap in its enacted budget by shifting educational costs to cities and counties.

5. Percentages of GDP are obtained using the estimate of UK GDP in 2009 in the IMF's April 2014 World Economic Outlook database (£1.417 trillion).
6. See the pages for Australia in the IMF's *Government Finance Statistics Yearbooks* and the data published by the Australian Bureau of Statistics at http://www.abs.gov.au/ausstats/abs@.nsf/PrimaryMainFeatures/5512.0?OpenDocument.
7. Personal communication from Yasemin Hürcan.

References

Alt, J.E. and Lassen, D.D. (2006) Fiscal transparency, political parties, and debt in OECD countries. *European Economic Review* 50(6): 1403–1439.

Alt, J.E., Lassen, D.D. and Skilling, D. (2002) Fiscal transparency, gubernatorial approval, and the scale of government: Evidence from the states. *State Politics and Policy Quarterly* 2(3): 230–250.

Alt, J.E., Lassen, D.D. and Rose, S. (2006) The causes of fiscal transparency: Evidence from the US States. *IMF Staff Papers* 53 (special issue): 30–57.

Alt, J.E., Lassen, D.D. and Wehner, J. (2014) It isn't just about Greece: Domestic politics, transparency, and fiscal gimmickry in Europe. *British Journal of Political Science* 44(4): 707–716.

Auerbach, A.J. (1994) The U.S. fiscal problem: Where we are, how we got here, and where we're going. In Fischer, S. and Rotemberg, Julio (eds.), *National Bureau of Economic Research Macroeconomics Annual 1994*, Vol. 9, (pp. 141–175). Cambridge, MA: MIT Press.

Auerbach, A.J. and Gale, W.G. (2014) Forgotten but not gone: The long-term fiscal imbalance. March 2015. Available at: http://www.brookings.edu/research/papers/2014/03/long-term-fiscal-imbalance-gale.

Auerbach, A.J., Gokhale, J. and Kotlikoff, L.J. (1991) Generational accounts: A meaningful alternative to deficit accounting. In Bradford, D. (ed.) *Tax Policy and the Economy* 5: 55–110.

Auerbach, A.J., Gokhale, J. and Kotlikoff, L.J. (1994) Generational accounting: A meaningful way to evaluate fiscal policy, *The Journal of Economic Perspectives* 8(1): 73–94.

Balassone, F. and Franco, D. (2000) Public investment, the stability pact and the 'golden rule.' *Fiscal Studies* 21(2): 207–229.

Balassone, F., Franco, D. and Zotteri, S. (2006) EMU fiscal indicators: A misleading compass. *Empirica* 33(2–3): 63–87.

Ball, I. and Pflugrath, G. (2012) Government accounting: Making Enron look good. *World Economics* 13(1): 9–26.

Barton, A. (2011) Why governments should use the government finance statistics accounting system. *Abacus* 47(4): 411–445.

Bentham, J. (1993) On public account keeping. In P. Schofield (ed.), *Official Aptitude Maximized; Expense Minimized* (pp. 293–301). Oxford: Clarendon Press.

Bifulco, R., Bunch, B., Duncombe, W., Robbins, M. and Simonsen, W. (2012) Debt and deception: How states avoid making hard fiscal decisions. *Public Administration Review* September/October: 72(5): 659–667.

Blanchard, O.J. and Giavazzi, F. (2008) Improving the stability and growth pact through proper accounting of public investment. In G. Perry, L. Servén, and R. Suescún (eds.), *Fiscal Policy, Stabilization, and Growth: Prudence or Abstinence?* 259–272. Washington, DC: World Bank.

Blejer, M.I. and Cheasty, A. (1991a) The measurement of fiscal deficits: Analytical and methodological issues. *Journal of Economic Literature* 29(4): 1644–1678.

Blejer, M.I. and Cheasty, A. (eds.) (1991b) *How to Measure the Fiscal Deficit*. Washington, DC: IMF.

Block, C.D. (2008) Budget gimmicks. In E. Garrett, E.A. Graddy, and H.E. Jackson, (eds.), *Fiscal Challenges: An Interdisciplinary Approach to Budget Policy*, Chap. 2. 39–67, Cambridge, UK: Cambridge University Press.

Blöndal, J. (2004) Issues in accrual budgeting. *OECD Journal on Budgeting* 4(1): 103–119.

Blondy, G., Cooper, J., Irwin, T., Kaufmann, K. and Khan, A. (2013) The role of fiscal reporting in public financial management. In M. Cangiano, T. Curristine, and M. Lazare (eds.), *Public Financial Management and its Emerging Architecture, Chap. 8.* 259–281, Washington, DC: IMF.

Bohn, H. (1992) Budget deficits and government accounting. *Carnegie-Rochester Conference Series on Public Policy* 37(1): 1–84.

Bohn, H. and Inman, R.P. (1996) Balanced-budget rules and public deficits: Evidence from the US states. *Carnegie-Rochester Conference Series on Public Policy* 45: 13–76.

Boskin, M. (2008) Economic perspectives on federal deficits and debt. In E. Garrett, E.A. Graddy, and H.E. Jackson (eds.), *Fiscal Challenges: An Interdisciplinary Approach to Budget Policy*, Chap. 5. 141–184, Cambridge, UK: Cambridge University Press.

Bradbury, S., Brumby, J. and Skilling, D. (1999) Sovereign net worth: An analytical framework. New Zealand Treasury Working Paper 99/3.

Brixi, H.P. and Mody, A. (2002) Dealing with government fiscal risk: An overview. In Brixi and A. Schick (eds.) *Government at Risk: Contingent Liabilities and Fiscal Risk*, 21–58, Washington: World Bank and Oxford University Press.

Budina, N., Kinda, T., Schaechter, A. and Weber A. (2013) Numerical fiscal rules: International trends. In M. Cangiano, T. Curristine, and M. Lazare (eds.), *Public Financial Management and its Emerging Architecture*, Chap. 3. 107–135, Washington, DC: IMF.

Buiter, W.H. (1983) Measurement of the public sector deficit and its implications for policy evaluation and design. *IMF Staff Papers* 30(2): 306–349.

Bunch, B. (1991) The effect of constitutional debt limits on state governments' use of public authorities. *Public Choice* 68(1): 57–69.

Buti, M., Martins, J.N. and Turrini, A. (2007) From deficits to debt and back: Political incentives under numerical fiscal rules. *CESifo Economic Studies* 53(1): 115–152.

Campbell, D.T. (1976) Assessing the impact of planned social change. Occasional Paper 8, Public Affairs Center, Dartmouth.

Campos, C.F.S., Jaimovich, D. and Panizza, U. (2006) The unexplained part of public debt. *Emerging Markets Review* 7(3): 228–243.

CBO (Congressional Budget Office) (2006) *Comparing Budget and Accounting Measures of the Federal Government's Fiscal Condition.*

Chan, J.L. and Zhang, Q. (2013) Government accounting standards and policies. In R. Allen, R. Hemming, and B.H. Potter (eds.), *The International Handbook of Public Financial Management*, Chap. 34. 742–766, New York: Palgrave Macmillan.

Chaney, B.A., Copley, P.A. and Stone, M.S. (2002) Effects of fiscal stress and balanced budget requirements on the funding and measurement of state pension obligations. *Journal of Accounting and Public Policy* 21: 287–313.

Cimadomo, J. (2014) Real-time data and fiscal policy analysis: A survey of the literature. *Journal of Economic Survey* forthcoming.

Costello, A., Petacchi, R. and Weber, J. (2012) The hidden consequences of balanced budget requirements. March 2015. Available at: http://rnchen.scripts.mit.edu/docs/AssetSale_CPW%209_24_12_Final.pdf.

Dafflon, B. and Rossi, S. (1999) Public accounting fudges towards EMU: A first empirical survey and some public choice considerations. *Public Choice* 101(1–2): 59–84.

Dechow, P. (1994) Accounting earnings and cash flows as measures of firm performance: The role of accounting accruals. *Journal of Accounting and Economics* 18(1): 3–42.

Dippelsman, R., Dziobek, C. and Gutiérrez Mangas, C.A. (2012) What lies beneath: Statistical definition of public debt. International Monetary Fund, Staff Discussion Note SDN/12/09, July 27.

Easterly, W. (1999) When is fiscal adjustment an illusion? *Economic Policy* 14(28): 55–86.

Easterly, W. and Servén L. (eds.) (2003) *The Limits of Stabilization: Infrastructure, Public Deficits, and Growth in Latin America.* Palo Alto, CA, and Washington, DC: Stanford University Press and World Bank.

Easterly, W., Irwin, T. and Servén, L. (2008) Walking up the down escalator: Public investment and fiscal stability. *World Bank Research Observer* 23(1): 37–56.

Efford, D. (1996) The case for accrual recording in the IMF's government finance statistics system, IMF Working Paper WP/96/73.

Eisner, R. (1984) "Which Budget Deficit? Some issues of measurement and their implications," *American Economic Review* 74(2): 138–143.

Ernst and Young (2012) Overview and comparison of public accounting and auditing practices in the 27 EU Member States. Prepared for Eurostat. Final Report. 19 December 2012.

Eslava, M. (2011) The political economy of fiscal deficits: A survey. *Journal of Economic Survey* 25(4): 645–673.

European Commission (2013) Report from the Commission to the Council and the European Parliament: Towards Implementing Harmonised Public Sector Accounting Standards in Member States—The suitability of IPSAS for the Member States, Brussels, March 6, COM(2013) 114.

European Commission, International Monetary Fund, Organisation for Economic Cooperation and Development, United Nations, and World Bank (2009) *System of National Accounts 2008*.

Eurostat (1996) European System of Accounts 1995.

Eurostat (2004) Revision of the Greek Government Deficit and Debt Figures, November 22.

Eurostat (2013a) EDP dialogue visit to the United Kingdom, 24–25 January 2013.

Eurostat (2013b) European System of Accounts 2010.

Eurostat (2013c) Manual on Government Deficit and Debt, 2013.

FASAB (U.S. Federal Accounting Standards Advisory Board) (2009) Reporting Extended Long-Term Fiscal Projections for the U.S. Government: Statement of Federal Financial Accounting Standards 36, September 28.

GASB (Governmental Accounting Standards Board) (1999) Basic Financial Statements—and Management's Discussion and Analysis—for State and Local Governments. Statement 34. June.

Gokhale, J. and Smetters, K. (2003) Fiscal and generational imbalances: New budget measures for new budget priorities. Federal Reserve Bank of Cleveland, Policy Discussion Paper No. 5. December.

Gokhale, J. and Smetters, K. (2006) Fiscal and generational imbalances: An update. *Tax Policy and the Economy* 20: 193–223.

Gokhale, J. and Smetters, K. (2007) Do the markets care about the $2.4 trillion US deficit. *Financial Analysts' Journal* 63(2): 37–47.

Government of France (2014) *Compte Générale de l'Etat*.

Government of Switzerland (2014) *Compte d'Etat: Rapport sur le compte de la Confédération*.

Greene, R. (1980) The joys of leasing. *Forbes*, November 24: 59.

Hameed, F. (2005) Fiscal transparency and economic outcomes. IMF Working Paper WP/05/225.

Haveman, R. (1994) Should generational accounts replace public budgets and deficits? *Journal of Economic Perspectives* 8(1): 95–111.

Heald, D. and Georgiou, G. (2011) The substance of accounting for public-private partnerships *Financial Accountability and Management* 27(2): 217–247.

Heald, D. and Hodges, R. (2014) Watch the public sector balance sheet: Guarantees as the next big thing in government accounting. In *Paper presented at the CIGAR workshop, "Whole of Government Accounting and Auditing: International Trends,"* Kristianstad University, Sweden, September, 8–9.

HM Treasury (2014) *Whole of Government Accounts*, Year Ended 31 March 2013.

Huther, J. (1998) An application of portfolio theory to New Zealand's Public Sector. New Zealand Treasury Working Paper 98/4.

IBP (International Budget Partnership) (2012) Open Budget Survey 2012.

IMF (International Monetary Fund) (1986) *A Manual on Government Finance Statistics* Washington, DC: IMF.

IMF (International Monetary Fund) (2001) *Government Finance Statistics Manual 2001* Washington, DC: IMF.

IMF (International Monetary Fund) (2012) *Fiscal Transparency, Accountability, and Risk*. Washington, DC: IMF.

IMF (International Monetary Fund) (2014a) *Fiscal Transparency Code*. Washington, DC: IMF.

IMF (International Monetary Fund) (2014b) *Government Finance Statistics Manual 2014*. Washington, DC: IMF.

IMF (International Monetary Fund) (various years) *Government Finance Statistics Yearbooks*. Washington, DC: IMF.

IPSASB (International Public Sector Accounting Standards Board), 2014, International Public Sector Accounting Standards.

Irwin, T.C. (2012) Some algebra of fiscal transparency: How accounting devices work and how to reveal them. IMF Working Paper WP/12/228.

Jackson, H.E. (2008) Counting the ways: The structure of federal spending. In E. Garrett, E.A. Graddy, and H.E. Jackson (eds.), *Fiscal Challenges: An Interdisciplinary Approach to Budget Policy*, Chap. 6. 185–220, Cambridge, UK: Cambridge University Press.

Joloza, T. (2013) Classification of Network Rail under European System of Accounts 2010.

Khagram, S., deRenzio, P. and Fung, A. (2013) Overview and synthesis: The political economy of fiscal transparency, participation, and accountability around the world in open budgets. In S. Khagram, P. deRenzio, and A. Fung (eds.), *Open Budgets: The Political Economy of Transparency, Participation, and Accountability*, 1–50, Brookings.

Khan, A. (2013) Accrual budgeting: Opportunities and challenges. In M. Cangiano, T. Curristine, and M. Lazare (eds.), *Public Financial Management and its Emerging Architecture*, Chap. 11. (pp. 339–359) Washington, DC: IMF.

Kharas, H. and Mishra, D. (2005) Looking beyond the budget deficit. In A. Shah (ed.), *Fiscal Management*, Chap. 6. Washington, DC: World Bank.

Kiewiet, D.R. and Szakaly, K. (1996) Constitutional limitations on borrowing: analysis of state bonded indebtedness. *Journal of Economics, Law and Organization* 12(1): 62–97.

Koen, V. and vanden Noord, P. (2005) Fiscal gimmickry in Europe: One-off measures and creative accounting. OECD Economics Department Working Papers 417.

Kopits, G. and Craig, J. (1998) Transparency in government operations, IMF Occasional Paper No. 158.

Kotlikoff, L.J. (1986) Deficit delusion. *The Public Interest* 84: 53–56.

Kotlikoff, L.J. (1988) The deficit is not a well-defined measure of fiscal policy. *Science* 241: 791–795.

Kotlikoff, L.J. and Burns, S. (2012) *The Clash of Generations: Saving Ourselves, Our Kids, and Our Economy*. Cambridge, MA: MIT Press.

Kotlikoff, L.J. and Raffelhüschen, B. (1999) Generational accounting around the globe. *American Economic Review* 89(2): 161–166.

Levin, J. (1991) The cash deficit: Rationale and limitation. In M.I. Blejer and A. Cheasty (eds.), *How to Measure the Fiscal Deficit*, Chap. 6. 103–112, Washington, DC: IMF.

Milesi-Ferretti, G.M. (2004) "Good, bad or ugly? On the effects of fiscal rules with creative accounting. *Journal of Public Economics* 88(1–2): 377–394.

Milesi-Ferretti, G.M. and Moriyama, K. (2006) Fiscal adjustments in EU countries: A balance sheet approach. *Journal of Banking and Finance* 30(12): 3281–3298.

Mohan, N. and Zhang, T. (2014) An analysis of risk-taking behavior for public defined benefit pension plans. *Journal of Banking and Finance* 40: 403–419.

Munnell, A.H. (2012) *State and Local Pensions: What Now?* Washington, DC: Brookings.

Nobes, C. (2006) *Penguin Dictionary of Accounting*. London, Penguin.

Novy-Marx, R. and Rauh, J.D. (2009) The liabilities and risks of state-sponsored pension plans. *Journal of Economic Perspectives* 23(4): 191–210.

Novy-Marx, R. and Rauh, J.D. (2011) Pension promises: How big are they and what are they worth? *Journal of Finance* 66(4): 1211–1249.

OECD (Organization for Economic Co-operation and Development) (2002) OECD Best Practices for Budget Transparency. *OECD Journal on Budgeting* 1(3): 7–14.

ONS (UK Office for National Statistics) (2014) *Public Sector Finances, August 2014*.

Penman, S.H. and Yehuda N. (2009) The pricing of earnings and cash flows and an affirmation of accrual accounting. *Review of Accounting Studies* 14(4): 453–479.

Perry, G., Servén, L., and Suescún, R. (eds.) (2008) *Fiscal Policy, Stabilization, and Growth: Prudence or Abstinence?* Washington, DC: World Bank.

Petersen, J. (2003) Changing red to black: Deficit closing alchemy. *National Tax Journal* 56(3): 567–577.

Phaup, M. (1993) Recent efforts to measure and control government risk-bearing In M.S. Sniderman (ed.), *Government Risk-Bearing* 167–176. New York: Springer.

Poterba, J.M. (1994) State responses to fiscal crises: 'Natural experiments' for studying the effects of budgetary institutions. *Journal of Political Economy* 102(4): 799–821.

Poterba, J.M. (1995) Capital budgets, borrowing rules, and state capital spending. *Journal of Public Economics* 56(2): 165–187.

Poterba, J.M. (1996) Budget institutions and fiscal policy in the US States. *American Economic Review* 86(2): 395–400.

Poterba, J.M. and vonHagen, J. (eds.) (1999) *Fiscal Institutions and Fiscal Performance*. Chicago: Chicago University Press.

Prammer, D. (2009) Public sector outsourcing: Creative accounting or a sustainable improvement? A case study for Austria. *Monetary Policy and the Economy* Q1: 118–135.

Quiggin, J. (2004) Risk, PPPs, and the Public Sector Comparator. *Australian Accounting Review*. 14(2): 51–61.

Rauch, B., Brähler, G., Engel, S. and Göttsche, M. (2011) Fact and fiction in EU-governmental economic data. *German Economic Review* 12(3): 243–255.

Savage, J.D. (2005) *Making the EMU: The Politics of Budgetary Surveillance and the Enforcement of Maastricht*, Oxford, Oxford University Press.

Sbragia, A.M. (1996) *Debt Wish: Entrepreneurial Cities, US Federalism, and Economic Development*, Pittsburg, PA: University of Pittsburg Press.

Schick, A. (2007) Performance budgeting and accrual budgeting: Decision rules or analytic tools? *OECD Journal on Budgeting* 7(2): 109–138.

Seiferling, M. (2013) Stock-flow adjustments, government's integrated balance sheet, and fiscal transparency. IMF Working Paper WP/13/16.

Sloan, R.G. (1996) Do stock prices fully reflect information in accruals and cash flows about future earnings? *The Accounting Review* 71(3): 289–315.

Stiglitz, J. (1989) On the economic role of the state. In Arnold Heertje (ed.), *The Economic Role of the State*. Oxford: Blackwell.

Stiglitz, J.E. and Bilmes, L.J. (2008) *The Three Trillion Dollar War: The True Cost of the Iraq Conflict*. New York: WW Norton.

Tirole, J. (2006) *The Theory of Corporate Finance*. Princeton: Princeton University Press.

United Nations (1968) *A System of National Accounts*. New York: United Nations.

United Nations (2012) Promoting transparency, participation and accountability in fiscal policies. Resolution adopted by the General Assembly on 21 December 2012.

U.S. Treasury (2011) *Financial Report of the US Government 2011*.

Velculescu, D. (2010) Some Uncomfortable Arithmetic Regarding Europe's Public Finances. IMF Working Paper WP/10/177.

Von Hagen, J. (1991) A note on the empirical effectiveness of formal fiscal restraints. *Journal of Public Economics* 44(2): 199–210.

Von Hagen, J. and Wolff, G.B. (2006) What do deficits tell us about debt? Empirical evidence on creative accounting with fiscal rules in the EU. *Journal of Banking and Finance* 30(12): 3259–3279.

Ward, M.P. (2004) Some reflections on the 1968–93 SNA revision. *Review of Income and Wealth* 50(2): 299–313.

Weber, A. (2012) Stock-flow adjustments and fiscal transparency: A cross-country comparison, IMF Working Paper WP/12/39.

7

RISE OF THE FIDUCIARY STATE: A SURVEY OF SOVEREIGN WEALTH FUND RESEARCH

William L. Megginson

University of Oklahoma, King Fahd University of Petroleum and Minerals

Veljko Fotak

University at Buffalo (SUNY), Sovereign Investment Lab, Baffi CAREFIN Centre, Bocconi University

Can governments ever act as objective, commercially oriented global investors managing their nations' wealth as investment fiduciaries? Over 25 national governments are now conducting such a natural experiment with state-led financial investment as sponsors of sovereign wealth funds (SWFs), which invest internationally in stocks, bonds, and real estate in search of a higher financial return than that offered by investment solely in sovereign bonds. These funds, which were assigned their vivid moniker by Andrew Rozanov 10 years ago (Rozanov, 2005), control over $5.4 trillion in investable assets and are growing more rapidly than any other class of large global investors—and thus appear set to strongly influence international investing for the foreseeable future. This paper surveys the academic and practitioner literature researching sovereign wealth funds and describes the issues that future researchers should address to better understand these important new financial agents.

The economic role of governments has, of course, been evolving rapidly over the past several decades. States have always and everywhere regulated private businesses to a greater or lesser degree, but many also chose to enter business as owners. Mostly from the Great Depression onwards, governments around the world launched (or nationalized) companies that produced goods and services sold to the nation's populaces, often under monopolistic regimes (Shleifer, 1998; Megginson, 2005). As these state-owned enterprises (SOEs) spread and citizens experienced the often poor quality of their output, disillusion with SOEs prompted governments to adopt a new policy of privatization. Since its introduction by Britain's Thatcher government in the early 1980s to a then-skeptical public, privatization now appears to be accepted as a legitimate—often a core—tool of statecraft by many of the world's over 190 national

A Collection of Surveys on Savings and Wealth Accumulation, First Edition. Edited by Edda Claus and Iris Claus.
Chapters © 2016 The Authors. Book compilation © 2016 John Wiley & Sons, Ltd. Published 2016 by John Wiley & Sons, Ltd.

governments. Since 1977, governments around the world have raised almost $3.0 trillion by selling state-owned enterprises to private investors and corporations (Megginson, 2014).

The historic rise of privatization as a core state policy has thus been well documented. As noted, what is far less appreciated is the high frequency with which governments have been buying equity in listed and unlisted private firms. Contrary to public perceptions and despite the worldwide success of state privatizations, over the 2001–2012 period governments acquired more assets through stock purchases ($1.52 trillion) than they sold through share issue privatizations and direct sales ($1.48 trillion).[1] Much of this state investment was channeled through SWFs and, as we describe in detail below, the vast bulk of these stock purchases have been cross-border transactions.

In many ways, this surge in government stock investment is puzzling, since a huge volume of published research on government ownership documents dramatic performance improvements for privatized enterprises, suggesting that states should be reducing their ownership of corporate equity, rather than increasing it. A large segment of this research, summarized in Shirley and Walsh (2001), Megginson and Netter (2001), Djankov and Murrell (2002), Sun and Tong (2003), and Estrin, Hanousek, Kočenda, and Svejnar (2009), suggests that governments are usually bad operating *managers* and that firm performance improves with privatization, while another stream of literature has looked at "mixed ownership" firms (Boardman and Vining, 1989, 2012; Shirley and Walsh, 2001; Lin and Su, 2008; Borisova *et al.*, 2012), generally finding that mixed ownership also has a negative impact on firm value. Figure 1

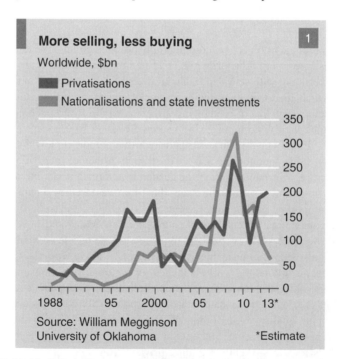

Figure 1. Worldwide Sales of State-owned Enterprises and Assets (Privatizations and Sales) and Purchases of Privately-owned Stock by Governments (Nationalizations and Investments), 1988–2011, US$ Billions.
Source: The Economist, Setting out the Store (January 11, 2014).
http://www.economist.com/news/briefing/21593458-advanced-countries-have-been-slow-sell-or-make-better-use-their-assets-they-are-missing

shows the annual value of state purchases of equity (nationalizations) and sales of assets and equity (privatizations) between 1988 and 2013. The world has thus been witnessing two powerful, simultaneous, and apparently contradictory economic phenomena over recent years: continuing sales of state-owned assets and enterprises to private investors by some governments, coupled with increasingly large purchases of private, often listed, corporate equity by other governments.

The key innovation that explains these apparent contradictions is that the recent government purchases of equity have been conducted mostly by state entities acting as investors rather than owners, buying noncontrolling stakes in foreign and domestic companies in order to realize a long-term financial return, rather than to own and operate these businesses as state enterprises. This phenomenon can be called the rise of the fiduciary state, and sovereign wealth funds are the single most important expression of this force, as, over the past decade, their total assets have grown to exceed those of hedge funds and private equity combined. What makes this phenomenon especially important, and perplexing, is the aforementioned fact that most government equity purchases have been acquisitions in foreign companies, where the state purchaser cannot exercise any sovereign regulatory or supervisory power. These state shareholders have no more authority to monitor target firm managers than do private investors—and may well have less ability to do so, if they are politically constrained from being too pushy.

Two economic phenomena have promoted the growth of SWFs since 1999. The first is the massive accumulation of foreign (mostly dollar-denominated) official reserves by central banks that was prompted by the devastating 1997–98 East Asian financial crisis. Governments have built up increasingly massive foreign exchange reserve holdings over the past 15 years—reaching $12.338 trillion at year-end 2012, according to the World Bank—and this has prompted them to reallocate some assets to SWFs, to seek a commercial return without having to convert out of dollars. The second major force fueling the recent growth of SWFs has been the nearly inexorable rise in the world price of oil, which increased from barely $10 per barrel in 1998 to over $148 a decade later, before stabilizing between $90 and 110 per barrel from late 2010 through June 2014. It remains to be seen whether the 50% drop in oil prices during the second half of 2014, to $55 per barrel at year-end, will permanently impact SWF funding and investment levels.

As discussed more fully in the following section, all of the largest SWFs receive their funding either from transfers of oil (and natural gas) revenues earned by national energy companies or from transfers of excess foreign exchange reserves earned from exports and managed by the national central bank or Treasury. SWFs are thus classified as either "oil based" or "trade surplus based," and we will follow this throughout the survey. However, we also stress another important method of classifying SWFs, which our reading of the empirical evidence suggests may in fact be even more relevant for explaining their investing behavior, operating philosophy, and how they are received by nations targeted for SWF investment— whether the funds are sponsored by democratic or nondemocratic nations and, closely related, whether the funds operate in a transparent or nontransparent manner.[2] We further note that there is tremendous heterogeneity among funds, and thus any attempt to neatly "classify" SWFs should be viewed with caution.

The key challenge for all survey article authors is to organize the great mass of published material on a topic into a series of discrete but connected topical treatments that fit within a holistic theme. The overarching question/theme we address in this survey is whether SWFs are fundamentally different in organization, behavior, and/or investment objectives from other types of large, internationally active institutional investors that are operated by or for private owners (Chen *et al.*, 2007; Ferreira and Matos, 2008; Cronqvist and Fahlenbrach, 2009; Aggarwal *et al.*, 2011). The answer to this question should guide all optimal public policy and financial valuation responses to the rise of SWFs. On one hand, SWFs resemble other internationally active investment vehicles such as pension funds, buy-out funds, and mutual funds that have been extensively researched by financial economists. SWFs are particularly similar in structure and expressed objectives to hedge funds, as described by Klein and Zur (2009); Brav *et al.* (2008); and Becht *et al.* (2009), in that SWFs are also stand-alone, unregulated pools of capital, managed by investment professionals, which often acquire large equity stakes in publicly traded companies. If SWFs are really just large, commercially minded financial investors, there is no compelling reason to establish regulatory barriers to their inward investments, demand greater disclosures from them than from other investors, or assess their financial performance any differently than one would a private institutional investor. However, if SWFs are inherently different because of their state ownership, as Truman (2008, 2011) and others suggest, then these funds will inevitably be viewed and regulated differently than other large institutional investors.

This survey is structured as follows. Section 1 addresses the difficulties of accurately defining a SWF, discusses the evolution of the original SWFs from stabilization to wealth funds, and examines how SWFs are organized and funded. We then document the surprising number of countries (26) that have proposed or launched new SWFs just since January 2008, usually in direct response to a major new natural resource discovery, and almost always using Norway's Government Pension Fund Global (GPFG) as an organizational and investment policy model.

Section 2 describes how SWFs are organized and operated, and details the key measures developed to assess the operational and informational transparency of different funds—the Sovereign Wealth Fund Institute's Linaburg-Maduell Index and the Truman (2008, 2011) SWF Scoreboard. This section concludes by comparing the organizational structures, corporate governance systems, and investment patterns observed for SWFs with those documented empirically for other internationally active institutional investors, both state-owned and private. Section 3 examines how SWFs make investment decisions. We describe how a fund's source of financing (oil versus trade surpluses) might be expected to impact its investment policies, and then survey the theoretical, normative, and empirical research examining how SWFs should and do allocate their funds across asset classes such as equity, fixed income, property, and alternative investments. The asset allocation policies of the largest and best managed SWF, Norway's GFPG, are described in some detail, and we then survey the empirical literature examining how SWFs allocate their investments geographically and across industries.

Section 4 addresses the valuation and corporate governance impact that SWF investments have on target companies, and in particular how SWFs' equity purchases affect target firm stock values in both the short term (at announcement) and long term. This is the "corporate finance" segment of the survey, which also happens to be the area that has attracted the most intense recent research, as evidenced by the large number of published studies and high-quality working papers we survey. While all relevant research is cited, we most prominently discuss findings from our own empirical study of SWF investment patterns and performance (Bortolotti *et al.*, 2014), which documents that SWF investments are associated with different announcement period wealth effects for target firms than are investments by similar large, but privately-owned, financial investors; in other words, we document a "SWF discount." Section 5 concludes the survey, summarizes the key lessons of extant SWF research, and points to issues that future researchers sorely need to address.

1. What are Sovereign Wealth Funds, and why do we care?

There is no consensus, in either the academic or practitioner literature, on exactly what constitutes a sovereign wealth fund. While SWFs are a heterogeneous group, most of the larger and more established SWFs evolved from funds set up by governments with revenue streams dependent on the value of one underlying commodity wishing to diversify investments to stabilize revenues. Accordingly, most SWFs have been established in countries that are rich in natural resources, with oil-related SWFs being the most common and largest group. These include the funds sponsored by the Arab Gulf countries, Russia and the ex-Soviet republics, Malaysia, Brunei, and Norway. A newer set of funds has recently been established in response to discoveries of major new resource endowments—particularly natural gas, but also oil, coal, diamonds, copper, and other minerals. A second important group of SWFs includes those financed out of accumulated foreign currency reserves resulting from persistent and large net exports, especially the funds based in Singapore, Korea, China, and other East-Asian exporters.

Because definitions vary and because few funds have disclosed key organizational details, heterogeneous funds are often grouped into the SWF category, even though there are significant differences between funds with respect to organizational structure (separately-incorporated holding companies versus pure state ministries), investment objectives (preservation of wealth versus wealth diversification and growth), compensation policies and status of fund managers (incentivized professionals versus fixed-wage bureaucrats), and degree of financial transparency (Norway's Government Pension Fund-Global and Australia's Future Fund versus almost all other large funds).

Most definitions of SWFs suggest these are state-owned investment funds (not operating companies) that make long-term domestic and international investments in search of commercial returns.[3] Some definitions are broader than this, as in Truman (2008), who defines a sovereign wealth fund as "a separate pool of government-owned or government-controlled financial assets that includes some international assets." Balding (2008) shows that an expansive definition encompassing government-run pension funds, development banks, and other investment vehicles would yield a truly impressive total value of "sovereign wealth."[4]

In this survey, we use the definition of a sovereign wealth fund employed by the Sovereign Investment Laboratory: (1) an investment fund rather than an operating company; (2) that is wholly owned by a sovereign government, but organized separately from the central bank or finance ministry to protect it from excessive political influence; (3) that makes international and domestic investments in a variety of risky assets; (4) that is charged with seeking a commercial return; and (5) which is a wealth fund rather than a pension fund—meaning that the fund is not financed with contributions from pensioners and does not have a stream of liabilities committed to individual citizens.[5] While this sounds clear-cut, ambiguities remain. Several funds headquartered in the United Arab Emirates are defined as SWFs, even though these are organized at the Emirati rather than the federal level, because the emirates are the true decision-making administrative units.[6] Table 1 presents the 33 SWFs that meet these criteria, the countries that sponsor the funds, their year of inception, their principal source of funds, and estimates of the value of assets under management (AUM) at year-end 2014. We also include Saudi Arabian Monetary Agency (SAMA) in this listing, since the Saudi government announced in June 2014 that it would establish a large SWF, partly encompassing SAMA's foreign assets.

There is some controversy regarding which is the largest SWF. Historically, the Abu Dhabi Investment Authority (ADIA) has been awarded that title, but that was mostly because

Table 1. Sovereign Wealth Funds in the Sovereign Investment Laboratory SWF Transaction Database. This table lists the 33 funds that meet the Sovereign Investment Laboratory definition of a sovereign wealth fund (SWF), plus the Saudi Arabian Monetary Agency's foreign assets, and offers information regarding country of origin; fund name; the year in which the fund was established; the principal source of funding for the fund; and estimated total assets under management in US$ billions as of December 31, 2014. Unless explicitly indicated as coming from the Sovereign Wealth Fund Institute, or as being Sovereign Investment Laboratory estimates, data are obtained from the funds' own websites.

Country	Fund name	Inception year	Source of funds	Total assets US$ billion
Norway	Government Pension Fund – Global	1997	Commodity (Oil)	$855.8
UAE-Abu Dhabi	Abu Dhabi Investment Authority[a]	1976	Commodity (Oil)	773.0
Saudi Arabia	Saudi Arabian Monetary Agency Foreign Assets	1963	Commodity (Oil)	747.6
China	China Investment Corporation	2007	Trade Surplus	652.7
Kuwait	Kuwait Investment Authority[a]	1953	Commodity (Oil)	548.0
Singapore	Government of Singapore Investment Corporation[a]	1981	Trade Surplus	320.0
Russia	National Wealth Fund and Reserve Fund	2006	Commodity (Oil)	168.9
Singapore	Temasek Holdings	1974	Trade Surplus	168.4
China	National Social Security Fund[a]	2000	Trade Surplus	201.6
Qatar	Qatar Investment Authority[a]	1974	Commodity (Oil)	256.0
Australia	Australian Future Fund	2006	Noncommodity	84.7
UAE-Dubai	Investment Corporation of Dubai[a]	2006	Commodity (Oil)	90.0
Kazakhstan	Kazakhstan National Fund[a]	1983	Commodity (Oil)	77.0
UAE-Dubai	International Petroleum Investment Company	1984	Commodity (Oil)	63.5
Libya	Libyan Investment Authority[a]	2003	Commodity (Oil)	66.0
Republic of Korea	Korea Investment Corporation	2006	Government-Linked Comps	72.0
UAE-Abu Dhabi	Mubadala Development Company PJSC	1993	Commodity (Oil)	60.8
Brunei	Brunei Investment Agency[a]	1983	Commodity (Oil)	40.0
Azerbaijan	State Oil Fund of Azerbaijan	1999	Commodity (Oil)	37.3
Malaysia	Khazanah Nasional Berhard	2000	Government-Linked Firms	31.7
Ireland	National Pension Reserve Fund	2001	Noncommodity	24.5
New Zealand	New Zealand Superannuation Fund	2001	Noncommodity	20.9
East Timor	Timor-Leste Petroleum Fund	2005	Commodity (Oil & Gas)	16.6
UAE-Dubai	Isthitmar World[b]	2003	Commodity (Oil)	11.5
Bahrain	Mumtalakat Holding Company	2006	Government-Linked Firms	10.7

Table 1. (*Continued*)

Country	Fund name	Inception year	Source of funds	Total assets US$ billion
UAE	Emirates Investment Authority[b]	2007	Commodity (Oil)	10.0
UAE-Abu Dhabi	Abu Dhabi Investment Council[b]	2005	Commodity (Oil)	10.0
Oman	State General Reserve Fund[b]	1980	Commodity (Oil & Gas)	8.2
UAE-Ras Al Khaimah	Ras Al Khaimah Investment Authority[b]	2005	Commodity (Oil & Gas)	2.0
Vietnam	State Capital Investment Corporation[b]	2005	Government-Linked Firms	0.6
Kiribati	Revenue Equalization Reserve Fund[b]	1956	Commodity (Phosphates)	0.5
São Tomé & Principe	National Oil Account[b]	2004	Commodity (Oil)	0.00063
Oman	Oman Investment Fund	2006	Commodity (Oil & Gas)	Unknown
Total, 21 oil-based funds (US$ billion)		$3,842.2		
Total, 12 nonoil based funds (US$ billion)		$1,588.3		
Total, all 33 funds (US$ billion)		$5,430.5		

[a]Sovereign Wealth Fund Institute (http://www.swfinstitute.org/fund-rankings) estimate of assets under management (AUM) as of December 31, 2014.
[b]Sovereign Investment Laboratory estimate of assets under management (AUM).

the fund has never reported its assets under management, and commentators assumed that Abu Dhabi's massive oil export revenues must translate into an equally massive fund, with AUM estimates often exceeding $800 billion. The Sovereign Wealth Fund Institute (http://www.swfinstitute.org/fund-rankings) estimates that ADIA has AUM of about $773 billion, which places it second in size behind Norway's Government Pension Fund-Global. The GPFG is growing very rapidly and has reported AUM of $855.8 billion as of December 31, 2014 (http://www.nbim.no/en/the-fund). If the Saudi Arabian Monetary Agency is reclassified as a SWF, it would be third largest, with total foreign assets of $747.6 billion as of May 26, 2014 (http://www.sama.gov.sa/sites/samaen/ReportsStatistics/ReportsStatisticsLib/5600_S_Monthly_Bulletin_AREN.pdf), but the China Investment Corporation [CIC, AUM of $652.7 billion at year-end 2013 (www.cina-inv.cn)] is now the third largest SWF, as defined by the Sovereign Investment Laboratory. Significantly smaller is fourth-ranked Kuwait Investment Authority [KIA, estimated AUM of $548.0 billion (http://www.swfinstitute.org/fund-rankings)], which is also the oldest SWF having been founded in 1953.[7] Amazingly, the small city state of Singapore itself sponsors the fifth and sixth largest SWFs, the Government of Singapore Investment Corporation [GIC, estimated AUM of $320.0 billion (http://www.swfinstitute.org/fund-rankings)], which is charged primarily with international investing, and Temasek Holdings (AUM of $168.4 billion as of March 31, 2014 (http://www.temasek.com.sg)], which focuses on domestic and regional investments. The United Arab Emirates alone accounts for six of the 33 SWFs on this list, and other Arabian Gulf states account for another four. Only four funds are from western-style democracies (Norway, Australia, New Zealand, Ireland), though many others are sponsored by countries meeting most definitions of being democratic (Korea, Malaysia, Singapore, Russia).[8] No fewer than 19 of the 33 funds have been launched since January 2000.

The 21 SWFs that are financed principally from oil revenues have combined year-end 2014 AUM of $3.842 trillion, or about 71 percent of the $5.431 trillion total for all funds, while trade-surplus-financed SWFs account for most of the rest. It should be noted that this fairly restrictive definition of SWFs yields a smaller number and total AUM value than do most other classifications. For example, the Sovereign Wealth Fund Institute lists 76 SWFs with AUM of $7.057 trillion on December 31, 2014. However the definitions of sovereign wealth funds vary, these funds have been growing much more rapidly over the past several years than have hedge funds, pension funds, and other private institutional investors.

1.1 *The Historical Evolution of SWFs—From Stabilization to Financial Investor*

Most of the well-established SWFs evolved in some way from commodity stabilization fund precursors. The main purpose of a stabilization fund is to offset revenue declines due to falling commodity prices or production levels, and most such funds are employed by countries whose budgets are highly dependent on natural resources, such as oil, copper, diamonds, or other commodities. A large portion of the existing literature regarding commodity stabilization funds has focused on their efficiency and on the related size question—that is, on whether current stabilization funds are under- or over-capitalized.[9] As Balding (2012) discusses in detail, the early pre-1980s stabilization funds often suffered from poor management and from the constant danger of politicians succumbing to the temptation to promote excessive domestic spending. A significant evolution was marked by the Chicago School economists charged with reforming the Chilean economy in the mid-1980s, who established the Chilean Social and Economic Stabilization Fund in 1985 with partial funding from the World Bank. The fund incorporated many of the characteristics of a modern SWF and, importantly, benefited from an independent board setting target levels of accruals and withdrawals, with the goal of minimizing political interference with the fund and thus restraining public spending. The subsequent success of the Chilean fund led the World Bank to advise other states to replicate this model. While the evolution from stabilization funds to SWFs was thus a gradual process, Balding (2012) notes that stabilization funds aim at promoting local development (by smoothing spending booms and busts related to volatile commodity prices), while SWFs aim at financial returns. As a consequence, stabilization funds tend to invest domestically, while SWFs attempt to diversify revenue streams by investing mostly abroad. In part, this foreign focus is also a result of governments using SWFs to reinvest commodity-originated funds abroad, perhaps to prevent the local currency from appreciating and, in general, to avoid what has come to be known as "Dutch disease"—or an overheating of the local economy that could hurt the development of other, noncommodity, sectors.[10] Yet we need to recognize that many of the modern SWFs, implicitly or explicitly, carry at least a partial stabilization mandate, as the domestic financial-sector recapitalizations seen in 2008 and 2009, and Russia's tapping of its SWFs in late 2014 all attest. As we have seen, the consensus in SWF-related research is that much of the growth in SWFs will originate from a reallocation of assets from stabilization funds; accordingly, the issue of optimal size of stabilization funds is very relevant to the overall discussion of SWFs.

While the older SWFs evolved out of stabilization funds, those established since 2000 were mostly created as *de novo* SWFs, even though the term itself had not yet been coined in many cases. However created, SWFs grew quietly but steadily through 2005. Since the start of 2006,

SWF total AUM have grown very rapidly, due to a shift in world trading patterns and the large rise in world oil prices that fueled dollar-denominated surpluses for mostly Asian countries running large trade surpluses and oil exporters in the Arabian Gulf, Asia and Europe. As noted in the Introduction, Andrew Rozanov coined the term "sovereign wealth fund" in 2005, which caught on slowly but inexorably.[11]

1.2 *The Evolving Political Response to Cross-Border SWF Investments*

SWFs first entered popular discourse during early 2007, when the newly-formed China Investment Corporation (CIC) purchased a $3 billion, nonvoting equity stake in Blackstone Group immediately prior to the group's highly touted (but subsequently under-performing) initial public offering. Later that same year, and again in early 2008, SWFs surged to the forefront of financial policy discussions when several, mostly Arabian Gulf-based SWFs effectively (if only briefly) rescued the western banking system by purchasing some $60 billion worth of newly issued stock in large American and European banks at the height of the subprime mortgage crisis. In total, SWFs invested almost $90 billion in the stock of U.S. and European financial institutions between July 2005 and October 2008, and CIC injected an additional $40 billion into recapitalizing two Chinese state-owned banks in late 2007 and 2008. These funds have thus collectively invested more new capital into the world's financial institutions recently than any other single entity except the entire United States government.

These episodes highlighted both the sheer financial firepower of SWFs and just how dependent on them western financial economies had become–and vice versa (Kunzel *et al.*, 2011; Bolton *et al.*, 2012). Early comments by public officials and analyses in the popular press tended to be very hostile towards SWFs, emphasizing perceived problems associated with their growth.[12] Political opposition to SWFs was exemplified by German Chancellor Angela Merkel who, in June 2007, publicly complained about Russian SWFs buying pipelines and energy infrastructure in Europe, and by a surge of discussions regarding SWFs in the U.S. Congress.

The issues raised by the early critics of SWFs included: (1) the possibility that their capital could be used to further political purposes and to acquire stakes in strategic industries; (2) the risk of equity price bubbles due to the sheer size of their investments and the related decline in demand for Treasury bonds; (3) the risk of an increase in volatility of financial markets; (4) the possibility that SWFs might have a detrimental effect on corporate governance because of political motives or lack of sophistication; and (5) the risk of the emergence of a new form of financial protectionism as a reaction to SWFs. The criticism most often mentioned was (6) the lack of transparency by SWFs—and this is one criticism that lingers to the present day. There was also great concern (7) that SWFs were growing at what appeared to be an exponential rate. By far the most important fear regarding SWFs was, and to some extent remains, (8) that as state-owned funds they would not act as strictly commercially-minded investors, seeking only the highest possible financial return, but would instead be forced to invest strategically by home-country governments seeking political influence or access to foreign technology. Most of these fears have proven groundless, as there have been no major documented cases of SWFs investing abroad as political agents of home-country governments; quite the reverse— SWFs have proven to be passive and nonconfrontational with target firm managers almost to a fault. As foreign, state-owned investment funds, any posture that SWFs take other than being purely passive investors might generate political pressure or a regulatory backlash from recipient-country governments (Dinç and Erel, 2013).[13] Even when SWFs do take majority stakes—which Miracky *et al.* (2008) show occurs almost exclusively when SWFs invest in domestic companies—the funds rarely challenge incumbent managers Mehrpouya *et al.* (2009). English *et al.* (2004) and Woitdke (2002) find similar behavior by U.S. public-sector pension funds and by California Public Employee Retirement System (CalPers) managers, respectively. More positively, SWFs provided invaluable liquidity to both global and domestic capital markets during the Financial Crisis of 2008–2009. Today, most governments actively court SWF investment, with Britain being the most successful by far.

1.3 *Countries Proposing or Launching SWFs Recently*

Despite the ambiguous political reaction to SWFs in the West, and notwithstanding the meager empirical evidence supporting their effectiveness (which we survey in Section 4), many countries have launched or proposed new funds in recent years. The Sovereign Wealth Fund Institute (SWFI) reports that 32 SWFs were created between 2005 and 2012, and that there were 76 funds in existence in December 2014 with assets of $7.05 trillion.[14] We identify and tabulate information on 26 new SWFs that have been announced since January 2008 (table available upon request). In most cases, the funds were proposed immediately after a major new natural resource reserve was discovered, or when administration of an existing resource base was restructured. Examples of countries that proposed or established a SWF after a new resource was proven include Brazil, Israel, Papua New Guinea, and Mongolia. These governments respectively proposed new SWFs after large oil deposits were discovered off Brazil's coast by Petrobras; after two immense natural gas fields were proven within Israel's Mediterranean territory; in anticipation of windfall payments—that ultimately might exceed 10 times Papua New Guinea's annual GNP—from a newly-built liquefied natural gas export project; and after mining concessions were granted to foreign companies to develop Mongolia's huge new mineral deposits.[15] Much the same experience motivated the governments of Ghana, Liberia, Sierra Leone, and Tanzania to propose new SWFs after new natural resource bases were proven. Greenland and Lebanon showed even greater anticipation, and proposed new SWFs after likely new natural gas fields in their territories were identified, but before their full commercial potential was even proven.

Angola, Chile, Iran, Nigeria, and Russia all launched new or restructured SWFs as a way to change how an existing stream of royalty payments would be administered. The stated rationales varied; Angola and Nigeria set up new funds to increase transparency and ensure that the nation's resource wealth would not be misappropriated; Iran set up a fund to help it circumvent international sanctions; and Chile and Russia re-oriented existing funds more towards making international investments.

A third common motivation for launching a SWF has been to allow "excess" foreign exchange reserves held by the central bank to be channeled away from static holdings of low-yielding sovereign (usually U.S. government) bonds and into higher-return equity and corporate debt investments. This impulse to "sweat" excess reserves motivated the governments (or at least governing parties) of India, Japan, Panama, Saudi Arabia, and South Africa to propose new SWFs.

Three patterns stand out regarding all of the instances of new and proposed SWFs described above. First, these governments usually proposed setting up a wealth fund to preserve and protect new monetary inflows, rather than using the new monies to launch spending programs or to channel windfall funds through existing state-owned financial entities. Relatedly, all these proposals reflect a strong desire to ensure that new resource flows would be channeled through a transparent, accountable, and professionally managed investment company rather than through existing—and often quite corrupt—state investment vehicles or state-owned banks (Jiang *et al.*, 2010; Lin *et al.*, 2011). Third, almost without exception, these new funds are being modeled after Norway's GPFG with respect to organizational design, transparency and managerial professionalism, and investment preference for listed shares and bonds of international companies.

2. How are Sovereign Wealth Funds Organized and Operated?

All modern governments play leading roles in their nations' economic affairs, and they conduct direct financial interventions through a wide range of entities. At one extreme are official state ministries, such as the Treasury and the Finance Ministry, while at the other extreme are legally separate, individually incorporated state owned enterprises (SOEs) through which states exert influence as the controlling shareholder. In between these organizational poles lie regulatory agencies, boards and commissions (such as the U.S. Securities and Exchange Commission and the Social Security Administration); state-owned but separately capitalized commercial and development banks (such as Brazil's BNDES and Germany's KfW); and, most important of all, central banks, which are integrated organs of government, even when granted substantial operating autonomy. There is a wide variation in the degree to which these institutions are under the direct political control of the national government, how much operational discretion the entity's managers can exercise, and even whether the entity's workers are state employees with civil service protection or are part of the private-sector workforce.

As described in Das *et al.* (2009), Jain (2009), and Al-Hassan *et al.* (2013), governments wishing to set up a SWF must confront all of these organizational, ownership, and personnel issues, beginning with the optimal degree of separation between the new SWF and the existing central bank and Finance Ministry. Stabilization funds and foreign exchange reserve management groups tend to be fairly tightly bound within existing entities, but when these funds evolve into SWFs most governments deliberately separate them—either legally or operationally, or both—from other ministries and agencies in order to shield the funds' managers from direct political pressure. There is, however, great variation between countries in how effectively SWFs are shielded from politics, and this is especially problematic for funds based in non-democratic countries and kingdoms. At one extreme lies Norway's GPFG, wherein investment policy is set by an independent board of experts based on strategic guidelines established by the nation's legislature (Towner, 2014). The fund's managers are fully protected from partisan political pressures, even though the fund is administered by Norges Bank (the central bank). At the other extreme (among large funds) lie Abu Dhabi's ADIA and Singapore's Government Investment Company, both of which report only to the nation's rulers and refuse to disclose even such basic information as total AUM. Other funds fall somewhere in between with respect to reporting lines of authority and mandated levels of disclosure. Figure 2 presents a stylized representation of how a new fund might be organized, funded, staffed, and operated. The nation's culture and political philosophy will be expressed through decisions regarding each variable in this flow diagram. Open, democratic societies typically establish funds through explicit legislation, endow them with financing from a dedicated revenue source, provide specific operating and investment objectives, mandate high standards of employee professionalism and information disclosure, and frequently also give them a mandate to invest ethically (Dimson *et al.*, 2013). Less democratic societies make different choices at these margins when

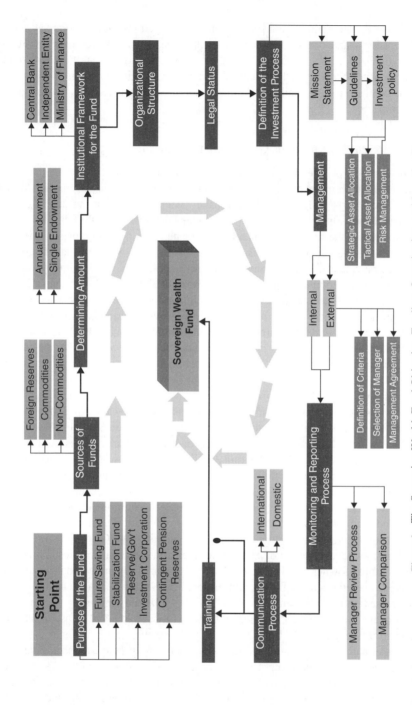

Figure 2. The Sovereign Wealth Fund Objective, Funding, Organization, and Investing Process

Source: Sameer Jain, "Integrating Hedge Fund Strategies in Sovereign Wealth Portfolios," Citi Capital Advisors (November 2009), p. 3.

establishing their funds, with varying emphasis being placed depending on the goals of the sponsoring regime.

2.1 *The Internal Governance and Staffing of SWFs—Why it Matters*

A key fact about all the larger SWFs is that they tend to have very small staffs, even though many funds control assets worth more than $100 billion. Norway's GPFG, China's CIC, and Abu Dhabi's ADIA collectively have fewer than 3000 employees, yet have combined AUM of over $2.28 trillion. In comparison, privately-owned Fidelity Investments has a comparable amount of assets under management [$2.02 trillion as of September 2014], but employs over 41,000 people. These meager SWF staffing levels have two important implications for fund operations and investment management. First, most large funds employ numerous external managers to actually invest the funds' money and oversee segments of their portfolios, as described in Clark and Monk (2009), Dixon and Monk (2013), and Al-Kharusi *et al.* (2014).[16] As in many other areas, Norway's GPFG and ADIA represent polar examples of this tendency. Since GPFG follows an almost purely index-matching investment strategy, it manages over 95 percent of its investment portfolio in-house (through Norges Bank Investment Management, or NBIM), whereas ADIA farms out over two-thirds of its total portfolio to external managers.

The second key implication of the fact that even large SWFs have small professional staffs is that these funds can play only limited direct corporate governance role in the companies in which they invest. At any point in time, Norway's GPFG owns stock in over 8000 companies, so it is unable to assign staff to sit on corporate boards or interact intensively with investee firm managers.[17] Other funds, which do not spread their equity investments as broadly as GPFG, can sometimes assign staff to sit on the boards of a few large investee firms, but almost always in domestic rather than foreign companies. Bortolotti *et al.* (2010) find that SWFs acquire seats in only 53 of 355 cases (14.9%) where director identities of investment targets could be verified, and most of these were domestic companies. Even in those cases, the funds are much more likely to nominate an employee of a fund subsidiary company than from the parent fund itself.

2.2 *Widely Varying Transparency Measures and Recent Changes*

SWFs have long fascinated corporate governance researchers, since their rise to global prominence brought forth a unique new class of major international investors: state-owned investment funds with massive capital bases, with demonstrated tastes for purchasing listed shares across borders, and with no real need to make liquid investments. Various measures of the transparency and internal corporate governance of SWFs have been suggested, but two have been embraced universally enough to be considered standards. The first measure is the continuously updated Linaburg-Maduell Transparency Index, which was developed by Carl Linaburg and Michael Maduell and is used by the Sovereign Wealth Fund Institute (Maduell is the SWFI's founder and current CEO). The second measure is the SWF Scoreboard, popularly called "Truman Scores" after Edwin Truman (2008, 2011), who defined and popularized the Scoreboard.

The two measures are quite similar in stressing how transparent the funds are with respect to their internal organization, the amount of information they disclose about fund investments, and their political distance from the host/sponsoring government. In constructing the index, Truman (2011) links together the following elements into four categories: "(1) structure of the fund, including its objectives, links to the government's fiscal policy, and whether the fund is independent from the countries' international reserves; (2) governance of the fund, including the roles of the government, the board of the fund and its managers, and whether the fund follows guidelines for corporate responsibility; (3) accountability and transparency of the fund in its investment strategy, investment activities, reporting, and audits; and (4) behavior of the fund in managing its portfolio and its risk management policies, including the use of leverage and derivatives" (http://www.iie.com/publications/briefs/truman4983.pdf). The maximum possible Truman score is 100 and the highest score assigned in 2011 (the last year available) is 96, for Norway's GPFG. The lowest assigned score is 15, for both Istithmar World and the Qatar Investment Authority (QIA).

Truman added another transparency/governance measure after 2008—how well individual SWFs complied with the "Santiago Principles" agreed to in September of that year by members of the International Working Group on Sovereign Wealth Funds at an IMF-sponsored conference in Chile (http://www.iwg-swf.org/pubs/gapplist.htm). This working group evolved into the International Sovereign Wealth Fund Forum, and includes the largest SWFs, as well as 25 host and sponsor countries. As with the Truman scores, the maximum "Santiago Principles" value is 100 and Norway's GPFG received a 96 score in 2011, while Qatar Investment Authority (QIA) came in last with a score of 15.

The Linaburg-Maduell Index (http://www.swfinstitute.org/statistics-research/linaburg-maduell-transparency-index/) is based on "ten essential principles that depict sovereign wealth fund transparency to the public." A value of either zero (absent) or one (present) is assigned for each essential principle for each fund, so the best score attainable is 10. The SWF Institute (sponsors and publishers of the index) recommends that a fund must have a minimum value of 8 to be considered adequately transparent, and 25 of the 53 SWFs to which the Institute assigns an Index value in December 2014 have scores of 8 or higher. Ten funds have Index values of 10, while six have Index values of only 1.

2.3 *How Do SWFs Differ from Other Large, Internationally Active Institutional Investors*

As discussed in the introduction, the key question regarding SWFs is whether they truly differ in form, motive, and effect from other large, internationally active institutional investors. In many ways, this question cuts across this survey and is reprised in each section. For example, an analysis of SWF portfolio allocations requires a private-sector comparison group, as in Chhaochharia and Laeven (2009), who compare SWFs to pension funds, and Avendaño and Santiso (2011), who compare SWFs to mutual funds; a discussion of the impact of SWFs on the behavior and governance of investment targets requires a private-sector benchmark, as in Karolyi and Liao (2011), or Bortolotti *et al.* (2014).

Yet, we would like to briefly summarize here the main characteristics that make SWFs truly distinct and that carry important implications of potential interest to academic observers. In this respect, the defining characteristic of SWFs is their state ownership. On the positive side, in terms of social welfare, governments could have broader goals than simple wealth maximization at the firm level—for example, the maximization of employment levels and promotion of broad national industrial interests. On the negative side, politicians might distort priorities through their rent-seeking influence and because they impose on enterprises multiple, perhaps conflicting objectives. As state-owned actors, SWFs might suffer from such deviations from the set of objectives normally associated with private-sector investors, and this, in turn, might translate political influence onto their investment targets. In this sense, SWFs investments suffer from the same problems of "multiple principals" and cognitive dissonance described in the "mixed ownership" model of Boardman and Vining (1989, 2012) and Vining *et al.* (2014). Yet, while many other examples of mixed ownership result in opaque entities, SWFs often apply mixed ownership to publicly traded, and hence transparent, firms allowing for a more data-rich investigation of the impact and efficiency of government investments. Whether this mixed ownership, as Vining *et al.* (2014) put it, results in the "best of both worlds"—merging government's concern for social welfare to private sector efficiency—or in the "worst of both worlds" (crony capitalism) is one of the lessons we can draw by investigating the impact of SWFs on their investment targets.

Second, SWFs, with rare exceptions, have no explicit liabilities—unlike, for example, heavily levered hedge funds or pension funds that have to budget for periodic cash outflows. In this sense, they have the potential to be true long-term shareholders, with very long investment horizons and very low liquidity requirements, possibly becoming the highly effective monitors described in Chen *et al.* (2007). Of course, whether that potential is realized or hampered by low staffing levels, political objectives, and a mistrust of a foreign government as a shareholder is a matter of empirical inquiry.

3. How SWFs Make Target Selection and Portfolio Allocation Decisions

With over $5.4 trillion worth of capital to invest, and a mandate to invest a large chunk of that cash internationally, it is unsurprising that many researchers have examined how SWFs allocate their investment dollars. This section surveys the academic and professional research examining how SWFs *should* allocate funds across different asset classes—based on the funding source and sponsor-country economic, financial and political characteristics—and then summarizes the research examining the asset allocations that SWFs actually do make.

3.1 *Normative Assessments of How SWFs Should Invest*

Many authors have presented normative, theoretical or empirical studies prescribing how SWFs should allocate their funds across asset classes. Twelve such articles are summarized in Table 2. Four of these papers (Martellini and Milhaup, 2010; Sa and Viani, 2011; Schena and Kalter, 2012; Bodie and Brière, 2014) describe optimal asset allocation models for SWFs based on general financial and economic principles relating to global investor preferences, contingent claims models of sovereign government funding sources and spending obligations, and/or the sponsoring nation's sensitivity to commodity price variability. The next three articles (Scherer, 2009; Balding and Yao, 2011; Bertoni and Lugo, 2013) focus on oil-financed SWFs and examine how this funding model should influence the asset allocation decisions of such funds. Two more studies describe the optimal investment policy followed by Norway's Government Pension Fund Global (GPFG) and assess whether the fund's actual asset allocations are consistent with the optimal design (Ang *et al.*, 2009; Chambers *et al.*, 2012). Finally, three studies present, first, a policy-oriented description of the "benchmarks" governments should take into account when establishing a SWF (Ang, 2010); second, an assessment of whether SWFs are and should be domestic "investors of last resort" (Raymond, 2012); and, third, a discussion of whether SWFs should promote domestic economic development by financing infrastructure investments in developing countries (Gelb *et al.*, 2014).

Table 2. Summary of Empirical, Theoretical and Normative Studies of How Sovereign Wealth Fund *Should* Select Asset Classes in Which to Invest. This table summarizes the findings, predictions and/or prescriptions of several recent empirical, theoretical and normative studies of how SWFs *should* allocate funds to different asset classes.

Study	Sample description, study period, and methodology	Summary of empirical findings and conclusions
Gelb, Tordo, and Halland (*OECD* 2014)	Assess whether SWFs should be used to fund the infrastructure financing gap in developing countries. Propose a system of checks and balances to ensure SWFs do not undermine macroeconomic management or make politicized investments.	Conclude that a well-governed SWF can improve the quality of a nation's public investment program, but the critical issue will always be limiting the SWF's investments to those proper for a wealth fund and not to supplant infrastructure investment that should come from other state agencies.
Bodie and Brière (*Journal of Investment Management* 2014)	Set out a new approach to sovereign wealth and risk management, based on contingent claims analysis (CCA). Note that state must solve an asset-liability management (ALM) problem between income and expenditures, and present applications for SWFs.	Propose analytical framework for optimal ALM based on analysis of sovereign balance sheet and extending CCA theory to sovereign wealth. Suggest using broadest possible definition of "sovereign entity" and specifically accounting for nation's financial, human, and resource wealth–and for risks of assets and liabilities. Apply model to Chile's SWF.
Schena and Kalter (*JIBS* 2013)	Ask whether it is time to rethink the "Endowment Model" of sovereign investment to focus on less liquid and relatively higher return assets, as do many university endowment funds.	Acknowledge endowment model's attractiveness, but stress the need for SWFs to consider how the "three Ls" of liabilities, liquidity, and definition of long-term impact the fund's specific needs and goals.
Chambers, Dimson, and Ilmanen (*Journal of Portfolio Management* 2012)	Discuss the management, investment policies, and transparency of the Norwegian Government Pension Fund Global (GPFG) and assess whether the fund has successfully achieved objectives. Assess how fund's strategy derives from Norwegian government's directives and examine fund's long-term investment performance.	Conclude that the GFPG is one of the best-managed large pension fund operating today, and that "the Norway Model" of investing only in listed debt and equity securities worldwide using in-house staff is both successful and is the antithesis of the "Yale Model" of investing in alternative assets and private equity through external managers.

Table 2. (*Continued*)

Study	Sample description, study period, and methodology	Summary of empirical findings and conclusions
Bertoni and Lugo (*WP* 2012)	Using a mean-variance framework, develop a model of the optimal strategic asset allocation for stabilization SWFs (funded by oil revenues). Then derive three sets of parsimonious tests to compare actual SAA of Norway's GPFG to its theoretical optimum.	Find that optimal SAA for an oil-funded SWF will deviate significantly from that of a general wealth-maximizing investor, and confirm that the static and dynamic deviations of the GPFG's SAA from the market equity portfolio are consistent with their theoretical predictions.
Sá and Viani (*WP* 2011)	Develop dynamic general equilibrium model to analyze the effects on target-country real and financial variables of a shift in portfolio preferences of foreign investors, and then calibrate model to examine increasing tendency of central banks to channel 'excess reserves' into SWFs for investments seeking commercial returns.	Derive two separate diversification paths for switching reserves into SWFs. One keeps same asset allocation as central banks, other keeps the same currency allocation. USD depreciates in both cases, but US net debt position differs. Both cause reduction in "exorbitant privilege" wherein US receives excess returns on its assets over what it pays for liabilities.
Balding and Yao (*WP* 2011)	Account for the fact that most SWFs depend heavily on oil revenues to increase their funding base by developing a dynamic portfolio risk-adjusted return maximizing model across many assets, accounting for continual depletion of natural resources.	Find that, given the high volatility and continuous depletion of oil as a portion of national wealth, SWFs should invest in low volatility liquid fixed income and indexed assets to balance their portfolios. Even then, find returns only maximized when oil drops to about 50% of national wealth.
Ang (*WP* 2010)	Presents policy-oriented description of the four "benchmarks" a nation should take into account when creating a SWF and defining the role it should play in overall national policy. These are the benchmarks (B/Ms) of legitimacy, integrated policy, performance and long-run equilibrium. States the essence of a SWF is as a vehicle for transferring sovereign wealth into the future.	The legitimacy B/M is the most important, and ensures fund's capital is not immediately spent. Integrated policy B/M accounts for broader policy environment in which SWF operates. Performance B/M implies fund's managers should be held accountable for maximizing risk-adjusted returns. Long-run equilibrium B/M ensures well-functioning capital markets, free cross-border capital flows and good corporate governance.

(*continued*)

Table 2. (*Continued*)

Study	Sample description, study period, and methodology	Summary of empirical findings and conclusions
Raymond (*Economie Internationale* 2012)	Analyzes whether SWFs are and/or should be domestic investors of last resort (ILR) during financial crises. Shows that such SWF interventions occurred frequently after the 2008–2009 Global Financial Crisis, and discusses SWFs' role as insurance funds against major crises.	Find that Gulf SWFs' interventions exerted a stabilizing short-term effect on local stock markets, though long-term impact much less obvious. Note that SWFs, contrary to central banks, can easily provide medium to long term financing to banking systems. SWFs may also be used for government spending during crises or to negate speculative financial attacks.
Martellini and Milhau (*EDHEC-Risk* 2010)	Propose quantitative dynamic asset allocation framework for SWFs, modeled as large long-term investors that manage fluctuating revenues typically emanating from budget or trade surpluses in the presence of stochastic investment opportunities. Suggest what optimal asset allocation should be.	Optimal asset allocation strategy should account for stochastic features of SWF endowment process (where money comes from) and the SWF's expected liability value (what money will be used for). Should make state-dependent allocations to (1) a performance-seeking portfolio, often heavy with equities; (2) an endowment-hedging portfolio; and (3) a liability-hedging portfolio heavy with bonds to mitigate interest rate and inflation risks.
Scherer (*Financial Market Portfolio Management* 2009)	Extends existing portfolio choice theories to SWFs in a strategic asset allocation model. Changing the existing analyses from single to multi-period framework allows for three-fund separation.	Optimal SWF portfolio should be split into speculative demand as well as demand against oil price shocks and short-term risk-free rate. All model terms also depend on investor's time horizon. Oil-rich countries should hold bonds and SWFs should determine and act on long-run covariance matrices that differ from correlation inputs that one-period investors use.
Ang, Goetzmann, and Schaefer (*NBIM* 2009)	Evaluate the role of active management by the Norges Bank Investment Management (NBIM) of the Norwegian GPFG over the period from inception in 1998 through early 2009. Also present review of efficient market hypothesis and apply lessons to evaluating GPFG's performance.	Find that active management has played a very small role in NBIM's superior long-term investment performance. Instead, a significant fraction of performance is explained by exposure to systematic factors that fared poorly during Crisis. They believe that exposure to such systematic factors is appropriate for a long term investor that can harvest illiquidity and other factor risk premiums over time.

3.1.1 *Financial and Macroeconomic Influences on Optimal SWF Investment Policies*

The studies described here extend existing financial models to incorporate SWF specificities. Martellini and Milhau (2010) propose a quantitative dynamic asset allocation framework for SWFs, modeling them as large long-term investors that manage fluctuating revenues typically emanating from budget or trade surpluses in the presence of stochastic investment opportunities. They show that the optimal asset allocation strategy should account for stochastic features of the SWF endowment process (where money comes from) and the SWF's expected liability value (what money will be used for). SWFs should make state-dependent allocations to (1) a performance-seeking portfolio, often heavy with equities; (2) an endowment-hedging portfolio; and (3) a liability-hedging portfolio heavy with bonds to mitigate interest rate and inflation risks.

Sa and Viani (2011) develop a dynamic general equilibrium model to analyze the effects of a shift in portfolio preferences of foreign investors on target-country interest rates, asset prices, investment, consumption, real output, exchange rates, and current account balances. They then calibrate this model to examine the increasing tendency of central banks to channel "excess reserves" into SWFs to make investments seeking commercial returns, and derive two separate diversification paths for switching reserves into SWFs. One keeps the same asset allocation as central banks, but moves fund flows away from dollar-denominated assets; the other keeps the same currency allocation but shifts investments from U.S. bonds to U.S. equities. The dollar depreciates in both cases, but the U.S. net debt position differs. Both cause reduction in the "exorbitant privilege," through which the United States government receives excess returns on its assets over what it pays for its liabilities.

Schena and Kalter (2012) take a different tack and ask whether SWFs should continue pursuing the "Endowment Model" of investment, which was popularized by David Swensen, Yale University's Chief Investment Officer (Lerner, 2007; Ferri, 2012) and has been followed by many U.S. private university endowments. This emphasizes investing in less liquid and relatively higher return assets rather than publicly traded stocks and bonds. The alternative would be to switch to the classic foundation model of investment in listed securities that Norway's GPFG has pursued so successfully. The authors acknowledge the endowment model's attractiveness, but conclude that the foundation model may be better for large institutional investors operating in today's environment of low risk-free returns, increased volatility, and higher return covariance across markets. Schena and Kalter particularly stress the need for SWFs to consider how the "three Ls" of liabilities, liquidity, and definition of long-term impact the fund's specific needs and goals.

Finally, Bodie and Brière (2014) develop a new approach to sovereign wealth and risk management, based on contingent claims analysis (CCA). They show that it is essential to analyze a sovereign's balance sheet, since the government must solve an asset-liability management (ALM) problem between income and expenditures. They present applications for SWFs and propose an analytical framework for optimal ALM based on analysis of the sovereign's balance sheet and extending CCA theory to sovereign wealth. Bodie and Brière suggest using the broadest possible definition of the "sovereign entity" and specifically accounting for a nation's financial, human, and resource wealth–and for the risks of the nation's assets and liabilities. They conclude by applying their model to Chile's SWF.

3.1.2 *How Oil Revenue-Funding Impacts a SWF's Optimal Asset Allocation Policies*

As noted in Section 2 above, the major SWFs are all funded in one of two ways, either through revenues from exports of oil (or other commodities, including natural gas) for the

Middle Eastern SWFs and Norway's GPFG, or through fiscal transfers from governments of mostly Asian countries that run persistent current account surpluses. Commodity-based funds are more common, both in terms of number of SWFs and aggregate size. Two papers explicitly analyze how this impacts optimal fund asset allocation. Scherer (2009) extends existing portfolio choice theories to SWFs in a strategic asset allocation model. In the model, changing the existing analyses from a single to a multi-period framework allows for three-fund separation; all model terms further depend on the investor's time horizon. The resulting optimal SWF portfolio should be split into a speculative component as well as a hedging component aimed at offsetting oil price shocks and short-term risk-free rate shocks. Oil-rich countries should hold bonds and SWFs should determine and act on long-run covariance matrices that differ from the correlation inputs that a one-period investor would use. Scherer also notes that SWFs seem ill-prepared for an oil price drop that would shrink the value of national cash inflows and increase the importance of the contribution SWF asset returns make to national income.

Balding and Yao (2011) suggest a better asset allocation policy for oil dependent SWFs than the one currently being followed. They account for the fact that most SWFs depend heavily on oil revenues to increase their funding base by developing a dynamic portfolio risk-adjusted return maximizing model across many assets, accounting for continual depletion of natural resources. Balding and Yao find that, given the high volatility and continuous depletion of oil as a portion of national wealth, SWFs should invest in low volatility, liquid, fixed income instruments and indexed assets. Even then, they find returns are only maximized when oil drops to about 50% of national wealth.

Bertoni and Lugo (2013) use a mean-variance framework to develop a model of the optimal strategic asset allocation for stabilization SWFs (those funded by oil revenues). They derive three sets of parsimonious tests to compare the actual allocation of Norway's GPFG to its theoretical optimum. They find that the optimal allocation for an oil-funded SWF will deviate significantly from that of a general wealth-maximizing investor, and confirm that the static and dynamic deviations of the GPFG's portfolio from the market equity portfolio are consistent with their theoretical predictions.

3.1.3 *The Norway Model of Asset Allocation*

The Norway GPFG, with over $850 billion assets under management, is the largest SWF and the second largest pension fund in the world (after Japan's Government Employees Pension Fund). The GPFG has long pursued an asset allocation policy akin to the classic foundation model of investing in publicly traded stocks and bonds, as opposed to the more recently developed endowment model of allocating fund resources much more towards illiquid/unlisted stocks and bonds, real estate, private equity, and alternative and absolute return investments. In addition to the aforementioned Bertoni and Lugo (2013), who develop a generalized model but test it on GPFG's portfolio, two studies focus explicitly on the optimal and actual asset allocations of the GPFG. The Ang et al. (2009) article is actually a report commissioned by the Norwegian government evaluating the role of active management by the Norges Bank Investment Management (NBIM) group of the Norwegian GPFG over the period from inception in 1998 through early 2009. Ang, Goetzmann, and Schaefer show that active management has played a very small role in NBIM's superior long-term investment performance. Instead, a significant fraction of performance is explained by exposure to systematic factors that fared poorly during the global financial crisis of 2008–2009. Approximately 70% of all active returns on the overall fund can be explained by exposure to systematic factors—and the authors believe that the fund *should* adopt a top-down, intentional approach to strategic and dynamic factor exposures. They conclude that the fund should provide volatility insurance to other investors and harvest volatility premiums as compensation. The key features of the GPFG that should influence deviation from market weightings are the fund's absence of any need for liquidity, its very long term investment horizon, and its freedom from explicit fund liabilities.

The Chambers, Dimson, and Ilmanen (CDI) article in the *Journal of Portfolio Management* (2012) has proven highly influential, since it analyses whether the "Norway Model" of investment has proven superior to the "Endowment Model" of investment followed by U.S. private university endowments. As discussed above, the Endowment Model emphasizes investing in alternative assets and private equity through external managers, whereas the Norway Model is virtually its antithesis—and instead mirrors the classic foundation investment approach of investing in publicly traded stocks and bonds, with a small allocation to real estate and other illiquid assets. The authors discuss the management, investment policies, and transparency of the Norwegian Government Pension Fund Global (GPFG) and assess whether the fund has successfully achieved its objectives. They also assess how the fund's strategy derives from the Norwegian government's directives and examine the fund's long-term investment performance. They conclude that the GFPG is one of the best-managed large pension funds operating today, and argue that the Norway Model is a much more appropriate investment strategy for SWFs. In their detailed analysis of the GPFG's performance, CDI point out that the fund resembles an index fund far more than one that is actively managed, and it relies on beta returns—reflecting exposure to systematic risk factors—rather than alpha returns resulting from superior stock picking (Dixon and Monk, 2013). They point out that six factors should and do drive the GPFG's investment strategy: (1) The fund has a long term horizon and little need for liquidity; (2) this long-term horizon makes the fund more tolerant of return volatility and short-term capital flows than most institutional investors; (3) the fund's size makes exploiting liquidity and volatility risk premiums impractical; (4) capacity issues, such as a small staff, favor benchmarks that are at least loosely linked to market capitalization; (5) the fund may most effectively earn liquidity and other premiums by serving as an opportunistic liquidity provider purchasing unpopular assets in illiquid markets; and (6) as long as oil remains a significant underground resource, the fund has less need for inflation hedging than most investors. It is worth noting that many SWFs, especially the larger ones, share all or most of these same features.

3.1.4 *Other Assessments of Optimal SWF Investment Policy*

What other aspects of SWF establishment, funding, and asset allocation have researchers considered normatively? Ang (2010) presents a policy-oriented description of the four "benchmarks" a nation should take into account when creating a SWF and defining the role it should play in overall national policy. These are the benchmarks (B/Ms) of legitimacy, integrated policy, performance and long-run equilibrium. He states the essence of a SWF is as a vehicle for transferring sovereign wealth into the future, and concludes that the legitimacy B/M is the most important, since this ensures the fund's capital is not immediately spent. The integrated policy B/M accounts for the broader policy environment in which a SWF operates, and the performance B/M implies a fund's managers should be held accountable for maximizing risk-adjusted returns. The long-run equilibrium B/M ensures well-functioning capital markets, free cross-border capital flows, and good corporate governance.

Raymond (2012) assesses whether SWFs are and/or should be domestic investors of last resort (ILR) during financial crises. She documents that such SWF interventions occurred frequently after the 2008–2009 Global Financial Crisis, and discusses SWFs' role as insurance funds against major crises. The author finds that Gulf SWFs' interventions exerted a stabilizing short-term effect on local stock markets during the global financial crisis, though the long-term impact has been much less obvious. She notes that SWFs, contrary to central banks, can easily provide medium- to long-term financing to banking systems, and concludes that SWFs may also be used for government spending during crises or to negate speculative financial attacks. In sum, Raymond concludes by answering her own question whether SWFs should be investors of last resort in domestic markets with a definitive "perhaps."

Finally, Gelb et al. (2014) assess whether SWFs should be used to fund the infrastructure financing gap in developing countries. They propose a system of checks and balances to ensure SWFs do not undermine macroeconomic management or make politicized investments. They conclude that a well-governed SWF can improve the quality of a nation's public investment program, but the critical issue will always be limiting the SWF's investments to those proper for a wealth fund and not to supplant infrastructure investment that should come from other state agencies.

3.2 Asset Allocations and Portfolio Selections Observed in Practice

While one set of academic studies examines how SWFs *should* invest, another stream of research documents and analyzes how funds actually *do* invest. We summarize eleven such papers in Table 3. Four of these papers (Chhaochharia and Laeven, 2009; Dyck and Morse, 2011; Karolyi and Liao, 2011; Avendano, 2012) document the actual portfolio decisions of SWFs using large samples of investment observations, examine what factors might be driving these decisions, and ask whether SWFs differ significantly from other large international investors with respect to how and in which types of companies they invest. The largest samples used in any type of SWF empirical studies are observed here. The next three articles (Candelon et al., 2011; Avendaño and Santiso, 2011; Knill et al., 2012b) assess whether political and macroeconomic factors significantly influence observed SWF investment decisions. Heaney et al. (2011) examine how SWFs select specific companies into which to invest and which factors influence that decision. Finally, two studies (Bernstein et al., 2013; Johan et al., 2013) measure how much SWFs invest in private equity (PE) worldwide, and assess why these funds seem to allocate less to PE than do other internationally active institutional investors.

3.2.1 Documenting SWF Portfolios and Assessing Factors Influencing Investment Decisions

The studies surveyed here employ large samples to document actual SWF portfolios and assess which factors significantly influence fund investment decisions. Chhaochharia and Laeven (2009) use a sample of 29,634 equity investments made by 27 SWFs and 38,880 stock investments made by public pension funds in firms from 56 countries over 1996–2008 to test whether SWFs show systematic investment biases compared to other large global investors. They find that SWFs do show strong biases vs other investors, specifically that: (1) SWFs tend to invest in countries that share a common culture, particularly religion; (2) this bias is more pronounced in SWFs than in other internationally active institutional investors; (3) this cultural bias disappears with repeated investments; (4) SWFs display industry biases, investing a disproportionally large fraction of their portfolios in oil company stocks; and (5) they tend to

Table 3. Summary of Empirical Studies of Sovereign Wealth Funds' Geographic and Industrial Investment Patterns. This table summarizes the findings of several recent empirical studies examining how SWFs allocate funds to different countries and different industries.

Study	Sample description, study period, and methodology	Summary of empirical findings and conclusions
Bernstein, Lerner, and Schoar (*JEP* 2013)	Use sample of 2662 direct private equity (PE) investments worth $198 bn made by 29 SWFs over 1984–2007 to analyze whether there exist differences in investment strategy and performance across funds regarding PE investing.	Find SWFs seem to engage in trend chasing, since they are more likely to invest in PE at home when domestic equity prices are higher, and invest abroad when foreign prices are higher—but SWFs invest at lower overall P/E ratios domestically. SWFs where politicians are involved are much more likely to invest at home than are SWFs with external managers.
Johan, Knill, and Mauck (*JIBS* 2013)	Examines empirically investments of 50 SWFs in 903 public and private global firms to see whether these funds are less likely to invest in private equity (PE) than other large institutional investors.	Find SWFs are less likely to invest in PE than are other investors, but economic significance surprisingly low. Find some evidence that SWFs invest internationally with political motivations in mind, perhaps to gain politically from corporate governance conflicts.
Avendaño (*WP* 2012)	Using sample of over 14,000 individual holdings of 22 SWFs in almost 8000 target firms in 65 countries over 2006–2009, studies how differences in funding source (commodity/noncommodity), investment guidelines (OECD/non-OECD), and investment destination (foreign/domestic) impact SWF investment decisions.	Finds SWFs prefer to invest in larger and internationally active firms, but OECD-based and non-OECD-based funds differ in their preferences about target-firm leverage, degree of internationalization, and profitability. SWFs prefer larger, more levered firms in foreign vs domestic investments, and find some evidence SWF ownerships positively impacts target's value. Home-country natural resource endowments help explain whether SWFs prefer to make foreign investments in these industries.
Knill, Lee, and Mauck (*Journal of Corporate Finance* 2012)	Use sample of over 900 acquisitions of public and private target firm stock by SWFs over 1984–2009 to test whether bilateral political relations significantly influence SWF investment decisions. Use Cragg Model to test whether political factors impact both decisions whether SWFs will invest and how much.	Find that political relations are an important factor in where SWFs invest, but matter less in determining how much. SWFs are more likely to invest in countries with which they have *weaker* political relations, contrary to the predictions of the FDI literature, suggesting that SWFs use—at least partially—nonfinancial motives in investment decisions.

(continued)

Table 3. (*Continued*)

Study	Sample description, study period, and methodology	Summary of empirical findings and conclusions
Avendaño and Santiso (*Book* 2011)	Examine whether SWF investments are politically biased by comparing almost 14,000 shareholdings of 17 SWFs to 11,600 shareholdings of the 25 largest mutual funds during 4Q2008. Ask whether SWF holdings show greater political influence than those by privately owned mutual funds.	Find that SWF investment decisions do not differ greatly from those of privately owned mutual funds, and conclude that the fear that sovereigns with political motivations will use their financial power to secure large stakes in Western companies is unfounded. Argue that double standards for SWFs and private institutional investors should be avoided.
Karolyi and Liao (*WP* 2011)	Study 4026 cross-border acquisitions over 1998–2008, worth $434 bn, that were led by government-controlled acquirers, and compare to 127,786 similar acquisitions worth $9.04 tr made by private acquirers and 733 deals worth $158 bn made by SWFs and other state-owned funds. Test whether state-controlled acquirers and SWFs/other funds selected targets in different industries or with different firms characteristics than did private acquirers.	Find surprisingly small, though often significant, differences between state-controlled acquirers' and private acquirers' investment patterns and preferences, but find somewhat larger differences with SWFs/other state funds. SWFs/other state funds pursue larger targets with higher growth options, and are more deterred by high insider or institutional share ownership. Conclude there is little reason for target-country policy-makers to discriminate against state-owned vs private acquirers.
Dyck and Morse (*WP* 2011)	Use sample of share holdings in 2008 by 20 SWFs in over 26,000 companies worth $2.04 tr to document SWF portfolio holdings and analyze objectives underlying observed investments. Also test whether SWF investments motivated by home-country portfolio diversification or industrial planning objectives.	Find SWF allocations are balanced across risky asset classes, very home-region biased, and biased towards the financial, transportation, energy, and telecommunications industries (especially finance). Measures capturing portfolio diversification and industrial planning objectives explain 14.4% of SWF portfolio variation; industrial motives account for 45% of this.

Table 3. (*Continued*)

Study	Sample description, study period, and methodology	Summary of empirical findings and conclusions
Candelon, Kerkour, and LeCourt (*WP* 2011)	Using sample of 1123 equity investments (849 foreign, 274 domestic) by SWFs in 73 countries over 1989–2011, examine whether and how macroeconomic factors influence SWFs' foreign and domestic equity investments. Also test whether decisions are based exclusively on profit-maximizing motives.	Find macroeconomic factors are important influences on SWFs' investing decisions. SWFs largely invest to diversify away from industries at home, but do so mostly in countries with economic and institutional stability. Use different criteria to decide on investments in OECD vs non-OECD countries, and tend to re-invest in a country once initial investment made.
Heaney, Li, and Valencia (*Australian Journal of Management*, 2011)	Document and analyze investments made by Temasek Holdings (TH) in 150 publicly listed Singaporean companies over the period 2000–2004.	Find that TH prefers to invest in companies that are relatively large, with lower systematic risk, that have few director block-holders, and use stock-based incentive compensation schemes.
Fernandes (*WP* 2011)	Uses sample of 8000 SWF share holdings in 58 countries over 2002–2007 to examine how SWFs select target firms, and test whether and how SWFs investments create value for target firms.	Documents that SWFs prefer large and profitable firms, they have a strong bias for highly visible companies with high analyst coverage. They prefer companies in countries with good governance standards and efficient institutions, but their holdings are unrelated to target firm's level of R&D.
Chhaochharia and Laeven (*WP* 2010)	Use a sample of 29,634 equity investments made by 27 SWFs and 38,880 stock investments made by public pension funds in firms from 56 countries over 1996–2008 to test whether SWFs show systematic investment biases compared to other large global investors.	Find SWFs do show strong biases vs other investors. They tend to chase past returns and hold conservative portfolios that are poorly diversified both geographically and across industries (SWF portfolios are heavily overweight oil companies). Biases are more pronounced for SWFs that are more activist, less transparent, and from less democratic countries. SWFs prefer to invest in countries with strong legal institutions.

invest mostly in large capitalization stocks. These biases are more pronounced for SWFs that are more activist, less transparent, and from less democratic countries. SWFs tend to chase past returns and hold conservative portfolios that are poorly diversified both geographically and across industries (SWF portfolios are heavily overweight in oil companies), and they prefer to invest in countries with strong legal institutions.

Dyck and Morse (2011) similarly use a large sample to document SWF portfolio holdings and analyze the objectives underlying these observed investments. Their sample captures holdings in 2008 by 20 SWFs in over 26,000 companies, with an aggregate value of $2.04 trillion. They find that SWF asset allocations are balanced across risky asset classes, are substantially home-region biased, and are very biased towards the financial, transportation, energy, and telecommunications industries—particularly finance (SWFs owned 4.8% of the world's listed financial company stocks in 2008). SWFs invest actively (with control rights) in both public and private sectors, but mainly exercise control in their home regions. Dyck and Morse also test whether SWF investments are motivated by home-country portfolio diversification or industrial planning objectives and find that measures capturing portfolio diversification and industrial planning objectives explain 14.4% of SWF portfolio variation; industrial motives account for 45% of this.

Karolyi and Liao (2011) employ a large number of cross-border equity investment observations to determine if state-controlled investors have a differential valuation impact on acquisition targets than do private, corporate acquirers. They study 4026 cross-border acquisitions over 1998–2008, worth $434 billion, that were led by government-controlled acquirers, and compare these to 127,786 similar acquisitions worth $9.04 trillion made by private acquirers and 733 deals worth $158 billion made by SWFs and other state-owned funds. They test whether state-controlled acquirers and SWFs/other funds select targets in different industries or with different firm characteristics than do private acquirers. They find surprisingly small, though often significant, differences between state-controlled acquirers' and private acquirers' investment patterns and preferences, but find somewhat larger differences with SWFs/other state funds. SWFs/other state funds pursue larger targets with higher growth options, and are more deterred by high insider or institutional share ownership. Karolyi and Liao conclude there is little reason for target-country policy-makers to discriminate against state-owned versus private acquirers.

Avendano (2012) uses a sample of over 14,000 individual holdings of 22 SWFs in almost 8000 target firms in 65 countries over 2006–2009 to study how differences in funding source (commodity/noncommodity), investment guidelines (OECD/nonOECD), and investment destination (foreign/domestic) impact SWF investment decisions. He finds SWFs prefer to invest in larger and internationally active firms, but OECD-based and non-OECD-based funds differ in their preferences about target-firm leverage, degree of internationalization, and profitability. SWFs prefer larger, more levered firms in foreign versus domestic investments, and Avendano finds some evidence that SWF ownership positively impacts the target firm's value. Home-country natural resource endowments help explain whether SWFs prefer to make foreign investments in these industries.

With over $5.4 trillion of assets under management, it is natural that most SWF research has focused on industrial and national influences on their investments, but Heaney, Li, and Valencia (2011) focus on the investments made by a single (albeit very important) fund, Singapore's Temasek, with a focus on firm selection criteria. They document and analyze investments made by Temasek Holdings (TH) in 150 publicly listed Singaporean companies over the period 2000–2004, and find that Temasek prefers to invest in companies that are relatively large, with low systematic risk, that have few director block-holders, and use stock-based incentive compensation schemes.

3.2.2 *Do Political and Macroeconomic Factors Influence SWF Asset Allocation Policies?*

One of the great fears surrounding SWF cross-border investments is that these will be made for noncommercial reasons and that political or macroeconomic forces will instead prove decisive. Two studies assess whether these fears are justified. Candelon *et al.* (2011) employ a sample of 1123 equity investments (849 foreign, 274 domestic) by SWFs in 73 countries over 1989–2011 to examine whether and how macroeconomic factors influence SWFs' foreign and domestic equity investments. They also test whether decisions are based exclusively on profit-maximizing motives. They find that macroeconomic factors are important influences on SWFs' investing decisions and that SWFs largely invest to diversify away from industries at home, but do so mostly in countries with economic and institutional stability. SWFs use different criteria to decide on investments in OECD vs non-OECD countries, and tend to re-invest in a country once an initial investment has been made.

Avendaño and Santiso (2011) examine whether SWF investments are politically biased by comparing almost 14,000 shareholdings of 17 SWFs to 11,600 shareholdings of the 25 largest mutual funds during the fourth quarter of 2008. They ask whether SWF holdings show greater political influence than stakes held by privately owned mutual funds. The authors find that SWF investment decisions do not differ greatly from those of privately owned mutual funds, and conclude that the fear that sovereigns with political motivations will use their financial power to secure large stakes in Western companies is unfounded. They argue that double standards for SWFs and private institutional investors should be avoided.

Knill *et al.* (2012b) use a sample of over 900 acquisitions of public and private target firm stock by SWFs over 1984–2009 to test whether bilateral political relations significantly influence SWF investment decisions. They find that political relations are an important factor in where SWFs invest, but matter less in determining the size of the investment. SWFs are more likely to invest in countries with which they have *weaker* political relations, contrary to the predictions of the foreign direct investment literature, suggesting that SWFs have—at least partially—nonfinancial motives in investment decisions.

3.2.3 *Do SWFs Invest in and through Private Equity?*

Many commentators, noting the political difficulties SWFs often encounter when they purchase large share blocs in publicly traded companies, have suggested that SWFs should invest indirectly instead, by channeling their assets through private equity funds. Two studies assess whether SWFs in fact do this. Bernstein *et al.* (2013) use a sample of 2662 direct private equity (PE) investments worth $198 billion made by 29 SWFs over 1984–2007 to analyze whether there exist differences in investment strategy and performance across funds regarding PE investing. They find SWFs seem to engage in trend chasing, since they are more likely to invest in PE at home when domestic equity prices are higher, and invest abroad when foreign prices are higher—but that SWFs invest at lower overall P/E ratios domestically. SWFs where politicians are involved are much more likely to invest at home than are SWFs with external managers, but greater domestic investment is a symptom of poor investment decision-making, since the funds are prone to home bias or have decisions distorted by political or agency considerations.

Johan *et al.* (2013) examine empirically investments made by 50 SWFs in 903 public and private global firms to see whether these funds are less likely to invest in private equity (PE) than are other large institutional investors. They find that SWFs are less likely to invest in PE than are other investors, but the economic significance of this is surprisingly low. The authors find some evidence that SWFs invest internationally with political motivations in mind, perhaps to gain politically from corporate governance conflicts or to avoid the intense scrutiny and criticisms of the public faced by Dubai World Ports and other investors caught up in controversial cross-border acquisitions (Dinç and Erel, 2013).

3.3 *Geographic and Industrial Distribution of SWF Investments*

So how have SWFs besides Norway's GPFG allocated their assets across countries and industries? Unfortunately, every discussion of SWF asset allocation must start with the recognition that most of these funds are fairly opaque in their allocations. Of course, notable exceptions exist, such as Norway's GPFG, but the norm is one of limited disclosure. Hence, it is impossible to say much about the large portion of SWF assets invested in corporate and sovereign debt and little is known about their real estate portfolios. Research has instead offered an analysis, and even that is incomplete, of SWF equity investments in publicly traded firms, as most regulatory regimes require disclosure of these.

Table 4 presents summary statistics on the investments documented in the Sovereign Investment Laboratory SWF database (presented in Table 1, except the Saudi Arabian Monetary Agency) over the period 1988–November 2012 (Bortolotti *et al.*, 2013). This table summarizes the 1634 investments of all types—in listed stock, real estate and private equity—contained in the SIL database, and reveals that Norway's GPFG made the largest number of investments (409), but since these were all quite small the total value was only $7.9 billion. The China Investment Corporation invested the largest aggregate amount ($98.96 billion in 74 deals), but this total is swollen by a handful of massive domestic investments required to recapitalize several state-owned banks preparatory to their partial privatization. The two Singaporean SWFs, Temasek and GIC, collectively made more (618 deals) investments than any other country, though the 211 deals by the five UAE-based funds on this list had an aggregate value, $168.1 billion, that exceeds Singapore's combined $156.2 billion total.

Columns 5 and 6 of Table 4, referencing the fraction of deals that were cross-border (foreign) rather than domestic, clearly support the common perception that SWFs target the vast bulk of their investments outside of their home markets (Megginson, 2013). Foreign investments represent 82.4% of all SWF investments by number and 69.1% by value over 1988–2012 and, if anything, this trend seems to be increasing recently. Many commentators have noted that SWFs tend to make more foreign than domestic investments and that domestic investments differ quite dramatically from the international investments these same funds typically make. Though this seems quite logical at first glance, such a pattern is actually well outside the norm of institutional investment long observed in western economies, which invariably show a decided "home equity bias" disproportionately favoring the stocks of companies headquartered in the same country (Hau and Rey, 2008; Bekaert and Wang, 2009). This literature shows that–apart from specialist investment vehicles, such as "emerging market" or "global growth" funds–the typical U.S. or European pension fund or mutual fund invests two to four times as much in their home equity markets as a portfolio diversification, risk-adjusted return maximizing strategy indicates they should. Although the motivations underlying SWFs' domestic versus international investment choices have not yet been fully examined empirically, the funds

Table 4. Investment Statistics for the Sovereign Wealth Funds in the Sovereign Investment Laboratory's SWF Database. This table describes the number and total value of investments made by the SWFs in the SIL database from 1988 to November 2012, as well as the fraction of those deals (by number and value) that are foreign rather than domestic, the average percentage stake purchased, the largest single investment for each SWF (and whether this was a domestic or foreign acquisition), and the average and median size investment documented for each fund.

Country	Fund name	# of deals	Value of deals, $million	Fraction of foreign deals		Avg stake purchased, %	Largest deal, $million	Average deal size, $million	Median deal size, $million
				by # deals	by $ value				
China	China Investment Corporation	74	98,961	66.7	39.6	14.02	20,000 (dom)	1,337	500
Singapore	Temasek Holdings	399	86,633	68.8	81.1	20.78	4,400 (dom)	217.1	25.1
Qatar	Qatar Investment Authority	89	83,204	66.3	68.2	11.29	13,260 (dom)	934.9	254.9
Singapore	Government Investment Corporation	219	69,487	98.0	95.3	7.70	9,760 (for)	317.3	90.0
UAE-Abu Dhabi	Mubadala Development Company	50	55,992	65.9	59.3	32.81	7,000 (for)	1119.8	500.0
UAE-Dubai	Intl Petroleum Investment Company	51	55,142	81.8	93.0	28.07	8,000 (for)	1081.2	310.1
UAE-Abu Dhabi	Abu Dhabi Investment Authority	48	32,929	82.9	63.6	5.35	8,000 (dom)	686.0	114.7
Kuwait	Kuwait Investment Authority	37	31,472	84.6	77.0	7.38	4,100 (for)	850.6	485.0
Malaysia	Khazanah Nasional Berhard	86	22,516	31.3	38.7	18.29	5,339 (for)	261.8	69.8
UAE-Dubai	Istithmar World	50	13,700	94.0	92.3	27.31	1,350 (for)	274.0	170.0

(continued)

Table 4. (*Continued*)

Country	Fund name	# of deals	Value of deals, $million	Fraction of foreign deals		Avg stake purchased, %	Largest deal, $million	Average deal size, $million	Median deal size, $million
				by # deals	by $ value				
UAE-Dubai	Dubai Intl Financial Corporation	12	10,306	91.7	92.1	23.95	3,397 (for)	858.6	413.0
Norway	Government Pension Fund – Global[1]	409	7,920	100.0	100.0	0.33	1,016 (for)	19.4	3.8
Libya	Libyan Investment Authority	39	7,387	87.2	51.7	21.91	2,000 (dom)	189.4	88.0
Australia	Australian Future Fund	14	5,283	62.5	39.7	1.13	1,973 (for)	377.4	228.6
China	National Social Security Fund	6	4,094	50.0	93.5	—	2,195 (for)	682.3	100.0
Korea	Korea Investment Corporation	13	3,051	70.0	85.0	8.47	2,000 (for)	234.7	99.0
Oman	Oman Investment Fund	14	2,915	100.0	100.0	10.62	645 (for)	208.2	127.7
Oman	State General Reserve Fund	5	1,360	100.0	100.0	30.0	900 (for)	292.0	128.0
	10 Other Funds	19	9,190	62.5	80.6	15.02	5,400 (for)	487.0	150.0
	Total, All Funds	1,634	601,542	82.4	69.1	7.90	20,000 (dom)	368.4	40.1
	Total Excluding Norway GPDF	1,225	593,622	75.9	68.7	16.25	20,000 (dom)	485.0	100.0

clearly seem to invest the majority of their funds internationally for two principal reasons. First, as wealth funds they are attempting to invest for the long term in financial assets with different macroeconomic and political exposures than their domestic economies, and the best way to achieve this is to invest in global equities—especially those of developed economies. Second, since many SWFs are very large funds based in relatively small economies, they are forced to invest abroad in order not to engender the monumental asset price bubble that would result from channeling investments into domestic stocks, bonds, and real estate.

We analyze, but in the interest of space do not present, the geographical distribution of SWF investments over this period. This analysis clearly reveals one important trend, but hides a second. The first, clear trend is SWFs' preference to invest in the developed economies of North America and, especially, Western Europe. The second, less clear trend is the tendency of SWFs to focus almost all of the investment that is not allocated to western countries on their domestic markets. Thus, the bulk of investment for the Asia-Pacific region actually represents Chinese investments by CIC, Singaporean investments by Temasek and GIC, Malaysian investments by Khazanah, and so on. Much as SWF managers might talk about desiring to invest regionally, or in emerging markets, in fact the vast bulk of these funds' investment that is not allocated domestically is funneled to the developed markets of America and Europe—particularly the English common law (La Porta *et al.*, 1998) countries of Canada, the United States, and Great Britain.

Finally, Figure 3 summarizes the industrial allocation of SWF investments over 1988–2012. This figure clearly reveals that SWFs favor investing in companies in the financial industry over all others. The 137 investments in banking and financial service firms account for only one-sixth (16.6%) of all deals by number, but their combined value represents almost two-thirds (65.3%) of the value of all acquisitions. This preference for financial investments is, however, a fairly recent phenomenon; sovereign funds allocated less than one-fifth of their investments to financial firms as recently as 2006, and allocated even smaller fractions to financial companies in previous years. Other industries attracting significant SWF investment

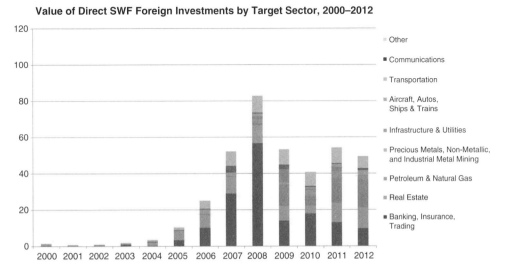

Figure 3. Value of Direct SWF Foreign Investment by Target Sector, 2000–2012
Source: Sovereign Investment Laboratory, 2013. *Sovereign Wealth Fund Annual Report 2012.*

are real estate development and services and REITs (7.9% of deals, 4.0% of value), oil and gas producers (4.1% of deals, 3.8% of value), chemicals (3.0% of deals, 3.2% of value) and general industrials (1.2% of deals, 3.2% of value).

3.4 *Recent Trends in SWF investments*

The Sovereign Investment Laboratory has now collected, but not yet publicized, SWF investment data for all of 2013, and the first part of 2014. Analyzing these data, as well as published summaries from other sources, allows us to highlight several key trends that have emerged regarding SWF investment patterns recently. These trends include the following: (1) Although the majority of SWF investment remains targeted towards developed markets with safe institutions and financial regulation, there has been a sharp divergence of investment away from North America and towards Europe, especially Britain; (2) There has been a surge of interest in acquiring real estate assets, which accounted for 26% of all SWF purchases in 2012. Once again, this has been targeted principally towards Europe and especially London (though the U.S. still remains a favored target for real estate investments, despite the trend previously mentioned); (3) Joint ventures and co-investing have increased in importance and attractiveness. This allows SWFs to directly invest in high-quality, big-ticket deals with western investment funds and developers at less risk than going-it-alone and with lower fees than fully out-sourcing investments; (4) There is an enduring interest in finance, which remains by far the most favored target, but there is also growing interest in allocating funds to private equity. This has long seemed to be a logical target as it finesses political problems with state-owned funds investing directly, while still accessing the best deal flow; (5) All large funds are bringing asset management in-house by building up internal analyst teams and bulking up with domestic or expatriate specialists. Some, especially GPFG, are much farther along than others, though even ADIA now manages one-third of new investments in-house; (6) the Norway Model (the classic foundation model) of investment, or variants thereon, are fast becoming the industry standard. This involves investing in mostly public equities (60–65%), traded fixed income (30–35%) and increasingly real estate (1–5%) and some alternative assets such as private equity. This involves mostly index-oriented, low cost investing rather than large direct stake purchases. Norway's managerial structure and internal governance are also becoming the model to emulate, especially for newly created funds; and (7) here has been major growth—albeit from a small base—in SWF funding and investment in sub-Saharan Africa. This is now the world's fastest growing continent and several countries there are launching new funds to protect resource endowments, all based to one degree or another on the Norway model.

4. The Impact of SWF Investments on Target Firms

4.1.1 *How State Ownership Itself Should Impact Firm Values*

A large literature examines empirically whether state ownership of domestic corporate equity is associated with increased or reduced firm value, and most of these studies conclude that government stockholdings tend to correlate with lower firm market values (Boubakri and Cosset, 1998; Chen, Schipper, Xu and Xue, 2012; Lin and Bo, 2012). The findings of this literature offer more support for the "political view" that state ownership is engineered to redistribute corporate wealth to connected groups and individuals (Megginson, Nash, van Randenborgh, 1994; Sapienza, 2004; Dinç, 2005; Avsar, Karayalcin, Ulubasoglu, 2013; Iannotta, Nocera,

Sironi, 2013; Acharya, Anginer, Warburton, 2013) than the competing "social view," which attributes socially benign intentions to state investors.

4.1.2 *Evidence on Different Types of State Owners*

There is as yet surprisingly little research examining whether all types of state owners have the same impact on target firm value, even though logic suggests a nation's finance ministry will have different motivations, capabilities, and effects than will its state-controlled pension fund. What little research examining the differential effect of various state actors that has been executed has focused largely on Chinese publicly traded companies. Chen *et al.* (2008), Lin and Su (2008), Jiang *et al.* (2010), Chen *et al.* (2009), Houston *et al.* (2010), and Berkman *et al.* (2010) all examine whether share ownership (or transfers from state to private ownership) by state ministries, state asset management bureaus, and state-owned enterprises are associated with differential impacts on target firms. These studies generally conclude that SOEs connected with the national government, or which have substantial private ownership, are associated with higher valuations than are shareholdings of and ownership transfers to asset management bureaus, local and regional governments, and SOEs affiliated with local and regional governments.

We are aware of only five non-Chinese empirical studies examining the valuation impacts of different types of state ownership or that compare the effects of comparable state and private investors. Woitdke (2002) shows that stock ownership by private, unaffiliated US pension funds enhances target firm values, whereas investment by public and affiliated pension funds do not. Gianetti and Laeven (2009) find that size and independence of Swedish pension funds seems to matter more than does a simple state-versus-private dichotomy, as only large, unaffiliated public and private funds are associated with value creation. Karolyi and Liao (2011) reach a similar conclusion in their study of cross-border stock acquisitions by state-owned entities and corporate acquirers; both are associated with nearly identical announcement period and long term target stock returns, though state-owned investment funds are associated with significantly less positive target firm stock returns. Lin *et al.* (2011) differentiate between four types of stockholders in their study documenting that a large control-cash flow wedge has a less substantial valuation impact for state controlled firms than for those controlled by families or for widely held companies. The fifth paper, by Oum *et al.* (2006), is the only non-Chinese study that examines the impact of multiple (six) types of majority-state ownership and mixed state and private ownership on the operating and financial performance of major airports in North America, Asia, and western Europe. They find that airports run by majority-private entities are the most efficient, whereas those run by multiple levels of governments and mixed majority-state/minority-private entities are least efficient.

To summarize, while empirical evidence strongly suggests that private ownership should generally be considered superior to state ownership, little existing research can guide our predictions of how different types of state owners might impact target firm value differentially. Some classes of government entities are more likely to be involved in the management and monitoring of their acquisition targets than are others. In particular, government entities such as SOEs are often more closely involved in the management of investment targets than are pure state actors, such as the central government or local/regional governments. To date, however, only the papers described below have studied the effect of SWF investment on target firms, and only two of these (Karolyi and Liao, 2011; Bortolotti *et al.*, 2014) compare the impact of SWF investments to those of comparable privately owned investors.

4.2 *The Impact of SWFs on Target Firm Financial Performance and Value*

Academic researchers and professional commentators have published a large number of mostly descriptive articles examining different aspects of the SWF phenomenon, and these studies have appeared in both scholarly and professional publications. Most of the corporate finance research on SWFs has, however, focused on the specific issue of how SWF investments have impacted the financial, operating, and corporate governance performance of the companies in whose stocks the funds invest. This section surveys 10 articles examining the impact that SWF investments have had on target firms' financial performance. We categorize these studies into three groups and present summaries of their methodologies and empirical findings in Table 5. The first group of studies employs event study methodology to examine the initial (announcement period) and long-run impact that news of SWF investment has on a target firm's stock price, while the second group studies how SWF investments affect the operating performance of investment targets and the third group studies how SWF stock purchases impact the longer term valuation and credit risk of investment targets.

4.2.1 *Event Studies of the Short and Long-Term Stock Price Effects of Investment in Listed Targets*

The five papers (Dewenter *et al.*, 2010; Kotter and Lel, 2011; Sojli and Tham, 2011; Karolyi and Liao, 2011; Bortolotti *et al.*, 2014) that examine how target firm stock prices react to news that a SWF has acquired an equity stake in the target all use standard event study methods to examine short (announcement-period) effects. All five studies reach generally similar conclusions, finding that the short term reaction to an announced SWF equity investment in a listed company yields significant positive announcement-period excess returns of 1–3%. Those which examine long-run returns generally document significantly negative excess returns, at least for some investment horizons. However, only two of these studies (Karolyi and Liao, 2011; Bortolotti *et al.*, BFM, 2014) explicitly test whether the average stock price reaction to news of a SWF investment is significantly different than the average reaction following announcements of investments in listed firms made by otherwise similar privately owned institutional and corporate investors. Both show that the average excess return associated with a SWF investment is less than half as large as that associated with investments by private investors; in other words, both document a "SWF discount."

Dewenter *et al.* (2010) analyze the short and long-term impact of SWF investments on target firm values using a sample of 227 stock purchases and 47 SWF stock sales over January 1987–April 2008. They examine whether there is a trade-off between SWF monitoring and lobbying benefits and tunneling and expropriation costs. They find significant announcement period (−1,+1) excess returns for SWF stock purchases (+1.52%) and divestments (−1.37%). They also document significantly negative median 1-year cumulative market-adjusted excess returns (−4.5%), but significantly positive median 3-year (+7.3%) and 5-year (+31.2%) returns for target firm stocks after SWF investments. Dewenter, Han, and Malatesta further find a nonmonotonic relationship between the size of the stakes purchased, with the abnormal returns first rising and then falling – and a similar result for their sample of divestments. Finally, the authors examine the behavior of investment targets and identify a series of events they associate with SWF monitoring or influence, including related-party investments and government regulatory actions affecting the investment target. They conclude that SWFs are active monitors, with over half of target firms experiencing one or more events indicating SWF monitoring or influence.

Table 5. Summary of Empirical Studies Examining Impact of Sovereign Wealth Fund Equity Investments on Target Firm Financial Performance. This table summarizes several recent empirical studies examining how SWF stock purchases impact the short and long-term stock return and financial performance of investee companies.

Study	Sample description, study period, and methodology	Summary of empirical findings and conclusions
Bortolotti, Fotak, and Megginson (*WP* 2014)	Construct a dataset of 1018 investments by SWFs (or by SWF-owned investment subsidiaries) in publicly traded firms completed over the 1980–November 2012 period. We generate a "benchmark" control sample of stock purchases by financial investors from the same home countries as our sample of SWFs, targeted at firms headquartered in the same countries as SWF investment targets, and executed over the same time period.	They find that announcements of SWF investments are associated with significant mean abnormal returns of 0.9% over $(-1,+1)$, including investments by Norway's GPFG, and 2.45% without Norway. However, these are significantly lower than the 5.02% mean abnormal returns generated by the private benchmark investors, implying the existence of a sovereign wealth fund "discount" due to their government ownership.
Borisova, Fotak, Holland, and Megginson (*WP* 2014)	Using a sample of 6671 credit spreads from 1723 bonds issued by 244 firms from 43 countries over 1991–2010, examine the impact that state ownership (including 1060 firm-years with SWF investment) of a firm's stock has on that company's cost of debt, as measured by the yield spread above treasuries. Examine for full sample period and after 2008 Financial Crisis.	In the full 1990–2010 sample, they find that state ownership (0/1) is associated with significantly higher (40 bp) cost of debt, and this is even larger during pre-crisis period, 1990–2007. From 2008 on, basic cost of debt rises sharply, and state ownership becomes associated with significantly lower (18bp) cost of corporate debt. SWFs specifically are associated with a higher cost of debt both before (46.7 bp) and after (26.1 bp) the Crisis begins.
Fernandes (*JACF* 2014)	Use sample of 8000 SWF share holdings in 58 countries over 2002–2007 to test whether and how SWFs investments create value for target firms.	Find that SWF investments are associated with a value (Tobin's q) premium of more than 15%, and that SWFs also positively impact target firm return on assets, return on equity, and net profit margin.
Bertoni and Lugo (*JCF* 2014)	Study the impact of SWF investments on the credit risk of their target companies by examining the evolution of credit default swap spreads (CDS) after 391 SWF investments over 2003–2010.	Find target company's credit risk decreases significantly after SWF investment. Suggests market perceives SWFs as investors that may protect target companies from bankruptcy risk.

(continued)

Table 5. (*Continued*)

Study	Sample description, study period, and methodology	Summary of empirical findings and conclusions
Knill, Lee, and Mauck (*Journal of Financial Intermediation* 2012a)	Use sample of 231 SWF acquisitions of listed firm stock over 1984–2009 to examine whether this investment significantly impacts the return-to-risk performance of target firms.	Find that target firm raw returns decline following SWF investment. Though risk also declines, find a net reduction in the compensation for risk assumed over 5 years after investment, suggesting SWFs may not provide monitoring benefits for targets offered by other institutional investors.
Kotter and Lel (*Journal of Financial Economics* 2011)	Use sample of 417 SWF investments into listed firms over 1980–February 2009 to examine the effect of SWF investment on the short and long term valuation and performance of target firms. Also study which types of target firms attract SWF investment.	Find that SWFs prefer large, poorly performing companies facing financial difficulties, and news of their investments yields significantly positive initial returns (+2.25%) that are higher for more transparent funds. Mean long-term stock returns after investment are insignificantly positive (3-yr significant); median returns insignificantly negative. Conclude SWFs are generally passive shareholders.
Sojli and Tham (*Book* 2011)	Examine the short and long-term performance impact of 66 SWF investments in US listed companies by comparing SWFs deals documented with 13D and 13G filings over 1997–2008 to a similar sample of investments made by US institutional investors.	Find that these large investments by SWFs where they plan to take active roles in target firm management yield significantly positive short and long-term stock returns and financial performance. Find the increase in target's Tobin's q post-deal results from the provision of government contracts.
Karolyi and Liao (*WP* 2011)	Study 4026 cross-border acquisitions over 1998–2008, worth $434 bn, that were led by government-controlled acquirers, and compare to 127,786 similar acquisitions worth $9.04 tr made by private acquirers and 733 deals worth $158 bn made by SWFs and other state-owned funds. Test whether investments by state-controlled acquirers and SWFs/other funds yield different short and long-run target firm stock returns than do acquisitions by private companies.	Find that announcement period (–5,+5) return for acquisitions by private companies (5.0%) is significantly higher than that for state-controlled acquirers (2.8%), and that the (–5,+5) return around SWF/other funds investment announcements (0.8%) is materially and significantly smaller than either. Also find the 3-yr mean and median buy-and-hold excess returns for SWFs/other funds (–50.3%; –62.8%) are significantly lower than for private acquirers (–9.4%; –40.3%) and state-controlled acquirers (–7.6%; –30.6%), though L-T excess returns post-deal are significantly negative for all groups over all time frames (1, 2, and 3 years).

Table 5. (*Continued*)

Study	Sample description, study period, and methodology	Summary of empirical findings and conclusions
Bertoni and Lugo (*WP* 2011)	Analyze the certification effect of SWF stock purchases on the credit risk of target firms by computing an adjusted measure of credit default swap (CDS) spread decrease (ADS) for 1-yr and 5-yr CDS for a sample of 371 direct SWF investments between 2003 and 2010.	Document a significant decline in target firm credit risk following SWF investments, especially for the 1-yr maturity CDS, even when investment is purely secondary (no new capital injected into target). Results consistent with market interpreting SWF investment as providing target with implicit insurance against short-term liquidity shocks.
Dewenter, Han, and Malatesta (*Journal of Financial Economics* 2010)	Analyze the short and long-term impact of SWF investments on target firm values using a sample of 227 stock purchases and 47 SWF stock sales over January 1987–April 2008. Try to determine whether there is a trade-off between SWF monitoring and lobbying benefits and tunneling and expropriation costs.	Find significant announcement period $(-1,+1)$ excess returns for SWF stock purchases $(+1.52\%)$ and divestments (-1.37%). Document significantly negative median 1-yr cumulative market-adjusted excess returns (-4.5%), but significantly positive median 3-yr $(+7.3\%)$ and 5-yr $(+31.2\%)$ returns for target firm stocks after SWF investments. Also find SWFs are active monitors, with over half of target firms experiencing one or more events indicating SWF monitoring or influence.

Kotter and Lel (2011) use a sample of 417 SWF investments into 326 listed firms over 1980–February 2009 to examine the effect of SWF investment on the short and long term valuation and performance of target firms. They also study which types of target firms attract SWF investment, finding that SWFs prefer large, poorly performing companies facing financial difficulties. News of SWF investments yield significantly positive initial returns $(+2.25\%)$ that are higher for more transparent funds, possibly because more transparent funds are more likely to invest in financially constrained firms. Mean long-term abnormal stock returns after SWF investments are positive but generally not statistically significant, whereas median long-term returns are negative, but similarly not statistically significant. They conclude that SWFs are generally passive shareholders whose stock purchases have limited impact on investment targets. Kotter and Lel (2011) also find that SWFs prefer large and poorly performing firms that are financially constrained or distressed.

Sojli and Tham (2011) examine the short and long-term performance impact of 66 SWF investments in US listed companies by comparing SWF deals documented with 13D and 13G filings over 1997–2008 to a similar sample of investments made by US institutional investors. They find that these large investments by SWFs where they plan to take active roles in target firm management yield significantly positive short and long-term stock returns and financial performance. The authors also show that the increase in a target's Tobin's q post-deal results from the acquisition of government contracts.

Although the principal focus of the study by Karolyi and Liao (2011) is not SWFs, they actually provide one of the most persuasive analyses of the differential valuation impact of stock investments by SWFs and other state-owned funds compared to stock purchases by private and state-controlled corporate acquirers. As discussed in Section 3, they study 4026 cross-border acquisitions over 1998–2008, worth $434 billion, that were led by government-controlled acquirers, and compare these to 127,786 similar acquisitions worth $9.04 trillion made by private acquirers and 733 deals worth $158 billion made by SWFs and other state-owned funds. They test whether investments by state-controlled acquirers and SWFs/other funds yield different short and long-run target firm stock returns than do acquisitions by private companies, and find that average announcement period (–5,+5) returns for acquisitions by private companies (5.0%) are significantly higher than those for state-controlled acquirers (2.8%), and that the (–5,+5) return around SWF/other funds' investment announcements (0.8%) is materially and significantly smaller than either. Karolyi and Liao also find the 3-year mean and median buy-and-hold excess returns for SWFs/other funds (–50.3%; –62.8%) are significantly lower than for private acquirers (–9.4%; –40.3%) and state-controlled acquirers (–7.6%; –30.6%), though the long-term excess returns post-deal are significantly negative for all groups over all time frames (1, 2, and 3 years).

The as-yet unpublished study by Bortolotti *et al.* (2014, BFM) examines the largest and most recent sample of SWF investments in the stocks of listed companies. They construct a dataset of 1018 investments by SWFs (or by SWF-owned investment subsidiaries) in publicly traded firms, with a total value of $352 billion, completed over the 1980–November 2012 period. Uniquely, they also generate a "benchmark" control sample of stock purchases by financial investors from the same home countries as their sample of SWFs, targeted at firms headquartered in the same countries as SWF investment targets, and executed over the same time period.[18] BFM thus compare the valuation impact of investments by SWFs to those of the full private benchmark sample, as well as to various private subsamples paired with the SWF sample by propensity score matching based on fund, country, and target-firm specific factors.

In all cases, BFM find that the announcement period abnormal returns associated with SWF stock purchases are positive but significantly lower than those observed for investments by the benchmark sample and propensity-score matched (PSM) subsamples. Specifically, they find that announcements of SWF investments are associated with significant mean abnormal returns of 0.9% over a three-day event window (–1,+1), including investments by Norway's GPFG, and 2.45% without Norway. However, these are significantly lower than the 5.02% mean abnormal returns generated by the private benchmark investors, implying the presence of a sovereign wealth fund "discount" apparently due to their government ownership. Even after an extensive set of year, country, industry, firm, and deal level controls are included in their analysis, BFM's main findings are confirmed. The market reaction to SWF investments is lower than that of comparable private-sector investments, by about 2.67 percentage points, and BFM verify the robustness of these results in data subsets and for both financial and nonfinancial targets.

4.2.2 *Impact of SWF Investment on the Operating Performance and Governance of Target Firms*

A stream of the literature investigating the impact of SWFs on target firms has analyzed the operating performance of investment targets. Many of the studies in this area have actually focused on the corporate governance impact of SWFs – and we will thus discuss the two, intersecting, research topics in unison. Fernandes (2014) studies the impact of SWF investments on the value and operating performance of firms in which SWFs invest and finds both a significant increase in firm value as well as significant improvements in operating performance, as measured by returns on equity, returns on assets and operating returns. The author further identifies the source of value provided by SWFs as originating from stronger monitoring, better access to capital, and improved access to foreign product markets. The findings of stronger monitoring are consistent with the results of Dewenter et al. (2010), who similarly find that SWFs are active investors and discuss the role of SWFs in managerial turnover, but also in the creation of valuable network effects. Sojli and Tham (2011) similarly attribute the improved performance of SWF investment target in the United States to, amongst other things, improvements in governance.

Rose (2013) describes in detail how SWFs tend to be disengaged from corporate governance matters in U.S. firms, as a reaction to regulatory and media opposition to their investments. Yet, as he discusses, this passivity has a dark side and it could have a negative impact on firm value by replacing other, potentially more engaged, shareholders–consistent with the results of Bortolotti et al. (2014).

4.2.3 *Impact of SWF Investment on Target Valuation, Credit Risk, and Stock Return Volatility*

Five studies examine how SWF equity investments impact the valuation, credit risk, and/or financial return volatility of target firms post-investment. Since these studies employ differing methodologies and samples, and examine different performance metrics, it is harder to draw general conclusions regarding their findings, except to say that two of these studies (Fernandes, 2014; Bertoni and Lugo, 2014) find that SWF investments generally increase target firm value and/or reduce the target's credit risk, while Knill et al. (2012a) find that both the risk and return of target firms' stocks decline following SWF investments. Borisova et al. (2014) document that SWF investment in target firms' stock is associated with an increase in those firms' bond yield spreads—and thus their cost of debt financing.

Fernandes (2014) examines a sample of 8000 SWF share holdings in 58 countries over 2002–2007 to test whether SWFs investments create value for target firms. He finds that SWF investments are associated with a value (Tobin's q) premium of more than 15%, and that SWFs also positively impact target firm return on assets, return on equity, and net profit margin. It should be pointed out that no other SWF empirical study finds a positive valuation impact anywhere near that large, although most do find that announcements of SWF stock purchases are associated with significantly positive returns in the 1–3% range.

Bertoni and Lugo (2014) study the effect of SWF stock purchases on the credit risk of target firms. The authors compute and analyze changes in credit default swap (CDS) spreads for a sample of 391 direct SWF investments over 2003–2010. They find the target company's CDS spreads decrease significantly after SWF investment and that the results are stronger when the SWF originates from a politically stable nondemocratic country. The authors interpret the results as suggesting that creditors expect SWFs to protect target companies from bankruptcy.

Knill et al. (2012a) use a sample of 231 SWF acquisitions of listed firm stock over 1984–2009 to examine whether this investment significantly impacts the return-to-risk performance of target firms, and find that target firm raw returns do indeed decline following SWF investment. Though risk also declines, they document a net reduction in the compensation offered to investors for the risk they assume over 5 years after investment, suggesting that

SWFs may not provide the same monitoring benefits for targets offered by other institutional investors.

Borisova *et al.* (2014, BFHM) examine the impact that state ownership of a firm's stock has on that company's cost of debt using a sample of 6671 credit spreads from 1723 bonds issued by 244 companies from 43 countries over 1991–2010. Although not the principal focus of their analysis, BFHM's sample includes 1060 firm-year observations with SWF ownership, representing 27% of their state ownership sample. They argue that government ownership of stock in a domestic company might carry an implicit guarantee on the debt of the firm, since it is not likely that a firm with significant state ownership will be allowed to fail. But this may be counteracted by factors resulting from state presence which could raise the firms' cost of debt financing such that government equity ownership may have a net negative effect on a firm's debt cost. Crucially, BFHM examine whether stock ownership by different state entities impact target firm yield spreads differently, and they predict that SWFs will have a less positive/more negative impact on target bond yields than will stock ownership by central banks, the national treasury, and state-owned nonfinancial enterprises. They also examine whether state ownership, including that by SWFs, impacts spreads differently during the period 1990–2007 than it does during the financial crisis beginning in 2008.

BFHM find that, in their full sample (1990–2010), the presence of a government shareholder is linked to an increase in the cost of debt, but that yield spreads decline as the size of the stake owned by the government rises. A binary variable related to the presence of government investors is associated with a 40 basis points (bp) increase in the cost of debt, while each percentage point of government ownership is associated with a corresponding 0.6 bp decrease. The presence of government shareholding thus seems, on balance, to increase the target firms' cost of debt during "normal times" (1990–2007) and for the full study period. The detrimental impact of specifically having a SWF as a state investor is even greater, since this presence is associated with a 46.7 bp higher spread for the full sample period (82.7 bp during 1990–2007), and each percentage point of SWF ownership is associated with a 4.7 bp increased spread for the full study period (6.2 bp during 1990–2007). And in all cases, stock ownership by a foreign state entity is associated with an increased cost of debt versus either domestic state or private ownership.

During the recent financial crisis, however, BFHM show that the overall cost of corporate debt soars by over 200 bp, and government presence becomes associated with lower spreads, by 18 bp, and each percentage point increase in government stake ownership translates into a 1 bp decrease in the cost of debt. Likewise, government ownership is associated with a 9 bp lower cost of debt during banking crises identified by Laeven and Valencia (2010, 2012), but with a 38 bp higher cost of debt outside of the banking crises. SWF ownership continues to be associated with higher yield spreads during the crisis, with its presence correlating to an increase of 26.1 bp and each percentage point of SWF ownership being associated with a 3.5 bp higher spread. This evidence contradicts other studies showing that SWF stock ownership is associated with a lower cost of debt; instead BFHM show that having a SWF as a stockholder correlates with a significantly higher cost of debt, except during financial crises.

5. Conclusions and Extensions

So what can we conclude about SWFs as financial actors, investors, and corporate monitors—and what research issues remain unresolved? We conclude this survey by first summarizing, in Section 5.1, the key lessons that extant research has taught us about SWFs. Then Section 5.2 describes the unresolved issues that we hope can be addressed by future SWF researchers.

5.1 *What Lessons Can Be Drawn from Existing SWF Research?*

The research published so far has led to some important lessons. First of all, though large, SWFs should not be frightening. Their assets under management, at $5.4 trillion, while large in absolute terms, are still only a small fraction of the total value of financial assets worldwide, estimated at $223 trillion in 2012 by McKinsey & Company (http://www.mckinsey.com/ insights/mgi/research/financial_markets). Further, while commentators often point out that SWFs are much larger than most hedge funds, they often fail to note that SWFs are dwarfed by banks, mutual funds, and insurance companies. Also, SWFs are often too politically constrained to be a serious financial threat, mostly due to the geopolitical goals of their governments that, far from pushing for influence abroad, often constrain their activities. Finally, SWFs are not only operationally and financially similar to other institutional investors, but often behave like big, passive pools of capitals (what cynics might call "big, dumb capital") due to low levels of internal staffing—or due to an explicit investment strategy aimed precisely at preventing undue influence and the resulting foreign backlash.

A second lesson emerging from this literature is that SWFs are not homogeneous—and should not be treated as such. Norway's GPFG stands apart, not just as the largest SWF, but also as the most transparent and diversified fund. GPFG has emerged as a true alternative to the "Yale Model" of endowment fund management, by limiting its investments to small stakes in a large number of firms diversified in both geography and industry. Qatar's fund, on the other hand, is the champion of a much more active role for SWFs, making fewer, larger and more visible investments both in equities and, even more, in iconic real-estate deals—and even playing the part of the deal-maker, as in the recent Glencore acquisition of Xstrata. Yet, to gain insight into SWF behavior, we should not be fooled by this heterogeneity, as SWFs are not idiosyncratic either; certain systemic differences can be identified and used to classify them into distinct groups. SWFs differ principally on funding source—with commodity-based funds on one side, clustering geographically around the Gulf area, and trade-imbalance funds more common in East Asia—and on sponsor-country characteristics. While many funds originate from nondemocratic regimes, there are big exceptions (Australia, Ireland, Norway, New Zealand) as well. Finally, we find substantial differences in transparency levels.

Third, while it would be naïve not to recognize that SWFs are state-owned entities that often make politicized capital allocations, we need to be mindful of the fact that no evidence exists, to date, of political interference in the behavior of the foreign targets in which SWFs invest. Of course, the same cannot be said for their domestic investments—but it is the foreign actions of these state-owned vehicles that trigger most fearful responses. Accordingly, while we recognize the need to keep monitoring and studying the behavior of these state-owned investment vehicles in foreign markets, the evidence to date does not justify the protectionist response that so many commentators and politicians have been advocating.

In some sense, SWFs are a "second best" organizational form as fiduciaries. As state-owned entities, they are constrained in their ability to invest abroad and to improve the governance of their investment targets through active monitoring, as other institutional investors have been shown to do. Small, under-motivated staffs, often associated with state-owned institutions, frequently compound the lack of monitoring activity induced by those constraints. As a result, while no definite statements can be made due to the distinctive lack of transparency of SWFs, what data is available indicates that private funds out-perform SWFs across the board in their investments. Extant research has amply shown that state ownership leads to a dramatic deterioration in efficiency, as SOEs are often managed by teams that are either undermotivated and "captured," at best, or incompetent and corrupt at worst. SWFs, when properly organized, can insulate investment targets from political oversight and influence and, in this way, mitigate some of the problems that plague SOEs. In some sense, a properly structured SWF—and Norway is the model, with its management team well insulated (but, even then, not completely insulated) from political pressures—is a hybrid structure, allowing for government ownership without government management. In societies in which the state plays a dominant economic role, SWFs might be the only real, feasible alternative to full governmental control. Regardless, with growing assets under management for existing funds and with many countries planning new inceptions, SWFs are a new form of organizational structure that is here to stay and that, accordingly, needs to be fully understood.

5.2 *Unresolved Issues and Areas for Future Research*

We conclude by claiming the survey article authors' prerogative of specifying what we believe are the key unresolved issues in SWF research and pointing where we believe the next group of researchers should target their efforts. We wish them good fortune.

First far too little is known about the details of SWF investments, with the notable exception of the activities of Norway's Government Pension Fund Global. Extant research has offered insights—and even those, incomplete—into investments in publicly traded firms and some glimpses into disclosed real estate and unlisted equity investments. The substantial fraction of SWF investments in bond markets has so far defied analysis and remains opaque. While little is known about the returns achieved by SWFs in their international equity and debt investments, even less is known about their domestic asset returns. This is partly because of inherently restricted information disclosure and partly because SWFs are often used to rescue local firms and industries during financial crises and recessions. SWFs can be employed as tools of domestic development far more easily than they can be used thusly in cross-border deals.

The lack of information and opaque nature of SWFs is, of itself, deserving of study. We strongly suspect that the secrecy surrounding most SWFs has actually been self-defeating, stoking the flames of those who see a foreign government investor with suspicion. Yet, there are perhaps valid reasons (domestic political short-term pressures but also the need to protect investment strategies) for opacity; it would be interesting to see what the optimal level of disclosure is and whether such heterogeneity among funds has rational justifications.

Despite the lack of truly comprehensive data, extant research has gained some insights into the performance of SWF investment portfolios. Most of this evidence indicates that the claimed returns of all but the most transparent funds are probably over-stated, perhaps wildly so. Yet this research relies on incomplete and certainly biased data—as it is the most transparent funds based in western countries that are most likely to provide sufficient disclosure, but those funds are also, on an average, the most sophisticated investors amongst their peer group.

Extant research on the impact of SWFs on target firm value has mostly relied on analysis of announcement-period abnormal returns—and found positive abnormal returns over short-term windows. However, a large literature documents the market reaction to investments by western mutual funds, pension funds, and other types of institutional investors and also finds positive abnormal returns. Yet, despite the abnormal performance of investment targets documented in this literature, most of the (to start with, scant) research on SWF performance has failed to compare the performance of SWF investment targets to that of a comparable, private-sector benchmark. Bortolotti *et al.* (2014) have offered a first attempt at constructing a benchmark of comparable private-sector investments and, while confirming that SWF investments are associated with positive abnormal returns, they have also shown that such returns are smaller than those to private-sector investment announcements. This "SWF discount" has thus been documented, yet it has not been fully explained—is the market reaction a rational response to the expectation of political interference by SWFs or is it perhaps a reaction to the stigma associated with the sovereign nature of these investors?

A related unanswered question is one of long-term impact. Empirical corporate finance literature has come to rely on short-term market reaction, under an assumption of market efficiency, to make inferences about the long-term value impact of corporate events—in this case, to make inferences about the long-term value impact of SWF investments in publicly traded firms. Yet is it reasonable to expect markets to efficiently and accurately assess the value impact of investments which are kept intentionally opaque by a group of funds who are, in the first place, little understood? Or is there perhaps more insight to be gained by long-term analysis of operating performance of investment targets, despite the added noise and econometric challenges inherent in long-term analyses?

In some sense, extant research has failed to provide answers to some of the most fundamental, and most important, questions surrounding SWFs. Foremost is the question whether SWFs can truly become vehicles financing economic development, to the benefit of the populations of the sponsoring countries. Of course, the evidence so far, suggesting that SWF capital flows are mostly directed to the financial industry in developed, western countries seems to reinforce this view of SWFs perpetuating Lucas' paradox and diverting resources that could perhaps be employed for domestic investments in countries often lacking infrastructure. Yet, such a view hinges on scant evidence: it is hard to draw any conclusion on the impact of SWF investments when their allocation, as previously discussed, is only partially known.

There are other related, specific, unanswered questions. Have SWFs strengthened the influence of government on their domestic economies—by virtue of direct asset acquisitions—or have they actually weakened such impact, by insulating those same assets from political interference? Have SWFs helped or hindered domestic financial and industrial development? While data constraints are one of the reasons for lack of clear answers, a contributing factor has been a 'western bias' in most of the related research – as western economists have been more interested in analyzing how SWFs impact target firms and target-firm economies, rather than questioning the rationale for SWF existence in the first place.

Finally, a critical issue is whether countries should set up SWFs in the first place—and, even more, whether there are certain countries for which a SWF is more appropriate. Should countries with large, and perhaps temporary, excess cash flows allocate a portion of these funds to a SWF? Should countries excessively dependent on a single commodity use a SWF to diversify their economic exposure? Should countries with aging populations use SWFs as a tool for inter-generational wealth transfer? We hope our research colleagues will vigorously pursue these issues going forward.

Acknowledgments

We thank Tor Bakke, Vee Barbary, Xuechen Gao, Joka Kusjlic, Hui Li, Valentina Milella, Laura Pelizzolla, Armando Rungi, Blaine Stansel, and Timothée Waxin for research assistance with this project. We also benefited from comments offered by Mohammed Alzahrani, Chris Balding, Ginka Borisova, Bernardo Bortolotti, Narjess Boubakri, Marie Brière, Craig Brown, Gilles Chemla, Rebel Cole, Serdar Dinç, Elroy Dimson, Mandy Duan, Louis Ederington, Nuno Fernandes, Chitru Fernando, Edith Ginglinger, Janya Golubeva, Kate Holland, Jason Kotter, Carl Linaburg, Stefano Lugo, Stefanie Kleimeier, April Knill, Ugur Lel, Diego Lopez, Stefano Lugo, Nathan Mauck, Aline Muller, Matthias van Randenborgh, Jay Ritter, Patrick Schena, Samer Sourani, Manuchehr Sharokhi, Aidan Vining, Vincenzo Verdoliva, Pradeep Yadav, two anonymous referees and the editor, Iris Claus. We also thank participants in the 2013 ECCE-USB Financial Globalization and Sustainable Finance conference in Cape Town, South Africa (keynote speech), the 2014 Global Finance Conference in Dubai (keynote speech), the 2014 Sovereign Investment Laboratory Sovereign Wealth Fund Conference (Florence), and seminar presentations at Université Paris Dauphine, Saudi Aramco headquarters (Dhahran, Saudi Arabia), King Fahd University of Petroleum and Minerals, the University of Liege, Università degli Studi di Napoli, and the European School of Management and Technology (Berlin).

Notes

1. Reported in Megginson (2013, Figure 3), based on data from the Thomson Reuters SDC Platinum M&A database and Privatization Barometer (http://www. privatizationbarometer.net). During 2013, state asset sales (privatizations) reverted to the pre-2001 historical pattern, exceeding state purchases by more than $50 billion.

2. Other researchers have classified SWFs in different ways. A common alternative is to classify funds according to the purpose for which they were launched. This approach is summarized in Bortolotti et al. (2013), distinguishing between inter-generational saving funds, aimed at investing incomes gained from harvesting finite resources such as oil, funds aimed at diversifying national reserves, and funds aimed at economic development.

3. Most definitions also exclude funds directly managed by central banks or finance ministries, as these often have very different priorities, such as currency stabilization, funding of specific development projects, or the development of specific economic sectors.

4. In ongoing research employing the Thomson Reuters Securities Data Corporation Mergers and Acquisitions database and other databases, we identify over 12,100 investments, worth over $1.67 trillion, just in listed-firm stocks by state-owned investment companies, stabilization funds, commercial and development banks, pension funds, and state-owned enterprises. If we add state purchases of government and corporate bonds, plus SWF holdings and foreign exchange reserves of roughly $12 trillion, the total value of state-owned financial assets may already exceed $25 trillion. David Marsh writes that global public investors now own about $30 trillion of assets worldwide. See David Marsh, "Sovereign-wealth funds must move out of shadows," MarketWatch (March 10, 2014, http://www.marketwatch.com/story/sovereign-wealth-funds-must-move-out-of-shadows-2014-03-10).

5. For a comparison of SWFs with state-run pension funds, see Blundell-Wignall et al. (2008).They conclude that SWFs and public pension reserve funds (PPRFs) are similar in some ways, but differ significantly with respect to objectives, investment strategies, sources of financing, and transparency requirements.

6. The sub-national UAE funds included in our list are the Abu Dhabi Investment Authority (the world's second-largest SWF), the Investment Corporation of Dubai, Istithmar World,

the Mubadala Development Company, the International Petroleum Investment Corporation (IPIC), and the Ras Al Khaimah Investment Authority.

7. The Kuwaiti SWF is also unusual among large funds in that it is funded based on a formulaic percentage of the sales of Kuwait National Oil Company. The fund is automatically granted 10% of the oil revenues of the state, and the finance ministry recently approved increasing the allocation to 25%. See Henny Sender, Kuwait Investment Authority: Integrity and caution are no handicap, *Financial Times* (April 24, 2013).

8. It is perhaps no surprise that so many oil-funded SWFs are from non-democratic countries, since it is well established that abundant oil reserves (which promote large SWFs) and the evolution of democratic societies are natural enemies. Tsui (2011) finds that discovering 100 billion barrels of oil (approximately the initial endowment of Iraq) pushes a country's democracy level almost 20 percentage points below trend after three decades. Wolf and Pollitt (2008) and Wolf (2009) also show clearly that national oil companies are significantly less efficient and innovative than privately-owned international oil companies—and thus document the scale of value-destruction associated with state ownership/control of petroleum reserves and production.

9. Commodity stabilization funds are discussed and analyzed in Arrau and Claessens (1992) while the U.S. equivalent, state "rainy day" funds, are described in Douglas and Gaddie (2002).

10. We thank Matthias Van Rendenborgh for his discussion on the topic. Kalter and Schena (2013) offer an in-depth analysis of emerging market economies needing to balance SWF asset growth, domestic development, and the risks related to recycling SWF assets domestically.

11. The slow take-up of "sovereign wealth fund" is illustrated by noting that the *Financial Times* first used the term on May 17, 2007, two years after Rozanov's article was published. Once the phrase reached a critical mass of usage—and the *FT* began employing the term—usage quickly became universal, to the point where a search of the *Financial Times* website (www.ft.com) on December 31, 2014 yielded 5,966 hits for "sovereign wealth fund".

12. See Lawrence Summers, "Sovereign wealth funds shake the logic of capitalism," *Financial Times*, July 30, 2007; Steven Weisman, "Concern about 'sovereign wealth funds' spreads to Washington," *International Herald Tribune*, August 20, 2007, and Krishna Guha, "Warning over sovereign wealth funds," *Financial Times*, June 22, 2007.

13. Active foreign government involvement in a domestic target is usually met with significant public opposition, and so governments often choose to be passive investors, especially in their foreign holdings. Prabakhar (2009), Masters (2013), and Jackson (2014) all show that involvement of a foreign state-owned entity in a large acquisition of a US company is certain to prompt scrutiny by the Committee on Foreign Investment in the United States (CFIUS).

14. The number of SWF start-ups is reported in Javier Blas, "Protecting Nigeria oil SWF is no easy task," *Financial Times* (October 10, 2013). The recent surge in setting up African SWFs is described in Triki and Faye (2011).

15. For descriptions of these countries' SWF launches, see Jonathan Wheatley and Richard Lapper, "Brazil in $200bn sovereign fund plan," *Financial Times* (June 9, 2008; http://www.ft.com/cms/s/0/625ea6ea-35bc-11dd-998d-0000779fd2ac.html#ixzz2DMtZy7xk); Amy Teibel, "Israel planning investment fund to turn natural gas into gold," Associated Press (January 24, 2012; http://usatoday30usatoday.com/money/world/story/2012-01-24/israel-natural-gas-sovereign-wealth-fund/52774108/1); Peter Korugl, "PNG announces

$30 billion sovereign wealth fund" (February 27, 2012; http://pidp.eastwestcenter.org/pireport/2012/February/02-27-01.htm); and Namitha Jagadeesh, "Mongolia to create $600 million sovereign fund in July," Bloomberg News (April 30, 2012; http://www.bloomberg.com/news/2012-04-30/mongolia-to-create-600-million-sovereign-fund-in-july.html).

16. Dixon and Monk (2013) and Al-Kharusi *et al.* (2014) also describe why many SWFs in distant (from major financial centers) regions might choose to set up satellite offices in financial centers or establish formal ties with asset managers located therein. Dixon and Monk note that many SWFs have grown disillusioned with paying high fees for mediocre returns; in their delicious phrase (page 42), "they [SWFs] were, and in most cases still are, paying for alpha but only receiving beta returns."

17. On the other hand, the Fund claims (http://www.nbim.no/) to have met with investee firm CEOs 77 times during 2013, and recently announced that it would reveal its voting intentions before general shareholder meetings [Richard Milne and Jonathan Guthrie, "Norway's oil fund to reveal voting intentions," *Financial Times* (August 7, 2014)].

18. In similar spirit, Kotter and Lel (2011) observe that the "magnitude of the market reaction is similar to the announcement effects of investments by institutional investors on stock returns for a comparable event window," but they offer no formal comparison. More comparably, Karolyi and Liao (2011) compare the market reaction to news of acquisitions by state-owned firms to acquisitions by state-owned funds (including SWFs) and by private-sector acquirers. Consistent with BFM's findings, Karolyi and Liao show that the market reaction to cross-border investments by state-owned funds is smaller than the market reaction to private-sector investments.

References

Acharya, V., Anginer, D. and Warburton, A.J. (2013) The end of market discipline? Investor expectations of implicit state guarantees. Working paper, New York University.

Aggarwal, R., Erel, I., Ferreira, M. and Matos, P. (2011) Does governance travel around the world? Evidence from institutional investors. *Journal of Financial Economics* 100: 154–181.

Al-Hassan, A., Papaioannou, M., Skancke, M. and Sung, C.C. (2013) Sovereign wealth funds: aspects of governance structures and investment management. International Monetary Fund Working Paper WP/13/231.

Al-Kharusi, Q.A., Dixon, A.D. and Monk, A.H.B. (2014) Getting closer to the action: why pension and sovereign funds are expanding geographically. Working Paper, Stanford University.

Ang, A. (2010) The four benchmarks of SWFs. Working Paper, Columbia University.

Ang, A., Goetzmann, W. and Schaefer, S. (2009) *Evaluation of active management of the Norwegian Government Pension Fund-Global.* Report to the Norwegian Parliament.

Arrau, P. and Claessens, S. (1992) Commodity stabilization funds. World Bank Policy Research Working Paper Series 835.

Avendaño, R. (2012) SWF Investments: firm-level preferences to natural endowments. Working Paper, Paris School of Economics.

Avendaño, R. and Santiso, J. (2011) Are sovereign wealth funds politically biased? A comparison with other institutional investors. In B. Narjess and C. Jean-Claude (eds), *Institutional Investors in Global Capital Markets* (pp. 313–353). Bradford, UK: Emerald Group Publishing Limited.

Avsar, V., Karayalcin, C. and Ulubasoglu, M.A. (2013) State-owned enterprises, political ideology, and redistribution. *Economics & Politics* 25: 387–410.

Balding, C. (2008) A portfolio analysis of sovereign wealth funds. Working Paper, University of California-Irvine.

Balding, C. and Yao, Y. (2011) Portfolio allocation for sovereign wealth funds in the shadow of commodity-based national wealth. In B. Narjess and C. Jean-Claude (eds), *Institutional Investors in Global Capital Markets* (pp. 293–312). Bradford, UK: Emerald Group Publishing Limited.

Balding, C. (2012) *Sovereign Wealth Funds: The New Intersection of Money and Politics*, 1st edn. New York: Oxford University Press.

Becht, M., Franks, J., Mayer, C. and Rossi, S. (2009) Returns to shareholder activism: evidence from a clinical study of the Hermes UK Focus Fund. *Review of Financial Studies* 22: 3093–3129.

Bekaert, G. and Wang, X.S. (2009) *Home bias revisited*. Working Paper, Columbia Business School.

Berkman, H., Cole, R.A. and Fu, L.J. (2010) Political connections and minority-shareholder protection: evidence from securities-market regulation in China. *Journal of Financial and Quantitative Analysis* 45: 1391–1417.

Bernstein, S., Lerner, J. and Schoar, A. (2013) The investment strategies of sovereign wealth funds. *Journal of Economic Perspectives* 27: 219–238.

Bertoni, F. and Lugo, S. (2013) Testing the strategic asset allocation of stabilization sovereign wealth funds. *International Finance* 16: 95–119.

Bertoni, F. and Lugo, S. (2014) The effect of sovereign wealth funds on the credit risk of their portfolio companies. *Journal of Corporate Finance* 27: 21–35.

Blundell-Wignall, A., Hu, Y.-W. and Yermo, J. (2008) Sovereign wealth and pension fund issues. OECD Working Papers on Insurance and Private Pensions 14.

Boardman, A.E. and Vining, A.R. (1989) Ownership and performance in competitive environments: a comparison of the performance of private, mixed and state-owned enterprises. *Journal of Law and Economics* 32: 1–33.

Boardman, E. and Vining, A.R. (2012) The political economy of public-private partnerships and analysis of their social value. *Annals of Public and Cooperative Economics* 83: 117–141.

Bodie, Z. and Brière, M. (2014) Sovereign wealth and risk management: a framework for optimal asset allocation of sovereign wealth. *Journal of Investment Management* 12: 45–61.

Bolton, P., Samama, F. and Stiglitz, J.E., eds. (2012) *Sovereign Wealth Funds and Long-Term Investing*. New York: Columbia University Press.

Borisova, G., Brockman, P., Salas, J. and Zagorchev, A. (2012) Government ownership and corporate governance: evidence from the EU. *Journal of Banking and Finance* 36: 2917–2934.

Borisova, G., Fotak, V., Holland, K. and Megginson, W. (2014) Government ownership and the cost of debt: evidence from government investments in publicly traded firms. Working Paper, University of Oklahoma.

Bortolotti, B., Fotak, V. and Pellizzola, L. (2013) SWF investment in 2013. In *Cautious Change– Sovereign Wealth Fund Annual Report 2012*. Sovereign Investment Lab, Università Bocconi, Milan, Italy.

Bortolotti, B., Fotak, V. and Megginson, W. (2010) Quiet leviathans: sovereign wealth fund investment, passivity, and the value of the firm. Working Paper. University of Oklahoma.

Bortolotti, B., Fotak, V. and Megginson, W. (2014) The sovereign wealth fund discount: evidence from public equity investments. Working Paper. University of Oklahoma and Sovereign Investment Lab.

Brav, A., Jiang, W., Partnoy, F. and Thomas, R.S. (2008) Hedge fund activism, corporate governance, and firm performance. *Journal of Finance* 63: 1729–1775.

Candelon, B., Kerkour, M. and Lecourt, C. (2011) Are sovereign wealth funds' investments determined by macroeconomic factors? University Maastricht Working Paper.

Chambers, D., Dimson, E. and Ilmanen, A. (2012) The Norway model. *Journal of Portfolio Management* 38: 67–81.

Chen, G., Firth, M., Yu, X. and Xu, L. (2008) Control transfers, privatization, and corporate performance: efficiency gains in China's listed companies. *Journal of Financial and Quantitative Analysis* 43: 161–190.

Chen, G., Firth, M. and Xu, L. (2009) Does the type of ownership control matter? Evidence from China's listed companies. *Journal of Banking and Finance* 33: 171–181.

Chen, X., Harford, J. and Li, K. (2007) Monitoring: which institutions matter? *Journal of Financial Economics* 86: 279–305.

Chhaochharia, V. and Laeven, L. (2009) Sovereign wealth funds: their investment strategies and performance. Working Paper, International Monetary Fund.

Clark, G. and Monk, A. (2009) The Oxford survey of sovereign wealth funds' asset managers. Working Paper, University of Oxford.

Cronqvist, H. and Fahlenbrach, R. (2009) Large shareholders and corporate policies. *Review of Financial Studies* 22: 3941–3976.

Das, U., Lu, Y., Mulder, C. and Sy, A. (2009) Setting up a sovereign wealth fund: some policy and operational considerations. IMF Working Paper WP/09/179.

Dewenter, K.L., Han, X. and Malatesta, P.H. (2010) Firm value and sovereign wealth fund investments. *Journal of Financial Economics* 98: 256–278.

Dimson, E., Karakaş, O. and Li, X. (2013) Active ownership. Working Paper, London Business School.

Dinç, I.S. (2005) Politicians and banks: political influences on government-owned banks in emerging markets. *Journal of Financial Economics* 77: 453–479.

Dinç, I.S. and Erel, I. (2013) Economic nationalism in mergers and acquisitions. *Journal of Finance* 68: 2471–2514.

Dixon, A.D. and Monk, A.H.B. (2013) Will collaboration and co-investment gain ground? In *Cautious Change–Sovereign Wealth Fund Annual Report 2012*, Sovereign Investment Lab, Università Bocconi, Milan, Italy.

Djankov, S. and Murrell, P. (2002) Enterprise restructuring in transition: a quantitative survey. *Journal of Economic Literature* 40: 739–792.

Douglas, J.W. and Gaddie, R.K. (2002) State rainy day funds and fiscal crises: rainy day funds and the 1990-1991 recession revisited. *Public Budgeting & Finance* 22: 19–30.

Dyck, A.I.J. and Morse, A. (2011) Sovereign wealth fund portfolios. Working Paper, Chicago Booth School of Business.

English, P.C., Smythe, T.I. and McNeil, C.R. (2004) The 'CalPERS effect' revisited. *Journal of Corporate Finance* 10: 157–174.

Estrin, S., Hanousek, J., Kočenda, E. and Svejnar, J. (2009) The effects of privatization and ownership in transition economies. *Journal of Economic Literature* 47: 699–728.

Fernandes, N. (2014) The impact of sovereign wealth funds on corporate value and performance. *Journal of Applied Corporate Finance* 26: 76–84.

Ferreira, M.A. and Matos, P. (2008) The color of investors' money: the role of institutional investors around the world. *Journal of Financial Economics* 88: 499–533.

Ferri, R. (2012) The Curse of the Yale Model, *Forbes.com* (April 16).

Gelb, A., Tordo, S. and Halland, H. (2014) Sovereign wealth funds and long-term development finance. Risks and opportunities, World Bank Working Paper 6776.

Giannetti, M. and Laeven, L., (2009) Pension reform, ownership structure, and corporate governance: evidence from a natural experiment. *Review of Financial Studies* 22: 4092–4127.

Hau, H. and Rey, H. (2008) Home bias at the fund level. *American Economic Review: Papers and Proceedings* 98: 333–338.

Heaney, R., Li, L. and Valencia, V. (2011) Sovereign wealth fund investment decisions: Temasek Holdings. *Australian Journal of Management* 36: 109–120.

Houston, J.F., Lin, C., Lin, P. and Ma, Y. (2010) Creditor rights, information sharing, and bank risk taking. *Journal of Financial Economics* 96: 485–512.

Iannotta, G., Nocera, G. and Sironi, A. (2013) The impact of government ownership on bank risk. *Journal of Financial Intermediation* 22: 152–176.

Jackson, J.K. (2014) The Committee on Foreign Investment in the United States (CFIUS). Congressional Research Service Report (January 2).

Jain, S. (2009) *Integrating Hedge Fund Strategies in Sovereign Wealth Portfolios*. Citi Capital Advisors (November).

Jiang, G., Lee, C.M.C. and Yue, H. (2010) Tunneling through intercorporate loans: the China experience. *Journal of Financial Economics* 98: 1–20.

Johan, S.A., Knill, A. and Mauck, N. (2013) Determinants of sovereign wealth fund investments in private equity vs public equity. *Journal of International Business Studies* 44: 155–172.

Kalter, E. and Schena, P. (2013) Into the institutional void: managing sovereign wealth of emerging economies. In J. Kamar (ed.), *Investing in Emerging and Frontier Markets*. London, UK: Euromoney Books 17–34.

Karolyi, A. and Liao, R. (2011) What is different about government controlled acquirers in cross-border acquisitions? Working Paper, Cornell University.

Klein, A. and Zur, E. (2009) Entrepreneurial shareholder activism: hedge funds and other private investors. *Journal of Finance* 64: 182–229.

Knill, A., Lee, B.-S. and Mauck, N. (2012a) Sovereign wealth fund investment and the return-to-risk relationship of their target firms. *Journal of Financial Intermediation* 21: 315–340.

Knill, A., Lee, B.-S. and Mauck, N. (2012b) Bilateral political relations and sovereign wealth fund investment. *Journal of Corporate Finance* 18: 108–123

Kotter, J. and Lel, U. (2011) Friends or foes? Target selection decisions of sovereign wealth funds and their consequences. *Journal of Financial Economics* 101: 360–381.

Kunzel, P., Lu, Y., Petrova, I. and Pihlman, J. (2011) Investment objectives of sovereign wealth funds—A shifting paradigm. IMF Working Paper WP/11/19.

Laeven, L. and Valencia, F. (2010) Resolution of banking crises: the good, the bad, and the ugly. Working Paper, IMF.

Laeven, L. and Valencia, F. (2012) Systemic banking crises database: an update. Working Paper, IMF.

LaPorta, R., López-de-Silanes, F., Shleifer, A. and Vishny, R.W. (1998) Law and finance. *Journal of Political Economy* 106: 1113–1150.

Lerner, J. (2007) *Yale University Investments Office: August 2006* (Harvard Business School Case, May 8).

Lin, C., Ma, Y., Malatesta, P. and Xuan, Y. (2011) Ownership structure and the cost of corporate borrowing. *Journal of Financial Economics* 100: 1–23.

Lin, C. and Su, D. (2008) Industrial diversification, partial privatization and firm valuation: evidence from publicly listed firms in China. *Journal of Corporate Finance* 14: 405–417.

Lin, H.-C. and Bo, H. (2012) State ownership and financial constraints on investment of Chinese-listed firms: new evidence. *European Journal of Finance* 18 [online].

Martellini, L. and Milhau, V. (2010) Measuring the benefits of dynamic asset allocation strategies in the presence of liability constraints. Working Paper, EDHEC-RISK Asset Management Research.

Masters, J. (2013) Foreign investments and U.S. national security. Council on Foreign Relations (New York).

Megginson, W. (2005) *The Financial Economics of Privatization.* 1st edn. New York: Oxford University Press.

Megginson, W., Randenborgh, M. and Nash, R.C. (1994) The financial and operating performance of newly-privatized firms: an international empirical analysis. *Journal of Finance* 49: 403–452.

Megginson, W. (2013) Privatization trends and major deals of 2012 and 1H2013. *Privatization Barometer 2012 Report. Privatization Barometer* (http://www.privatizationbarometer.net). Milan.

Megginson, W. (2014) Privatization trends and major deals of 2013 and 2014. *Privatization Barometer 2013 Report. Privatization Barometer* (http://www.privatizationbarometer.net). Milan.

Megginson, W.L. and Netter, J.M. (2001) From state to market: a survey of empirical studies on privatization. *Journal of Economic Literature* 39: 321–389.

Megginson, W.L., You, M. and Han, L. (2013) Determinants of sovereign wealth fund cross-border investments. *Financial Review* 48: 539–572.

Mehrpouya, A., Huang, C. and Barnett, T. (2009) An analysis of proxy voting and engagement policies and practices of sovereign wealth funds. RiskMetrics Group Report.

Miracky, W.F., Dyer, D., Fisher, D., Goldner, T., Lagarde, L. and Piedrahita, V. (2008) *Assessing the Risks: The Behaviors of Sovereign Wealth Funds in the Global Economy* (Monitor Group).

Oum, T.H., Adler, N. and Yu, C. (2006) Privatization, corporatization, ownership forms and their effects on the performance of the world's major airports. *Journal of Air Transport Management* 12: 109–121.

Prabhakar, R. (2009) Deal-breaker: FDI, CFIUS, and Congressional response to state ownership of foreign firms. Working Paper (Harvard College).

Raymond, H. (2012) Sovereign wealth funds as domestic investors of last resort during crises. *International Economics* 123: 121–159.

Rose, P. (2013) Sovereign investing and corporate governance. Working Paper, Ohio State University Moritz

Rozanov, A. (2005) Who holds the wealth of nations. *Central Banking Journal*, Volume XV, Number 4.

Sá, F. and Viani, T. (2011) Shifts in portfolio preferences of international investors: an application to SWFs. Working Paper, Bank of England.

Sapienza, P. (2004) The effects of government ownership on bank lending. *Journal of Financial Economics* 72: 357–384.

Schena, P.J. and Kalter, E. (2012) On the need to rethink the endowment model... Again. Working paper, Fletcher School Tufts University.

Scherer, B. (2009) A Note on portfolio choice for sovereign wealth funds. Working Paper, EDHEC Business School.

Shirley, M. and Walsh, P. (2001) Public vs private ownership: the current state of the debate. Working Paper, World Bank.

Shleifer, A. (1998) State versus private ownership. *Journal of Economic Perspectives* 12, 133–150.

Sojli, E. and Tham, W.W. (2011) The impact of foreign government investments: sovereign wealth fund investments in the United States. In B. Narjess and C. Jean-Claude (eds). *Institutional Investors in Global Capital Markets* (pp. 207–243). Bradford, UK: Emerald Group Publishing Limited.

Sun, Q. and Tong, W. (2003) China's share issue privatization: the extent of its success. *Journal of Financial Economics* 70: 183–222.

Towner, M. (2014) Norway's summit on responsible investing. *Journal of Investment Management* 12.01: 33–44.

Truman, E.M. (2008) A blueprint for sovereign wealth fund best practices. Peterson Institute for International Economics Policy Brief.

Truman, E.M. (2011) Are Asian sovereign wealth funds different? *Asian Economic Policy Review* 6: 249–268.

Tsui, K.K. (2011) More oil, less democracy: evidence from worldwide crude oil discoveries. *Economic Journal* 121: 89–115.

Vining, A.R., Boardman, A.E. and Moore, M.A. (2014) The theory and evidence pertaining to local government mixed enterprises. *Annals of Public and Cooperative Economics* 84: 53–86

Woidtke, T. (2002) Agents watching agents? Evidence from pension fund ownership and firm value. *Journal of Financial Economics* 63: 99–131.

Wolf, C. (2009) Does ownership matter? The performance and efficiency of state oil vs. private oil (1987-2006). *Energy Policy* 37: 2642–2652.

Wolf, C. and Pollitt, M. (2008) Privatising national oil companies: assessing the impact on firm performance. Working Paper, University of Cambridge.

8

GENUINE SAVINGS AND SUSTAINABILITY

Nick Hanley, Louis Dupuy and Eoin McLaughlin

University of St. Andrews

1. Introduction

The purpose of this paper is to set out the theoretical and empirical under-pinnings for a savings-based measure of the sustainability of economic development, known as *Genuine Savings*. Genuine Savings (GS) is also known as Adjusted Net Savings, Comprehensive Investment and as the change in Comprehensive Wealth (all of these terms are explained below). GS is a measure of how a nation's total capital stock changes year-on-year in real terms. It is thus firmly based on the idea of wealth accounting (Hamilton and Hepburn, 2014).

Total capital includes all assets from which people obtain well-being, either directly or indirectly. It thus comprises produced capital (machines, buildings, telecommunication networks), human capital, natural capital and social capital. Natural capital comprises all 'gifts of nature': non-renewable and renewable resources such as oil reserves and fisheries, but also ecosystems, the functions of which generate flows of ecosystem services over time (UKNEA, 2011). The values we obtain from natural capital are priced by the market in many cases (coal, timber) but not in others (nutrient cycles, landscape quality, biodiversity). Social capital is a measure of the quality of institutions and social networks. The addition of all these capital stocks (or *instruments of wealth*, to use the terminology of Section 2), under a defined set of shadow prices (see below), composes comprehensive wealth. Changes in total capital then define changes in future well-being.

Why 'Genuine Savings'

The economics of sustainable development is typically viewed as being based around two alternative definitions of what characterizes sustainable development:

- Capabilities based: sustainable development is a path for an economy where the (per capita) real value of changes in the capital stocks (wealth instruments) is non-negative.
- Outcome based: sustainable development is a path for an economy where utility or real consumption per capita is not declining; or where utility or consumption can potentially be sustained over time.

A Collection of Surveys on Savings and Wealth Accumulation, First Edition. Edited by Edda Claus and Iris Claus.
Chapters © 2016 The Authors. Book compilation © 2016 John Wiley & Sons, Ltd. Published 2016 by John Wiley & Sons, Ltd.

At any point in time, the possibility set for an economy will depend on its resources, technology, the current level of consumption and population. This possibility set is reflected in the Resource Allocation Mechanism (RAM), which may or may not be *optimal* and may or may not yield a *sustainable* path for development. If governments wish to intervene on behalf of citizens on normative grounds they need to know what 'rules' will move the economy closer to a sustainable path, and how to measure progress towards and along such a path.

It is this desire for such a measure of progress that gave rise to the *capabilities-based* definition and the GS literature (Pearce and Atkinson, 1993). An existing measure of capabilities-based sustainability is green Net National Product (NNP) which measures the productive capacity of the economy. As Pezzey *et al.* (2006) show, green NNP is an expanded measure of GS, whilst the relationship between green NNP and GS was set out in Asheim and Weitzman (2001). Introducing concerns about equity between generations first led to a famous sustainability rule, the Hartwick rule, discussed below.

Equity concerns also led to the *outcome-based* definition of sustainability. Under restrictive assumptions regarding the optimality of sustainable paths for development (Pezzey, 1997) outcome-based and capabilities-based sustainability can be both assessed using GS. This explains the lead taken by GS as an indicator of sustainability and the progressive incorporation of the indicator in accounting settings. Since the System of National Accounts (SNA) framework is the dominant global approach to measuring national economic performance in a consistent manner, it would be of advantage if GS could be shown to be consistent with the principles of the SNA.

Underlying GS is an assumption about how the different forms of capital combine to produce a stream of well-being over time and to maintain the functioning of the economy-environment system. This assumption is known as weak sustainability (WS). One of the first publications to explore the concept of WS was Pearce *et al.* (1989) in *Blueprint for a Green Economy*. They define sustainable development as a situation where well-being for a given population is not declining, or preferably is increasing over time. Based on Solow (1986), they state that this requires that each generation passes on an undiminished stock of total capital to the next generation, meeting a requirement for intergenerational fairness and non-declining consumption over time. They note arguments over the extent to which a decline in natural capital, e.g. a loss of forests, can be compensated for by an increase in produced or human capital, leading to two cases for this intergenerational rule:

1. Sustainable development requires non-declining total wealth.
2. Sustainable development requires non-declining natural wealth.

We now view the first as representing the idea of WS, and the second as representing the idea of strong sustainability. As explained below, WS implies that a $1 decline in the value of any asset (any instrument of wealth) can be potentially offset by an increase in the value of some other asset or assets. That is, a country just needs to worry about what is happening to the value of its total capital or comprehensive wealth, not what is happening to any individual component of this total. Since it is difficult to test empirically whether the WS hypothesis is supported by the data (Markandya and Pedroso-Galinato, 2007), adherence to either paradigm is largely a matter of beliefs.

The work of Pearce and Atkinson (1993) in developing the idea of GS as an indicator of sustainability moves away from a strict strong sustainability perspective since GS allow for reductions in natural capital to be offset by increases in human or produced capital. The

GS concept does not rest *formally* on WS (Dasgupta, 2009). The only critical assumption regarding substitutability for GS is acceptance of the monetary valuation of natural capital.[1] However, GS is typically viewed as an empirical measure of the WS of an economy.

We present in Section 2 the underlying model of WS on which most economic analysis of sustainable development is based. Section 3 explains how GS is calculated in practice. Section 4 of the paper is concerned with empirical testing of GS as a predictor of changes in future well-being, and Section 5 concludes by setting out ways in which the theory and practice of GS could be usefully improved.

2. The Weak Sustainability Model and Genuine Savings

The WS model links variations in future well-being to changes in the value of capital stocks. It uses the Brundltand Report definition (World Commission on Environment and Development, 1987) to define a path satisfying a criterion for intergenerational equity, through the ideas of consumption and wealth (Arrow *et al.*, 2012). A necessary step before presenting the model is to lay a common ground in the terminology used.

Fisher (1906) made the first attempt at defining wealth and its instruments.[2] In his view, wealth is simply a physical capital stock, *an instrument of wealth* multiplied by an observable, *current* price. It includes all the elements that are consumed or used in the production processes composing the economy. This wealth estimated with observed prices we call *Fisherian* wealth.

Consumption represents the share of income destroyed every period to satisfy human needs and wants. Following Arrow *et al.* (2012), our definition of consumption is again Fisherian, i.e. it includes all the services, marketed and non-marketed produced from the available wealth instruments.[3]

2.1 *The General Model: Capabilities-Based Sustainability*

The intuition that savings and investment should be the prime indicator of sustainability comes from the late David Pearce (Hamilton and Atkinson, 2006).

The formal relation between well-being, wealth and consumption is presented in a general model of sustainability. The WS model reviews potential paths characterized by levels of wealth and consumption. Paths are then classified based on an equity criterion. These paths may or may not be optimal/efficient depending on the structure of the economy and the information content of prices. The GS indicator emerges from this model. GS are affiliated to the *capabilities-based* view on sustainability: they are the real value of changes in the capital stocks/instruments of wealth.

The theoretical basis for the WS model goes back to the presentation of the DHS or DHSS model[4] and has been subsequently expanded in many contributions. The model we present here is based on this rich tradition, from the seminal contributions by Weitzman (1976) and Hartwick (1977) to the more recent contributions of Hamilton and Clemens (1999), Dasgupta and Maler (2000), Asheim and Weitzman (2001), Pezzey (2004), Asheim (2007), Atkinson and Hamilton (2007), Dasgupta (2009) and Arrow *et al.* (2012). Our main reference for this section is the presentation in Dasgupta (2009). Consider a simple economy where production takes the form:

$$Y(t) = A(t)F(K(t), L(t), R(t)) \tag{1}$$

K, L, R are inputs used in the economy, K being reproducible (man-made) capital, L labour or human capital used in production and R a flow from a natural capital stock $N(t)$ used in the production process. F only needs to be non-decreasing and twice differentiable in each argument.[5] Each argument is essential in production, so that $F = 0$ if A, K, L or $R = 0$. A represents total factor productivity, the general effectiveness of institutions and the ability of the economy to combine inputs in an efficient fashion. A also represents the state of technology.

The representative agent maximizes *intergenerational well-being* at t, $V(t)$, which depends on the succession of *instantaneous well-being* $U(t)$ as a function of consumption, so that $U(t) = U(C(t))^6$ with $U'(C) > 0$ and $U'' < 0$. The value of V in t is given by:

$$V(t) = \int_t^\infty [U(C(\tau))e^{-\beta(\tau-t)}]d\tau \tag{2}$$

with β the discount rate ($\beta > 0$) and τ instantaneous utility in future periods. As mentioned in Dasgupta (2009), integral (2) can also be defined recursively (Stokey *et al.*, 1989) for ease of computation, without discretization altering the argumentation. Each and every 'wealth instrument' in the economy has an idiosyncratic pattern of accumulation and depletion. Man-made capital K depreciates at a given rate $\lambda > 0$. The stock of human capital L depreciates at a rate μ as people die. This yields the following budget constraint:

$$A(t)F(K(t), L(t), R(t)) = C(t) + \frac{dL(t)}{dt} + \mu L(t) + \frac{dK(t)}{dt} + \lambda K(t) \tag{3}$$

A balanced budget means that output is consumed, invested to expand the productive base or used to offset the depreciation ('wear and tear') of wealth instruments.

$R(t)$ represents the services from natural capital used in the production process, when the stock $N(t)$ regenerates at a natural growth rate M:[7]

$$\frac{dN(t)}{dt} = M(N(t) - R(t)) \tag{4}$$

We follow Dasgupta (2009) in giving the natural renewal rate a quadratic form:

$$M(N(t)) = -b + mN(t)\left[\frac{1 - N(t)}{Q}\right], \quad \text{for } N(t) > 0 \tag{5}$$

$$M(N(t)) = 0 \quad \text{for } N(t) = 0 \tag{6}$$

Total depletion of the stock wipes out natural capital without the possibility of regeneration and therefore halts any production.[8] A given *state* for the economy is defined in this example by the triplet (K, L, N) by $\underline{S} = (K, L, N)$.[9]

We now introduce the concept of a RAM from Dasgupta and Maler (2000). A RAM characterizes all the constraints on a given economy (whether they be technical, institutional or environmental) that co-evolve over time with the economy and form the superstructure for decisions regarding resource allocation.[10] Formally, α represents the RAM that maps a given state $\underline{S}$ in t to an observed broader set of economic variables[11] in τ (with $\tau > t$) defined as $\{E\}_t^\infty \equiv \{C(\tau), R(\tau), J(\tau), K(\tau), L(\tau), N(\tau)\}_t^\infty$:

$$\alpha : \{\underline{S}(t), t\}\{E(\tau)\}_t^\infty \tag{7}$$

α is time dependent as superstructures co-evolve over time with economic conditions. Under a given (and unobservable) α, equation (2) can be written as:

$$V(\underline{S}, t) \equiv \int_t^\infty [U(C(\underline{S}, \tau))e^{-\beta(\tau-t)}]d\tau \tag{8}$$

So that the value function V depends on time and exogenous shocks are possible.[12]

Sustainability is introduced in our framework via the use of discounted utilitarianism to describe intergenerational well-being through the value function. *Optimality* is associated with the conditions of the RAM of the economy.

The properties of the price system are related to the mathematical transcription of the 'imperfections' of the economy. Some RAM are so imperfect as to prevent the definition of shadow prices altogether. If the RAM is merely 'inefficient', the marginal contribution of a given instrument of wealth will differ across industries. Shadow prices for the same wealth instruments will then differ across sectors.

We then define shadow prices associated with our three 'instruments of wealth', capital stocks K, L and N:

$$p(bS, t) = \frac{\partial V(\underline{S}, t)}{\partial K(t)} \tag{9}$$

$$q(bS, t) = \frac{\partial V(\underline{S}, t)}{\partial L(t)} \tag{10}$$

$$n(bS, t) = \frac{\partial V(\underline{S}, t)}{\partial N(t)} \tag{11}$$

Those expressions take felicity (well-being) as the *numéraire*. The evolution of shadow prices may be explained by variations in the marginal utility of consumption and the allocation process using equations (2) or (8) and (9) to (11).

If shadow prices can be computed for *all* the wealth instruments in the economy, then what we called *Fisherian wealth* becomes *Comprehensive wealth*, that is wealth assessed using shadow prices. Using shadow prices, we can propose a formal definition for GS, in two broad categories of RAM: (time) autonomous and non-autonomous. Let us assume temporarily that changes in total factor productivity $A(t)$ are exogenous and the RAM does not co-evolve with the economy over time. The value function defined in (2) is now equal to the RAM-contingent value function in (8). Differentiating $V(t)$ with respect to t using the definition of shadow prices in (9) to (11) gives:

$$\frac{dV(\underline{S}(t))}{dt} = p(t)\frac{dK(t)}{dt} + q(t)\frac{dL(t)}{dt} + n(t)\frac{dN(t)}{dt} \tag{12}$$

We now define GS as the rate of change in stocks multiplied by shadow prices:

$$I(t) = p(t)\frac{dK(t)}{dt} + q(t)\frac{dL(t)}{dt} + n(t)\frac{dN(t)}{dt} \tag{13}$$

which leads to the logical conclusion that:

$$\frac{dV(\underline{S}(t))}{dt} = I(t) \tag{14}$$

The quite powerful conclusion of the general model is therefore that the level of GS at time t, $I(t)$, corresponds to variations in intergeneration well-being $V(t)$ in t.

We obtained this result under the assumption that the RAM (including total factor productivity evolution) is time invariant (the autonomous case). Starting with Pemberton and Ulph (2001), various authors considered that a time-dependent RAM could be formalized considering the effect of 'time passing' as an investment. Let us relax the autonomy assumption so that V is now time dependent: $V = V(\underline{S}(t), t)$ Differentiating V now adds the time derivative of V to equation (12):

$$\frac{dV(\underline{S}(t))}{dt} = \frac{\partial V}{\partial t} + p(t)\frac{dK(t)}{dt} + q(t)\frac{dL(t)}{dt} + n(t)\frac{dN(t)}{dt} \tag{15}$$

$$\frac{dV(\underline{S}(t))}{dt} = \frac{\partial V}{\partial t} + I(t) \tag{16}$$

Defining this new instrument of wealth as Z, its accumulation dynamics is simply $dZ/dt = 1$. This conceptual trick allows us to account for the unobservable (or observable but yet unaccounted for) characteristics of a given RAM, such as exogenous technological progress.

Assessing sustainability means assessing *changes* in the pool of instruments of wealth (capital stocks) priced using the relevant shadow prices, so that the rate of change of comprehensive wealth (i.e. GS) will indicate evolutions in intergenerational well-being. GS is therefore an indicator of sustainability at a given point t looking forward over a succession of τ periods. GS can inform about the future sustainability and the sustainability of a given consumption path or pattern of resource use.

Particular forms of this general model aim at either extracting observable characteristics of the RAM (so they can be incorporated into the pool of known instruments of wealth with an associated shadow price), or deriving a better understanding of the structure of the economy, that is exogenous elements in the RAM itself.

2.2 Outcome-Based Sustainability: Consumption, Prices and Discounting, NNP and the Hartwick Rule

Starting from the general form of the DHSS model, authors have imposed restrictions on either the production function or the set of production possibilities to offer both *prescriptions for* and *descriptions of* sustainability. This includes additional assumptions on the price index used to estimate shadow prices and the treatment of technical change, population growth and international trade.

Practical implementation of sustainability requires rules that can be assessed and followed, grounded in welfare/utilitarian theory while taking into account physical and environmental constraints. The most prominent of these sustainability rules based on the DHSS model is the Hartwick (1977) rule, linking conditions on consumption and wealth instruments. Hartwick (1977) shows that a sufficient condition to maintain consumption *constant over time in value terms* is that all rents and profits from the depletion of instruments of wealth available in the economy are reinvested into man-made (renewable) capital. This result is based on the Solow (1974) model. Hartwick (1977) assumed a Cobb–Douglas production function,[13] constant returns to scale in production and optimality in the exhaustible resource extraction plan.

As a consequence, sustainability is obtained when net savings in each period are equal to zero so that total capital is maintained.[14] The Hartwick rule is associated with the optimal path for constant consumption in an open economy, but does not effectively yield a rule for local deviations from the path. Does this make the Hartwick rule a prescriptive rule? Solow (1986) supports the prescriptive use of the Hartwick rule. He shows how, consumption being the interest on comprehensive wealth, maintaining the productive base constant over time naturally leads to constant consumption over time.

Asheim *et al.* (2003) offer to clarify the terms of the debate over the prescriptive character of the rule. A first important observation is that both descriptions and prescriptions are obtained in a competitive and autonomous context.[15] A useful difference can be made between the *investment rule* and the *Hartwick result*. The *investment rule*, as in the original Hartwick (1977) contribution, is a prescription to hold the value of net investments constant and equal to zero. The *Hartwick result* shows how this prescription leads to constant utility.[16]

The authors show how in a perfectly competitive economy, following the investment rule yields constant utility and sustainability if and only if the Hartwick rule applies to all periods $\tau \in (0, \infty)$. However, should the Hartwick rule only be applied over an interval (t_1, t_2) then the corresponding level of constant utility cannot be sustainable forever, so that the investment rule does not yield the Hartwick result. As a consequence, the Hartwick rule should not be considered to be prescriptive as the assumptions needed to yield the desired results (constant utility/consumption in value terms/sustainability) are out of reach.

Asheim *et al.* (2003)'s argumentation rests on more than two decades of work on the properties of competitive settings, defining sustainable levels of consumption and investment. Dasgupta and Mitra (1983) formulate the challenge clearly: the model should be defined so that it is efficient in economic terms (i.e. yielding an optimal path) and equitable (i.e. yielding basic conditions for sustainability such as distributive justice between generations).

First in this line of works is the seminal contribution of Weitzman (1976) who showed, in a framework with no technical change or population growth that Net National Product[17] (NNP) is the stationary equivalent of future consumption.[18] As a consequence, NNP can be used as a predictor of the maximum sustainable level of consumption reachable over future time.

The work of Weitzman (1976) associated with the Hartwick rule led to the definition of *outcome based sustainability*. A sustainable path is a path where consumption per capita (measured in terms of utility) is not declining in real terms. Thereafter, the literature focused on characterizing optimal paths that would satisfy conditions of equity, and used NNP (and its rate of change) as the indicator of sustainability in this optimal context. Unless stated otherwise, all the contributions listed below assume an autonomous (time independent) RAM.

Dixit *et al.* (1980) define equity as the Maximin criteria from Rawls[19] (1971) and endeavour to relate the Hartwick rule to Maximin-efficient paths. They conjecture that any Maximin efficient path satisfies the Hartwick rule, so that the Hartwick rule is a necessary but not sufficient condition for equity on an optimal (competitive) path. This result was proved many years later by Mitra (2002). Buchholz *et al.* (2005) show how conversely, an equitable competitive path must follow the Hartwick rule.

Two important assumptions of the competitive settings need to be discussed here. Intertemporal optimization is the core of the competitive setting, so what would be an appropriate parameter for discounting future flows? The Hartwick rule is linked to the NNP to derive the Hartwick result. But as Brekke (1994) wonders: what actual prices should be used to measure NNP?

Following Asheim *et al.* (2003)'s interpretation of the Hartwick rule, we may weight all future periods the same way, as violation of the Hartwick rule at *any* time nullifies the Hartwick result. Without discount rates, Ramsey (1928) proposes to use an upper-bound to the maximum level of utility it is possible to reach, as a way to ensure stable equilibria.

We may alternatively decide to weight future flows less than the present, but at varying rates. Asheim (1994) investigates the potential impact of a non-constant rate for utility discounting, while Gollier (2010) argues that changes in consumption and changes in wealth instruments should be discounted differently. See Gollier (2012) for a review of the different interpretations and computation methods for discount rates.

What about price indexes? The importance of measuring prices to maintain the welfare measurement properties of NNP led Asheim and Weitzman (2001) to propose a Divisia (1925) price index. Divisia price indexes apply weights based on consumption and investment flows, so that the path followed by prices is taken into account, not only the start and ending points (Asheim, 2007). This is the solution to the objection (Brekke, 1994) that current prices do not represent welfare changes accurately. The use of a Divisia price index will yield shadow prices in a competitive setting, in discrete or continuous time.

The divisia price index simply starts from nominal prices to obtain real prices that are effectively shadow prices. Shadow prices for instruments of wealth do not change much over the short run (as they reflect changes in large stocks) even though observed nominal prices may be more volatile. To build an empirical sustainability indicator, a full characterization of shadow prices is not required as the rate of change in prices will be mostly driven by the observable and more volatile components. This is the reason why Arrow *et al.* (2003a) define sustainability as 'non-negative growth of wealth in *constant capital prices*' (our emphasis). Asheim (2010) notes how the potential discrepancy gets worse at the international level, when purchasing power parity measures need to be used.

Pezzey (2004) provides us with a clear account of the Asheim and Weitzman (2001) results, describing a sustainability rule in the autonomous case. We call $C(t)$ a vector of multiple consumption goods, including environmental amenities. Consumption is the sole argument in the utility function $U(C(t))$ with U the instantaneous utility function.[20] Instruments of wealth in the economy are summarized by a vector $K(t)$. Investment (net of depreciation) is defined as $I(t) = \dot{K}(t)$. Values for K are obtained in a set $S(K)$ starting from a given $= K(0) = K_0$. The agent maximizes inter-temporal welfare which is the present value of instantaneous utilities in all t, using a constant discount rate:

$$V(C(t)) = \int_0^\infty U[C(t)]e^{-\beta t}dt \qquad (17)$$

Subject to:

$$(C(t), I(t)) \in S(K(t)) \qquad (18)$$

with $\beta > 0$. Assuming all externalities are internalized, this program yields an optimal path. The current value Hamiltonian of the problem is:

$$H(C, I, \Psi) = U(C) + \Psi I \qquad (19)$$

As in Weitzman (1976), $\Psi(t)$ are the shadow prices for investment in each instrument of wealth at period t. Consumption and investment along the optimal path are priced using the marginal utility of consumption $\lambda(t) > 0$ and a divisia price index $\pi > 0$ so that:

$$P(t) = \frac{[\nabla U(C)(t)]}{[\lambda(t)\pi(t)]} \qquad (20)$$

$$Q(t) = \frac{[\Psi(t)]}{[\lambda(t)\pi(t)]} \qquad (21)$$

Using this definition[21] for prices along the optimal path, 'Green' NNP can be expressed as:

$$Y(t) \equiv P(t)C(t) + Q(t)I(t) \tag{22}$$

with $Q(t)I(t)$ the real value of investment, effectively representing GS. An economy is sustainable at time t if $U(C(t)) \leq U^m(t)$, where $U^m(t)$ is the maximum sustainable utility at time t, i.e. the instantaneous utility level delivered on the optimal path. Any value below $U^m(t)$ is sustainable, but only $U^m(t)$ would be both optimal and sustainable.

The logic of the argument is that if the current positive level of utility $U(C(0))$ is sustainable while the current value of investment at shadow prices $\Psi(0)I(0)$ is negative, we reach a contradiction. The current value Hamiltonian computed starting in period 0 would then yield higher inter-temporal utility than the same Hamiltonian computed from any subsequent period. It follows from this that an economy is unsustainable if $Q(t)I(t) \leq 0$ *on the optimal path*.

As a result, outcome-based sustainability and capabilities-based sustainability are two sides of the same coin in an optimal setting. A path where consumption expressed in utility is constant in real terms and the path where the value of changes in the wealth instruments is non-negative are one and the same path. The World Bank (2006) uses the outcome based definition to obtain a value for wealth from consumption flows, while GS are obtained estimating the change in the value of the wealth instruments (see Section 3 below). This result is also critical for what it *does not* say, namely that positive GS *necessarily* implies sustainability (Asheim, 1994). As in the Hartwick rule, the unsustainability test presented here is slightly more general as optimal instantaneous utility is not assumed to be constant.

As a consequence of this, negative GS implies unsustainability in a competitive framework, but does not seem to be able to bring information on sustainability. It is thus a 'one-sided indicator' (Pezzey, 2004). Even worse, observed consumption is increasing over time, making tests based on constant or capped consumption of little practical use. This interrogation translated into concerns about a potential peak in consumption, where a trend of increasing consumption peaks before collapsing (Sato and Kim, 2002; Hartwick *et al.*, 2003).

Hamilton and Hartwick (2005) show how, in consumption peak models, GS prior to the peak is effectively a predictor of future consumption. GS will fall and then become negative before consumption peaks. Positive GS indicate that consumption will not peak in the near future. A positive value of GS is an indicator of rising future consumption, as long as savings are not 'too high': that is, so long as GS is growing at a slower rate than the real interest rate. Hamilton and Withagen (2007) then show how a negative value for GS in time t implies that well-being is likely to decline in future time periods. This is the procedure used to test the predictive power of GS, in the final section of this contribution.

In perfectly competitive economies with welfare assessed on the basis of an intergenerational equity criterion and constant consumption, sustainability can be assessed interchangeably with 'green' NNP or GS. We will now discuss extensions of the framework for the non-autonomous cases.

2.3 GS Extensions: Population Growth and Technical Change

The two main sources of time dependence in competitive settings are technical change and population growth. Technical change as a source of time dependence was first explored by Weitzman (1997) and then used to propose a definition of unsustainability tests in non-autonomous contexts in Pezzey (2004). Using the model in Section 2.2 it is easy to see how technical change can be considered as one of the unaccounted time-dependent productive stocks $\frac{\partial V}{\partial t}$ that affects the RAM, as in Section 2.1. Capital stocks are now $K' = (K, t)$ so that *time-augmented* net investment is $I' = (\dot{K}', 1) = (I, 1)$. The Hamiltonian becomes:

$$H(C, I, \Psi) = U(C) + \Psi'I' = U(C) + \Psi I + \Psi' \tag{23}$$

As in the general model, time-dependent capital stocks can be linearly separated from non-time-dependent ones, technical change is the equivalent of introducing a new time-dependent capital stock for which investment is 1 in every period. The 'augmented' unsustainability test (Pezzey *et al.*, 2006) straightforwardly becomes:

$$Q'(t)I'(t) \le 0 \quad \text{or} \quad Q(t)I(t) + Q'(t) \le 0 \tag{24}$$

Technical progress acts as another instrument of wealth or capital stock and increases the maximum level of sustainable consumption. Technical change is therefore unequivocally good for sustainability. Population growth is intuitively less obviously beneficial.

Higher population increases the quantity of human capital available (capability side),[22] while it increases resource consumption (and congestion), with negative consequences for present and future utility. Arrow *et al.* (2003b) include population growth showing that under the assumption that growth is exponential, sustainability criteria should be considered in per capita terms. Other growth profiles require more complex amendments. Using again the framework from Pezzey (2004) we present the reasoning for the case of a given constant growth rate. Assume that population in t $N(t)$ enters the utility function ($U(C, N)$) and the production set ($S(K, N, t)$).[23] $N(t)$ is exogenous and time-dependent. Assume that the objective is to maximize individual utility $u(C, N)$ multiplied by a weighting function $G(N)$. It is then possible to show, under quite restrictive assumptions that the following *individual* unsustainability criterion holds:

$$Q(t)[i(t) - nk(t)] + q'(t) \le 0 \tag{25}$$

with n the rate of population growth and k the per capita stock of man-made capital and q the individual price of time. It is then possible to obtain the global rule by multiplying the individual rule by $N(t)$:

$$Q(t)I(t) - nQ(t)K(t) + Nq'(t) \le 0 \tag{26}$$

With population growth, a share equal to the growth rate of the existing stock of produced capital must be deducted and the global increase of time dependent stocks added to obtain a revised measure of GS. The impact of population is further explored in Asheim *et al.* (2007) where the authors show that population growth needs to be quasi-arithmetic to be compatible with sustainability in a competitive framework. Li and Löfgren (2013) then show how uncertainty regarding population growth requires us to subtract a term from GS reflecting the welfare loss from risk aversion.

Extensions of the competitive models tried to combine the approaches presented here. Man-made capital is subject to wear and tear so that the stock depreciates over time. Cheviakov and Hartwick (2009) study how technical change can compensate man-made capital depreciation in the DHSS model with two patterns of population growth. They conclude that technical change should be maintained sufficiently high to compensate for produced capital depletion and avoid economic collapse. D'Autume and Schubert (2008) consider the case where natural capital is an argument in the utility function. They show how this creates an incentive to preserve a minimum critical stock of natural capital and how higher amenity values lead to lower depletion rates and a higher stock of natural capital over time.

2.4 Trade Openness and Beyond: Does Structure Matter?

The impact of trade openness on WS models is somewhat tough to comprehend, although not for technical reasons as in the population growth case. International trade is first a question of scale: shall we assess sustainability at the country level or the global level? In an integrated world (Samuelson, 1949) with factor price equalization, the law of one price, and no border frictions, the answer is simple. A competitive setting makes national borders, if not *de jure*, *de facto* irrelevant.

Still, international borders matter. Institutional differences and trade costs set open economy issues in the realm of non-optimal RAMs. In a closed economy, institutions (governments or others) exist to promote intergenerational equity concerns. No such institutions exist yet at the international scale, which begs the question of who is ultimately responsible for the use and depletion of resources. Forming and then maintaining a comparative advantage is imperative for open economies with consequences for optimal growth, consumption and depletion paths. International trade is therefore a complex problem where aggregate sustainability results are hard to obtain.

Asheim (1986) first examined the consequences of economic openness for the Hartwick rule. From a sustainability perspective, openness introduces an element of uncertainty regarding resource prices as single countries are price takers. Countries can expect a long run improvement in the terms of trade (the ratio of import prices to export prices) for natural resources as scarcity starts to bite. Economic openness acts as a violation of the constant technology assumption so that terms of trade variations have been considered as 'capital gains' from trade.

This result was then adapted to different modelling structures in Hartwick (1990) and Hartwick (1995), the latter exploring the consequences of endogenously determined world prices in a two country setting. Vincent *et al.* (1997) propose an assessment of the capital gains based on the example of Indonesia. Using the model from Pezzey (2004) we call $\Sigma(t)$ a non-renewable resource stock in t whose depletion rate is $V(t)$ so that $\dot{\Sigma} = -V$. The resource is exported at a time varying exogenous world price $Q^V(t)$.[24] Assume the economy's total domestic endowment is composed of the non-renewable resource and all man-made capital $K(t)$ is owned and maintained abroad earning an interest rate R. Total capital evolution (domestic and foreign) is:

$$\dot{K} = RK + Q^V(t)V - C - X(V) \tag{27}$$

with $X(V(t))$ the extraction cost and $U(C)$ the utility function. Augmented net investment becomes:

$$Q'(t)I'(t) = \dot{K} - Q^\Sigma V + Q' \tag{28}$$

$$Q'(t)I'(t) = \dot{K} - [Q^V(t) - X_V]V + \int_t^\infty \dot{Q}^V(s)V(s)e^{-R(s-t)}ds \tag{29}$$

See Pezzey (2004) for more details. GS including the terms of trade is therefore the sum of net investment, net extraction and the impact of the world resource price evolution considering a given level of extraction $V(t)$. The amendment is somewhat similar to the amendment for technical change, only more volatile with resource prices and even harder to assess in its forward-looking component. Pezzey *et al.* (2006) offers a method to include capital gains for natural resources in GS, and calculate the impact this adjustment implies for GS.

Considering the volatility of commodities market, capital gains are sometimes considered to have a small impact over the long run and could/should therefore be neglected. Hamilton and Bolt (2004) find them to be a sizeable share of GS for low income countries, transition and emerging economies. Rubio (2004) and Van der Ploeg (2010) investigate some specific cases, wondering whether capital gains could correct apparent unsustainability. They both conclude capital gains alone do not alter significantly overly negative or positive GS. Although capital gains can theoretically be a reason to violate the Hartwick rule, they do not appear to be large enough empirically.

Chichilnisky (1994) showed how ill-defined property rights in one trading partner may bias trade flows and increase depletion in an institutionally weaker country. Based on the intuition that property rights and rent seeking behaviour may foster over-depletion, Proops *et al.* (1999), Atkinson and Hamilton (2002) and Atkinson *et al.* (2012) estimated the natural resources content of imports and exports for a selection of regions and individual economies. They offer the concept of 'virtual sustainability' to characterize the sum of GS and the consumption-induced depletion in trading partners.

In the same vein Okumura and Cai (2007) show how when instruments of wealth enter as complements in the production process, countries favour depletion of the non-renewable factor in the foreign country before using up domestic resources. This strategic result is further explored by Oleson (2011) who suggests that export dependence may undermine sound domestic management and compromise long run sustainability by increasing reliance on unsustainable partner countries. Those results, although not yet as formal as those obtained in competitive frameworks, suggest that GS should be amended for resources trade strategies, to factor in the risks associated with dependence on foreign assets. However, this will be very difficult to implement empirically.

The final consequence of trade for GS estimates is related to the notion of comparative advantage. Economic openness is not neutral for an economy, as economic structures need to adapt to develop and foster comparative advantages. The literature on the resource curse illustrates how trade patterns may set economies on unsustainable patterns of resource depletion with (a) the sole intent of maintaining a comparative advantage and (b) at the cost of potential growth and future consumption (Van Der Ploeg, 2011). Bogmans and Withagen (2010) show how variations in the discount rate of future utility flows between trading economies may also modify economic structures and impact the location of polluting industries.

The resource curse is now depicted mostly as a consequence of poor quality institutions or low levels of social capital (Acemoglu and Robinson, 2012; Van Der Ploeg, 2011). Examining the impact of trade on economic structure and sustainability would be a way to better understand the RAM and reduce the influence of the time-dependent term in equation (12), potentially through accounting for a new instrument of wealth, namely institutional capital. A trade-induced economic specialization may lead to path dependence in GS, as the economy develops an economic structure that is optimal from a global perspective, but less so from a national perspective. Combining inputs from the resource curse, sustainability literature and neoclassical growth theory (Ventura, 1997), Dupuy (2015) shows how countries with a strongly asymmetric distribution of instruments of wealth may be better-off in autarky than free-trade, considering the induced pattern of economic specialization.

The study of the consequences of trade on sustainability is therefore promising. It may lead to new amendments of GS to account for indirect trade effects. It may also be an interesting way to understand the sustainability consequences of non-optimal RAMs and the dependence on scarce, exhaustible wealth instruments.

2.5 Other Issues: Strong Sustainability and Equity Concerns

In Fisher's (1906) original definition of wealth there was a clear dissociation between capital theory (Victor, 1991) and the theory of value.[25] The core of the WS paradigm is therefore not so much in capital theory but in the theory of value used to assign prices to instruments of wealth. As a result, GS do not carry any particular assumption regarding the potential substitutability of the *physical* stocks. They rest on the degree of substitutability as measured by shadow prices. The WS paradigm sees the problem of substitutability as a dilemma akin to the famous macro-Trilemma. It is impossible to have simultaneously a constant or growing population, imperfect substitution between instruments of wealth and no technical progress. But assuming that population is growing 'slowly enough', or that technical progress is 'fast enough' or that physical substitutability is 'high enough' then there is no real issues with critical levels for a given instrument of wealth. Use of GS rests on the existence of a RAM, however imperfectly this produces shadow prices. It remains to be seen whether a system where critical physical limits (or safe minimum standards) have been reached would still rely on market mechanisms and prices to construct a sustainability indicator.

The very issue of incommensurable instruments of wealth is therefore by assumption, a different question. The 'weak versus strong sustainability' question has been the background of sustainability studies since at least the Meadows *et al.* (1972) report.[26] Hartwick (1978) tried to estimate the consequences of multiple exhaustible resources for the DHSS model and found no incompatibility. Asheim *et al.* (2003) studied the importance of perfect substitutability in an optimal setting. They find that perfect substitutability is not required as long as the technology exists for an 'eventual productivity path' (i.e. as long as the sustainability macro-Trilemma can be solved). The World Bank (2006) and Markandya and Pedroso-Galinato (2007) consider empirical evidence on the substitutability and find high substitutability so far.

The common view today is that WS is in essence a special, regular case in what would be a unified strong sustainability (Hediger, 2006) paradigm. The WS model seems suitable for most historical situations. Strong sustainability indicators could be used instead of GS when dealing with irreplaceable ecosystem services or irreversible biodiversity losses, where shadow prices cannot be computed.

A more potent criticism of the strong sustainability paradigm has to do with the links between physical constraints/substitutability and equity. Any model based on the notion of value has a *normative* perspective. Norms characterize the properties of economic states and paths between states in what Dasgupta (2001) calls after Meade (1989) the 'good enough society' where institutions exist to promote and implement first-best solutions so that optimal paths form a realistic aim for the considered economy. We showed how the WS model is also workable in *kakotopia* the 'not-so-good society' of inefficient RAMs that is the reality of most developing countries today.

In the original Solow (1974) model, equity is based on Rawls (1971)'s criterion for inter-generational equity.[27] Solow also shows that the Maximin criterion is highly dependent on the initial condition: 'if the initial capital stock is very small, no more will be accumulated and the standard of living will be low forever' (Solow, 1974, p. 11).

An application of the Maximin in economics[28] is therefore (a) an objective of constant consumption over time as the condition for intergenerational equity and (b) an underlying condition on the capital stock from which the flows of services (i.e. consumption) are to be derived. Early generations can have a higher consumption/capital ratio, because what they need to pass on is a sufficient *technical progress adjusted capital* to the next one.

The version of the Maximin proposed by Solow delivered a criterion for *outcome based sustainability*: some definition of consumption should be kept constant over time. Its formalization is detailed above. But the transmission of capital from a better-off individual in the (theoretical) early generation should also be scrutinized to make sure this transmission will be to the benefit of the 'least advantaged members of society'.

In the RAMs scrutinized by the strong sustainability paradigm, the problem is entirely different. Individuals in a generation own instruments of wealth that are either non-substitutable or imperfectly substitutable, for physical reasons or lacking trading possibilities. Should the share of these non-substitutable wealth instruments owned by each individual not be the same[29], intragenerational inequalities will endure. They may feed into intergenerational inequalities depending on the evolution of physical substitutability.

Although the DHSS model would become the basis of the WS model, intragenerational equity is, to our knowledge, not addressed in it. It is usually argued that intragenerational equity is addressed with different tools and in different models with an ambition to tackle this particular issue. It should be dealt with using relevant redistributive policy (depending on the preferences of voters) as 'No reliable theory exists to integrate those to a comprehensive economic development approach' (Arrow *et al.*, 2012).

Intragenerational equity is discussed in the literature on the resource curse (Van Der Ploeg, 2011) and the many commentaries on the best possible use for resource windfalls (Oleson, 2011; Kuralbayeva and Stefanski, 2013). Reinvestment of resource windfalls could be tailored for redistributive purposes, but in the literature on GS, emphasis is put on optimal reinvestment (Van der Ploeg, 2010) to counter rent-seeking and corruption. Windfall management and redistribution should be undertaken to fulfil the equity imperative of constant consumption (in value terms) over time within *and* between generations.

It is not clear whether this equity rule for consumption, as in Hartwick (1977), was defined primarily as a desirable contract between current generations to preserve far-off future generations capabilities to maintain utility levels. In value terms, the constant consumption target is also an incentive to increase productivity (hence sparing resources via increased efficiency) so that consumption of *physical* quantities can effectively increase at constant value. Future generations experience physical gains on top of value gains for effort and thrift.

The trade-off between consumption and investment in the productive base (the wealth instruments) is ethically indefensible if not grounded in robust intra- and intergenerational equity criteria. This leaves the amount of needed reinvestment and the actual level of constant consumption attainable to be quantified.

3. Genuine Savings: Empirical Methods

The World Bank produces estimates of GS and wealth for most of the world's economies (World Bank, 1997, 2006, 2011) for an extensive sample of countries and regions in the world. The World Bank method is based on a series of publications by Kirk Hamilton and his coauthors (Hamilton, 1994, 1996; Hamilton and Clemens, 1999).

Besides yearly estimates of GS using accounting data, the World Bank provides an estimate of comprehensive wealth, or total capital (which are viewed as being equal to each other). The method is best explained in World Bank (2011, p. 94). Wealth is defined as:

$$W_t = \int_t^\infty C(s)^{-r(s-t)} ds \tag{30}$$

where C is consumption, s in the current period and r is the social rate of return. r is calculated using the Keynes–Ramsey formula. This value of wealth is obtained by assuming that the original observed level of consumption is sustainable, and gives an upper bound to the estimate of wealth for a given country. The next step is to estimate the relative size of the instruments of wealth (types of capital) within this total. Indeed, the very rationale for looking for an upper bound for wealth is precisely that some instruments of wealth cannot be estimated in their entirety, or are completely ignored. This claim is backed by the very high implicit rate of return on wealth if wealth was only composed of produced capital.[30] Estimates of the subcomponents of intangible capital can be found in the previous report (World Bank, 2006, chap. 7, p. 87). The authors show that the biggest component of intangible capital is likely to be the quality of institutions, followed by human capital. For the World Bank, GS is the year-on-year change in the value of a country's total capital.[31]

3.1 Empirical Evidence on GS

A number of studies have constructed empirical estimates of GS, and these are summarized in Table 1. There are a number of challenges to produce empirical values which correspond closely to their theoretical equivalents. One of the biggest challenges is the measurement of natural capital resource rents, as in theory the marginal costs should be deducted from the market price, whereas in practice it is the average costs that are deducted from market prices.[32] Hamilton (1994, p. 162) argues that this deviation will be small if it is assumed that there are distinct extraction costs for a number of resources and if for any given resource the difference in marginal cost between the first and last unit extracted is small. Other measurement issues are the units of measure, spatial resolution, aggregation, abatement costs and lack of WTP

Table 1. Empirical Estimates of Genuine Savings Measures.

Authors	N	Time Period	Variables Constructed
Pearce and Atkinson (1993)	20	1 year (c. 1990)	[1], [2], [3]
Hamilton (1994)	n/a	1961–1991	[5]
World Bank (1995)	n/a	1961–1991	[5]
Hamilton and Clemens (1999)	103	1970–1993	[4], [5]
Rubio (2004)	2	1936–1985	[1], [2], [3], [8]
World Bank (2006)	123	2000	[1], [2], [3], [4], [5]
Pezzey et al. (2006)	1	1992–1999	[1], [2], [3], [7], [8]
Mota and Martins (2010)	1	1990–2005	[1], [2], [3], [4], [5], [7]
Ferreira and Moro (2011)	1	1995–2005	[2], [3], [4], [5]
Lindmark and Acar (2013)	1	1850–2000	[2], [3], [4], [5]
Greasley et al. (2014)	1	1765–2000	[2], [3], [4], [5], [6], [7]
Oxley et al. (2014)	3	1870–2000	[4], [7]
Pezzey and Burke (2014)	Global (Σ120)	2005	[5], [6], [7]

(willingness to pay) measures for non-market impacts (Hamilton 1994, p. 163–164). Also, for cross-country comparisons, the choice of exchange rates, deflators and discount rates are problematic. Given these issues, there is a trade-off between depth and scale: in order to obtain comparable estimates for as broad a range of countries and regions as possible it is necessary to make a trade-off in the accuracy of data (e.g. using international estimates of costs instead of country specific costs). For individual country studies it is possible to get more refined data but it is then difficult to make direct cross-country comparisons as data are not of similar consistency.

The following indicators of changes in the 'instruments of wealth' are commonly constructed, with [3] and [4] the most common examples presented:

1. Gross investment (savings): Gross fixed capital formation + inventories + net foreign investment
2. Net investment (savings): [1] – depreciation of reproducible capital
3. Green investment (savings): [2] + Δ natural capital
4. Genuine investment (savings) (GS): [3] + Δ human capital
5. Pollutant adjusted GS: [4] – damage from pollutants (typically CO2)
6. Malthusian savings/wealth dilution: [3] or [4] adjusted for population growth
7. Technology augmented GS: [3] or [4] augmented by the present value of total factor productivity (TFP)
8. Trade adjusted GS: [3] or [4] augmented by the present value of Capital Gains from Trade

For all of these measures, the changes in capital are evaluated between adjacent years t and $t + 1$. In [3], renewable and non-renewable natural capital are treated differently. Renewables such as forestry and fisheries are added to the measure if there is an increase in stocks and subtracted if there is a decrease. However, depletion of non-renewables are subtracted whereas new discoveries are either not counted or treated as windfalls. Hamilton (1994, p. 167) and Hamilton *et al.* (1997, pp. 17–18) argue that new discoveries should not be treated separately as they appear in [1] in the form of investment in exploration. In addition to [1]–[6] listed above, Hamilton *et al.* (1997) illustrate ways in which these indicators can be further expanded to take account of endogenous technological progress, resource discoveries and how to account for critical levels of natural capital. Commonly, only the most important market-orientated forms of natural capital are included in these measures and as a result non-market resources (such as many ecosystem service values) are not included and thus are undervalued.

Technological change is an important concept in constructing sustainability indicators and a number of questions arise empirically: should it be included, how can it be measured, and how can it be incorporate into the GS framework. Theoretically, Weitzman (1997, p. 2) argues for the inclusion of a measure of technological progress because 'future growth is driven by the rate of technological progress, however it is conceptualised'. However, this leads to the issue of how to measure technological progress. A number of indicators are available such as patents, research and development (R & D) expenditure, energy intensity and total factor productivity. Incorporating some of these indicators is empirically difficult given the monetary unit of measurement of GS. In the existing literature two different approaches have been adopted to incorporate technological change, both based on TFP. Changes in TFP are used as an indicator of technological progress. Pezzey *et al.* (2006), following Weitzman (1997), calculate the present value contribution of TFP growth to future income. In contrast Arrow *et al.* (2012) incorporate a measure of TFP by adding the TFP growth rate to the wealth per capita growth rate; see Greasley *et al.* (2014) for more discussion. However, as TFP is a growth accounting residual, in the words of Abromovitz (1956) a 'measure of our ignorance', future research could attempt to incorporate alternative indicators of technical change such as patents, R & D expenditure and energy intensity.

Another empirical issue relates to the choice of discount rate. This is important for any variable that is measured by discounting (e.g. pollution damages, TFP, values of resource depreciation). The underlying theory considers a social discount rate which is empirically not possible to observe (Gollier, 2012). In practice, empirical studies incorporate proxies such as measures of long-run real discount rates using long-run growth rates, long-run interest rates and central bank discount rates.

One of the first measures of GS was by Pearce and Atkinson (1993) who constructed measures for 18 countries to determine if they were on sustainable (positive values) or unsustainable (negative values) development paths. The measures constructed were [1], [2] and [3] but they noted the difficulty of accurately measuring and valuing natural capital, a theme which is persistent in all estimates. Contemporaneously, Hamilton (1994) reported estimates of [4] for OECD countries and sub-Saharan countries from 1961 to 1991. Hamilton (1994, p. 166) compared various green accounting measures and argued that although measures of green national income were useful in their own right, measures of [2]–[4] 'provide a current measure of trends towards or away from sustainability, with concomitant signals for policy'.

Since the mid-1990s the World Bank has reported GS estimates for various countries (World Bank 1995, pp. 52–56; Hamilton *et al.*, 1997). Data for World Bank GS estimates are available for almost every country from 1970 and these are annually updated (World Bank, 2006, 2011).[33] World Bank (2006, p. 37) outlines the methods used to calculate these estimates. Natural capital is valued at world prices minus total costs of production. Non-renewable natural capital (fuel, metal and minerals) included in the estimates are 'oil, natural gas, and coal, bauxite, copper, gold, iron ore, lead, nickel, phosphate, silver, tin, and zinc'. Renewable natural capital, mainly forestry, is treated differently in that only extraction that exceeds natural growth is subtracted from net savings. Pollution damages from CO_2 and particulate damage are also subtracted from net investment. Expenditure on education is also included in the measure as a proxy for human capital formation. The World Bank (2006) urges caution when interpreting the resulting savings measures as there are a number of omitted assets, such as diamonds, fisheries, soil erosion and many ecosystem service values. Other limitations of the World Bank measure are also evident, as resource rents in most cases do not rely on country specific prices or costs and forestry growth is not added to GS estimates. The human capital proxy is an underestimate as education expenditure does not equate to all investments in human capital, nor does the measure capture on the job-training or private education expenditure. The excluded intangible assets are also very difficult to measure and value. Essentially, the construction of GS by the World Bank is a step towards a sustainability metric rather than an end in itself.

Hamilton and Clemens (1999) present and analyse GS data constructed at a national level and for different geographic regions. They provide information on how these estimates were constructed.[34] The database constructed is for the period 1970–1993 and covers developing and developed countries. GS was constructed from national accounts using [1], depletion of natural resources, CO_2 emissions and also education expenditure. Hamilton and Clemens (1999) inferred from their data whether a country was on a sustainable/unsustainable path if it had a positive/negative value of GS.

More recently, Pezzey and Burke (2014) have constructed a global estimate of GS ([5]) using the World Banks country-level data set. Pezzey and Burke (2014) include measures of technological change and population growth ([6] & [7]), and compare conventional WB estimates of GS, which, on the whole, suggest global sustainability whilst other indicators of sustainable development, such as the Ecologial footprint, suggest the opposite. An innovation of Pezzey and Burke (2014) to resolve this discrepancy is through the selection of CO_2 prices. Rather than using a literature based estimate of the social cost of carbon (e.g. Tol, 2009), they modify the underlying DICE (Dynamic integrated model of Climate and the Economy) models on which the World Bank's carbon price estimate was based. They find that a DICE model in which future CO_2 emissions are optimally controlled leads to conclusions of sustainability not too dissimilar from the World Bank. However, a DICE model where future CO_2 emissions are uncontrolled (business as usual) leads to significantly different (i.e. unsustainable) conclusions to the WB measure of GS.

There are also a number of country specific estimates of GS in addition to the cross-country estimates. For example, Hanley *et al.* (1999) and Pezzey *et al.* (2006) have constructed measures of GS for Scotland over the periods 1980–1993 and 1992–1999, respectively. Using country-specific data they were able to calculate more refined variants of the natural capital than the cruder cross-country comparisons. The purpose of Hanley *et al.* (1999) was to construct a variety of sustainability indicators for Scotland over the period 1980–1993, one of which was GS. The measure of GS presented was [3] above with no inclusion of education expenditure. Hanley *et al.* (1999) found that inclusion/exclusion of offshore oil had a big impact on the GS estimate because the inclusion of oil extraction suggested an unsustainable path. However, when discoveries were included this suggested a more sustainable path. Pezzey *et al.* (2006) also constructed a variant of [3] with natural capital data including a variety of data on coal and other minerals, fisheries, forestry and oil. Pollution was calculated by sector of the Scottish economy. An innovation in this study was the inclusion of the value of time and terms of trade effects. The resulting estimates were positive and indicated that Scotland was not on an unsustainable development path.

In a similar vein to Pezzey *et al.* (2006), Mota and Martins (2010) constructed time-series estimates of GS for Portugal over the period 1990–2005. They include a basket of pollutants and detailed data on forestry and other forms of natural capital. Also, as with Pezzey *et al.* (2006), they incorporate a measure of technological progress. Mota and Martins (2010) argued that the message of sustainability depended on the variant of GS used: excluding education expenditure resulted in a downward trend of GS resulting in negative values in the early 2000s; whereas including education and TFP signalled sustainable levels of development.

Likewise, Ferreira and Moro (2011) construct comprehensive estimates of GS for Ireland and found negative estimates of GS from 1995 to 1997 which they attributed to environmental degradation. Their GS calculations were also significantly lower than the World Bank estimates for Ireland and they argued that this illustrated the importance of expanding the comprehensiveness of the World Bank estimates as they overestimated Ireland's sustainability path. However, Edens (2013) is critical of the findings of Ferreira and Moro (2011) and outlines how they made errors in their calculations of the pricing of pollutants. Yet, Ferreira and Moro (2013) illustrate how their finding of negative GS for two consecutive years were still valid when environmental damages were priced accordingly.

Longer-run estimates of GS have also been constructed. Rubio (2004) constructed long-run indicators of [1],[2],[3] and [8] for Venezuela and Mexico from the 1930s to the 1980s, but natural capital only considered one asset: oil. However, in the case of Venezuela, the subtraction of oil rents from net capital resulted in negative GS throughout almost the entire period of the study. Mexico also experienced large negative GS in the early 1980s. Rubio (2004) attempted to reconcile these persistent negative GS with historical experience of both countries that indicated neither had in fact been 'unsustainable'. Rubio (2004) addressed this by incorporating capital gains in the measures of GS, [8] above, but even here calculations did not indicate positive GS. A result Rubio (2004) attributed to the fact that technological change was not included in the measure of GS.

Lindmark and Acar (2013) construct long-run time-series estimates of Swedish GS ([2], [3], [4], [5]) over the period 1850–2000. They incorporate pollutants (CO_2, SO_2 and NOx). They found a negative trend in GS in the 1800s and a gradual transition to positive GS around 1910 and continuing positive throughout the twentieth century. Lindmark and Acar (2013) argue that this shift from negative to positive supported their hypothesis that industrialization was preceded by a shift from negative to positive GS. However, as with Ferreira and Moro (2011), this seems to be a reflection of how pollutants were priced when incorporated into the measures of GS.

Greasley and coauthors have also constructed long-run time series for Britain (1765–2000), Germany (1850–2000) and the US (1869–2000) (Greasley *et al.*, 2014; Kunnas *et al.*, 2014; Oxley *et al.*, 2014). They find that for Britain there were times of negative GS in the early industrial revolution and during the two World Wars in the 20th century but that GS was positive for the most part. GS was also predominantly positive in the US except during the World Wars and the Great Depression. German GS was also mostly positive except during the aftermath of the Second World War.

Empirical work has also focused more explicitly on estimates and decompositions of wealth. Examples in this literature include World Bank (1995); World Bank (2006, 2011), UNU-IHDP and UNEP (2012), Arrow *et al.* (2012) and McLaughlin *et al.* (2014).[35] There are essentially two approaches to the measurement of wealth. First, capital stocks (Reproducible, Natural, Human and Health) are estimated and a measure of comprehensive wealth is aggregated. Alternatively, a measure of wealth is constructed from the present value of total consumption over a lifetime and estimates of the capital share of wealth are derived from available data. Using the latter approach, the World Bank (2006, 2011) finds a growing importance of what it deems 'intangible capital' which is approximated to be human capital and other factors not accounted for. Arrow *et al.* (2012), using the former approach, find that health capital is the most dominant form of wealth. These approaches are in similar vein to the GS approach as they view changes in wealth (i.e. investment/disinvestment) as indicating sustainable/unsustainable development.

As various studies indicate, there are numerous ways of measuring sustainable development (income, savings or wealth based), however each measure offers different signals to policy makers for improving sustainability paths. The World Bank's preferred measure of GS is not without criticism. For example Vincent (2001) is critical of the consensus regarding the reporting and collecting of green national accounting estimates without regard to their predictive power. Ferreira and Vincent (2005) are also critical of the underlying assumptions in the construction of GS estimates.

Elsewhere, Pillarisetti (2005) argues that GS is conceptually and empirically weak. From a conceptual perspective, Pillarisetti (2005) takes the view that, as GS is a national measure of WS, it overlooks key international externalities. From an empirical perspective, Pillarisetti (2005) is highly critical of the World Bank data and argues that the findings of sustainability/unsustainability are drawn from a small number of outliers that are mainly fuel-rich countries. Pillarisetti (2005) illustrates that 50 developed countries indicate positive GS but when ecological indicators are used they display negative signals. He thus argues that GS 'by ignoring global externalities, portrays a positive picture of sustainability for advanced countries and vice versa [for developing countries]'. Furthermore, since conventional net investment [2] and GS [4] are highly correlated, GS adds little additional value to conventional concepts. However, from a predictive perspective, it is not the correlation between the indicators that is important but the slope of the regression line involving the indicator and a measure of future well-being. In this scenario, GS may be a useful measure if it 'corrects' the slope and aligns it with the theoretical properties of the GS model outlined above.

4. Testing the Predictive Power of GS

Whilst thanks to the efforts of the World Bank there are GS estimates available for almost every country, empirical tests of its predictive power are less common. Table 2 compiles a number of studies that have explicitly tested the theoretical properties of GS. However, an issue with comparability of these results is the lack of consistency of the variables under consideration. For the most part, studies have used data over different time periods and different countries. In general, tests to date have differed in their methods (panel versus time series), time horizon and choice of discount rates. The formal framework for econometrically testing the theoretical properties of GS was set out by Ferreira and Vincent (2005):[36]

$$PV\Delta C_{it} = \beta_0 + \beta_1 g_{it} + \epsilon_{it} \tag{31}$$

$$PV\Delta C_{it} + PV(\Delta y_{it} w_{it}) = \beta_0 + \beta_1 g_{it} + \epsilon_{it} \tag{32}$$

where PV ΔC_{it} is the present value of future changes in consumption and PV $(\Delta y_{it} w_{it})$ is the present value of future changes in wealth per capita adjusted for population growth.

From these econometric specifications, Ferreira and Vincent (2005) set out 4 testable hypotheses:

1. $\beta_1 = 0$ and $\beta_1 = 1$
2. $\beta_1 > 0$ and $\beta_1 \Rightarrow 1$ as the measure of S is extended to include more types of capital
3. $\beta_1 > 0$
4. The model will better predict $\overline{C}_{it} - C_{it}$ when a broader measure of S_{it} is used.

The first hypothesis is the most stringent test of GS in that it tests for a 1-for-1 relationship between the savings indicator and future consumption, the second is less stringent but implies a relationship closer to 1 as more types of capital are included in the explanatory variable, the third is the least stringent of all and only implies that a positive relationship exists between the savings indicator and future well-being. As most tests do not find evidence for hypothesis 1, the discussion below focuses on hypotheses 2 and 3, and Table 2 presents the β_1 coefficients from the various studies implicitly or explicitly using this framework.

One of the first tests is by Vincent (2001) using data constructed from 13 Latin American countries over the period 1973–1986. Vincent tests the predictive power of Green Net National Product and 'Genuine Savings', although for the sake of consistency this is labelled as 'Green Savings' in Table 2 as it does not include a measure for human capital. Vincent (2001) tests both aggregate measures and disaggregate measures of Green Savings. For the aggregate data, Vincent (2001) finds a positive β_1 coefficients using both OLS and GLS panel estimators. For the disaggregate measure in Vincent (2001, table 8), the various components of GS have their

Table 2. Summary of Tests of the Predictive Power of Genuine Savings.

	Vincent (2001)	Ferreira and Vincent (2005)	World Bank (2006)	Ferreira, Hamilton and Vincent (2008)	Mota and Domingo (2013)	Mota and Domingo (2013)	Greasley et al. (2014)	Greasley et al. (2014)
N	13	93	54; 69; 74; 74; 78	64	1	1	1	1
Time coverage of data	1973–1997	1970–2001	1970–2000	1970–2001	1990–2005	1990–2005	1765–2000	1870–2000
Test time horizon (years)	10	10	20	20	5;10	5;10	20:30:100	20; 30; 100
Time coverage in test	1973–1986	1970–1991	1976–1980	1970–1982	n/a	n/a	1765–1989; 1765–1959; 1765–1909	1870–1989 1870–1959; 1870–1909
Estimation	Panel	Panel	Yearly cross-sections	Panel	Time-series	Time-series	Time-series	Time-series
Discount rate (%)	2	3.5	5	Country-specific; minus population growth rate	4	4	2.5; minus population growth rate	2.5
Dependent variable	$\bar{C}_{it} - C_{it}$	$\bar{C}_{it} - C_{it}$	PV ΔC	PV ΔC	$\bar{C}_{it} - C_{it}$	PV ΔC	PV ΔRW	PV ΔC
Gross Savings (β_1)	–	–0.02	1.02; 0.76; 1.05; 1.23; 0.83	–0.64	–0.11; –1.9	–0.11; –0.87	–	–
Net Savings (β_1)	–	0.128	0.66; 0.21; 0.65; 0.98; 0.71	–0.64	3.03; 2.76	0.62; 1.24	2.32; 0.37; 2.39	1.46; –0.22; 0.40
Green Savings (β_1)	0.492	0.129	1.28; 0.85; 1.26; 0.78; 0.99	0.43	1.66; 2.66	0.40; 1.28	1.62; –0.20; 2.89	0.65; –0.28; 0.68
Genuine savings (β_1)	–	0.037	–	–	–	–	1.85; 0.81; 2.71	1.14; 0.20; 1.04
Green Wealth	–	–	0.78; 0.57; 0.47; 0.36; 0.52	0.56	–	–	1.15; –0.69; –4.00	–
dilution adjustment (β_1)	–	–						
GS Wealth	–	–	–	–	–	–	1.34; –0.10; –3.99	–
dilution adjustment (β_1)	–	–						
Green TFP (β_1)	–	–	–	–	2.19; 2.15	0.56; 1.13	0.97; 1.64; 1.37	0.79; 1.29; 1.13
GS TFP (β_1)	–	–	–	–	2.51; 2.56	0.70; 1.44	0.83; 1.50; 1.30	0.69; 1.18; 1.12
GS TFP wealth	–	–	–	–	–	–	0.71; 1.43; 2.41	–
dilution adjustment (β_1)	–	–			–	–		–

expected sign (+ Savings, - depreciation, + Natural capital appreciation, - Natural resource rents) and are closer to 1 than the β_1 coefficients of the regression from the aggregated data.

In their benchmark results, Ferreira and Vincent (2005) did not find any support for hypothesis 1, but did find some support for hypotheses 2 and 3. However, the coefficient on β_1 when education expenditure was included was a fourth of the size of the coefficient for Green Savings. Ferreira and Vincent (2005) argue that this reflects the shortcomings of this variable as a proxy for human capital formation. When using alternative specifications, they found that increasing the time horizon increased the β_1 coefficients but that they were still significantly less than 1. Also, when the panel was disaggregated between OECD and non-OECD countries the resulting β_1 coefficients were significantly different and had opposing signs (e.g. for GS the β_1 coefficient for OECD v non-OCED was –0.274 v 0.322). Ferreira and Vincent (2005) suggest that the reason for the negative coefficient for OECD countries is due to the absence of any measure of technological progress and that net investment by itself underestimates average future consumption. In sum, Ferreira and Vincent (2005, p. 751) stated that 'results from our pooled analysis reject the hypothesis that even the broadest of the World Bank's net investment measures coincides with the difference between current and average future consumption'.

Building on these findings, Ferreira *et al.* (2008) focus on a sample of 64 developing countries. A key difference between Ferreira *et al.* (2008) and Ferreira and Vincent (2005) is a change in the specification of the dependent variable which is now the present value of changes in future consumption per capita and also the incorporation of 'wealth dilution'. The inclusion of the wealth dilution effect incorporates population growth into a GS framework. Over 20 year time horizons, Ferreira *et al.* (2008) find weakly negative β_1 coefficients for Gross and Net investment but they find much stronger positive β_1 coefficients for Green and population adjusted measures. Ferreira *et al.* (2008, p. 246) conclude that the results indicate that the GS indicators published by the World Bank should be interpreted 'as signals of future consumption paths if and only if the rates include this adjustment for natural capital'. However, Ferreira *et al.* (2008, p. 246) also note that better estimates of capital stocks are needed before it can 'confidently be stated that this adjustment significantly improves the performance of GS as an indicator of future consumption changes'.

World Bank (2006) provides an alternative test of the GS using yearly cross-sections from 1977 to 1980 to test the relationship between savings indicators and the present value of changes in future consumption.[37] However, as with Ferreira *et al.* (2008), these tests of GS use metrics that do not include education expenditure or pollutant damages. World Bank (2006) uses a 20-year time horizon for the present value of future changes in consumption and finds reasonably consistent positive β_1 coefficients for gross and 'genuine saving'. Furthermore, in line with Ferreira and Vincent (2005), World Bank (2006) finds that the various savings measures tested do not provide good predictors for future changes in consumption in developed countries arguing that this is a reflection of factors other than savings, such as technological innovation, learning by doing and institutional capital, being important in the growth performance of developed countries. However, World Bank (2006) also warns about the hazards inherent in attempting to test data given potential measurement error.

Mota and Domingos (2013) test Portuguese data over the period 1990–2005 using time-series methods. They test both specifications of the consumption variable with a host of GS measures, including models that incorporate technological progress. The tests were conducted over 5- and 10-year horizons and as with the finding of Ferreira and Vincent (2005) and Ferreira *et al.* (2008) the indicators performed better over longer-term horizons. Although it is unclear from the text what the time horizon, or rather the sample size, to perform these tests was. In all, Mota and Domingos (2013) find that incorporating TFP does not improve the explanatory power of their tests as they argue that the underlying production function does not incorporate green capital.

Greasley *et al.* (2014) test British data over a much longer time frame – 1765–2000 – and focus primarily on testing hypotheses 1 to 3. They use time-series methods, especially cointegration, to test the strength of correlation coefficients and conduct tests over much longer time horizons: 20, 50 and 100 time horizons. As the underlying theory is set in infinite time these time horizons are closer to the theoretical specification than the shorter horizons adopted by the other tests listed in Table 2. The tests were based on two welfare indicators, the present value of changes in real wages and the present value of changes in consumption per capita. Results were influenced by both the time horizon and the choice of discount factor over the period. In terms of real wages, the β_1 coefficients for net and GS were consistently positive over all time horizons but performed poorly over 50 year horizons, when notably cointegration was absent. Furthermore, measures of green investment performed poorly over all specifications. In terms of consumption, the various measures did not perform well. For net investment the β_1 coefficients ranged from -0.22 to 1.46 and for green the range was also broad from -0.28 to 0.68. All indicators performed especially poorly over the 50 year horizon and in no specification was a cointegrating relationship displayed.

Greasley *et al.* (2014) then incorporate a measure of technological progress by augmenting GS with the present value of changes in TFP over 20- and 30-year horizons. β_1 coefficients for the 20-year horizons are reported in Table 2. They found that technology augmented measures of GS (and Green investment) had a significant impact on the resulting coefficient estimates and also found evidence of cointegrating relationships, thus strengthening the findings. In addition, Greasley *et al.* (2014) introduced a wealth dilution effect and found this had a dramatic impact on the resulting coefficients and in many cases reversed the sign of the β_1 coefficients. However, when technology was included in these specifications the resulting β_1 coefficients reverted to positive and displayed cointegrating relationships. Thus, Greasley *et al.* (2014) argued for the inclusion of measures of technological change in GS estimates.

In contrast to the studies above that focus on monetary measures of future well-being, Gnegne (2009) adopts an alternative testing framework and focuses on the relationship between GS and non-monetary well-being indicators: infant mortality and the human development index. Using a panel of 36 developing countries over the period 1971–2000, the econometric model is specified as:

$$W_{it} = \beta_0 + \beta_1 S_{it} + \epsilon_{it} \tag{33}$$

where W is a well-being measure and S is a GS measure. The model is estimated over 5, 10 and 15 year sub-periods with the focus of the test being changes in the dependent variable. Gnegne (2009) finds positive correlations between measures of [3] and changes in the HDI and IMR and also that the coefficients are higher the longer the time horizon used. In addition, Gnegne (2009) tested [2], [3], [4] and [5] and found that [2] had a higher coefficient than the other measures but for changes in infant mortality [2] had the lowest coefficient. Gnegne (2009) noted that 'these results support the idea of a broader view of savings that includes human and natural capital'. When tests are expanded to include other explanatory variables Gnegne (2009) still finds a positive relationship between the savings indicators and well-being indicators. Overall, Gnegne (2009) concludes that there is a positive relationship between [4] and future changes in well-being and that the results would be more consistent with theory if they could be tested over a longer time horizon.

As illustrated in Table 2, there are a variety of tests but a lack of consistency across studies. There are also inconsistencies depending on whether tests are performed on panel or time-series data. However, there is an emerging consensus that longer-term horizons are better for testing GS. In terms of panel data, the various tests cited that excluded OECD countries from panels found greater support for hypotheses 1 and 2. However, the longest and widest panels are only available to test for relatively short time-horizons. In terms of time-series tests, tests over short horizons (5, 10 and 20) perform poorly. However, over the longest horizon (50, 100 years) GS performs best when there is an adjustment for technological progress.

5. Conclusion

This paper surveys the current literature on GS and the WS model. The combination of capital theory and equity concerns in the neoclassical theory of value in the 1970s set the theoretical foundations for the indicator. Empirical work from the late 1980s onwards demonstrated the practical applications. The indicator then gradually entered widespread use in the early 2000s, propelled by World Bank publications.

We discuss the theoretical underpinnings of GS in Section 2. GS can be most naturally derived from a *capabilities-based* definition of sustainability. GS emerges as the rate of change, using shadow prices, of total capital: it indicates future change in intergenerational well-being. An important result as it shows that a negative value for GS implies falling future well-being, as measured by consumption. GS are robust to limited physical substitutability in its intergenerational dimension, but fails to take intragenerational equity issues into account. We showed how, within the limiting assumptions of a competitive framework, GS can be amended for technical change, population growth and international trade.

In Section 3 we outline various empirical measures of GS including a presentation of the World Bank's method to compute GS. We review extant GS estimates for many countries and regions. We find these studies are not directly comparable, as different authors tend to use different versions of GS. As a rule of thumb, greater accounting of all instruments of wealth (including human capital, TFP growth) tends to bring about a message of probable sustainability for many countries over the long run.

We discussed in Section 4 how, as a predictor of future consumption, GS tends to perform poorly when a limited number of instruments are considered over short horizons. Longer time horizons typically improve the predictive power of the measure. So does the addition of measures of the gradual improvement of productivity and technology (mostly via the addition of an extra total factor productivity term in econometric tests).

More work could be done to improve the indicator. The better performance of the indicator on longer time horizons and the important empirical role of technical change both suggest that a better way to account for the economic structure for which GS is measured is needed. Institutions matter, but how to include measures of change in the quality of institutions over time is unclear. It is not yet clear whether the solution goes through the inclusion of more and more instruments of wealth, so as to 'shrink' the impact of the total factor productivity term, or if a more fundamental amendment of the approach is needed.

In the short run, some avenues for theoretical research seem to be promising. The first comes through a better understanding of the impact of international trade on sustainability. It is not yet clear whether economic specialization in a narrow range of productive activities is fostering or hindering sustainability. The second important avenue comes from the renewed interest in wealth inequalities. More investigation should be made on the impact on sustainability of an asymmetric distribution of instruments of wealth across agents.

GS as a concept is essentially forward looking; however, the only way to effectively test the implications of the theory is to use long run historical data. The scarcity of tests of GS suggests that the literature can benefit from more research in this direction. For example, there are geographic regions which are driving the cross-country comparisons – namely countries in Latin America, Africa and Asia – but more detailed country-specific studies would help expand our existing knowledge as to why this is the case. Is it simply the Pillarisetti (2005) critique that outliers are driving results or can GS say more about individual country experiences and future sustainability? Also, more needs to be done pre-1970s, as the GS estimates may be picking up price shocks from the various oil crises. In general, the sensitivity of GS estimates to how changes in capital stocks – especially natural capital – are valued is problematic.

Furthermore, attention needs to focus on countries that do not fit neatly into the GS framework. The solution heretofore has been to exclude them in cross-country studies but if the GS theoretical framework does not fit their economic record, then more needs to be done to explain why this is the case (e.g. see Ferreira and Vincent, 2005). Moreover, issues such as how governments influence consumption and savings can be informative to the study of sustainability. Also, historical peculiarities may shed light on future sustainability such as the collapse of consumption in post-War Germany, low TFP growth in Latin America and regulatory differences affecting savings rates in various countries such as Switzerland. Finally, the theoretical GS framework is set in infinite time, thus more long-run data for as broad a range of countries would help get a better understanding of the predictive power of GS and how well they match the historical record, as in Greasley *et al.* (2014). An obvious limitation here is the lack of standardized national accounts pre-dating the 1940s both in terms of savings or consumption. Vincent (2001) in particular was critical of the conventional measures of reproducible capital in Latin American countries, so more could be done in this direction. Lastly, attention could be directed toward ways to include non-monetary measures of well-being, such as anthropometric indicators, into the testing framework.

Acknowledgements

We thank the three referees for comments on an earlier version of the paper.

Notes

1. And indeed, acceptance that the notion of natural capital itself makes sense!
2. 'Wealth is wealth only because of its services. And services are services only because of their desirability in the mind of the man, and of the satisfactions which man expects them to render' (Fisher, 1906, p. 41).
3. This is what Fisher calls *income* (services rendered by (any)one wealth instrument) *outgo* and (services rendered to (any)one wealth instrument). Leisure is understood in this context as a reduced contribution to the maintenance of some instruments of wealth (lower use of labour services), and an increased use of services from leisure-related wealth instruments such as parks and gardens.
4. For Dasgupta-Heal–Solow or Dasgupta-Heal-Solow–Stiglitz, after authors contributing to the all important 1974 seminar on exhaustible resources (Dasgupta and Heal, 1974; Solow, 1974; Stiglitz, 1974a, b).

5. The function F is not assumed to be concave at this stage.

6. Considering the richness of the literature on amenities entering as arguments in the utility function (Krautkraemer, 1985) using only C seems limiting. As shown in Dasgupta (2009) and Arrow *et al.* (2012), adding more arguments to the utility function merely affects the structure of shadow prices. So we can consider C as an expanded vector of consumption goods. As stated above, consumption is the consumption of services, including leisure. All services are assumed to behave and yield utility the same way. In a similar vein, any effort reducing technology will be captured by the $A(t)$ term or the characterization of the RAM (see below).

7. This dynamic can be altered to reflect exhaustible resources. Using this general form from Dasgupta (2009) nests the non-renewable exhaustible resources case into the renewable exhaustible resources case.

8. For N to be positive, we assume also that $Q > 4b/m$ so that the renewal threshold is $Q[1 - (1 - 4b/mQ^{1/2}]$. Should N reach a value below this level, the stock will converge towards 0 over time and production would halt.

9. As we did not assume concavity in production, we do not assume a convex set of production or an optimal economy.

10. As stressed by Dasgupta (2009), this superstructure does not need to be efficient, include a benevolent social planner or exclude any real life distortions.

11. Which Dasgupta (2009) calls an 'economic programme'.

12. The only constraint put on the mathematical properties of α is that V must be differentiable. See Dasgupta (2009, p. 14) for a full discussion of the mathematical properties of the value function.

13. So that each input in the production function is essential.

14. This proposition is valid in a closed economy context. It holds in an open setting in general equilibrium.

15. So that again, technology and population are both constant over time.

16. And, by means of definition, constant consumption.

17. Defined as the sum of consumption and net investment.

18. This result hold under discounted utilitarianism if NNP and consumption are measured in terms of utility (or if the utility function is linearly homogeneous). Otherwise, NNP is the present value of the interest on future consumption, where the interest rate need not be constant.

19. Or more precisely the Solow (1974) interpretation of it as an intergenerational equity criterion.

20. Satisfying the usual conditions: concave, twice differentiable.

21. $\nabla U(C)(t)$ is a vector of partial derivatives as C is a vector of multiple consumption goods.

22. Although it might lower average quality depending on available education.

23. Population affects both the production function and the maximand as it is both population and the labour force. Hence, population size determines how total utility is divided to yield per capita utility. The rationale for including population as an argument in the utility function is presented in full in Arrow *et al.* (2003b).

24. Exchange rates are not considered: the world economy works under a single price system.

25. Fisher defined a system centred on the needs and wants of human-beings, assuming that there is no value as we understand it outside of human perception, so that valuation is necessarily performed through the prism of the definition of value by human stakeholders.

There is no intrinsic value in nature in that sense: the expression becomes, in the framework we lay here, an oxymoron, an opposition in the terms.

26. See Sabin (2013) for a historical discussion of the debates.

27. 'Each person has an equal right to the most extensive scheme of equal basic liberties for all' and 'social and economic inequalities are to meet two conditions: they must be (a) to the greatest expected benefit of the least advantaged members of society (the Maximin equity criterion) and (b) attached to offices and positions open to all under conditions of fair equality of opportunity' (Rawls, 1974, p. 142).

28. Note that Solow used the Maximin criterion to tackle intergenerational equity when Rawls opposed it being used this way (Rawls, 1974).

29. See Hanley *et al.* (2014) for a presentation of the links between intragenerational equity and strong sustainability.

30. In the example of Canada presented in World Bank (2011, p. 94) the implicit rate of return on produced capital is 35.9%.

31. The use of the Maximin criteria also imposed restrictions on consumption so that consumption is kept constant over time. As Dasgupta (2009) reminds us, the second-order derivative of consumption is assumed to be constant and not negative in most papers. Using the NNP or GS is equivalent in a competitive setting. In this scenario, the two indicators of the WS model yield a similar information on dynamic welfare and sustainability. GS are less demanding in imperfect economies.

32. Atkinson and Hamilton (2007) discuss issues measuring nonrenewable natural resources and pollution.

33. Data are available online at: http://data.worldbank.org/topic/environment

34. See Bolt *et al.* (2002) for a manual of how to construct GS.

35. See also the recent special issue on Wealth in *Oxford Review of Economic Policy*, 2014, 30.

36. Ferreira and Vincent (2005) use $\overline{C}_{it} - C_{it}$, average future consumption minus current consumption, as a measure of future well-being, however later studies incorporate an alternative dependent variable PV ΔC_{it}, the present value of future changes in consumption.

37. The tests draw on Hamilton (2005).

References

Abramovitz, M. (1956) Resource and Output Trends in the United States Since 1870, NBER, chapter Resource and output trends in the United States since 1870, pp. 1–23.

Acemoglu, D. and Robinson, J.A. (2012) *Why Nations Fail: The Origins of Power, Prosperity, and Poverty.* New York: Crown Publishers.

Arrow, K.J., Dasgupta, P. and Mäler, K.-G. (2003a) Evaluating projects and assessing sustainable development in imperfect economies. *Environmental and Resource Economics* 26(4): 647–685.

Arrow, K.J., Dasgupta, P. and Maler, K.G. (2003b) The genuine savings criterion and the value of population. *Economic Theory* 21(2-3): 217–225.

Arrow, K.J., Dasgupta, P., Goulder, L.H., Mumford, K.J. and Oleson, K. (2012) Sustainability and the measurement of wealth. *Environment and Development Economics* 17(03): 317–353.

Asheim, G.B. (1986) Hartwick's rule in open economies. *The Canadian Journal of Economics* 19(3): 395–402.

Asheim, G.B. (1994) Net national product as an indicator of sustainability. *Scandinavian Journal of Economics* 96(2): 257.

Asheim, G.B. (2007) Can NNP be used for welfare comparisons? *Environment and Development Economics* 12(1): 11.

Asheim, G.B. (2010) Global welfare comparisons. *Canadian Journal of Economics-Revue Canadienne D Economique* 43(4): 1412–1432.

Asheim, G.B. and Weitzman, M.L. (2001) Does NNP growth indicate welfare improvement? *Economics Letters* 73(2): 233–239.

Asheim, G.B., Buchholz, W. and Withagen, C.A. (2003) The Hartwick rule: myths and facts. *Environmental and Resource Economics* 25(2): 129–150.

Asheim, G.B., Buchholz, W., Hartwick, J.M., Mitra, T. and Withagen, C. (2007) Constant savings rates and quasi-arithmetic population growth under exhaustible resource constraints. *Journal of Environmental Economics and Management* 53(2): 213–229.

Atkinson, G. and Hamilton, K. (2002) International trade and the 'ecological balance of payments'. *Resources Policy* 28(1-2): 27–37.

Atkinson, G. and Hamilton, K. (2007) Progress along the path: evolving issues in the measurement of genuine saving. *Environmental and Resource Economics* 37(1): 43–61.

Atkinson, G., Agarwala, M. and Mu noz, P. (2012) Are national economies (virtually) sustainable? An empirical analysis of natural assets in international trade. In *Inclusive Wealth Report 2012 Measuring Progress Toward Sustainability* (pp. 87–117). Cambridge, UK: Cambridge University Press.

Bogmans, C. and Withagen, C.A. (2010) The pollution haven hypothesis. A dynamic perspective. *Revue Economique* 61(1): 93–114.

Brekke, K.A. (1994) Net national product as a welfare indicator. *Scandinavian Journal of Economics* 96(2): 241.

Buchholz, W., Dasgupta, S. and Mitra, T. (2005) Intertemporal equity and Hartwick's rule in an exhaustible resource model. *Scandinavian Journal of Economics* 107(3): 547–561.

Cheviakov, A.F. and Hartwick, J. (2009) Constant per capita consumption paths with exhaustible resources and decaying produced capital. *Ecological Economics* 68(12): 2969–2973.

Chichilnisky, G. (1994) North-south trade and the global environment. *The American Economic Review* 84(4): 851–874.

Dasgupta, P. (2001) *Human Well-Being and the Natural Environment.* Oxford: Oxford University Press.

Dasgupta, P. (2009) The welfare economic theory of green national accounts. *Environmental & Resource Economics* 42(1): 3–38.

Dasgupta, P. and Heal, G. (1974) The optimal depletion of exhaustible resources. *Review of Economic Studies* 41(128): 3.

Dasgupta, P. and Maler, K.-G. (2000) Net national product, wealth, and social well-being. *Environment and Development Economics* 5(1): 69–93.

Dasgupta, S. and Mitra, T. (1983) Intergenerational equity and efficient allocation of exhaustible resources. *International Economic Review* 24(1): 133–153.

D'Autume, A. and Schubert, K. (2008) Hartwick's rule and maximin paths when the exhaustible resource has an amenity value. *Journal of Environmental Economics and Management* 56(3): 260–274.

Divisia, F. (1925) L'indice monétaire et la théorie de la monnaie. *Revue d'économie Politique* 39: 842–864.

Dixit, A.K., Hammond, P. and Hoel, M. (1980) On Hartwick's rule for regular maximin paths of capital accumulation and resource depletion. *The Review of Economic Studies* 47(3): 551–556.

Dupuy, L. (2015) International trade and structural change: a dynamic model of weak sustainability. University of St. Andrews Discussion Papers in Environmental Economics 2015-12.

Edens, B. (2013) Comments on Ferreira and Moro (2011) Constructing genuine savings indicators for Ireland, 1995-2005. *Journal of Environmental Management* 127: 335–336.

Ferreira, S. and Moro, M. (2011) Constructing genuine savings indicators for Ireland, 1995-2005. *Journal of Environmental Management* 92(3): 542–553.

Ferreira, S. and Moro, M. (2013) Response to the comments on Ferreira and Moro (2011) 'Constructing genuine savings indicators for Ireland, 1995-2005'. *Journal of Environmental Management* 127: 337–338.

Ferreira, S. and Vincent, J.R. (2005) Genuine savings: leading indicator of sustainable development? *Economic Development and Cultural Change* 53(3): 17.

Ferreira, S., Hamilton, K. and Vincent, J.R. (2008) Comprehensive wealth and future consumption: accounting for population growth. *The World Bank Economic Review* 22(2): 233–248.

Fisher, I. (1906) *The Nature of Capital and Income*. London: Macmillan and Company Limited.

Gnegne, Y. (2009) Adjusted net saving and welfare change. *Ecological Economics* 68: 1127–1139.

Gollier, C. (2010) Ecological discounting. *Journal of Economic Theory* 145(2): 812–829.

Gollier, C. (2012) *Pricing the Planet's Future: The Economics of Discounting in an Uncertain World*. Princeton, NJ: Princeton University Press.

Greasley, D., Hanley, N., Kunnas, J., McLaughlin, E., Oxley, L. and Warde, P. (2014) Testing genuine savings as a forward-looking indicator of future well-being over the (very) long-run. *Journal of Environmental Economics and Management* 67: 171–188.

Hamilton, K. (1994) Green adjustments to GDP. *Resources Policy* 20(3): 155–168.

Hamilton, K. (1996) Pollution and pollution abatement in the national accounts. *Review of Income and Wealth* 42(1): 13–33.

Hamilton, K. (2005) Testing genuine savings. World Bank Research Working Paper 3577.

Hamilton, K. and Atkinson, G.D. (2006) *Wealth, Welfare and Sustainability*. Cheltenham, UK: Edward Elgar Publishing Ltd.

Hamilton, K. and Bolt, K. (2004) Resource price trends and development prospects. *Portuguese Economic Journal* 3(2): 85–97.

Hamilton, K. and Clemens, M. (1999) Genuine savings rates in developing countries. *World Bank Economic Review* 13(2): 24.

Hamilton, K. and Hartwick, J.M. (2005) Investing exhaustible resource rents and the path of consumption. *Canadian Journal of Economics-Revue Canadienne D Economique* 38(2): 615–621.

Hamilton, K. and Hepburn, C. (2014) Wealth. *Oxford Review of Economic Policy* 30(1): 1–20.

Hamilton, K. and Withagen, C. (2007) Savings growth and the path of utility Croissance de l'épargne et sentier d'utilité. *Canadian Journal of Economics/Revue canadienne d'économique* 40(2): 703–713.

Hanley, N., Moffatt, I., Faichney, R. and Wilson, M. (1999) Measuring sustainability: a time series of alternative indicators for Scotland. *Ecological Economics* 28(1): 55–73.

Hanley, N., Dupuy, L. and Mclaughlin, E. (2014) Genuine savings and sustainability. University of St. Andrews Discussion Papers in Environmental Economics 2015-09.

Hartwick, J.M. (1977) Intergenerational equity and the investing of rents from exhaustible resources. *The American Economic Review* 67(5): 972–974.

Hartwick, J.M. (1978) Investing returns from depleting renewable resources stocks and intergenerational equity. *Economics Letters* 1: 85–88.

Hartwick, J.M. (1990) Natural resources, national accounting and economic depreciation. *Journal of Public Economics* 43: 291–304.

Hartwick, J.M. (1995) Constant consumption paths in open economies with exhaustible resources. *Review of International Economics* 3(3): 275–283.

Hartwick, J.M., Long, N.V. and Tian, H. (2003) On the peaking of consumption with exhaustible resources and zero net investment. *Environmental and Resource Economics* 24: 235–244.

Hediger, W. (2006) Weak and strong sustainability, environmental conservation and economic growth. *Natural Resource Modeling* 19(3): 359–394.

Krautkraemer, J.A. (1985) Optimal growth, resource amenities and the preservation of natural environment. *Review of Economic Studies* 52(1): 153–170.

Kunnas, J., McLaughlin, E., Hanley, N., Greasley, D., Oxley, L. and Warde, P. (2014) Counting carbon: historic emissions from fossil fuels, long-run measures of sustainable development and carbon debt. *Scandinavian Economic History Review* 62(3): 243–265.

Kuralbayeva, K. and Stefanski, R. (2013) Windfalls, structural transformation and specialization. *Journal of International Economics* 90(2): 273–301.

Li, C.-Z. and Löfgren, K.-G. (2013) Genuine savings measurement under uncertainty and its implications for depletable resource management. *Environmental Economics* 4(3): 20–25.

Lindmark, M. and Acar, S. (2013) Sustainability in the making? A historical estimate of swedish sustainable and unsustainable development 1850–2000. *Ecological Economics* 86: 176–187.

Markandya, A. and Pedroso-Galinato, S. (2007) How substitutable is natural capital? *Environmental and Resource Economics* 37(1): 297–312.

McLaughlin, E., Hanley, N., Greasley, D., Kunnas, J., Oxley, L. and Warde, P. (2014) Historical wealth accounts for britain: progress and puzzles in measuring the sustainability of economic growth. *Oxford Review of Economic Policy* 30(1): 44–69.

Meade, J.E. (1989) *Agathotopia: The Economics of Partnership.* Aberdeen: Aberdeen University Press.

Meadows, D.H., Meadows, D.L., Randers, J. and Behrens III, W.W. (1972) *The Limits of Growth.* London : Earth Island Ltd.

Mitra, T. (2002) Intertemporal equity and efficient allocation of resources. *Journal of Economic Theory* 107(2): 356–376.

Mota, R.P. and Domingos, T. (2013) Assessment of the theory of comprehensive national accounting with data for Portugal. *Ecological Economics* 95: 188–196.

Mota, R.P. and Martins, D.T. (2010) Analysis of genuine savings and potential net national income: Portugal, 1990–2005. *Ecological Economics* 69: 1934–1942.

Okumura, R. and Cai, D. (2007) Sustainable constant consumption in a semi-open economy with exhaustible resources. *The Japanese Economic Review* 58(2): 226–237.

Oleson, K.L.L. (2011) Shaky foundations and sustainable exploiters: problems with national weak sustainability measures in a global economy. *Journal of Environment and Development* 20(3): 329–349.

Oxley, L., Hanley, N., Greasley, D., Blum, M., McLaughlin, E., Kunnas, J. and Warde, P. (2014) Empirical testing of genuine savings as an indicator of weak sustainability: a three-country analysis of long run trends. Stirling Economics Discussion Paper 2014-03.

Pearce, D.W. and Atkinson, G.D. (1993) Capital theory and the measurement of sustainable development: an indicator of "weak" sustainability. *Ecological Economics* 8(2): 103–108.

Pearce, D.W., Markandya, A. and Barbier, E.B. (1989) *Blueprint for a Green Economy.* London: Earth-scan Publications Ltd.

Pemberton, M. and Ulph, D. (2001) Measuring income and measuring sustainability. *Scandinavian Journal of Economics* 103(1): 25–40.

Pezzey, J. (1997) Sustainability constraints versus "optimility" versus intertemporal concern, and axioms versus data. *Land Economics* 73(4): 448–466.

Pezzey, J.C. (2004) One-sided sustainability tests with amenities, and changes in technology, trade and population. *Journal of Environmental Economics and Management* 48(1): 613–631.

Pezzey, J.C.V. and Burke, P.J. (2014) Towards a more inclusive and precautionary indicator of global sustainability. *Ecological Economics* 116: 141–154.

Pezzey, J.C., Hanley, N., Turner, K. and Tinch, D. (2006) Comparing augmented sustainability measures for Scotland: is there a mismatch? *Ecological Economics* 57(1): 60–74.

Pillarisetti, J.R. (2005) The World Bank's 'genuine savings' measure and sustainability. *Ecological Economics* 55(4): 599–609.

Proops, J.L.R., Atkinson, G., Schlotheim, B.F.V. and Simon, S. (1999) International trade and the sustainability footprint: a practical criterion for its assessment. *Ecological Economics* 28(1): 75–97.

Ramsey, F.P. (1928) A mathematical theory of savings. *The Economic Journal* 38(152): 543–559.

Rawls, J. (1971) *A Theory of Justice.* Cambridge, MA: University of Harvard Press.

Rawls, J. (1974) Some reasons for the maximin criterion. *The American Economic Review* 64(2): 141–146.

Rubio, M.D.M. (2004) The capital gains from trade are not enough: evidence from the environmental accounts of Venezuela and Mexico. *Journal of Environmental Economics and Management* 48(3): 1175–1191.

Sabin, P. (2013) *The Bet: Paul Ehrlich, Julian Simon, and Our Gamble over Earth's Future.* Yale, CT: Yale University Press.

Samuelson, P.A. (1949) International factor-price equalisation once again. *The Economic Journal* 59(234): 181–197.

Sato, R. and Kim, Y. (2002) Hartwick's rule and economic conservation laws. *Journal of Economic Dynamics and Control* 26(3): 437–449.

Solow, R.M. (1974) Intergenerational equity and exhaustible resources. *The Review of Economic Studies* 41: 29–45.

Solow, R.M. (1986) On the intergenerational allocation of natural resources. *The Scandinavian Journal of Economics* 88(1): 141–149.

Stiglitz, J.E. (1974a) Growth with exhaustible natural resources: efficient and optimal growth paths. *The Review of Economic Studies* 41: 123–137.

Stiglitz, J.E. (1974b) Growth with exhaustible natural resources: the competitive Economy. *The Review of Economic Studies* 41: 139–152.

Stokey, N.L., Lucas Jr, R.E. and Prescott, E.C. (1989) *Recursive Methods in Economic Dynamics.* Cambridge, MA: Harvard University Press.

Tol, R.S.J. (2009) The economic effects of climate change. *Journal of Economic Perspectives* 23(2): 29–51.

UKNEA (2011) The UK National Ecosystem Assessment. Technical report, UNEP-WCMC, Cambridge.

UNU-IHDP and UNEP (2012) *Inclusive Wealth Report 2012: Measuring Progress toward Sustainability.* Cambridge: Cambridge University Press.

Van der Ploeg, F. (2010) Why do many resource-rich countries have negative genuine saving? Anticipation of better times or rapacious rent seeking. *Resource and Energy Economics* 32(1): 28–44.

Van Der Ploeg, F. (2011) Natural resources: curse or blessing? *Journal of Economic Literature* 49(2): 366–420.

Ventura, J. (1997) Growth and interdependence. *The Quarterly Journal of Economics* 112(1): 57–84.

Victor, P.A. (1991) Indicators of sustainable development: some lessons from capital theory. *Ecological Economics* 4(3): 191–213.

Vincent, J.R. (2001) Are greener national accounts better? Centre for International Development at Harvard University working papers 63.

Vincent, J.R., Panayotou, T. and Hartwick, J.M. (1997) Resource depletion and sustainability in small open economies. *Journal of Environmental Economics and Management* 33(3): 274–286.

Weitzman, M.L. (1976) On the Welfare Significance of National Product in a Dynamic Economy. *The Quarterly Journal of Economics* 90(1): 156–162.

Weitzman, M.L. (1997) Sustainability and technical progress. *The Scandinavian Journal of Economics* 99(1): 1–13.

World Bank (1995) *Monitoring Environmental progress: A Report on Work in Progress.* Washington, DC: World Bank.

World Bank (1997) *Expanding the Measure of Wealth: Indicators of Environmentally Sustainable Development.* Washington, DC: The World Bank.

World Bank (2006) *Where Is the Wealth of Nations? Measuring Capital for the 21st century.* Washington, DC: The World Bank.

World Bank (2011) *The Changing Wealth of Nations: Measuring Sustainable Development in the New Millennium.* Washington, DC: World Bank.

World Commission on Environment and Development (1987) Our common future, Technical report, The United Nations, New York.

9

SAVINGS IN TIMES OF DEMOGRAPHIC CHANGE: LESSONS FROM THE GERMAN EXPERIENCE

Axel Börsch-Supan

Munich Research Institute for the Economics of Aging (MEA) at MPISOC, Technical University of Munich, Germany, and National Bureau of Economic Research (NBER), Cambridge, Massachusetts

Tabea Bucher-Koenen

Munich Research Institute for the Economics of Aging (MEA) at MPISOC and Netspar

Michela Coppola and Bettina Lamla

Munich Research Institute for the Economics of Aging (MEA) at MPISOC

1. Introduction

In order to cope with demographic change, far reaching reforms of the pension systems have been implemented in many countries in the past decades. These reforms have in common that they shift part of the responsibility for income after retirement from the state to the individual. This requires individuals to make their own provisions for income in old age. Most reforms involve three dimensions: They raise the statutory retirement age; decrease public pillar replacement rates; and transform monolithic public pensions into multipillar systems by fostering private and occupational pensions.

Will such a fundamental change in saving behavior and financial market allocation actually take place? The prediction of the classical life-cycle savings hypothesis is clear: If income from the public pension pillar is decreasing, individuals should adjust their labor market decisions as well as their consumption and saving choices to the new situation. But does this prediction really hold? Are people sufficiently farsighted to increase private and occupational saving for

We would like to thank Johanna Schütz for excellent research assistance.

old age? Will they retire later? Or will procrastination of saving prevail, paired with finding new loopholes to escape later retirement?

Germany attempted a very consistent transition from a monolithic public pension system with relatively early retirement ages to a multipillar system with a substantial increase in the statutory retirement age. It has not, however, escaped fierce opposition. It is therefore an excellent case study for the ambivalence of recent reform attempts and the link between such reforms and their consequences for householdsá labor market choices and saving behavior. The public pension system in Germany used to be very generous such that pre-retirement living standards could be secured even after retirement. Precipitated by demographic pressures, the system underwent a series of reforms in the last two decades. Major reforms took place in 1992, 2001, 2004, and 2007. They induced substantial cuts in public pension benefits and created an increasing gap in old-age income relative to past benefits levels. Germans have therefore been urged to postpone retirement and adjust their saving behavior to fill this looming pension gap.

The objective of this paper is to survey the economic research analyzing this transition and to draw lessons about how households adjust their saving, financial, and retirement decisions. We will treat the German pension reforms and the political situation leading to those reforms as exogenous shocks, and will interpret the evidence on German households' reactions to those reforms as outcomes of a large-scale historical experiment. Frame of reference is the life-cycle framework as the fundamental theory predicting life-course behavioral adjustments.

This survey is therefore structured as follows: In Section 2 we summarize the life-cycle framework structuring our discussion of saving behavior and juxtapose it to international evidence. Section 3 sketches the German pension system and its recent reforms. Section 4 reviews how retirement decisions and savings behavior have changed in response to those reforms. In Section 5, we summarize the general lessons learned from the German experience and comment on recent political discussions.

2. Review of the Literature on the Reactions to Pension Reforms

The common framework to analyze the effect of pensions on individuals' behavior is the so-called life-cycle/permanent income (LC/PI) hypothesis inspired by the works of Modigliani and Brumberg (1954) and Friedman (1957). In the most simple version of the model, fully rational and forward looking individuals decide how much to consume (and thus to save) in each period based on their permanent income, that is on the total lifetime resources available to them. More specifically, over the life-cycle consumption is smoothed so that its marginal utility stays constant over time. As a consequence, saving is higher in phases where individuals enjoy high income so that the saved amount can be used to sustain consumption levels in periods with lower or no income at all. In such a simplified framework, the availability of public pensions reduces the need for private reserves thus reducing private savings (Friedman, 1957). By the same token, if public pension benefits are reduced, individuals fill potential gaps in their old-age provision by saving more.

The role of social security was acknowledged in Friedman's early study; however, it was not until the seminal paper of Feldstein (1974) that the potential effect of public pensions has been formally incorporated into the life-cycle model. Feldstein (1974) recognized that availability and generosity of public pensions affect individuals' labor supply, setting an incentive to retire early. He therefore extended the basic life-cycle model to make the event of retirement endogenous. In such a framework, public pensions have an ambiguous effect on personal savings. On the one hand, the pension benefits substitute for household assets, so that an increase (decrease) in their generosity should be compensated by a decrease (increase) in individual savings. On the other hand, however, higher (lower) public pensions might also increase (decrease) personal savings, as the induced earlier (later) retirement lengthens (shortens) the period over which the accumulated assets will be spread.

The literature on retirement and saving behavior has grown dramatically since Feldstein's article. Unlike the earlier models – static in their nature – recent models account for the sequential nature of behavior adjustment to the unfolding of the events. Furthermore, they have been progressively augmented with more realistic features, like imperfections in capital markets (e.g., Rust and Phelan, 1997), health status (e.g., Diamond and Hausman, 1984) or heterogeneous preferences (e.g., Gustmann and Steinmeier, 2005). Other studies have focused on the effect of means-tested social insurance programs on savings and labor supply. Hubbard *et al.* (1995) and more recently Sefton *et al.* (2008) show that the existence of means-tested welfare programs reduce savings among households with low expected lifetime incomes. More recently, Van der Klaauw and Wolpin (2008) have developed a model which includes also expectations over changes in social security policy as well as subjective longevity and retirement expectations. It is based on the ideas that, first, subjective data provide useful information about individuals' decision processes and that, second, the magnitude of behavioral responses to changes in the pension system depend on the extent to which these changes are anticipated.

Haan and Prowse (2014) develop a dynamic life-cycle model of employment, retirement, and consumption, where individuals' optimal behavior depends on life expectancy and the design of the public pension system. According to their model, individuals react to the increase in life expectancy, by optimally increasing employment and postponing retirement. This change is however not enough to completely offset the negative consequences for the government budget of a rise in life expectancy. Their results thus underline the need for policy reforms addressing the additional fiscal requirements created by an aging society. A very recent extension of the classical life-cycle model incorporates investments into financial knowledge (Lusardi *et al.*, 2013). The basic prediction of this model is that individuals facing a larger drop in income at retirement, for example due to a less generous social security system, will accumulate larger amounts of private wealth and at the same time invest more in financial knowledge which is needed to make wise investment decisions.

However, whether and to what extent households' savings react to pension reforms remains an empirical question. The evidence so far is mixed. Although several studies find that pension wealth is a substitute for private assets, no consensus has been reached on the order of magnitude of the substitutability parameter. Although some studies find limited substitutability between public pensions and private savings (e.g., Kotlikoff, 1979; Dicks-Mireaux and King, 1984), other studies find an almost perfect substitutability (Gale, 1998). More recent results indicate that the effect of pensions on private wealth differs significantly across households. So, for example, Attanasio and Rohwedder (2003), using microeconomic data covering a time span that encompasses several major pension reforms in the United Kingdom, find a higher degree of substitutability among workers close to retirement. Alessie *et al.* (2013) find that among individuals with low education pension wealth does not displace private wealth, whereas for the high educated the displacement is almost complete. The authors suggest that a lack of financial literacy might explain why for some households public pensions do not completely offset private assets. Little research has examined the reasons for the less than perfect substitution between public pension and private assets in detail. Still, this fact has important policy implications, as it means that a reduction in public pension benefits might not be compensated by an equivalent increase in private savings, thus leaving some individuals without sufficient provisions for the old-age (unless they postpone their retirement age). Concerned about the lack of response to pension cuts and the inadequate level of old-age provision, many governments have thus subsidized private pension plans (via matching contributions or tax credits), to foster their uptake. However, whether these programs are effective in increasing savings is still a matter of debate. From a theoretical point of view, even simple consumption behavior models yield ambiguous results (for a detailed discussion, see Bernheim, 2002). As the subsidies increase, the return rate of retirement savings in comparison with other saving forms increases and individuals face the classical income and substitution effect when choosing the optimal saving amount. On the one hand side, consumption today becomes more expensive and therefore saving should increase (substitution effect); on the other hand, the higher interest rate increases the value of the actual resources, making saving less attractive (income effect). As the income effect may compensate and even outstrip the substitution effect, it is not possible to draw a firm conclusion. In more complex consumption models that take into account risk preferences or differences in liquidity, the effect of the subsidies is even harder to discern, and the answer is likely to depend on the magnitude of several preference parameters.

Empirically, the effect of subsidized saving contracts on household savings and in particular the degree to which the introduction of private pension plans displaced other forms of savings have been tested several times, leading to a wide range of results. In the United States, for example, Engen *et al.* (1994, 1996) and Attanasio and DeLeire (2002) find that only a very small fraction of the contributions in such subsidized contracts represents new saving and the great part of these accounts are funded by decreasing investments in other assets. On the contrary, Venti and Wise (1990) and Poterba *et al.* (1995, 1996) conclude that such contracts do not feature any displacement effect on conventional savings; Engen and Gale (2000) and Benjamin (2003) find mixed effects: subsidized contracts represent new savings for some households (as low-income households or less financially sophisticated households) and simple reshuffling of different assets for other households (as high-income households or homeowners). However, Abadie (2000) does not only find no evidence of displacement effects, but also concludes that subsidized contracts even have positive effects on other savings. Gelber (2011) reaches similar conclusions. The discussion about the efficacy of the subsidies as a saving device has accompanied pension reforms in almost all developed countries, generating an interest in cross-national analyses. However, evidence on the issue outside the United States is scarce. In the United Kingdom, Guariglia and Markose (2000), looking at the effect of the tax favored Personal Pension Plans (PPPs) on private savings find no displacement effects, whereas Rossi (2009) finds that PPPs even enhance other forms of saving. In Italy, Paiella and Tiseno (2014) find little effects of tax-favored accounts on overall household savings and substantial substitution of non-tax-favored for tax-favored assets.

To summarize, the behavioral responses to pension reforms are extremely difficult to model and to measure. As retirement is an endogenous choice, the effect of changes in the public pension systems on savings cannot be clearly predicted by a theoretical model. Empirical estimations suggest that a reduction in public pension benefits is not fully compensated by an increase in private savings, and that this effect is stronger among certain groups, possibly also because of a lack of financial literacy. Saving incentives (in the form of matching contributions or tax credits) are a widely used tool to foster savings through private pension plans. The literature analyzing the efficacy of this instrument also produces ambiguous results, and no clear-cut conclusions are possible. In the next section, we will give an overview of the German pension system and its recent reforms before turning to German households' reactions to these reform measures.

3. Regimes of Retirement Policies in Germany

Germany introduced the first formal national pension system worldwide in the 1880s. The quintessential Bismarckian pension system began as a funded disability insurance scheme some 120 years ago but was quickly broadened into a general old-age pension system. The funded system was formally transformed into a pay-as-you-go system in 1957 after about half of the capital stock was lost in two world wars and a hyperinflation. There are many descriptions of the history of the German pension system (e.g., Eichenhofer *et al.*, 2011; Masuch *et al.*, 2014). We will restrict this section on its essence and focus on the reform process starting in the 1990s, drawing from Börsch-Supan and Wilke (2004) and Börsch-Supan and Jürges (2012).

As opposed to other countries such as the United Kingdom and the Netherlands, which originally adopted a Beveridgian social security system that provided only a base pension, public pensions in Germany are designed to extend the standard of living that was achieved during work life also to the time after retirement. Individual pension benefits are therefore proportional to individual labor income averaged over the entire course of the working life and feature only few redistributive properties, in particular, a minimum pension at the social assistance level. Benefits in the disability branch are identical to benefits for old-age pensions. They are, however, calculated as if the working life had extended to the early retirement age.

The following brief post-war history of the German pension system distinguishes four phases: (1) a relatively stable phase after the introduction of the pay-as-you-go system in 1957 until 1972; (2) a phase of increasing generosity precipitated by the 1972 pension reform; (3) a phase of modest retrenchment, especially affecting disability benefits in the mid-1980s; (4) a phase of cost cutting reforms after 1992 leading to a sustainable pension system by 2007. Current discussion in Germany shows first signs that we may actually experience a phase of reform backlash. We will discuss this briefly in our conclusions.

3.1 *Phase 1 (1957–1972): Stability*

Initially, the pay-as-you-go system introduced in 1957 had a single eligibility age for old age pension, age 65 for men and age 60 for women (conditioned on a minimum number of years of service). Earlier retirement was impossible unless one could prove a disability. Disability rates were very high after World War II and then declined. Disability insurance was the main entry path into the German pension system until 1972 for both men and women (see Figure 1).

3.2 *Phase 2 (1972–1984): Increasing Generosity*

The 1972 reform was a major change in policy. It introduced "flexible retirement for the long-term insured" by providing old age pension benefits at age 63, given that workers had a minimum of 35 years in which they contributed to the system. These benefits were not actuarially adjusted. Average retirement age dropped by more than 2 years (Börsch-Supan, 2000b), and the "flexible retirement" pathway partly substituted for the disability pathway into retirement, see Figure 1. At the same time, the "old-age pension for disabled workers" was

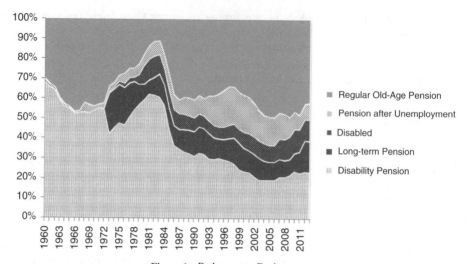

Figure 1. Pathways to Retirement.
Source: Own calculation based on data from the German pension provider (Rentenversicherung in Zeitreihen 2013).

introduced, first with an earliest entry age of 62, then, after 1978, it was reduced in two steps to age 60.

Between 1984 and 1987, early retirement was further extended by creating a 'bridge to retirement'. The government introduced more generous unemployment insurance benefits for older workers which were especially attractive in the age range from 55 to 59 years, up to 32 months of unemployment insurance benefits at 63% or 68% of former net wages. These benefits were neither means tested nor were job-search activities required for those unemployed who were aged 55 and older. In addition, severance pay became tax advantaged for the employers. As a result of the 'bridge to retirement', the pathways to retirement changed again: Registered unemployment of elderly (age 55–59) rose – particularly dramatically between 1991 and 1996 – and the uptake of disability benefits declined (see Figure 1).

3.3 *Phase 3 (1984–1992): Modest Retrenchment*

In 1984, the balance between old-age and disability pensions was changed by reducing the eligibility requirement for old-age pensions (at regular retirement age 65) from 15 to 5 contribution years. At the same time, restrictions on the eligibility for disability pension were strengthened. This included the introduction of a minimum of three contribution years in the last 5 years and stricter medical examinations.

3.4 *Phase 4 (1992– 2007): Sustainability Reforms*

Threatened by demographic change, Germany began in the early 1990s a 15-year lasting process of reform steps. These reform steps were not master-minded; some 'happened' due to budget crises and new political constellations. Seen from hindsight, however, the reform steps follow an astoundingly consistent common thread.

Step 1: Towards actuarial adjustments (1992). The first step in the long German reform process was the 1992 reform. It anchored benefits to net wages, that is net of taxes and social security contributions, rather than to gross wages.[1] This removed an odd mechanism that would have created a vicious cycle of increasing pension benefits in response to increasing contribution rates. At the same time, credits for higher education were abolished and survivor benefits reduced.

The second important element in the 1992 reform was the introduction of 'actuarial' adjustments of benefits to retirement age. Actuarial is set in quotes because the adjustments factors have been set discretionarily at 3.6% for each year of earlier retirement and are not directly linked to changes in life expectancy. They are about 1.5 percentage points lower than current life tables and a 3% discount rate would imply.[2] Nevertheless, their gradual introduction between 1998 and 2006 reduced incentives to retire early, and retirement age and labor force participation of older individuals has indeed increased since then, almost symmetrically to the decline after the 1972 reform (see evidence presented in Section 4.1).

Step 2: Towards a genuine multipillar system (2001). The financial situation of the pension system worsened rather quickly after the 1998 elections that brought the Social Democrats to power in Germany. As a remarkable irony in politics, the former union leader, then secretary of labor, Walter Riester, successfully passed a major reform bill through parliament in 2001.[3]

The Riester reform is a major change of the German public pension system. It transformed the monolithic pay-as-you-go retirement insurance into a genuine multipillar system by partially substituting pay-as-you-go financed pensions with funded pensions. The reform aimed to achieve three main objectives. First, the reform was to stabilize contribution rates. The Riester reform law actually states that contribution rates to the public retirement insurance scheme must stay below 20% until 2020 and below 22% until 2030 whereas the net replacement rate must stay above 67%. Failure must precipitate further government action. Second, a new pillar of supplementary funded pensions was introduced. Contributions to this pillar are subsidized, either by tax deferral and tax deduction, or by direct subsidies. These supplementary pensions are, however, not mandatory. The plans can be separated into Rürup and Riester pensions. We will focus here on explaining the Riester pensions, because they are the far more common form of private supplementary pension plans. Riester pensions are state subsidized private saving plans with a (largely) annuitized payout plan. The subsidies are bound to eligibility criteria. Basically everyone who is affected by the decreasing statutory pensions is eligible for subsidies (for the specific eligibility rules, see Börsch-Supan *et al.*, 2012). For certified Riester products, subsidies exist in two forms: a basic benefit matching the own contribution and a tax deduction which depends on the amount contributed to the contract and the marginal tax rate of the owner of the contract; the maximum of the two will be applied. Low-income individuals receive a relatively high subsidy due to the matching mechanism whereas higher income individuals benefit from tax deductions. Furthermore, there is an additional subsidy for each child. On average, the subsidies amount to about 45% of contributions, depending on income and number of children. Additionally, occupational pension schemes have been significantly promoted (second pillar), most importantly by the introduction of a legal right to convert salary into pension contributions in the so-called 'Entgeltumwandlung' scheme (Börsch-Supan *et al.*, 2007). Finally, the third element of the reform was that benefits of the pay-as-you-go system were scheduled to be gradually reduced in proportion to the maximum subsidized contribution to the new supplementary pensions.

Step 3: Towards sustainability (2004). Although praised as a 'century reform', it quickly became obvious that the cost-cutting measures of the Riester reform would not suffice to meet the contribution rate targets. A new reform commission, the 'Commission for Sustainability in Financing the German Social Insurance Systems', was established in November 2002.[4] Its twin objectives were those of the Riester reform. To stabilize contribution rates while at the same time ensuring appropriate future benefit levels.

The Commission met in 2003 under very different circumstances than Riester had faced just a few years earlier. Unexpectedly high unemployment rates and the poor performance of the German economy with extremely low growth rates precipitated a short-run financial crisis of the pension system and created a sense of urgency for reform. Moreover, the electorate became increasingly aware that stabilizing social security contributions and thus limiting the increase of total labor compensation will be essential for enhancing future growth. This paradigm shift away from thinking in pension claims toward thinking in financing possibilities had a noticeable impact on the Commission's reform proposals.

The Commission proposed an entire reform package (Kommission, 2003). In addition to a gradual shift of the retirement age in proportion to the expected change of life length after retirement, the key element of the Commission's reform proposal was a new pension benefit indexation formula linking benefits to the system dependency ratio, called 'sustainability formula'.[5] It will lead to further decreases in pension benefits vis-à-vis the path planned by the Riester reform. Most of the Commission proposals, and most significantly the introduction of the sustainability formula, were quickly passed by the German parliament in May 2004.

In parallel, the government also passed major changes to the unemployment insurance system, called 'Hartz reforms'.[6] They dramatically shortened the duration of unemployment benefits, especially for older individuals, to 18 months (rather than 32 months) and made unemployment insurance much less attractive as a substitute for early retirement and disability insurance benefits. This was accompanied by shifting the age limit for 'old-age pensions due to unemployment' from age 60 to 63.

Step 4: Towards later retirement ages (2007). The Commission also proposed an increase of the normal retirement age from 65 to 67 years according to a schedule from 2011 to 2035 reflecting expected future changes in life expectancy. The underlying rationale was to divide the life time gained in proportion to the current division between life time in work and in retirement, namely two-to-one. In order to prevent substitution into early retirement and disability pensions as a result of the increase in the retirement age, the Commission also proposed to increase the early retirement ages (to the same extent and on the same schedule as the normal retirement age) and to increase the actuarial adjustments for disabled and long-term insured workers.

The shift in the retirement age was deemed politically too dangerous and was excluded from the legislation package in March 2004. The unions heavily opposed this adaptation of retirement age to life expectancy, using the argument that it would lead to higher unemployment and take jobs away from the young.

Nevertheless, in yet another ironic move, just 2 years later, with population aging high on the political agenda, the then labor secretary Franz Müntefering unilaterally announced an accelerated increase of the retirement age, being fully effective in 2029. It was legislated in March 2007. The age limit for 'old-age pensions for disabled' was shifted to 65 years, and the 'old-age pension for women' effectively phased out.

The government change in 2013[7] precipitated some reform backlash. For example, a new early retirement pathway was created for workers with very long contribution histories, allowing them to retire at age 63 after 45 years of contributions. This measure is temporary and will be phased out in parallel to the gradual shift of the normal retirement age. The basic reform elements – the long-term increase of the normal retirement age and the reduction of benefits due to the sustainability factor – were explicitly confirmed by the new government.

Summing up, the reforms have the following consequences for German households

- The generosity of state-financed public pensions has been reduced and will decrease further thereby lowering income from the PAYG pillar. Börsch-Supan and Gasche (2010a) find that compared to a situation without reforms the public pension level will be lower by about 16% in 2040.
- The statutory retirement age will increase gradually.
- Additional occupational and private pillars have been strengthened. In particular, the state subsidized Riester and Rürup pensions create additional incentives to save privately for retirement.

Thus, in order to fill the arising pension gap, individuals will have to adjust their expectations about the point of retirement and the level of their pension income from the public pillar. They will have to shift retirement ages and adjust private savings in both subsidized and unsubsidized contracts if they want to keep the consumption profile stable under the new circumstances. In the following section, we summarize the empirical evidence on the adaptations of German households to this new institutional environment.

4. Empirical Evidence from Germany

In times of decreasing pension income, individuals need to reoptimize their labor market and saving choices. In order to compensate for the reduction in retirement income they can postpone their retirement age, increase their old-age saving provisions, or choose a combination of both in order to smooth consumption under the new circumstances. In this section we will look into both aspects: changes in retirement behavior and changes in saving behavior of the Germans as a response to the new situation.

A big challenge in empirically capturing the behavioral responses to pension reforms is represented by the data requirements. Behavioral reaction will feature considerable heterogeneity not only across income classes but also within. Micro-data on saving and labor supply are therefore essential. Attanasio and Rohwedder (2003) stress datasets with individual-level information on savings are rare. Furthermore, pension wealth accumulated in government programs and employer-provided pension plans is difficult to measure (Brugiavini *et al.*, 2005; Gustman and Steinmeier, 2014). Although the information necessary to estimate public pension wealth (such as occupation, age or unemployment spells) can reliably be collected in a household survey, panels covering the whole employment life of the respondents are quite rare. Therefore, researchers either have to make strong assumptions on the value of the relevant variables in the years not covered by the survey, or rely on retrospective data, which might be quite noisy. Information on occupational pension wealth requires respondents to know if they are involved in an occupational pension plan and, if yes, to know the details of their plan. Individuals however often ignore if they are covered by such pensions (e.g., Dummann, 2008; Lamla and Coppola, 2014) and are not familiar with the type of pension coverage they have (Gustman and Steinmeier, 2004). The data situation for analyzing households' financial behavior has been for a long time particularly limited in Germany, as the existing databases did not record detailed data on the variables needed to properly capture the behavioral responses to pension reforms.

Most of the evidence provided especially in Sections 4.2 and 4.3 is based on the SAVE[8] survey. The study was initiated in 2001 with the main goal to create an empirical base specifically targeted at understanding households' saving behavior and asset choices. It was thus designed to collect detailed information on income, financial, and real assets and debt, together with a rich set of psychological questions, questions on health status, expectations, and attitudes. The survey has been set up as a longitudinal study to follow up developments in the saving behavior over time.[9] After the first wave in 2001, a second wave was put on field in 2003/2004. Between 2005 and 2011 the survey has been conducted on an annual basis. In 2013 the tenth and last wave of the study has been collected. SAVE has therefore monitored the adaptation process of German households over a period of fundamental changes in the pension system. From time to time the set of core questions repeated in each wave has been complemented with extra modules dealing with up-to-date topics. In 2009 and 2010, for example, specific questions have been inserted to capture the effects of the economic and financial crisis on households' saving behavior. Furthermore, in the wave conducted in 2011 the participants have been asked to provide their written consent to link the SAVE questionnaire to administrative data from the Federal Employment Agency, which includes also information on the respondents' employer (Coppola and Lamla, 2012).

4.1 *Changes in Retirement Behavior*

One dimension along which individuals can adjust their behavior when facing changes in the pension system is the retirement age. Changes in the retirement age might be induced by two elements of the reforms described in Section 3. On the one hand, the changes in the age eligibility rules require individuals to shift the time of entering retirement. On the other hand, reductions in the expected pension income due to actuarial adjustments and a lower growth rate of pensions might cause backward shifts in the pension age in order to compensate for those losses. If individuals shift their age of retirement to later ages the pension income will be higher for three reasons: first, pensions when retiring later are higher due to actuarial adjustment. Specifically, if Germans retire before the statutory retirement age,[10] their pension is reduced by 3.6% per year of early retirement. Note that this adjustment is lower than required for actuarial neutrality, see Börsch-Supan (2004) and Werding (2007), creating a barrier to retiring later. If they shift their retirement past the statutory retirement age anyway, their pension rises by 6% per year of later retirement. Second, when postponing retirement, the pension increases because of additional contributions to the pension system; more earnings points which are used to calculate the pension are accrued. Finally, because income from work is usually higher than retirement income, additional private savings can be accumulated when postponing retirement.

There is an extensive literature on the expected and actual changes in retirement behavior of Germans due to the pension reforms in the last decades. Much of the literature predicting the reactions to proposed and implemented reforms is based on the option value model by Stock and Wise (1990). To put it simply, the option value describes the financial incentives to retire by modeling the trade-off that individuals face when they decide to retire today vs. to postpone retirement to the future by comparing the income streams resulting from these alternatives. Individuals will stay in the labor force as long as the utility from retiring now is below the utility from continuing to work. The option value model has been very useful in showing that financial incentives matter a great deal in Germany, see Börsch-Supan (2000a, 2001), and this finding is robust to alternative linear and nonlinear econometric specifications.

Berkel and Börsch-Supan (2004) as well as Börsch-Supan *et al.* (2004) estimate the effects of the 1992 and 1999 reforms as well as additional hypothetical increases of the adjustment factors. The results of the various reforms are normalized in the sense that they are translated into the financial incentives exerted by the option value; the metric is thus always the utility change of the corresponding future income streams. Börsch-Supan *et al.* (2004) estimate that the 1992 reform will increase the average retirement age by about 8 months; a hypothetical increase of adjustment factors to 6% would shift the average retirement age by 17 months. Berkel and Börsch-Supan (2004) find that the same reforms would increase men's (women's) average retirement age by 1.9 (0.8) years. In the same paper, two hypothetical increases of the retirement age are simulated as well. If all age limits for early and regular retirement are increased by 1 year on average men (women) will shift retirement by 0.3 (0.2) years; if all age limits are shifted by 2 years, men will adjust retirement by 0.7 years, whereas there is no effect for women. The authors argue that this is because women, under these circumstances, more frequently select disability insurance as an alternative pathway to retirement.

Haan and Prowse (2014) implement their theoretical model (see Section 2) in Germany and explore the consequences of a reduction in the generosity of the public pension system comparing two revenue-equivalent policies: (i) an increase in the full pensionable age and (ii) a cut in the yearly pension benefits. They find that increasing the legal retirement age leads to a greater response in terms of employment and retirement behavior than a (budget-equivalent) reduction in pension benefits. Furthermore, according to their simulations, the life-time consumption of individuals is higher when the first measure is implemented. On the contrary, when the pension benefits are cut, Haan and Prowse (2014) estimate a relatively modest postponement of the retirement entry and a substantial increase in wealth accumulation prior to retirement. The latter is, however, not enough to counter the income effects of the reduction in the pension benefit, so that life-time consumption of individuals is lower.

Turning to the development of actual retirement ages, Figure 2 gives a first impression. It shows the average retirement age by year of retirement for men and women in east and

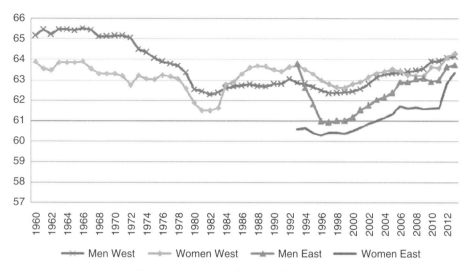

Figure 2. Retirement Ages in Germany (Old Age Retirement).
Source: Own calculation based on data from the German pension provider (Rentenversicherung in Zeitreihen 2013).

west Germany and illustrates the effects of the reforms described in Section 3 quite nicely. Although retirement ages were pretty high before 1972, they dropped rapidly when the pension provisions became more generous and reached a low point in the beginning of the 1980s. The retirement age stayed around 63 for men until the late 1990s, when the average age started to rise due to the actuarial adjustments implemented in the 1992 reform and the closing of certain pathways to retirement (see Figure 1). In 2013, west German men on average retired at age 64.1 and hence still well below the statutory retirement age, which was at 65 and 2 months for those born in 1948, which is the cohort that reached their statutory retirement age in that year. West German women follow roughly the same pattern: average retirement ages declined after 1972. However, they were somewhat above the retirement ages of men. This is most likely due to a massive selection among West German women who are in the labor force.[11] On the one hand, many West German women of those cohorts did not work and, on the other hand, those women who had some pension claims very often had interrupted careers and thus did not qualify for early retirement as often as men. The development of women's average retirement age is more or less similar to men's for the years from 1999 onwards. Retirement ages in east Germany were very low during the 1990s mostly as a result of the labor market transitions after unification. Unemployment was very high and many older employees retired early. However, average retirement ages have risen rapidly and in 2013 almost matched the west German average ages.

Besides this descriptive evidence Hanel (2010) estimates the actual effects of the German pension reforms during the 1990s on retirement behavior. She uses data from the German public pension provider and finds that the changes in accrued social security wealth led to a postponement of individual retirement entries by about 14 months and a shift in the exit from the labor market by about 10 months. Thus, there is an increase of the gap that arises between the age at which individuals leave the labor force and the age at which they start receiving pension benefits. The resulting gap in income has to be filled either by private savings or other social transfers like, for example, unemployment benefits. Furthermore, Hanel (2012) estimates the effect of the 2001 reform of the disability pension system on claiming such pensions. The reform reduced benefit levels and the author finds that this significantly affected the probability to claim benefits among those in better health. Individuals with bad health conditions did not adjust their behavior. This result is very plausible if some (healthy) individuals were using the disability route to enter early retirement before.

The effects of pension reforms on retirement behavior develop over time and are fully observable only with a lag of several years, especially if the reforms are implemented in a gradual fashion. As a consequence, today it is possible to observe and measure the behavioral reactions of the pension reforms implemented in the 1990s. The effects of the most recent adjustments to the legal retirement age will be therefore observable only in a couple of decades. Nonetheless, understanding to what extent people will adjust to a higher legal retirement age is crucial to policy makers. Especially young people have to make decisions in important areas like saving or investment in further education where retirement expectations play an important role.

Although several studies have analyzed the relationship between retirement expectations and realizations (e.g., Chan and Stevens, 2004; Benitez-Silva and Dwyer, 2005), very few papers have looked at the effect of policy changes on expectations (Bottazzi *et al.*, 2006; Michaud and Van Soest, 2008; Barret and Mosca, 2013). Coppola and Wilke (2014) investigate how the raise in the statutory retirement age from 65 to 67 influences people's retirement expectations in Germany. Using the longitudinal structure of the SAVE survey (waves 2005–2009), the authors apply a difference-in-difference approach to estimate if the magnitude of the expectation revision due to the German pension reforms is in line with the magnitude implied by the law change. Their results show that persons affected by the reform on average expect to retire about two years later. However, certain social groups are faster in changing their expectations whereas other groups are more resilient to the reform. In particular, respondents with low educational levels did not or not yet adjust their expectations about their retirement age adequately.

Despite the fact that an increase in the retirement age is one of the most straightforward and efficient options to reform the pension system, a large fraction of the population opposes such reforms. Opposition to increasing retirement ages could be driven by expectations about low work abilities at retirement or a fundamental opposition to reforms of the welfare state. Scheubel *et al.* (2013) exploit the discussion about the increase in statutory retirement age from 65 to 67 years in Germany in combination with a controlled experiment embedded into the SAVE survey. They find that individual expectations clearly reflect a major concern in the public discussion – namely, that people become increasingly unable to work beyond age 65. Furthermore they find evidence of a downward bias in the expected ability to work caused by a fundamental opposition to an increase in the retirement age. These results have important implications for pension reforms. They underline the need for the policy maker to seriously tackle public concerns if they want to successfully increase the legal retirement age. To boost the acceptance of such a reform individuals' awareness of the rising life expectancy and of the growing need to work at older ages has to be increased.

Overall, the evidence on the shifts in retirement ages indicates that Germans reacted to the changes in incentives and raised their actual retirement age as well as expectations about when to retire in the future. However, there is still a substantial fraction of individuals retiring before the statutory retirement age and a considerable fraction of individuals who plan to retire early even if retirement ages rise. Those individuals will either have to reduce their consumption level at retirement substantially in the future or they will have to build up adequate private savings in order to bridge the gap arising in benefits levels. In the next section we turn to adjustments of savings behavior.

4.2 *Changes in Savings Behavior*

German households have traditionally had high saving rates. For example, since 1960 saving rates have always been higher in Germany than in the United States, with the discrepancy increasing over time (Börsch-Supan, 1994a, Table 4.1). According to the OECD, in the year 2000 – right before the introduction of the Riester pension reform, German households saved on average 9.4% of their disposable income, whereas the equivalent figure in the United States was only 4% (Figure 3). The distribution of saving rates, however, has been rather skewed, with the median saving rate being lower than the mean (Börsch-Supan, 1994b). Börsch-Supan *et al.* (2005) use a micro-simulation model based on the 2003 SAVE wave to estimate how many households would be able to fill the pension gap created by the Riester reform, if they would keep their (at that time) current saving behavior. On average, the projected savings were enough to fill the gap between what they would have received as public pension under the old and the new pension system. However, although about one quarter of the households was over annuitized, about one third had no private wealth at all, thus being completely dependent on the shrinking public pension benefits during retirement. The crucial question is therefore if and to what extent the saving behavior of German households changed in the last decade.

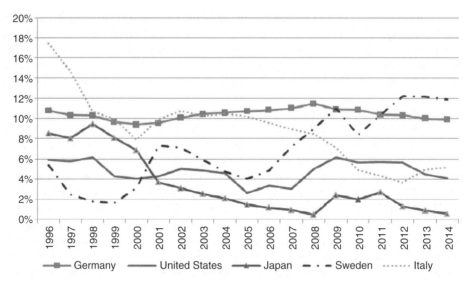

Figure 3. Household Net Saving Rates (in % of Disposable Household Income).
Source: OECD Economic Outlook (2014).

After the Riester pension reform households' saving rates have slightly increased, reaching a peak of 11.5% in 2008, only to decrease again in the last few years (Figure 3). Thus, no major changes in terms of average household saving rates are observable in the aggregate data. National saving rates have shown a similar pattern; they actually increased during the time when the subsidies for the Riester pensions increased as well. Although there have been many other developments in these years, there is at least no prima facie evidence that the government expenditures for Riester subsidies have offset the increase in household saving.

However, and partially as a response to the pension reforms, the composition of financial assets in the portfolio of German households changed dramatically in the last decade. Until the turn of the century, financial portfolios have been dominated by relatively safe assets (e.g., checking and saving accounts and domestic bonds), and life insurances represented the main asset for the old-age provision (Börsch-Supan and Essig, 2002). Although private and occupational pensions had a very long tradition in Germany, they made up only a small part of the household savings and they have been simply the icing on the cake (Börsch-Supan and Gasche, 2010b).

After a relative lackluster start, which led to a simplification of the initial design in 2005, the demand for Riester pensions rose significantly. Currently, the coverage rate among eligible households is around 40%. Börsch-Supan *et al.* (2012) provide a measure of the effectiveness of the subsidies. The authors estimate that for each €1 of subsidies between €1.9 and €2.2 of new saving for the old age have been created. Thus, after subtracting the costs of the subsidies, it appears to be a net positive effect of the incentives at an aggregate level.

Börsch-Supan *et al.* (2012) also explore the coverage rates of supplementary pensions using the SAVE data. Updating the results of that paper, we find that the share of households that do not own any supplementary old-age provision decreased continuously from more than 70% in SAVE 2003 to less than 40% in SAVE 2013 (Figure 4). The reduction in the share of households without private supplementary pensions is mainly due to the dynamic development

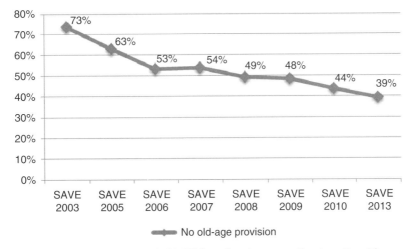

Figure 4. Fraction of Households Without Supplementary Pensions Over Time.
Source: SAVE 2003–2013. Own calculations as in Börsch-Supan et al. (2012).

of the Riester pensions together with the increased uptake of occupational pensions. In contrast, the coverage rates with other (not subsidized) private pensions have been relatively stable – hovering around 16% over the past 10 years (Figure 5). Furthermore, households now combine different savings instruments. About a quarter of households have at least two different forms of supplementary pensions (Börsch-Supan *et al.*, 2012).

Uptake rates of supplementary pension schemes are however very heterogeneous across socio-economic groups. Looking at the distribution of occupational pensions, for example, it

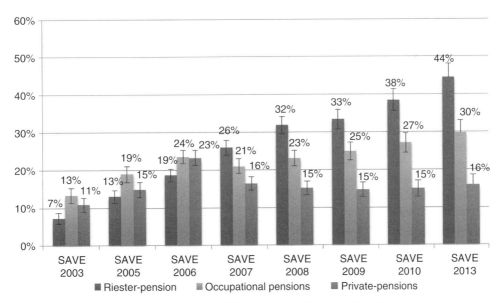

Figure 5. Uptake Rates of Supplementary Pensions Over Time.
Source: SAVE 2003–2013. Own calculations as in Börsch-Supan et al. (2012).

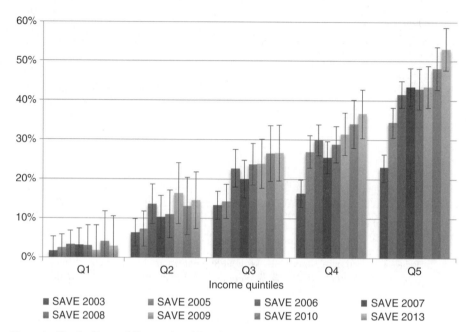

Figure 6. Uptake Rates of Occupational Pensions by Quintiles of Monthly Household Disposable
Income.
Source: SAVE 2003–2013. Own calculations.

can be observed that households in the upper 20% of the income distribution have not only
higher coverage rates, but exhibit also a much stronger dynamic over time (Figure 6). On the
contrary, in the bottom income quintile coverage rates are extremely low and basically flat
over time.

A similar heterogeneity across household income quintiles can be observed if we look at
coverage rates of Riester-pensions. Here we can also observe a huge difference between the
top and the bottom quintile of the income distribution in terms of coverage. According to
the SAVE survey 2013, almost 60% of the households in the upper income quintile have at
least a Riester-pension in their portfolios, whereas in the bottom quintile less than 20% have
such products. However, in contrast to the available evidence for the occupational pensions,
the uptake of Riester-pensions has been quite dynamic also in the bottom income quintiles
(Figure 7). Nonetheless, given the generosity of the subsidies for low-income households, the
relatively low uptake rates are puzzling. A key lesson is therefore that high subsidies alone are
not enough to reach low-income households. The next paragraph will highlight how crucial
the role of information is in reaching this group.

As highlighted in Section 2, a relevant empirical question which has still not been resolved is
to what extent the successful uptake of the Riester contracts has displaced other saving forms,
in particular other types of private pensions. Corneo *et al.* (2009) and Pfarr and Schneider
(2011) provide econometric analyses that cannot refute the hypothesis that subsidizing Riester
pensions produces only displacement effects. Both papers, however, make strong implicit
assumptions in order to overcome the problem of a missing counterfactual (due to the design

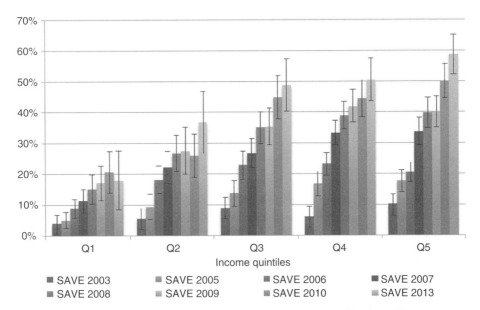

Figure 7. Uptake rates of Riester Pensions by Income Quintiles Over Time.
Source: SAVE 2003–2013. Own calculations as in Börsch-Supan et al. (2012).

of the Riester scheme, virtually everyone is eligible, so there is no natural control group). They assume, for example, that having a Riester pension and having other savings are independent decisions. Coppola and Reil-Held (2010) follow a different approach, they ask households directly about the extent to which savings increased or decreased after the purchase of a subsidized product. Responses to questions about changes in behavior may be subjective and contain elements of wishful thinking or ex post justification. Nevertheless, the evidence provided by Coppola and Reil-Held (2010) is unambiguous (Figure 8): Only a minority of the households reports saving less in total since enrolling in a Riester pension plan, and most households report saving more. Particularly striking is the fact that a very large proportion of low-income households indicate that they are saving more.

Börsch-Supan *et al.* (2008) provide an econometric analysis of supplemental pensions. Using the wave 2006 of the SAVE study, a bivariate probit regression model is estimated, where the decisions to take up a Riester-pension plan and to enroll in other unsubsidized private pension plans are modeled simultaneously. Besides controlling for the usual socio-economic indicators (such as age, education, income and wealth), for the degree of financial knowledge, and for the relevance of different saving reasons, the authors also introduce a variable indicating the presence of additional vehicles for supplemental old-age-provision (such as occupational pension plans or life insurance products). The coefficient on this variable turns out to be positive and statistically significant, revealing that households which are already covered by one of these alternative pension plans are also more likely to have a Riester-contract. The result, therefore, gives evidence for a form of "crowding in" among pension products. At the same time, Börsch-Supan *et al.* (2008) point also to possible displacement effects between old-age provision and real estate purchase.

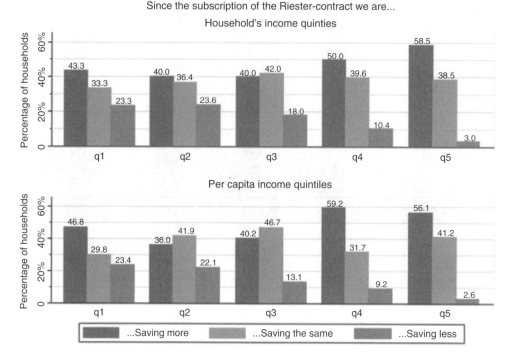

Figure 8. Change in Total Saving After Enrolling in a Riester Plan.
Source: Coppola and Reil-Held (2010), based on SAVE (2008).

4.3 *Heterogeneity in Planning and Saving for Retirement*

Making life-cycle saving choices is a quite complex task and many aspects have to be considered. Individuals have to be well informed about their expected income from the public pension system and potential other sources. Moreover, they have to evaluate different saving opportunities and form expectations about their future returns. Finally, they have to form expectations about their future health and life-expectancy to determine the planning horizon. A substantial literature in the past years evolved aiming at evaluating individuals' capabilities to deal with this increase in responsibility to plan for old age.

One aspect that has repeatedly been linked to retirement planning is financial literacy (see Lusardi and Mitchell, 2014, for a review of the recent literature). A central empirical finding of this literature is that financial knowledge is not widespread in many countries (Lusardi and Mitchell, 2011) and Germany is no exception (see Bucher-Koenen, 2011; Bucher-Koenen and Lusardi, 2011; Bucher-Koenen and Lamla, 2014). In particular, women, East Germans, those with low levels of education, the unemployed and persons with low income display low levels of financial literacy. Bucher-Koenen and Lusardi (2011) examine the consequences of financial literacy for retirement planning. They find that in general the level of financial planning for retirement is very low in Germany. In 2009, less than a quarter of the German population below age 65 attempted to find out how much they needed to save to finance retirement. The propensity to plan is significantly higher with higher levels of financial literacy.

The role of knowledge about finance and pensions has been found to be crucial also in more specific contexts. Despite the fact that financial incentives for taking up private pensions have been in place for some time, it appears that some households have not reacted. However, people only respond to incentives they know about (Chan and Stevens, 2008). In the German context, Coppola and Gasche (2011) show that a large share of the population is not well-informed about the incentives provided by the Riester scheme. The authors compare the self-assessed eligibility for state-subsidies under the Riester scheme with respondents' de facto eligibility, which can be observed in the SAVE data. Results demonstrate that especially low-income households are ignorant of their eligibility for subsidies under the Riester scheme. Moreover, the authors find that low knowledge of the pension system is associated with a higher probability to misreport the household's eligibility for the Riester subsidies. In a similar context, Ziegelmeyer and Nick (2013) analyze the reasons behind the termination of Riester contracts finding that in about one third of the cases miscounseling or bad products were the only cause for terminating or stopping contributions to Riester contracts. This indicates that individuals were not well-informed when making their plan choices.

Similarly, Lamla and Coppola (2013) investigate the determinants of perceived access to occupational pensions among German workers. For their analysis, the authors link wave 2011 SAVE data with administrative data from the German Federal Employment Agency, thus creating an employer-employee data set. They find that the current regulation that gives every employee the right to participate in an occupational pension scheme, has not resolved the problem of workers' ignorance of their access to occupational pensions: Only about half of the workers are aware of having access to an occupational pension.

In addition, many households are not well informed about the institutional context for receiving public pensions and thus, may form incorrect expectations on which they base their decisions. Honekamp and Schwarze (2010) show that people have problems to predict their public pension entitlement. Using SAVE data from 2005 to 2008 they show that women, persons with low educational background, persons not working full time or having low wages are less able to make predictions about their income-replacement rates. Moreover, Lamla and Gasche (2014) find that 38% of the households expect to rely on means-tested social assistance in the old age (i.e., 'Grundsicherung im Alter'). For these individuals it would appear rational not to save for old age, because all savings will be considered when applying the means test. Indeed, Lamla and Gasche (2014) find that individuals who expect to rely later on social assistance are less likely to currently save for retirement. However, more than half of those households misjudge their future eligibility as they have already accumulated enough public pension rights today to place them above the threshold of the means test. Those households may as a consequence make incorrect savings decisions.

Aside from being well informed about the potential income from public, occupational, and private sources individuals have to form expectations about their planning horizon and adjust to increases in life expectancy. Bucher-Koenen and Kluth (2012) reveal that women and men underestimate their individual life expectancy substantially. Women on average expect to live about 7 and men about 6.5 years shorter compared to the (cohort-adjusted) official life tables for Germany. This might have substantial consequences for private savings, because individuals might not accumulate adequate reserves to finance the extra years they might live. Bucher-Koenen and Kluth (2012) find that women with higher subjective life expectancy are significantly more likely to own Riester pension contracts; no such selection effect is determined for men. Similarly, Doerr and Schulte (2012) use SAVE data from 2005 to explore which role subjective life expectancy plays for the uptake of nonsubsidized private pensions.

They find evidence for adverse selection of the private pension market: The probability of buying a private pension is positively correlated to anticipated life spans.

To summarize, one crucial element in the reaction to reforms is the available information on which individuals can base their decisions. They need to be well informed about eligibility rules and their claims from the public system. Additionally, households need the information about the eligibility for certain (potentially subsidized) schemes that provide them with beneficial means to save for their old age, like, for example, occupational pensions and subsidized private schemes. Finally, individuals need to be well informed about their longevity risk in order to save adequately for the extra years they might live.

5. Conclusion: Lessons Learned and Current Developments

Germany provides an excellent 'historical experiment' to analyze households' saving, financial, and retirement decisions. The German pension reforms between 1992 and 2007 have created a very large exogenous shock. We now observe how German households react to this shock.

They reacted indeed. We observe a significant adjustment of retirement behavior. Both actual and expected retirement age increased. German households also responded to the private saving incentives. Since 2001, the start of the Riester plans, the fraction of individuals without any source of supplementary income has decreased from 73% to 39%. Thus, on average German households responded to the expected cuts in the pension levels and to the incentives provided in the private schemes. This response is in line with the predictions of the life-cycle theory and adequate from a social policy point of view. On average, the emerging gap between future public pension benefits and the accustomed benefit level will be closed by private and occupational pensions.

However, the heterogeneity in this response is very large. Although households with higher income and education responded to shifts in retirement ages and built up substantial private savings, very often using multiple sources, there is a substantial fraction of households, in particular those with low education, low income and less financial education, who did not respond to the reforms. From a social policy point, this creates worries. These households are less likely to plan for retirement, have wrong expectations about future benefit levels, do not adjust retirement ages and do not respond to incentives provided by the Riester scheme. Thus, although a large fraction of the German population seems to be well equipped to face the new challenges posed by the reformed pension system there is a fraction of the population that appears to be less well informed and might not be able to make the adequate choice about retirement age and savings. The predictions of the life-cycle theory fail to describe their behavior even in first approximation.

This lack of adjustment is in line with other information gaps. For instance, the average German underestimates her or his life expectancy, and this by a very substantial margin, women by 7 and men by 6.5 years. This underestimate corresponds to roughly a third of life spent in retirement and is therefore likely to cause serious problems when planning for retirement.

The life-cycle model also fails as guidance for a rational pension policy approach. The political climate in Germany is showing signs of a reform backlash, similar to tendencies in France and Italy. Although it would be rational to adapt the normal retirement age to the increased life expectancy, and use all available human resources in times of population aging, there is loud and forceful opposition in all three countries. In Germany, the increase of the retirement age legislated in 2007 irritated the left wing of the social democratic party.

When they entered the government after the 2012 elections, they took revenge and watered the increase down by introducing exemptions for those workers who have 45 years of service. Other actions may also indicate the beginning of a period of reform backlashes. Under increasing pressure from the newly founded 'Left Party', the grand coalition government reversed the decision to shorten the duration of unemployment insurance benefits for older workers which was part of the 'Hartz-IV' labor market reform. Moreover, the government decided in the spring of 2008 to have a two-year exemption from the sustainability formula to increase pension benefits in 2008 and 2009 when Federal elections were held. Finally, the issue of 'blockwise partial retirement' – essentially an early retirement device – is back on the agenda. It is too early to judge whether these changes will end the phase of sustainability reform and begin a phase of reform roll-backs. In any case, they do not conform well to the assumptions of long-term foresight that is essential for the life-cycle hypothesis to describe actual behavior.

Rationality may be improved by better informing individuals about the demographic situation, by providing easier to understand information about individuals' life expectancy, and by more aggressively showing the opportunities of eligibility for private and occupational schemes and their high subsidy rates. This would also require more transparency in the often rather intransparent pricing schemes of those pension plans.

The large heterogeneity in the households' response to pension reform is an important insight in itself. For economic research it implies the urgent need for better micro data on households' finances. Only such data permits the understanding of the large qualitative and quantitative variance in the effects of pension reform on saving behaviors.

Notes

1. The actual calculation was rather complicated and has been changed since. Currently pension benefits are anchored to gross wages and adjusted for changes in the contribution rate.
2. Actuarial computations depend on a discount or interest rate which makes payments made or received at different points in time commensurable. Usually, a rate of 3% is assumed, sometimes 4% or 5%. The German computations rest on a discount rate of about 1%.
3. The 2001 reform is therefore popularly referred to as the Riester reform.
4. Popularly referred to as the Rürup commission after its chairman, Bert Rürup. The Commission was in charge of making reform proposals for the pension system, health care, and long-term care insurance. We only refer to the proposals of the pension group which was co-chaired by one of the authors of this paper.
5. Technical details are described in Börsch-Supan and Wilke (2004).
6. Peter Hartz, former chief personnel officer at Volkswagen, headed the commission.
7. Before 2013, Angela Merkel lead a coalition of the conservative CDU/CSU and the liberal FDP parties. In 2013, the FDP was not reelected and a grand coalition was formed between the CDU/CSU and the socialdemocratic SPD with Angela Merkel as the chancellor.
8. SAVE stands for "Sparen und AlterVorsorgE in Deutschland", which can be roughly translated into "Saving and Old-Age Provision in Germany"
9. For a detailed description of the scientific background of the study and of its design see Börsch-Supan et al. (2009).
10. The statutory retirement age is 65 for cohorts born before 1947. It will increase gradually and reach 67 for the cohorts born after 1964. Thus, the reference age for the calculation of the adjustments is changing currently for each cohort reaching retirement.

11. During the 1950s and 1960s less than 50% of all West German women between age 15 and 65 participated in the labor force; and participation rates only increased gradually during the 1970s and 1980s (see https://www-genesis.destatis.de/genesis/online/link/tabelleErgebnis/12211-0001).

References

Alessie, R., Angelini, V. and vanSanten, P. (2013) Pension wealth and household savings in Europe: evidence from SHARELIFE. *European Economic Review* 63: 308–328.

Abadie, A. (2000) Semiparametric estimation of instrumental variable model for causal effects. *NBER Technical Working Paper* 260.

Attanasio, O. and DeLeire, T. (2002) The effect of individual retirement accounts on household consumption and national saving. *Economic Journal* 112(7): 504–538.

Attanasio, O. and Rohwedder, S. (2003) Pension wealth and household saving: evidence from pension reforms in the United Kingdom. *American Economic Review* 93(5): 1499–1521.

Barret, A. and Mosca, I. (2013) Increasing the state pension age, the recession and expected retirement ages. *The Economic and Social Review* 44(4): 447–472.

Benitez-Silva, H. and Dwyer, D.S. (2005) The rationality of retirement expectations and the role of new information. *The Review of Economics and Statistics* 87: 587–592.

Benjamin, D. (2003) Do 401(k)s increase saving? Evidence from propensity score subclassification. *Journal of Public Economics* 87(5–6): 1259–1290.

Bernheim, B.D. (2002) Taxation and saving. In: A. Auerbach and M. Feldstein (eds.), *Handbook of Public Economics*. Vol. 3 (pp. 1173–1249). Amsterdam: Elsevier.

Berkel, B. and Börsch-Supan, A. (2004) Pension reform in Germany: the impact on retirement decisions. *FinanzArchiv* 60: 393–421.

Börsch-Supan, A. (1994a) Savings in Germany - Part I, incentives. In: J. Poterba (ed.), *Public Policies and Household Saving* (pp. 81–104). Chicago: University of Chicago Press.

Börsch-Supan, A. (1994b) Savings in Germany - Part II, behavior. In: J. Poterba (ed.), *International Comparisons of Household Savings* (pp. 207–236). Chicago: University of Chicago Press.

Börsch-Supan, A. (2000a) Incentive effects of social security on labor force participation: evidence in Germany and across Europe. *Journal of Public Economics* 78: 25–49.

Börsch-Supan, A. (2000b) A model under siege: a case study of the German retirement insurance system. *The Economic Journal* 110: 24–45.

Börsch-Supan, A. (2004) Faire Abschläge in der gesetzlichen Rentenversicherung. *Sozialer Fortschritt* 53(10): 258–261.

Börsch-Supan, A. and Essig, L. (2002) Stockholding in Germany. In: L. Guiso, M. Haliassos and T. Jappelli (eds.) *Stockholding in Europe*. New York: Palgrave MacMillan.

Börsch-Supan, A. and Gasche, M. (2010a) Kann die Riester-Rente die Rentenlücke in der gesetzlichen Rente schließen? *MEA Discussion Paper* 201–2010, MEA Universität Mannheim.

Börsch-Supan, A. and Gasche, M. (2010b) Zur Sinnfähigkeit der Riester-Rente. *MEA Discussion Paper* 197–2010, MEA Universität Mannheim.

Börsch-Supan, A. and Jürges, H. (2012) Disability, pension reform and early retirement in Germany, In: D. Wise (ed.), *Social Security and Retirement around the World: Historical Trends in Mortality and Health, Employment, and Disability Insurance Participation*. Chicago: University of Chicago Press.

Börsch-Supan, A. and Wilke, C.B. (2004) The German Public Pension System. How It Was, How It Will Be. NBER Working Paper 10525.

Börsch-Supan, A., Schnabel, R., Kohnz, S. and Mastrobuoni, G. (2004) Micro-modeling of retirement decisions in Germany. In J. Gruber and D. Wise (eds.), *Social Security Programs and Retirement Around the World* (pp. 285–343). Chicago: University of Chicago Press.

Börsch-Supan, A., Essig, L. and Wilke, C. (2005) Rentenlücken und Lebenserwartung. Wie sich die Deutschen auf den Anstieg vorbereiten. Deutsches Institut für Altersvorsorge, Köln.

Börsch-Supan, A., Reil-Held. A., and Wilke, C. (2007) Zur Sozialversicherungsfreiheit der Entgeltumwandlung. MEA Discussion Paper 117–2007, MEA Universität Mannheim.

Börsch-Supan, A., Reil-Held, A. and Schunk, D. (2008) Saving incentives, old-age provision and displacement effects: evidence from the recent German pension reform. *Journal of Pension Economics and Finance* 7(3): 295–319.

Börsch-Supan, A., Coppola, M., Essig, L., Eymann, A. and Schunk, D. (2009) The German SAVE Study: Design and Results, MEA Study n. 5, University of Mannheim.

Börsch-Supan, A., Coppola, M., and Reil-Held, A. (2012) Riester pensions in Germany: design, dynamics, targeting success and crowding-in. *NBER Working Paper* 18014.

Bottazzi, R., Jappelli, T. and Padula, M. (2006) Retirement expectations, pension reforms, and their impact on private wealth accumulation. *Journal of Public Economics* 90: 2187–2212.

Brugiavini, A., Maser, K. and Sundén, A. (2005) Measuring Pension Wealth. Paper prepared for LWS Workshop: Construction and Usage of Comparable Microdata on Wealth: the LWS, Banca d'Italia, Perugia, Italy, 27–29 January 2005.

Bucher-Koenen, T. (2011) Financial Literacy, Riester Pensions, and Other Private Old Age Provision in Germany. MEA-Discussion-Paper 250–2011. MEA-Max Planck Institute for Social Law and Social Policy.

Bucher-Koenen, T. and Kluth, S. (2012) Subjective Life Expectancy and Private Pensions. MEA-Discussion-Paper 265–2012. MEA-Max Planck Institute for Social Law and Social Policy.

Bucher-Koenen, T. and Lamla, B. (2014) The Long Shadow of Socialism: On East-West German Differences in Financial Literacy. MEA-Discussion-Paper *282–2014*. MEA-Max Planck Institute for Social Law and Social Policy.

Bucher-Koenen, T. and Lusardi, A. (2011) Financial literacy and retirement planning in Germany, *Journal of Pension Economics and Finance* 10(4): 565–584.

Chan, S. and Stevens, A. (2004) Do changes in pension incentives affect retirement? A longitudinal study of subjective retirement expectations. *Journal of Public Economics* 88: 1307–1333.

Chan, S. and Stevens, A. (2008) What you don't know can't help you: pension knowledge and retirement decision making. *Review of Economics and Statistics* 90(2): 253–266.

Coppola, M. and Lamla, B. (2012) Empirical Research on Household's Saving and Retirement Security: First Steps towards an Innovative Triple-Linked-Dataset. MEA Discussion Paper 07–2012.

Coppola, M. and Reil-Held, A. (2010) Jenseits staatlicher Alterssicherung: die neue regulierte private Vorsorge in Deutschland. In L. Leisering (ed.), *Die Alten der Welt. Neue Wege der Alterssicherung im globalen Norden und Süden* (pp. 215–243). Frankfurt: Campus Verlag.

Coppola, M. and Gasche, M. (2011) Die Riester-Förderung – Mangelnde Information als Verbreitungshemmnis. *Wirtschaftsdienst* 91(11): 792–799.

Coppola, M. and Wilke, C.B. (2014) What age do you expect to retire? Retirement expectations and increases in the statutory retirement age. *Fiscal Studies* 35: 165–188.

Corneo, G., Keese, M. and Schröder, K. (2009) The Riester scheme and private savings: an empirical analysis based on the German SOEP. *Schmollers Jahrbuch* 129(2): 321–332.

Diamond, P.A. and Hausman, J.A. (1984) Individual retirement and savings behavior. *Journal of Public Economics* 23: 81–114.

Dicks-Mireaux, L. and King, M. (1984) Pension wealth and household savings: tests of robustness. *Journal of Public Economics* 23(1–2): 115–139.

Doerr, U. and Schulte, K. (2012) Betting on a long life – the role of subjective life expectancy in the demand for private pension insurance of German households, *Schmollers Jahrbuch* 132: 233–263.

Dummann, K. (2008) What determines supply and demand for occupational pensions in Germany? *Journal of Pension Economics and Finance* 7(2): 131–156.

Eichenhofer, E., Rische, H. and Schmähl, W. (2011) Handbuch der Gesetzlichen Rentenversicherung SGB VI, Luchterhand, Köln.

Engen, E. and Gale, W. (2000) The Effects of 401(k) Plans on Household Wealth: Differences Across Earnings Groups. NBER Working Paper 8032.

Engen, E., Gale, W. and Scholz, J.K. (1994) Do saving incentives work? *Brookings Papers on Economic Activity* 1994(1): 85–151.

Engen, E., Gale, W. and Scholz, J.K. (1996) The illusory effects of saving incentives on saving. *Journal of Economic Perspectives* 10(4): 113–138.

Feldstein, M.S. (1974) Social security, induced retirement, and aggregate capital accumulation. *Journal of Political Economy* 84: 905–926.

Friedman, M. (1957) *A Theory of the Consumption Function.* Princeton, NJ: Princeton University Press.

Gustman, A.L. and Steinmeier, T.L. (2004) What people don't know about their pensions and social security. In: W.G. Gale, J.B. Shoven and M.J. Warshawsky (eds.), *Private Pensions and Public Policies* (pp. 57–125). Brookings Institution: Washington, DC.

Gustman, A.L. and Steinmeier, T.L. (2005) The social security early entitlement age in a structural model of retirement and wealth. *Journal of Public Economics* 89(2–3): 441–463.

Gustman, A.L. and Steinmeier, T.L. (2014) Mismeasurement of pensions before and after retirement: the mystery of the disappearing pensions with implications for the importance of social security as a source of retirement support. *Journal of Pension Economics and Finance* 13(1): 1–26.

Gale, W. (1998) The effects of pensions on household wealth: A reevaluation of theory and evidence. *Journal of Political Economy* 106(4): 706–723.

Gelber, A. (2011) How do 401(k)s affect saving? Evidence from changes in 401(k) eligibility. *American Economic Journal: Economic Policy* 3(4): 103–122.

Guariglia, A. and Markose, S. (2000) Voluntary contributions to personal pension plans: evidence from the British household panel survey. *Fiscal Studies* 21(4): 469–488.

Haan, P. and Prowse, V. (2014) Longevity, life-cycle behavior and pension reform. *Journal of Econometrics* 178(P3): 582–601.

Hanel, B. (2010) Financial incentives to postpone retirement and further effects on employment evidence from a natural experiment. *Labour Economics* 17(3): 474–486.

Hanel, B. (2012) The effect of disability pension incentives on early retirement decisions. *Labour Economics* 19(4): 595–607.

Honekamp, I. and Schwarze, J. (2010) Pension reforms in Germany: have they changed savings behavior? *Pensions: An International Journal* 15(3): 214–225.

Hubbard, G., Skinner, J. and Zeldes, S. (1995) Precautionary savings and social insurance. *Journal of Political Economy* 103(2): 360–399.

Kommission – Kommission für die Nachhaltigkeit in der Finanzierung der Sozialen Sicherungssysteme (2003). Abschlussbericht, Berlin.

Kotlikoff, L.J. (1979) Testing the theory of social security and life-cycle accumulation. *The American Economic Review* 69(3): 396–410.

Lamla, B. and Coppola, M. (2013) Is it all about access? Perceived access to occupational pensions in Germany. MEA-Discussion-Paper 277–2013. MEA- Max Planck Institute for Social Law and Social Policy.

Lamla, B. and Gasche, M. (2014) Erwarteter Bezug von Grundsicherung im Alter: Verhaltensunterschiede und Fehleinschätzungen. *Schmollers Jahrbuch* 133(4): 539–562.

Lusardi, A. and Mitchell, O.S. (2011) Financial literacy around the world: an overview. *Journal of Pension Economics and Finance* 10(4): 497–508.

Lusardi, A. and Mitchell, O. (2014) The economic importance of financial literacy: theory and evidence. *Journal of Economic Literature* 52(1): 5–44.

Lusardi, A., Michaud, P. and Mitchell, O. (2013) Optimal Financial Literacy and Wealth Inequality. NBER Working Paper 18669.

Masuch, P., Spellbrink, W., Becker, U. and Leibfried, S. (2014) *Grundlagen und Herausforderungen des Sozialstaats.* Erich Schmidt Verlag: Berlin.

Michaud, P.C. and vanSoest, A. (2008) How did the elimination of the earnings test above the normal retirement age affect labour supply expectations? *Fiscal Studies* 29: 197–231.

Modigliani, F. and Brumberg, R. (1954) The *Collected Papers of Franco Modigliani – The Life-Cycle Hypothesis of Saving*. Cambridge, MA: MIT Press.

Rust, J. and Phelan, C. (1997) How social security and medicare affect retirement behavior in a world of incomplete markets. *Econometrica* 65(4): 781–832.

Pfarr, C. and Schneider, U. (2013) Choosing between subsidized or unsubsidized private pension schemes: evidence from German panel data. *Journal of Pension Economics and Finance* 12(1): 62–91.

Paiella, M. and Tiseno, A. (2014) Evaluating the impact on saving of tax-favored retirement plans. *Journal of Pension Economics and Finance* 13: 62–87.

Poterba, J., Venti, S. and Wise, D. (1995) Do 401(k) plans crowd out other personal saving? *Journal of Public Economics* 58(1): 1–32.

Poterba, J., Venti, S. and Wise, D. (1996) How retirement saving programs increase saving. *Journal of Economic Perspectives* 10(4): 91–112.

Rossi, M. (2009) Examining the interaction between saving and contribution to personal pension plans. Evidence from the BHPS. *Oxford Bulletin of Economics and Statistics* 71(2): 253–271.

Scheubel, B., Schunk, D. and Winter, J. (2013) Strategic responses: a survey experiment on opposition to pension reforms. *Scandinavian Journal of Economics* 115: 549–574.

Sefton, J., vande Ven, J. and Weale, M. (2008) Means testing retirement benefits: fostering equity or discouraging savings? *The Economic Journal* 118: 556–590.

Stock, J.H. and Wise, D.A. (1990) Pensions, the option value of work, and retirement. *Econometrica* 58: 1151–1180.

vander Klaauw, W. and Wolpin, K.I. (2008) Social security and the retirement and savings behavior of low-income households. *Journal of Econometrics* 145(1–2): 21–42.

Venti, S.F. and Wise, D.A. (1990) Have Iras increased US saving? Evidence from consumer expenditure surveys. *Quarterly Journal of Economics* 422: 661–698.

Werding, M. (2007) Versicherungsmathematisch korrekte Abschläge. *Ifo Schnelldienst* 16–2007: 19–32.

Ziegelmeyer, M. and Nick, J. (2013) Backing out of private pension provision: lessons from Germany. *Empirica* 40: 505–539.

10

ECONOMIC DETERMINANTS OF WORKERS' RETIREMENT DECISIONS

Courtney C. Coile

Wellesley College

"Retirement is as necessary to me as it will be welcome" – George Washington
"The question isn't at what age I want to retire, it's at what income" – George Foreman

The retirement decision is complex and multifaceted, involving considerations of health, family, work and leisure opportunities, and retirement income. Retirement is one of the most financially significant decisions an individual makes during his or her lifetime, as it typically marks the end of labor earnings and the beginning of the drawdown of retirement resources accrued over the worker's career. A worker's calculation of whether he or she has saved enough to be able to retire at a particular age is complicated by uncertainty about longevity, out-of-pocket medical expenditures, and investment returns. Yet retirement has important nonfinancial consequences also, as it may bring relief from the strain of working while in declining health as well as the opportunity to spend more time with a spouse or grandchildren or to engage in leisure activities.

When aggregated, the retirement decisions of individual workers have important consequences for the economy as a whole. Workers aged 55 years and above make up an increasing share of the U.S. labor force – 22% in 2014, versus 12% in 1992 (Coy, 2014). Any change in their behavior will therefore impact the overall labor force participation rate as well as Gross Domestic Product (GDP). Population aging is responsible for an estimated 1.5–2 percentage point decline in the U.S. labor force participation rate since 2007 (CBO, 2014; Munnell, 2014), as participation rates tend to be lower for older groups. Changes over time in retirement behavior can partially offset this decline, if workers are working longer, or exacerbate it if they are retiring earlier.

Retirement decisions can have important implications for government budgets as well, though the picture is complex. The United States and other developed countries devote a large share of government revenues to funding old age pensions and health care for the elderly, but some of these entitlements are independent of workers' retirement decisions. Retirement behavior matters for payroll and income tax revenues, and may also affect spending on old age pensions, depending on how benefits are adjusted for age of claiming.

A Collection of Surveys on Savings and Wealth Accumulation, First Edition. Edited by Edda Claus and Iris Claus.

Chapters © 2016 The Authors. Book compilation © 2016 John Wiley & Sons, Ltd. Published 2016 by John Wiley & Sons, Ltd.

Researchers have been actively engaged in exploring the economic determinants of retirement decisions for the past several decades. Dramatic declines in the labor force participation of older men after World War II provided an important source of motivation for this work, as did the aging of the baby boomers and resulting financial pressure on old age pension and health care programs. Two rich longitudinal data sets made much of the work possible – the Retirement History Survey (RHS) of the 1970s was used in much of the early literature, while the Health and Retirement Study (HRS), which began in 1992 and is still ongoing, has been an important resource for more recent work. The success of the HRS has encouraged the creation of similar surveys in other countries, including the Survey of Health, Ageing and Retirement in Europe (SHARE) as well as aging studies in England, Ireland, Israel, Mexico, Japan, Korea, China, and India. Over the past 20 years, more than 2000 articles on the economics of retirement have been published in academic journals indexed by *EconLit*.

This paper summarizes theory and evidence regarding the economic determinants of retirement decisions. Section 1 discusses the definition of retirement and Section 2 documents retirement patterns and trends. Section 3 focuses on the effect of public and private pensions on retirement. Section 4 looks at other factors, including wealth and savings, health and health insurance, and labor demand. Section 5 concludes with some thoughts about the future of retirement behavior and retirement research.

1. Defining Retirement

While retirement may seem like a straightforward concept, it is surprisingly difficult to define. Perhaps the simplest option is to define retirement as occurring when an individual stops working for pay. This definition works well when a worker with a full-time career job that he or she has held for many years leaves this job and never works again. However, workers with career jobs may also retire gradually, in stages, often working for a period of time at a bridge job that offers a part-time schedule, more flexibility, or fewer responsibilities. While these individuals would be considered workers under the standard retirement definition, they may have more in common with fully retired individuals than they do with full-time workers.

Alternatively, retirement could be defined as occurring when an individual leaves his or her career job. But not all workers have career jobs, and it is not clear how to classify workers who switch to part-time status at their same job. A third option is to allow individuals themselves to define whether or not they are retired. This sidesteps some issues, but raises the concern that individuals with the same level of labor force participation could be classified differently. A final option is to focus on the initial claim of public or private pension benefits. While obviously an important milestone, benefit receipt need not be related to work, because individuals may be able to claim pension benefits while they are still working or to delay benefit receipt after they have stopped working.

In the end, most analysts define retirement as withdrawal from the labor force, as this is conceptually straightforward and easy to implement using most survey data. Analysts tend to treat retirement as an absorbing state and ignore the possibility of labor force re-entry, and often do not distinguish between transitions that include a period of time working at a bridge job and those that do not. Ultimately, given that no two definitions will give the same date of retirement for every individual, it is most important to acknowledge the complexity of retirement transitions and to select a consistent definition that may be used to explore patterns in and correlates with retirement behavior.

2. Retirement Trends and Patterns

While the discussion of retirement trends often focuses on the period since the end of World War II, it is possible to look back further, thanks to Dora Costa's seminal economic history of retirement (1998). Using the decennial census, she documents that from 1850 to 1880, more than three-quarters of U.S. men ages 65 years and above were in the labor force (defined as gainful employment and based on reporting an occupation in the previous year). After 1880, this figure began to decline markedly, reaching a value of about 45% in 1950. Interestingly, she documents similar declines of 20–40 percentage points over this time span in Great Britain, Germany, and France. Costa attributes much of these early changes in retirement behavior in the U.S. to rising incomes, but also documents a role for occupational shifts, health improvements, and changes in leisure opportunities.

The period since World War II has been characterized by a continuation of the dramatic decline in the labor force participation of older men. As illustrated in Figure 1 using U.S. Bureau of Labor Statistics data, the share of men ages 65 years and above in the labor force (defined as working or looking for work) fell from 47% in 1948 to 16% in 1984 and then remained roughly constant through the early 1990s. The share in the labor force at ages 55–64 years fell by a similar amount, from 90% in 1948 to 66% in the mid-1990s. Since then, the labor force participation of older men has risen slowly but steadily, reaching a value of 24% for men ages 65 years and above and a value of 70% for men ages 55–64 years in 2013.

For older women in the United States, the trend is much different. As shown in Figure 2, labor force participation of women ages 55–64 years has risen continuously over the past 60 years, from 24% in 1948 to 59% in 2013. Participation for women ages 65 years and above dipped slightly between 1960 and the mid-1990s but has doubled since then, from 7% to 15%.

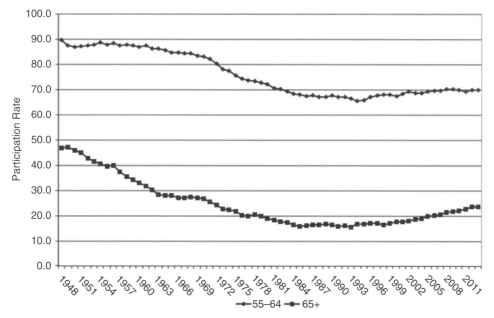

Figure 1. Men's Labor Force Participation, Ages 55–64 and 65+, 1948–2013.
Source: Bureau of Labor Statistics (Series LNU01300199 and LNY01300199).

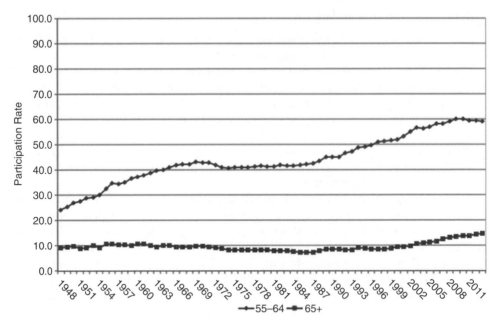

Figure 2. Women's Labor Force Participation, Ages 55–64 and 65+, 1948–2013.
Source: Bureau of Labor Statistics (Series LNU01300347 and LNY01300354).

The societal trend of greater labor force participation by women of all ages appears to have essentially swamped any movement towards earlier retirement for women.

Looking back at retirement behavior over the past century and a half, it is evident that although retirement is now a well-established phase of life, it is actually a fairly modern concept. In the 19th century, many men worked until their deaths or close to it. Since then, the duration of retirement has skyrocketed, due both to rising life expectancies and earlier retirement. Leonesio *et al.* (2012) estimate that between 1950 and 2000, the average duration of retirement increased from 11 to 19 years for men and from 13 to 23 years for women, based on changes in the median age of labor force exit and life expectancy. Of this increase, roughly one-third was due to increasing longevity and two-thirds to earlier labor force exit.

A second notable aspect of retirement behavior is the pattern of retirement by age. This is generally measured using the retirement hazard, or probability that a worker still in the labor force at a given age will exit the labor force at that age. If work becomes more difficult as workers age due to declining health, one might expect the hazard to rise smoothly with age. In fact, the hazard does rise with age, but also exhibits sharp spikes at ages 62 and 65 years, as shown in Figure 3 using data from the March Current Population Survey (CPS) for the period 2000–2014. These spikes correspond to the ages at which Social Security benefits are first available (62 years) and the age of Medicare eligibility and historical full retirement age (FRA) for Social Security (65 years).

There are distinct patterns in retirement behavior by education as well. Figure 4 illustrates the labor force participation rate of men by age and education level during the period 2000–2014. By age 50, there is already a 20-point gap in men's labor force participation, with only three-quarters of high school dropouts in the labor force, versus 94% of college graduates. The

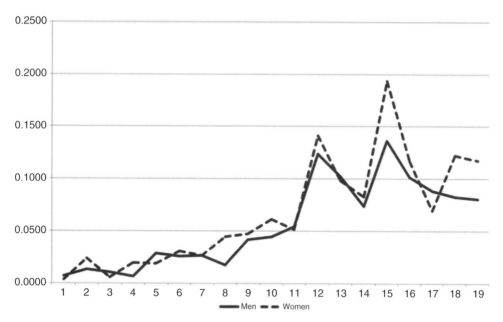

Figure 3. Retirement Hazard by Age, 2000–2014, CPS.
Source: Author's Calculation from March CPS, Stimulated Retirement Hazard Based on Age-Specific
Declines in Labor Force Participation.

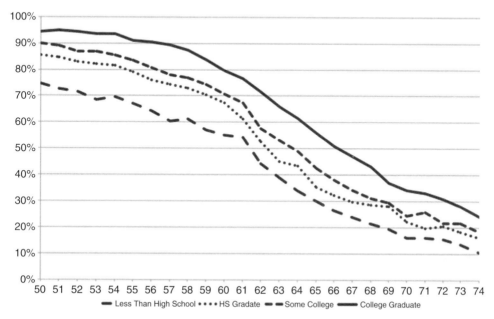

Figure 4. Labor Force Participation by Education, 2000–2014, CPS Men.
Source: Author's calculation from March CPS.

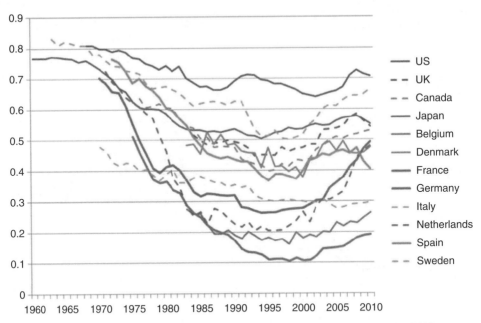

Figure 5. Employment Rates of Men Ages 60–64 by Year and Country, 1960–2010.
Source: Coile *et al.* (forthcoming).

gap subsequently widens to nearly 30 points, as men with less education exit the labor force at earlier ages than their more educated counterparts. At age 62, for example, the retirement hazard is 18% for high school dropouts and 7% for college graduates. By age 62, more than half of high school dropouts are out of the labor force; for college graduates, this occurs at age 67. A sizeable share of college graduates work into their 70s, roughly twice the share of high school dropouts who do so. For women (not shown), patterns are similar, with even bigger gaps in labor force participation between the highest and lowest education, particularly before age 62. The reasons for these differences across education groups are not well understood, but could include differences in health and life expectancy, the nature of work, or wages.

Retirement behavior in other developed countries displays many of the same patterns seen in the U.S. Coile *et al.* (forthcoming) tabulate data for a dozen countries including the United States, Canada, Japan, and nine European countries. They document a decline in men's employment in Europe from about 1970 until the mid-to-late 1990s that was similar to, if not steeper than, that in the United States.[1] As seen in Figure 5, by 1995 only 10–30% of men ages 60–64 were employed in Belgium, France, Germany, Italy, and the Netherlands, with employment rates somewhat higher in the United States and Sweden (50%) and Japan (70%).[2] Since the late 1990s, many of these countries have experienced a substantial rise in older men's employment, with increases in employment of at least 10 percentage points in eight of the twelve countries. Other aspects of retirement behavior are also similar across developed countries. As documented in Gruber and Wise (1999), the retirement hazard by age in other countries is like that in the United States but exhibits even larger spikes at the early and normal ages for public pension plans, with as many as 60–80% of remaining workers retiring when they reach these critical ages, as opposed to about 20% in the United States. Coile *et al.* (2014)

report that differences in employment by level of education in other countries are also quite similar to those in the United States.

As noted earlier, retirement transitions are complex and often include employment in a bridge job or a return to the labor force after some period of retirement. Cahill *et al.* (2015) find that about 60% of workers leaving a career job move to a bridge job, whereas 40% go directly to full retirement. There is some evidence that the use of bridge jobs is increasing for women (though not for men) over time and that bridge jobs are increasingly likely to be full-time jobs.[3] Maestas (2010) reports that over one-quarter of retirees return to the labor force within the first 6 years after retirement, most commonly about 2 years after retirement, whereas Cahill *et al.* (2011) find that 15% of older workers who held career jobs and have been retired for at least 2 years re-enter the labor force.

3. The Effect of Public and Private Pensions on Retirement

The steep decline in men's labor force participation following the end of World War II that was seen in Figure 1 occurred during a time of expansion of public and private pension plans. After the passage of the Social Security Act in 1935, both the share of workers eligible for Social Security benefits and the real value of benefits grew rapidly. From 1956 to 2012, the number of workers fully insured for Social Security retired worker or survivor benefits rose from 74 to 208 million, an increase of 181% during a period when the size of the U.S. population increased by 86%. During that same period, the inflation-adjusted average monthly benefit for retired workers rose from $533 to $1,262 (in 2012), an increase of 137%.[4] The increase in private pension coverage was equally dramatic. Between 1975 and 2012, the number of participants in private pension plans rose from 12 to 91 million (U.S. Department of Labor, 2014).

The coincidence of these trends spawned a large literature on the effect of public and private pensions on retirement. As in some other areas of economic research, different approaches developed to explore this question. Some researchers followed a structural approach, positing a specific form for the individual or household utility function and using data to estimate parameters of the utility function such as the discount rate and level of risk aversion. A clear advantage of this method is that the estimated parameters can be used to simulate the effect of policies outside the scope of real world experience, such as how retirement behavior would change if public pensions were eliminated. By contrast, other researchers relied on natural experiments such as policy changes or other real-world phenomena to generate plausibly exogenous variation in pension benefits and estimated reduced form models relating benefits to retirement behavior. An advantage of the latter approach is that it does not rely on correctly specifying the form of the utility function and its key assumptions are transparent – for example, that there would be no other reason for the retirement behavior of two groups to differ except that one group received larger pension benefits. Where possible, it is desirable to compare results from reduced form and structural models, as conclusions about the effects of pensions on retirement will be strengthened when the two literatures are in agreement.

3.1 *Why public pensions may affect retirement in theory*

Before proceeding to discuss the empirical literature, it is useful to recall why pension benefits might be expected to influence retirement behavior, beginning with public pensions. If workers receive social security benefits of equal value to their payroll tax contributions plus a market rate of return, the existence of social security would not alter the incentive to retire in a perfect market setting (Blinder *et al.*, 1978). However, in the real world social security systems may create income effects, as benefits received may be greater or less than payroll tax contributions, as well as substitution effects, as additional work may increase or decrease net pension wealth.

Public pension systems often feature intercohort and intracohort redistribution that generates income effects. The introduction of Social Security in the United States as a pay-as-you-go system advantaged early beneficiaries, who did not contribute over their full working lives, at the expense of later cohorts (Leimer, 1999). Within a cohort, low earners receive higher benefits relative to contributions than do high earners because of the progressivity in the benefit formula,[5] though the tendency of higher earners to have longer lives offsets this to some extent, because Social Security is a real annuity (Liebman, 2002). Dependent spouse and survivor benefits also create intracohort redistribution, as a married, one-earner family receives more benefits than a single worker with the same payroll tax contributions.[6]

The process by which a public pension plan creates substitution effects is complex. By working one more year, the worker makes payroll tax contributions and gives up a year of benefits (once past the early retirement age). However, the extra year of work is incorporated into the benefit calculation, which may raise the benefit amount. Further, the benefit amount is often raised for delaying benefit claim beyond the early eligibility age (EEA). If that adjustment is actuarially fair, lifetime benefits are similar regardless of claiming age, but if it is less (or more) than fair, this aspect of the system penalizes (or rewards) additional work. Whether the pension system as a whole taxes or subsidizes additional work depends on the net of all these factors, and may vary across individuals depending on their earnings history and other characteristics. Coile and Gruber (2001) report that although the median male worker faces a near zero tax rate between the early and full eligibility age and a large tax thereafter, there is substantial heterogeneity in tax rates and significant non-monotonicities in Social Security wealth accruals.

Relaxing the assumptions of perfect capital markets, rationality, and certain lifetimes further complicates the picture. Consider two types of individuals who on their own would save little for retirement: a rational, forward-looking individual who gets little utility from retirement consumption and a myopic individual who fails to plan. For both types, the pension plan raises retirement income, leading to earlier retirement. Because workers cannot borrow against future pension income, there may be a spike in the retirement hazard at the EEA, when benefits become available. On the other hand, incorporating longevity risk may have an opposite effect. Public pension benefits are generally paid as an annuity, providing protection against the risk of outliving one's resources in retirement; if benefits are indexed for inflation, as Social Security benefits in the United States are, they offer protection against inflation risk as well. With private annuity markets plagued by adverse selection (Finklestein and Poterba, 2004), workers may not have access to annuities outside the social security system and may therefore choose to delay retirement in order to purchase a larger annuity (Crawford and Lilien, 1981).

With employer-sponsored private pensions, there is no income effect, because the pension is simply part of the worker's total compensation package. But defined benefit (DB) pensions typically contain strong incentives for work and retirement at particular ages. Specifically, Stock and Wise (1990a, 1990b) note that many pensions feature large annual pension wealth accruals in the years before the plan's early or normal retirement age and negative accruals thereafter. Lazear (1979, 1983) argues that this structure may be part of an optimal employment contract in which workers are paid less than their marginal product when young and more than their marginal product when old, in order to induce the young worker (whose effort is not perfectly observable) to exert more effort; because an older worker being paid more than his or her marginal product would be reluctant to retire, negative pension wealth accruals after the plan retirement age provide an important inducement. By contrast, defined contribution (DC) pension plans such as 401(k) plans feature smooth pension wealth accruals, with contributions fixed as a share of earnings or employee contributions, and thus do not provide strong incentives to work to or retire at particular ages.

3.2 *Empirical Evidence on Pensions and Retirement Based on Reduced Form Models*

Turning to the empirical evidence, trends in the evolution of retirement behavior and pensions over time suggest a link between the two. As noted earlier, the labor force participation rate for older men in the United States and other developed countries declined rapidly after the end of World War II, at a time when pension coverage was becoming more ubiquitous and real benefits were rising. Labor force participation then began to rise in the mid-1990s, at a time when many European countries adopted pension reforms, such as raising the retirement age or scaling back the generosity of benefits (Gern, 2002). The fact that labor force participation first fell and then rose as developed countries expanded and then cut back their public pension systems strongly suggests a link between pensions and retirement, and has provided powerful motivation for much of the empirical work on this topic.

Research that highlights the spikes in the retirement hazard at public pension plans' early and normal retirement ages provides additional evidence of a role for pensions in retirement decisions. There are generally few if any other reasons to expect spikes at those ages, and many authors make this point by using the variation in eligibility ages over time. Burtless and Moffitt (1986) and Costa (1998) show that the spike in retirement at age 62 in the United States only emerged once age 62 became the EEA for Social Security. The same phenomenon occurred in France, where first some workers gained access to pensions at age 60 and then age 60 became the normal retirement for all, and a large spike at age 60 subsequently developed (Gruber and Wise, 1999). Similarly, in Germany, the 1972 introduction of a more flexible system that allowed some workers to retire at ages 60 and 63 years, rather than the traditional age of 65 years, was followed by the emergence of spikes at ages 60 and 63 years where none had existed before and a sharp decline in the age-65 spike (Börsch-Supan and Schnabel, 1998).

Turning back to the United States, Blau (1994) finds that there is a large spike in retirement in the precise quarter in which workers turn 65, the Social Security FRA at this time, relative to adjacent quarters; Lumsdaine and Wise (1994) conclude that the spike cannot be explained by private pension plan incentives or access to Medicare and suggest that Social Security plays a key role by setting up the "focal point" of a normal retirement age. More recently, Mastrobuoni (2009) finds that the increase in the FRA from ages 65 to 66 years led the retirement age for affected cohorts to rise by about half as much.

In addition to inferring the effect of Social Security on retirement decisions from evidence such as this, researchers have been interested in estimating the effect of benefits on retirement directly. The earliest work, summarized in Mitchell and Fields (1982), often used RHS data and featured Social Security wealth (SSW) as the key regressor of interest. Subsequent studies (Quinn and Burkhauser, 1983; Hausman and Wise, 1985) added the 1-year accrual, or change in SSW from working an additional year, in order to capture substitution effects. These early studies generally found that Social Security has a significant effect on retirement, but can explain only a modest share of the time series decline in labor force participation.

Kruger and Pischke (1992)'s study of Social Security "notch babies," however, cast doubt on previous estimates of the relationship between SSW and retirement. The notch cohort, born between 1917 and 1921, unexpectedly received lower benefits than earlier cohorts due to a 1977 law change, but their labor force participation did not deviate from the long-term downward trend.

This study highlights one of the key challenges facing researchers working in this area. Social Security is a national program, and thus lacks the state-level differences in program provisions that have proven useful in estimating the effects of other public programs, such as unemployment insurance and welfare. Social Security benefits (and thus SSW, which is the present discounted value of benefits) are a nonlinear function of average lifetime earnings, which themselves may affect retirement behavior directly or be correlated with unobservable factors that affect retirement. Estimating the effect of SSW on retirement may result in biased coefficients unless the researcher controls for average earnings, but doing so may absorb most of the variation in SSW. Exploring this issue, Coile and Gruber (2001) find that there is substantial variation in the 1-year accrual of SSW (though less variation in the level of SSW) even after controlling for lifetime and current earnings as well as other factors that may affect both incentives and retirement, such as spouse's age. They note that this variation arises from nonlinearities in the Social Security benefit formula, the particulars of each individual's earnings history (such as earnings in the lowest earnings year), and the interaction of all of these factors, and suggest that this variation makes it possible to estimate the effect of Social Security incentives on retirement while controlling flexibly for earnings and other direct determinants of retirement.

A second important critique of the early empirical literature is its focus on the single-year accrual, or change in lifetime pension benefits arising from an additional year of work. Coile and Gruber (2001) report that many workers experience positive SSW accruals between the EAA of 62 years and the FRA, accruals larger than those available in the years prior to the EEA, due to the increase in the monthly benefit amount from delayed claiming. Focusing on the 1-year financial gain to work at, say, age 55, overlooks these subsequent larger accruals. Coile and Gruber (2001, 2007) therefore develop a forward-looking "peak value" (PV) measure that captures the financial gain from working to the future retirement date that maximizes the PDV of SSW. They find their measure to be strongly correlated with retirement, with those who have a greater incentive to continue working being less likely to retire; the estimated elasiticity of nonparticipation with respect to benefits is 0.15.[7]

Liebman et al. (2009) employ a similar methodology that relies only on variation arising from discontinuities in the Social Security benefit formula; they use this approach to examine labor supply responses to Social Security incentives along both the extensive and intensive margins, finding stronger evidence for the former. Asch et al. (2005) estimate PV models for federal civil service workers who are covered by a DB-style plan and not by Social Security, and find results in line with previous studies. Friedberg and Webb (2005) estimate PV models to explore the effects of the shift in pensions from DB to DC style on retirement behavior.

International comparisons also provide evidence of the effect of public pensions on retirement. Gruber and Wise (1999) calculate "tax force," which is the sum of the tax/subsidy rate (or 1-year SSW accrual scaled by earnings) at ages 55–69 years, for the median worker in a dozen developed countries. They show that it varies dramatically across countries, with particularly large penalties on additional work in Belgium, France, Italy, and the Netherlands. The tax force measure also correlates strongly with the labor force participation rates of older men, as it can explain 80–85% of the differences in participation across countries in a simple regression. In subsequent work, Gruber and Wise (2004) use microdata to estimate reduced form PV models and find that they are key predictors of retirement in virtually all countries in their sample.[8]

Several studies have made use of changes in public pension systems in recent decades in various countries as natural experiments that can be used to explore the effect of public pensions on retirement. For example, Atalay and Barett (2014) find that a 1-year increase in the eligibility age for women in Australia is associated with a 12–19 percentage-point decrease in the probability of retirement. Euwals *et al.* (2010) find that a Dutch policy reform that made early retirement schemes less generous and more actuarially fair induced workers to postpone retirement. Staubli and Zweimuller find that raising the early retirement age in Austria led to increases in employment for men and women, but also to similar if not larger increases in the use of the unemployment insurance system, pointing to the possibility of substitution among various public programs that serve as de facto early retirement schemes. Börsch-Supan *et al.* (2004) have a similar finding in Germany, where decreased use of a flexible retirement program was accompanied by growth in the use of unemployment insurance after age 60.

3.3 *Structural Models of Social Security and Retirement*

In addition to the literature estimating reduced form models, there is a robust literature on Social Security and retirement that employs a structural approach. This approach became popular in the early 1980s, when advances in computing began to make the estimation of such models easier. Since then, researchers have been building more complex models that incorporate many additional features not present in the earliest models, for example uncertainty in asset returns or out-of-pocket medical expenses.

Structural models of retirement are generally based on a life cycle model of retirement behavior. A rational, forward-looking individual is presumed to maximize a lifetime utility function subject to a lifetime budget constraint. The form of the utility function is specified by the researcher, though its parameters, such as the degree of risk aversion, are estimated empirically. The individual receives labor earnings while working and public and private pension benefits when retired, where pension benefits are generally a function of retirement age. The lifetime budget constraint requires that initial assets plus any savings or dissavings in each period and investment returns on assets sum to zero over the individual's life. These models are estimated using micro data via maximum likelihood techniques. The model is validated based on its ability to generate reasonable utility parameter estimates and to match observed retirement behavior, such as the spikes in the retirement hazard at the Social Security early and normal retirement ages.[9] Public and private pensions enter the model as a source of retirement income, and these models may be used to infer the importance of pensions through simulations of changes in pension policy.

Gustman and Steinmeier (1986) is an important early paper in this literature and the first in a series of contributions by these authors. They find that their model can replicate the peaks in the retirement hazard and estimate that Social Security and private pensions have a strong negative effect on labor supply. Later related studies have added to this framework by incorporating complexity in a number of ways, for example by allowing for heterogeneity in the consumption parameter (Van der Klaauw and Wolpin, 2008) or time preference (Gustman and Steinmeier, 2005) or by allowing reverse flows into employment (Gustman *et al.*, 2010). Other important extensions to the structural retirement literature are discussed later.

Another important early structural model of retirement is the option value model of Stock and Wise (1990a, 1990b). In the context of employer-provided DB pensions, they note that the PDV of pension wealth in a DB plan often rises sharply just before the plan's early or normal retirement age and declines substantially thereafter. Thus, by working in a given year, the worker is effectively retaining the option of working in future years that may have higher accruals. They develop an option value model in which the worker compares the utility of retiring today to that available at all future retirement dates. This model is also estimated structurally, with utility parameters chosen to maximize the likelihood of observing the retirement transitions that occurred in the sample. They conclude that pensions have substantial effects on retirement behavior.

A number of studies have used structural models to predict the effects of changes in Social Security policy on retirement behavior. Gustman and Steinmeier (2005) predicts that raising the Social Security early entitlement age to 64 years would cause many people to delay retirement from age 62 to 64 years. By contrast, French (2005) estimates that moving the early entitlement age would have little effect on retirement, but that eliminating the earnings test (which prevents individuals from receiving benefits while working) would lead individuals to work longer.

The structural approach has proven popular for analyses of pensions outside the United States as well. For example, Börsch-Supan (1992) estimates an option value of retirement in Germany and concludes that the pension system has contributed to earlier retirement by having less than actuarially fair incentives. Manoli and Weber (2011) estimate a dynamic model of retirement in Austria, making use of discontinuous changes in retirement benefits by years of job tenure, and find relatively low labor supply elasticities.

3.4 *Social Security Claiming and the Earnings Test*

Another decision facing older workers, related to but potentially distinct from the labor supply decision, is the choice of when to initiate receipt of Social Security benefits. In many countries, the monthly benefit amount depends on the age of initial benefit receipt. In the United States, currently, for example, a worker claiming at the EAA of 62 years receives a benefit that is 25% lower than that received if he or she claims at the FRA of 66 years, whereas a worker waiting until age 70 would receive a benefit that is 32% higher than the FRA benefit.[10] Depending on how these adjustment factors are set and which types of people claim early versus late, claiming decisions may have an impact on the budget of the pension program. Claiming decisions may also affect the likelihood of poverty in old age, because earlier claiming is associated with a lower monthly benefit.

For the adjustment of benefits with claiming age to be actuarially fair, it must be just large enough so that the expected present discounted value of benefits over the average worker's lifetime is the same regardless of claiming age. Although conventional wisdom has long held that this is roughly true in the United States, Shoven and Slavov (2014) argue that the gains from delay have increased dramatically since the 1990s due to a combination of low interest rates, increasing longevity, and legislated increases in the adjustment for claiming beyond the FRA. Even if the adjustment is actuarially fair for the population as a whole, it will be more than fair for those individuals who have long life expectancies and less than fair for those with short life expectancies. There may also be differences in actuarial fairness across groups if there are systematic mortality differences; Brown *et al.* (2002) show that mortality rates are higher for lower educated individuals and blacks. Finally, it may be appropriate to consider the gains to delayed claiming in a utility framework rather than in the context of a financial calculation due to the annuity value of Social Security. That is, it may be useful to think of the individual as choosing a claiming date so as to maximize expected utility from the stream of future retirement income rather than to maximize the expected PDV of benefits. Delaying claiming effectively allows the individual to purchase more of a real annuity (which may be unavailable on the private market), and the value of this to a risk averse individual facing an uncertain date of death is understated in a purely financial calculation.

Although researchers once essentially assumed that all workers claimed benefits as soon as they retired (or at the EAA, if retiring before this), several recent studies have examined claiming behavior more closely. Coile *et al.* (2002) use an expected utility framework to show that in many cases it is optimal to delay claiming and that gains from delay can be large. They find that 10% of men retiring before age 62 delay claiming for at least 1 year, whereas delays are less common for later retirees; delays are also found to be consistent with utility-maximizing behavior, as men with longer life expectancies (proxied by *ex post* mortality) and men with younger spouses are more likely to delay. Similarly, Hurd *et al.* (2004) find that the great majority of workers claim as soon as they are eligible and that those with low subjective survival probabilities retire and claim earlier. Gustman and Steinmeier (2008) report that 85–95% of fully retired males (age 63 and above) are receiving Social Security benefits, suggesting that claiming delays are fairly uncommon, relatively short, or both. However, many full-time working males – 25% at age 64, 60% at age 65, and 75% or more at ages 66 years and up – are in receipt of benefits, indicating that there is some claiming prior to retirement, particularly as workers near the FRA.

More recently, several papers have examined the claiming decision in the context of behavioral economics. Behaghel and Blau (2012) show that the spike in claiming at age 65 moved in lockstep along with the FRA, a finding similar to that of Song and Manchester (2007); they attribute this to reference dependence with loss aversion. Brown *et al.* (2013) provide experimental evidence on the impact of the framing of the claiming decision on behavior. In their experiment, participants are randomly assigned to see information presented in either a "breakeven" frame that emphasizes the number of years one would need to survive to make up for the benefits lost by delayed claiming or a "symmetric" frame that simply shows facts about claiming ages and benefit amounts. They find that using the breakeven frame leads individuals to select a claiming age that is on average 15 months earlier. By contrast, Liebman and Luttmer (2015) find that sending a brochure with information about Social Security provisions had no statistically significant effect on claiming, but did increase labor force participation by seven points among women.

In social security systems where an earnings test applies to benefit receipt, this may affect the claiming decision and potentially the retirement decision as well. In the United States, for example, workers between the EAA of 62 and the FRA are subject to an earnings test in which benefits are reduced by \$1 for each \$2 of earnings above a threshold amount (\$15,720 in 2015)[11]; beneficiaries above the FRA were subject to an earnings test until the year 2000. In fact, the earnings test in the U.S. system is not a true tax because upon reaching the FRA, the worker's benefit is recomputed to treat any lost months of benefit receipt as months of claiming delay. If beneficiaries fail to understand this provision, however, they may respond to the earnings test as if it was a tax.

A number of methods have been employed to assess the effect of the earnings test on labor supply, including looking for a concentration of workers with earnings just below the earnings test limit ("bunching"), using the kinks in the budget constraint generated by the test to structurally estimate labor supply models, and using changes over time in the earnings test in reduced form labor supply regressions. The evidence from these studies is mixed. While there is evidence of bunching (Friedberg, 2000), most projections based on structural estimates suggest that removing the earnings test would have a relatively small effect on labor supply;

Friedberg's (2000) estimate of a 5% increase in hours of work is on the high end of estimates from this literature. In the reduced form literature, Gruber and Orszag (2003) use changes in the structure of the earnings test prior to 2000 to explore its influence and conclude that it exerts no robust influence on men's labor supply decisions, though loosening the test does accelerate benefit receipt. However, Baker and Benjamin (1999) find that the removal of earnings test in Canada was associated with shifts from part-time to full-time work, whereas Disney and Smith (2002) find that eliminating the test above age 65 in the United Kingdom led to a 4-hour increase in average weekly hours for affected men. Haider and Loughan (2008) attempt to reconcile these disparate estimates by showing that measurement error and labor market rigidities tend to depress the amount of bunching at the kinks, which will affect structural estimation that uses these kinks; they also use longitudinal data to show that men increase earnings when the earnings test is removed, with larger responses for younger men.

4. Other Factors

4.1 *Wealth and Savings*

The retirement decision is likely to depend on all of the worker's financial resources, not only on pension benefits. Economists generally believe that leisure is a normal good and thus expect wealthier individuals to retire earlier, ceteris paribus. One challenge in testing this hypothesis empirically is that wealth is determined in large part by the savings decisions individuals make over time. If wealthier workers retire earlier, this might reflect the fact that these workers wanted to retire early and saved accordingly rather than a causal effect of wealth on retirement. More generally, wealthy individuals may differ from less wealthy individuals in ways that are unobservable to the researcher, creating bias in the estimate.

To surmount these challenges, the primary strategy adopted by researchers who favor a natural experiments approach is to identify unanticipated changes to wealth and test whether these wealth shocks are associated with an increased probability of retirement. Researchers have made use of several sources of wealth shocks. Imbens *et al.* (2001) show that large lottery gains lead to a reduction in labor supply, particularly for those near retirement age. Brown *et al.* (2010) find that the receipt of an inheritance increases the probability of retirement, particularly when the inheritance is unexpected and thus more likely to represent a true shock to wealth.

Another source of wealth shocks is the boom-bust cycles in the stock market over the past twenty years, which have created large, unexpected fluctuations in the value of equities. Evidence from this literature is more mixed. Focusing on the late 1990s and early 2000s, Hurd *et al.* (2009) find no evidence that workers in households with large stock market gains retired earlier than expected, compared to those without such gains. Coile and Levine (2006) find no evidence that changes in the stock market drive aggregate trends in labor supply, which they attribute to the fact that few workers have large stock holdings.[12] However, Coile and Levine (2011a) find that college-educated workers age 62 and above – who are more likely to own stocks and may be more easily persuaded to retire – do reduce retirement in response to long-term declines in the value of stocks. The effect is economically meaningful, with a one-standard-deviation increase in the 10-year return raising the probability of retirement by 12% relative to the mean.

On the structural side, researchers who estimate structural models of retirement have augmented their models to incorporate savings and wealth in more sophisticated ways. French

(2005), for example, introduces borrowing constraints, which may limit a household's ability to perfectly smooth consumption. Van der Klaauw and Wolpin (2008) also incorporate limited borrowing and uncertain wages in their analysis of the retirement and savings behavior of low-income households. These authors continue to use their estimates to assess the effect of public pensions on retirement, but do so in a more realistic setting in terms of savings decisions.

4.2 Health and Health Insurance

At the simplest level, a decline in health status is expected to increase the disutility of work and therefore increase the worker's probability of retirement. There may be other effects as well – a decline in health status may lead the worker to update his or her mortality expectations, require an increase in medical expenditures, or change how much the worker values consumption in retirement. Any of these could also affect the retirement decision.

Researchers have used several approaches to assess the effect of health on retirement. One method is to include self-reported health status or work limitations in the retirement model. Studies using this method, such as Diamond and Hausman (1984), find large effects of health on retirement. However, this method is subject to the concern that self-reported health is a subjective measure, as individuals' judgments of what constitutes poor health may vary substantially. Moreover, this measure may be influenced by retirement status if people justify being retired by reporting a health problem. A second method is to use objective measures of health, such as diagnoses of particular diseases. Studies using this method, such as Anderson and Burkhauser (1985), find smaller effects, but these measures are only imperfectly correlated with working capacity. A third method is to combine subjective and objective data, including by using one type of measure to instrument for the other.

The subsequent literature has largely confirmed the concerns about these methods. Bound (1991) uses a statistical model to show that bias can arise using any of the three methods. Kerkhofs et al. (1999) find an endogenous relationship between health and retirement in the Dutch context, although Dwyer and Mitchell (1999) reach the opposite conclusion for the United States. Baker et al. (2004) report that objective, self-reported measures of health are subject to considerable measurement error, resulting in large attenuation bias when used as explanatory variables. Kalwij and Vermeulen (2008) find that objective health measures are important determinants of labor force participation in some of the 11 European countries in their study and thus may not be an appropriate instrument for endogenous self-reported health.

A final approach is to focus on negative shocks to health. As in the wealth shocks literature, the appeal of this approach is that it exploits the arrival of unexpected new information. By focusing on changes in health, this approach avoids the concern that people who are generally in worse health may differ from those in better health in ways that are unobservable to the researcher. McClellan (1998) uses this approach and finds that workers who experience a health shock such as a heart attack or new cancer diagnosis are much more likely to retire, particularly when the shock is accompanied by a large decline in functioning.[13] Similarly, Disney et al. (2006) find that adverse shocks to an individual's "health stock" are strongly predictive of retirement for workers in Britain, whereas Bound et al. (1999) show that controlling for lagged health, poorer contemporaneous health is strongly associated with labor force exit.

A more recent literature has explored the effect of retirement on health. This is a challenging question to explore empirically because of the dual causality between retirement and health. Charles (2004) and several subsequent studies make use of the spikes in the retirement hazard at key public pension ages to explore whether the health of the older population changes at these points. Charles (2004) and Johnston and Lee (2009) both find positive effects of retirement on mental health, whereas Bound and Waidmann (2007) find some evidence of a positive effect on physical health for men. By contrast, in their study of the mortality effects of reduced Social Security payments to the "notch" generation, Snyder and Evans (2006) note that younger cohorts responded to the benefit cut by increasing their post-retirement work effort with positive effects on mortality, suggesting that moderate work at older ages may be beneficial for health.

Access to health insurance may also play a role in retirement decisions, particularly in the United States, where most individuals rely on their employer or a family member's employer for access to insurance. Madrian *et al.* (1994) finds that workers whose employers offer retiree health insurance retire on average 5–16 months earlier; Rogowski and Karoly (2000) have similar findings. Gruber and Madrian (1996) find that continuation of coverage mandates that allow retirees to purchase insurance through a previous employer for a period of time after leaving the firm raise retirement rates substantially, particularly for workers close to Medicare eligibility. Health insurance plays less of a role in countries with universal insurance coverage, and the recent passage of the Patient Protection and Affordable Care Act in the United States may lessen its impact in the United States as well. In fact, Sanzenbacher (2014) shows that following the passage of the Massachusetts health reform law in 2006, the labor force participation of men age 55–64 fell by over one percentage point, relative to participation in neighboring states, findings consistent with a lessening role for job lock in retirement decisions.

On the structural side, a number of authors have explored the role of health insurance. Rust and Phelan (1997) augment the standard structural model by designating a share of the population as "health insurance constrained," meaning that they have no source of retiree health insurance except Medicare or private purchase, and also incorporate uncertainty about future health status and health expenditures. They conclude that Medicare plays an important role in explaining the spike in retirement at age 65. Blau and Gilleskie (2006) estimate their own model that extends the work of Rust and Phelan (1997) in several ways and find that it can explain a significant share of the differences in employment among married men with and without access to retiree health insurance, though this is less true for married women. French and Jones (2011) build on earlier studies by allowing individuals to smooth consumption through saving and also allow Medicaid to provide a substitute for other means of health insurance. They find that raising the Medicare eligibility age would lead workers to work longer.

4.3 *Retirement in a Family Context*

Although the preceding discussion largely treats retirement as an individual decision, many workers today are part of married, dual-career couples. It seems likely that workers in such families might make retirement decisions jointly, or at least that each spouse might be influenced to some extent by the other spouse's decision, for several reasons. First, individuals in a married couple have access to common financial resources. Second, individuals who are married may have similar preferences – for example, both may have low discount rates, making them patient with respect to tradeoffs between present and future income. Third, each spouse's enjoyment of his or her leisure time may depend on whether the other spouse is present. One key empirical fact motivating the literature on couples' retirement is that many spouses do retire together – Coile (2004) finds that in approximately one-third of working couples, both spouses retire within 1 year of each other.

Several authors estimate structural models of joint retirement by husbands and wives, including Hurd (1990), Gustman and Steinmeier (2000), and Maestas (2001). These authors employ different models, but all find that complementarity of leisure is a key factor driving retirement decisions. Other studies, such as Coile (2004) and Baker (2002) test for joint decision-making more indirectly, estimating reduced form regressions that explore whether retirement incentives for one spouse have "spillover effects" on to the retirement behavior of the other spouse; both find that they do.[14]

4.4 *Labor Demand*

The discussion to this point has focused on factors affecting the individual's willingness to supply labor, including public and private pension incentives, wealth, health and health insurance, and a spouse's retirement status. Yet one should not assume that all older individuals who wish to work will be able to do so. Labor demand factors may also influence the labor force participation and retirement behavior of older individuals.

Economists have long been interested in the relationship between age, wages, and productivity. In two influential papers, Lazear (1979, 1983) pointed to two puzzles in the employment of older workers: employer-sponsored DB pensions that penalize work beyond some age through negative pension wealth accruals and mandatory retirement rules requiring many workers to retire by a certain age, commonly age 65. Why would employers want to discourage or forbid work beyond some age? Such behavior is inconsistent with standard human capital theory, where workers are paid wages equal to (or less than) the value of their marginal product of labor. As Hutchens (1989) explains, Lazear suggests that workers and firms enter into long-term contracts in which workers are paid less than their marginal product when young and more than their marginal product when old, in order to discourage shirking in situations where it is difficult to monitor worker effort. Negative pension accruals and mandatory retirement are important parts of the agreement, as they induce the worker to retire at the appropriate time.

The evidence suggests that there is divergence in workers' wages and productivity with age, a pattern that cannot be explained by standard human capital theory but is consistent with Lazear's theory. Using individual and plant-level data that allow for the comparison of marginal product and wages for groups of workers, Hellerstein *et al.* (1999) find that older workers are less productive than younger workers but paid more. Similarly, Skirbekk (2004) concludes from his summary of the literature on age and productivity that earnings increase until relatively late in work life while job performance peaks in mid-career. Hutchens (1986) notes that the structure of contracts posited by Lazear could lead to a situation where firms employ older workers but do not hire new older workers for the same jobs and presents evidence consistent with this hypothesis.

If the wages of older workers exceed their productivity, firms may be reluctant to hire older workers or may seek to shed older employees from their payrolls. Concerns about the treatment of older workers in the labor market led to a key policy intervention, the Age Discrimination in Employment Act (ADEA). Passed in 1968, the ADEA protects workers age 40 and above from age-based discrimination in hiring, firing, or promotion.

Has the ADEA been helpful in combatting age-based discrimination? Using data covering the period before and after the ADEA's introduction, Neumark and Stock (1999) find that the law boosted employment of all protected workers (ages 40 and above) only slightly, but raised employment among those 60 and above more substantially. Adams (2004) uses a similar approach, making use of both state laws that predated the ADEA and the federal law, and finds somewhat larger effects. However, Lahey (2008a) finds that having both a state and federal age discrimination law, which effectively lengthens the time period during which claims can be filed, is associated with lower employment, which she suggests could reflect firms hiring fewer older workers in order to avoid potential future litigation by employees.

Separate from any potential effect on age discrimination, the ADEA has affected the labor market for older workers by ending mandatory retirement. In the 1970s, about 40% of male workers in the U.S. faced mandatory retirement at age 65 (von Watcher, 2002). Amendments to the ADEA in 1978 and 1986 first raised the age of mandatory retirement to age 70 and then eliminated age limits on work entirely. Von Watcher (2002) estimates that the labor force participation of workers age 65 and above rose by 10–20% as a result of the abolishment of mandatory retirement, though Burkhauser and Quinn (1983) emphasize that the effect was relatively small because Social Security and private pension incentives cause many workers to choose to retire at age 65 even in the absence of a mandate.

Does age discrimination persist despite the ADEA? Although older job seekers may perceive that they face discrimination when looking for work, establishing whether such discrimination is real is more difficult. Lahey (2008b) conducts a field experiment in which resumes for fictional female job applicants are randomly assigned different ages and sent to employers. She finds that resumes for younger workers are substantially more likely to result in an interview offer. She concludes that this is more likely due to statistical discrimination, in which employers use the average characteristics of a group as a proxy for the unknown characteristics of an individual in that group (and thus may assume that an older worker would have weak computer skills or be more difficult to train, for example), than of taste-based discrimination, in which the employer, firm's existing employees, or customers prefer interacting with younger people.

The recent recession has heightened fears about the ability of older job seekers to find employment. Nearly one in six U.S. workers reported losing a job during the Great Recession (Farber, 2011). Although older workers experienced lower rates of job loss, displaced older workers also experienced longer spells of unemployment and lower re-employment rates, as compared to their younger peers. Even during normal economic times, there will be older job losers who struggle to find new work, perhaps more so than suggested by official economic statistics if some discouraged older workers drift into (involuntary) retirement.

The effect of labor market conditions on retirement is a relatively new branch of the retirement literature. Chan and Stevens (2001) find that older U.S. workers who experience a job loss are 20 percentage points less likely to be employed four years after the job loss than similar nondisplaced workers. Coile and Levine (2007) show that downturns in the U.S. labor market increase retirement transitions, particularly for workers who are eligible to claim Social Security benefits. Using industry-level variation in employment in Sweden, Hallberg (2011) similarly finds that retirement is counter-cyclical. Late-career job loss has implications beyond retirement – Coile and Levine (2011b) show that experiencing weak labor market conditions near the age of retirement lowers retiree income, whereas Sullivan and von Wachter (2009) and Coile et al. (2014) find that job loss and recessions are associated with higher long-term mortality. Beyond the United States, Dorn and Sousa-Poza (2008) conclude that involuntary early retirement due to employment constraints is widespread in continental Europe, particularly in countries facing recessions and having strict employment protection legislation.

In sum, there is reason to believe that labor demand factors may impede some older individuals who wish to work to work. Older workers' declining productivity (whether real or imagined) may make it difficult for them to find work unless they adjust their wage expectations accordingly. Instances of age discrimination may persist despite the ADEA. And as highlighted by the recent recession, older workers who experience a late-career layoff may retire involuntarily and earlier than planned. As future changes to public pension programs are likely to be based on the expectation that workers will remain in the labor force longer, it is important for policy makers to be cognizant of the fact that some older individuals who wish to work may face difficulties finding employment.

5. Discussion

Retirement trends since 1850 suggest that retirement behavior has rarely been static, and that is as true now as it has ever been. The landscape is shifting in any number of ways for cohorts nearing retirement age. The number of older women in the labor market continues to rise, as part of a wider societal trend towards greater labor force participation among women. The economy in the United States and other developed countries continues to shift towards service sectors and production based on intellectual capital and away from manufacturing and other traditional blue-collar industries. In the United States and other countries, retirement ages in public pension plans are going up, and benefits have been cut or may need to be further reduced or delayed in the future in order to put pensions systems on firmer financial footing. Private pensions are increasingly shifting from DB to DC type pensions, putting more responsibility on the worker to decide whether to participate in the pension plan, how much to contribute, where to invest those contributions, and how to draw down savings in retirement, and exposing individuals to investment risk in their pension. During the past two decades, the boom-and-bust cycles in equity and housing markets have been far bigger than in earlier decades, holding out the prospect of windfalls but also subjecting households to the risk that asset values will fall just as they need to begin drawing down assets to finance retirement consumption. There are continuing improvements in mortality and morbidity (Cutler *et al.*, 2014), so individuals are living longer and having more years of good health at older ages.

How have these different factors affected retirement trends in recent decades, and how is retirement behavior likely to evolve in the future? To begin with women's labor force participation, there is as yet little evidence that the trend towards greater participation is abating (Goldin, 2006). In terms of shifts in the economy, evidence suggests that having computer skills is associated with an increase in the probability of continuing to work at older ages and that gaps in computer use by age are declining over time, so the importance of this factor is perhaps more likely to decline than to increase as time passes (Friedberg, 2001). Increases in the Social Security FRA seem to be leading individuals to claim benefits later and to retire later as well (Mastobuoni, 2009; Behaghel and Blau, 2012). Cuts in public pension benefits may also lead workers to work longer, though the effects of changes in benefit levels seem to be small relative to the effect of changes in the eligibility age, judging by the findings of Kruger and Pischke (1992). The switch to DC style pensions is estimated to increase the median retirement age by roughly a year for workers in their 50s today compared to workers in their 50s three decades ago (Friedberg and Webb, 2005). Fluctuations in equity markets do not appear to be a major driver of retirement decisions. As health continues to improve over time, it seems likely that fewer workers will experience health shocks that will force them into retirement earlier than planned, though there may be pockets of workers who struggle to extend their work lives as governments raise eligibility ages for public pensions.

In spite of the wealth of research on retirement in recent decades, many important questions remain. The retirement literature, as yet, has done relatively little to incorporate the insights of behavioral economics. The effects of retirement on health and well-being more generally are also not yet well understood. With life expectancy in the U.S. forecast to rise by a decade by the end of this century (Population Reference Bureau, 2006), more research is needed to understand how improvements in health are likely to affect retirement behavior. Finally, as policy makers consider changes to old age programs, they will require input from economists, founded on a solid base of research, to understand the consequences of policy changes and the tradeoffs inherent in the choices facing them. For all these reasons and more, future research on all the issues reviewed above is essential.

Notes

1. Patterns in labor force participation are similar, as can be seen in Gruber and Wise (1999).
2. Interestingly, Japan has historically had a mandatory retirement age of 60 years for many workers, but workers are often rehired by their career employer as a contract employee or able to find work at a smaller company. See Clark *et al.* (2008) for an analysis of the labor supply of older Japanese workers.
3. See Cahill *et al.* (2013) for a recent summary of the bridge job literature. As the authors note, the pattern of bridge job use with respect to wages is U-shaped, with those at the low end of the wage scale moving to a bridge job because they had to, according to survey questions, whereas those at the high end do so because they wanted to. Those who leave their career jobs when they are younger and in better health are also more likely to use bridge jobs.
4. The figures for these calculations come from the Social Security Administration's 2013 *Annual Statistical Supplement*, Tables 4.C1 and 5.B8. 1956 and 2012 are the earliest and more recent years for which all data are available.
5. Specifically, the formula that converts average indexed monthly earnings (AIME, which is meant to reflect lifetime earnings and is calculated by applying a wage index to each year of past earnings, selecting the 35 highest years of indexed earnings, and calculating 1/12 of the average) to primary insurance amount (PIA, the monthly benefit amount received if the worker claims at the full retirement age) in 2015 replaces 90% of the first $826 of AIME, 32% of the next $4,154, and 15% of earnings beyond $4,980. Thus, the replacement rate falls with AIME, even though the monthly benefit amount rises with AIME.
6. Much of the progressivity in the U.S. Social Security system actually arises from Disability Insurance (DI) benefits, as shown by CBO (2006).
7. Samwick (1998) and Coile and Gruber (2007) also use an option value (OV) measure, which is a reduced form version of Stock and Wise's (1990a, 1990b) structural option value model (described below), calculated using assumed utility parameters. In brief, OV measures the utility gain from working to the future retirement age that maximizes expected utility, while PV measures the financial gain from working to the future retirement age that maximizes the PDV of SSW. The key differences between PV and OV are that PV does not directly incorporate earnings [which account for a large share of the variation in OV, as shown by Coile and Gruber (2001)] and that PV is a financial rather than utility-based measure. Samwick (1998) and Coile and Gruber (2007) find that larger values of OV measure are associated with a reduced probability of retirement, indicating that those with the most to gain from delaying retirement are the most likely to delay.
8. Gruber and Wise (2004) estimate reduced form OV models as well.

9. These models generally do not include age dummies, so their ability to match spikes relies on having the model predict that retiring at these ages is optimal for a substantial share of the sample.

10. As benefits are reduced for claiming prior to the FRA and increased for claiming after the FRA, there is, in fact, no particular reason to claim at the FRA (so long as adjustments are actuarially fair, as discussed next), although the FRA may nonetheless serve as a focal point for both retirement and claiming decisions.

11. The application of the earnings test is more complicated in the year the worker attains the FRA, but these details are omitted here for simplicity.

12. These findings are at odds with Sevak (2001) and Coronado and Perozek (2003), who find that households that experienced larger stock market gains during the stock market boom of the late 1990s had an increased probability of retirement; however, these studies are subject to the concern that stockholdings may be correlated with preferences for retirement. Subsequent studies whose sample period included the "dot com" bust period that followed the late 1990s boom fail to find an effect of market gains and losses on retirement.

13. In an earlier study, Anderson *et al.* (1986) finds that deterioration in health induced retirement, as did unanticipated increases in Social Security benefits, whereas the recession of the 1970s tended to delay retirement.

14. In terms of the magnitude of these effects, Baker (2002) finds that the introduction of the Spouse's Allowance benefit in Canada (an income support program for spouses of old age pensioners) reduced the labor force participation of men in families where the wife was eligible for this benefit by 6–7 percentage points, relative to the participation of ineligible males; the effect on eligible females is similar. Coile (2004) finds that men are more responsive to financial incentives their wives face due to the structure of Social Security and private pensions than vice versa, and estimates that the effect of a policy change on the probability of men working at age 65 may be biased by up to 20% if spillover effects are omitted.

References

Adams, S.J. (2004) Age discrimination legislation and the employment of older workers. *Labour Economics* 11: 219–240.

Anderson, K.H. and Burkhauser, R.V. (1985) The retirement-health nexus: a new measure of an old puzzle. *Journal of Human Resources* 20(3): 315–330.

Anderson, K.H., Burkhauser, R.V. and Quinn, J.F. (1986) Do retirement dreams come true? The effect of unanticipated events on retirement plans. *Industrial & Labor Relations Review* 39(4): 518–526.

Asch, B., Haider, S.J. and Zissimopoulus, J. (2005) Financial incentives and retirement: evidence from federal civil service workers. *Journal of Public Economics* 89(2-3): 427–440.

Atalay, K. and Barrett, G.F. (2014) The impact of age pension eligibility age on retirement and program dependence: evidence from an Australian experiment. *The Review of Economics and Statistics* 97(1): 71–87.

Baker, M., Stabile, M. and Deri, C. (2004) What do self-reported, objective measures of health measure? *Journal of Human Resources* 39(4): 1067–1093.

Baker, M. (2002) The retirement behavior of married couples evidence from the spouse's allowance. *Journal of Human Resources* 37(Winter): 1–34.

Behaghel, L. and Blau, D.M. (2012) Framing social security reform: behavioral responses to changes in the full retirement age. *American Economic Journal: Economic Policy* 4(4): 41–67.

Blau, D.M. (1994) Labor force dynamics of older men. *Econometrica* 62(1): 117–156.

Blau, D.M. and Gilleskie, D. (2006) Health insurance and retirement of married couples. *Journal of Applied Econometrics* 21(7): 935–953.

Blinder, A., Gordon, R. and Wise, D. (1978) An empirical study of the effect of pensions and the saving and labor supply of older men. Report submitted to the U.S. Department of Labor.

Börsch-Supan, A. (1992) Population aging, social security design, and early retirement. *Journal of Institutional and Theoretical Economics* 148(4): 533–557.

Börsch-Supan, A., Schnabel, R., Kohnz, S. and Mastrobuoni, G. (2004) Micro-modeling of retirement decisions in Germany. In J. Gruber and D.A. Wise (eds.), *Social Security Programs and Retirement Around the World: Micro-Estimation*. Chicago: University of Chicago Press.

Börsch-Supan, A. and Schnabel, R. (1998) Social security and declining labor-force participation in Germany. *American Economic Review* 88(2): 173–178.

Bound, J. (1991) Self-reported objective measures of health in retirement models. *Journal of Human Resources* 26: 103–138.

Bound, J., Schoenbaum, M., Stinebrickner, T.R. and Waidmann, T. (1999) The dynamic effects of health on the labor force transitions of older workers. *Labour Economics* 6(2): 179–202.

Bound, J. and Waidmann, T. (2007) Estimating the health effects of retirement. *Michigan Retirement Research Center Working Paper*, pp 2007–2168, University of Michigan.

Brown, J.R., Coile, C.C. and Weisbenner, S.J. (2010) The effect of inheritance receipt on retirement. *The Review of Economics and Statistics* 92(2): 425–434.

Brown, J.R., Kapteyn, A. and Mitchell, O.S. (2013) Framing and claiming: how information-framing affects expected social security claiming behavior. *Journal of Risk and Insurance* doi: 10.1111/j.1539-6975.2013.12004.x

Brown, J.B., Liebman, J.B. and Pollet, J. (2002) Estimating life tables that reflect socioeconomic difference in mortality. In M. Feldstein and J.B. Liebman (eds.), *The Distributional Aspects of Social Security and Social Security Reform* (pp. 447–357). Chicago: University of Chicago Press.

Burkhauser, R.V. and Quinn, J.F. (1983) Is mandatory retirement overrated? Evidence from the 1970s. *Journal of Human Resources* 18(3): 337–358.

Burtless, G. and Moffitt, R. (1986) Social security, earnings tests, and age at retirement. *Public Finance Quarterly* 14: 3–27.

Cahill, K.E., Giandrea, M.D. and Quinn, J.F. (2015) Retirement Patterns and the Macroeconomy, 1992–2010: the prevalence and determinants of bridge jobs, phased retirement, and reentry among three recent cohorts of older Americans. *Gerontologist* 55(3): 384–403.

Cahill, K.E., Giandrea, M.D. and Quinn, J.F. (2013) Bridge jobs. In M. Wang (ed.), *The Oxford Handbook of Retirement*. Oxford: University of Oxford Press.

Cahill, K.E., Giandrea, M.D. and Quinn, J.F. (2011) Reentering the labor force after retirement. *Monthly Labor Review* 134(6): 34–42.

Chan, S. and Stevens, A.H. (2001) Job loss and employment patterns of older workers. *Journal of Labor Economics* 19(2): 484–521.

Charles, K. (2004) Is Retirement Depressing? Labor Force Inactivity and Psychological Well-Being in Later Life. *Research in Labor Economics* 23: 269–299.

Clark, R.L., Ogawa, N., Sang-Hyop, L. and Matsukura, R. (2008) Older workers and national productivity in Japan. *Population and Development Review* 34: 257–274.

Coile, C.C. (2004) Retirement incentives and couples' retirement decisions. *B.E. Press Journal of Economic Analysis & Policy* 4(1): 1–30.

Coile, C., Diamond, P., Gruber, J. and Jousten, A. (2002) Delays in claiming social security benefits. *Journal of Public Economics* 84(3): 357–385.

Coile, C.C. and Gruber, J. (2001) Social Security incentives for retirement. In D.A. Wise (ed.), *Themes in the Economics of Aging*, Chicago: University of Chicago Press.

Coile, C.C. and Gruber, J. (2007) Future social security entitlements and the retirement decision. *Review of Economics and Statistics* 89(2): 234–246.

Coile, C.C. and Levine, P.B. (2011a) The market crash and mass layoffs: how the current economic crisis may affect retirement. *B.E. Press Journal of Economic Analysis & Policy* 11(1): 1–22.

Coile, C.C. and Levine, P.B. (2011b) Recessions, retirement, and social security. *American Economic Review* 101(3): 23–28.

Coile, C.C. and Levine, P.B. (2007) Labor market shocks and retirement: do government programs matter? *Journal of Public Economics* 91(10): 1902–1919.

Coile, C.C. and Levine, P.B. (2006) Bulls, bears, and retirement behavior. *Industrial and Labor Relations Review* 59: 408–429.

Coile, C.C., Levine, P.B. and McKnight, R. (2014) Recessions, older workers, and longevity: how long are recessions good for you? *American Economic Journal: Economic Policy* 6(3): 92–119.

Coile, C.C., Milligan, K.S. and Wise, D.A. (2014) Introduction and summary. In D.A. Wise (ed.), *Social Security Programs and Retirement Around the World: Disability Insurance Programs and Retirement*, Chicago: University of Chicago Press.

Coile, C.C., Milligan, K.S. and Wise, D.A. (forthcoming) Introduction and Summary. In D.A. Wise (ed.), *Social Security Programs and Retirement Around the World: The Capacity to Work at Older Ages.* Chicago: University of Chicago Press.

Congressional Budget Office (2006) Is Social Security Progressive? *Economic and Budget Issue Brief*, December.

Congressional Budget Office (2014) An Update to the Budget and Economic Outlook: 2014 to 2024. Pub. No. 5005, August.

Coronado, J. and Perozek, M. (2003) Wealth Effects and the Consumption of Leisure: Retirement Decisions During the Stock Market Boom of the 1990s. Board of Governors of the Federal Reserve System Finance and Economics Discussion Series no. 2003–20.

Costa, D.L. (1998) *The Evolution of Retirement: An American Economic History, 1880–1990*. Chicago: University of Chicago Press.

Coy, P. (2014) American workers are older than ever. Bloomberg Business Week, August 4. Available at: http://www.businessweek.com/articles/2014-08-04/a-record-22-dot-2-percent-of-of-u-dot-s-dot-workers-are-55-or-older (Last accessed July 9, 2015)

Crawford, V.P. and Lilien, D.M. (1981) Social security and the retirement decision. *Quarterly Journal of Economics* 96(3): 506–529.

Cutler, D.M., Ghosh, K. and Landrum, M.B. (2014) Evidence for significant compression of morbidity in the elderly U.S. population. In D.A. Wise (ed.), *Discoveries in the Economics of Aging*. Chicago: University of Chicago Press.

Diamond, P. and Hausman, J. (1984) The retirement and unemployment behavior of older men. In G. Burtless and H. Aaron (eds.), *Retirement and Economic Behavior*. Wa shington, DC: Brookings Institution Press.

Disney, R., Emmerson, C. and Wakefield, M. (2006) Ill health and retirement in Britain: A panel data-based analysis. *Journal of Health Economics* 25(4): 621–649.

Disney, R. and Smith, S. (2002) The labor supply effect of the abolition of the earnings rule for older workers in the United Kingdom. *Economic Journal* 112(478): C136–C152.

Dorn, D. and Sousa-Poza, A. (2008) 'Voluntary' and 'involuntary' early retirement: an international analysis," *Applied Economics* 42(4): 427–438.

Dwyer, D. and Mitchell, O.S. (1999) Health problems as determinants of retirement: are self-rated measures endogenous? *Journal of Health Economics* 18(2): 173–193.

Euwals, R. and VanVuuren, D.J. and Wolthoff, R.P. (2010) Early retirement behavior in the Netherlands: evidence from a policy reform. *De Economist* 158(3): 209–236.

Farber, H.S. (2011) Job loss in the great recession: historical perspective from the displaced workers survey, 1984–2010. NBER Working Paper #17040, National Bureau of Economic Research.

Finklestein, A. and Poterba, J. (2004) Adverse selection in insurance markets: policyholder evidence from the U.K. annuity market. *Journal of Political Economy* 112(1): 183–208.

French, E. (2005) The effects of health, wealth, and wages on labor supply and retirement behavior. *The Review of Economic Studies* 72(2): 395–427.

French, E. and Jones, J.B. (2011) "The Effects of Health Insurance and Self-Insurance on Retirement Behavior," *Econometrica* 79(3): 693–732.

Friedberg, L. (2000) The labor supply effects of the social security earnings test. *Review of Economics and Statistics* 82(1): 48–63.

Friedberg, L. (2001) The impact of technological change on older workers, evidence from data on computer use. *Industrial and Labor Relations Review* 56(3): 511–529.

Friedberg, L. and Webb, A. (2005) Retirement and the evolution of the pension structure. *Journal of Human Resources* 40(2): 281–308.

Gern, K.-J. (2002) Recent developments in old age pension systems: an international overview. In M. Feldstein and H. Siebert (eds.), *Social Security Pension Reform in Europe*, Chicago: University of Chicago Press.

Goldin, C. (2006) The quiet revolution that transformed women's employment, education, and family. *American Economic Review* 92(2): 1–21.

Gruber, J. and Madrian, B. (1996) Health insurance and early retirement: evidence from the availability of continuation coverage. In D.A. Wise (ed.), *Advances in the Economics of Aging*. Chicago: University of Chicago Press.

Gruber, J. and Orszag, P. (2003) Does the social security earnings test affect labor supply and benefits receipt? *National Tax Journal* 56(4): 755–773.

Gruber, J. and Wise, D.A. (1999) Introduction and summary. In J. Gruber and D.A. Wise (eds.), *Social Security and Retirement Around the World* (pp. 1–35). Chicago: University of Chicago Press.

Gruber, J. and Wise, D.A. (2004) *Social Security Programs and Retirement Around the World: Microestimation*. Chicago: University of Chicago Press.

Gustman, A.L. and Steinmeier, T.L. (1986) A structural retirement model. *Econometrica* 54(3): 555–584.

Gustman, A.L. and Steinmeier, T.L. (2000) Retirement in dual-career families: a structural model. *Journal of Labor Economics* 18(3): 503–545.

Gustman, A.L. and Steinmeier, T.L. (2005) The social security early entitlement age in a structural model of retirement and wealth. *Journal of Public Economics* 89(2–3): 441–463.

Gustman, A.L. and Steinmeier, T.L. (2008) Projecting behavioral responses to the next generation of retirement policies. *Research in Labor Economics* 28: 141–196.

Gustman, A.L, Steinmeier, T.L. and Tabatabai, N. (2010) What the stock market decline means for the financial security and retirement choices of the near-retirement population. *Journal of Economic Perspectives* 24(1): 162–181.

Haider, S.J. and Loughran, D.S. (2008) The effect of the social security earnings test on male labor supply. *Journal of Human Resources* 43(1): 57–87.

Hallberg, D. (2011) Economic fluctuations and retirement of older employees. *Labour* 25(3): 287–307.

Hausman, J. and Wise, D. (1985) Social security, health status, and retirement. In D. Wise (ed.), *Pensions, Labor, and Individual Choice* (pp. 159–192), Chicago: University of Chicago Press.

Hellerstein, J.K., Neumark, D. and Troske, K. (1999) Wages, productivity and worker characteristics: evidence from plant-level production functions and wage equations. *Journal of Labor Economics* 17(3): 409–446.

Hurd, M.D. (1990) The joint retirement decision of husbands and wives. In D.A. Wise (ed.), *Issues in the Economics of Aging* (pp. 231–258). Chicago: University of Chicago Press.

Hurd, M.D., Smith, J.P. and Zissimopoulos, J. (2004) The effects of subjective survival on retirement and social security claiming. *Journal of Applied Econometrics* 19(6): 761–775.

Hurd, M.D., Reti, M. and Rohwedder, S. (2009) The effect of large capital gains or losses on retirement. In D.A. Wise (ed.), *Developments in the Economics of Aging* (pp. 127–171). Chicago: University of Chicago Press.

Hutchens, R.M. (1986) Delayed Payment Contracts and a Firm's Propensity to Hire Older Workers, *Journal of Labor Economics* 4(4): 439–457.

Hutchens, R.M. (1989) Seniority, wages, and productivity: a turbulent decade. *Journal of Economic Perspectives* 3(4): 49–64.

Imbens, G.W., Rubin, D.B. and Sacerdote, B. (1999) Estimating the effect of unearned income on labor earnings, savings, and consumption: evidence from a survey of lottery players. *American Economic Review* 91(4): 778–794.

Johnston, D.W. and Lee, W.-S. (2009) Retiring to the good life? The short-term effects of retirement on health. *Economic Letters* 103(1): 8–11.

Kalwij, A. and Vermeulen, F. (2008) Health and labour force participation of older people in Europe: what do objective health indicators add to the analysis. *Health Economics* 17(5): 619–638.

Kerkhofs, M., Lindeboom, M. and Theeuwes, J. (1999) Retirement, financial incentives, and health. *Labour Economics* 6(2): 203–227.

Krueger, A.B. and Pischke, J.-S. (1992) The effect of social security on labor supply: a cohort analysis of the notch generation. *Journal of Labor Economics* 10(4): 412–437.

Lahey, J.N. (2008a) Age, women, and hiring: an experimental study. *Journal of Human Resources* 43(1): 30–56.

Lahey, J. (2008b) State age protection laws and the age discrimination in employment act. *Journal of Law and Economics* 51(3): 433–460.

Lazear, E.P. (1979) Why is there mandatory retirement? *Journal of Political Economy* 87(6): 1261–1284.

Lazear, E.P. (1983) Pensions as severance pay. In Z. Bodie and J.B. Shoven (eds.), *Financial Aspects of the United States Pension System* (pp. 57–90). Chicago: University of Chicago Press.

Leimer, D.R. (1999) Lifetime redistribution under the social security program: a literature synopsis. *Social Security Bulletin* 62(2): 43–51.

Leonesio, M.V., Bridges, B., Gesumaria, R. and Bene, L.D. (2012) The increasing labor force participation of older workers and its effect on the income of the aged. *Social Security Bulletin* 72(1): 59–77.

Liebman, J.B. (2002) Redistribution in the current U.S. social security system. In M. Feldstein and J.B. Liebman (eds.), *The Distributional Aspects of Social Security and Social Security Reform* (pp. 11–48). Chicago: University of Chicago Press.

Liebman, J.B. and Luttmer, E.F.P. (2015) Would people behave differently if they better understood social security? Evidence from a field experiment. *American Economic Journal: Economic Policy* 7(1): 275–299.

Liebman, J.B., Luttmer, E.F.P. and Seif, D. (2009) Labor supply responses to marginal social security benefits: evidence from discontinuities. *Journal of Public Economics* 93(11–12): 1208–1223.

Lumsdaine, R. and Wise, D. (1994) Aging and labor force participation: a review of trends and explanation. In Y. Noguchi and D. Wise (eds.), *Aging in the United States and Japan: Economic Trends*. Chicago: University of Chicago Press.

Madrian, B., Burtless, G. and Gruber, J. (1994) The effect of health insurance on retirement. *Brookings Papers on Economic Activity* 1994(1): 181–252.

Maestas, N. (2001) *Labor, Love, and Leisure: Complementarity and the Timing of Retirement by Working Couples*. Berkeley: U.C. Berkeley.

Maestas, N. (2010) Back to work: expectations and realizations of work after retirement. *Journal of Human Resources* 45(3): 718–748.

Manoli, D.S. and Weber, A. (2011) Nonparametric evidence on the effects of financial incentives on retirement decisions. *NBER Working Paper* No. 17320, August, National Bureau of Economic Research.

Mastrobuoni, G. (2009) Labor supply effects of the recent social security benefit cuts: empirical estimates using cohort discontinuities. *Journal of Public Economics* 93(11–12): 1224–1233.

McClellan, M.B. (1998) Health events, health insurance, and labor supply: evidence from the health and retirement survey. In D.A. Wise (ed.), *Frontiers in the Economics of Aging* (pp. 301–349). Chicago: University of Chicago Press.

Mitchell, O.S. and Fields, G.S. (1982) The effects of pensions and earnings on retirement. In *Research in Labor Economics*, Vol. 5. Greenwich, Connecticut: JAI Press.

Munnell, A.H. (2014) The impact of aging baby boomers on labor force participation: A review. *Center for Retirement Research Issue Brief* 14–4: 115–155.

Munnell, A.H. (2006) Employer-sponsored plans: the shift from defined benefit to defined. *The Oxford Handbook of Pensions and Retirement Income* 13: 359–380.

Neumark, D. and Stock, W.A. (1999) Age discrimination laws and labor market efficiency. *Journal of Political Economy* 107:1081–1125.

Quinn, J.F. and Burkhauer, R.V. (1993) Influencing retirement behavior: a key issue for social security. *Journal of Policy Analysis and Management* 3(1): 1–13.

Rogowski, J. and Karoly, L. (2000) Health insurance and retirement behavior: evidence from the health and retirement survey. *Journal of Health Economics* 19(4): 529–539.

Rust, J. and Phelan, C. (1997) How social security and Medicare affect retirement behavior in a world of incomplete markets. *Econometrica* 65(4): 781–831.

Samwick, A.A. (1998) New evidence on pensions, social security, and the timing of retirement. *Journal of Public Economics* 70(2): 207–236.

Sanzenbacher, G.T. (2014) What we know about health reform in Massachusetts. *Center for Retirement Research Issue Brief* 14–19.

Sevak, P. (2001) Wealth shocks and retirement timing: evidence from the nineties. *Michigan Retirement Research Center Working* Paper no. WP00D1, University of Michigan.

Shirbekk, V. (2004) Age and individual productivity: a literature survey. *Vienna Yearbook of Population Research* 2: 133–153.

Shoven, J. and Slavov, S. (2014) Does it pay to delay social security? *Journal of Pension Economics and Finance* 13(2): 121–144.

Song, J. and Manchester, J. (2007) Have people delayed claiming retirement benefits? Responses to changes in social security rules. *Social Security Bulletin* 67(2): 1–23.

Snyder, S.E. and Evans, W.N. (2006) The effect of income on mortality: evidence from the social security notch. *The Review of Economics and Statistics* 88(3): 482–495.

Staubli, S. and Zweimuller, J. (2012) Does raising the retirement age increase employment of older workers? *University of Zurich Department of Economics* Working Paper 20.

Stock, J. and Wise, D. (1990a) Pensions, the option value of work, and retirement. *Econometrica* 58: 1151–1180.

Stock, J. and Wise, D. (1990b) The pension inducement to retire: an option value analysis. In D.A. Wise (ed.), *Issues in the Economics of Aging* (pp. 205–229). Chicago: University of Chicago Press.

Sullivan, D. and Wachter, T.V. (2009) Job displacement and mortality: an analysis using administrative data. *The Quarterly Journal of Economics* 124(3): 1265–1306.

U.S. Department of Labor, Employee Benefits Security Administration (2014) *Private Pension Plan Bulletin Historical Tables and Graphs*, September. Available at http://www.dol.gov/ebsa/pdf/ historicaltables.pdf, accessed January 2, 2015.

Vander Klaauw, W. and Wolpin, K.I. (2008) Social security and the retirement and savings behavior of low-income households. *Journal of Econometrics* 145(1): 21–42.

VonWachter, T. (2002) *The End of Mandatory Retirement in the US: Effects on Retirement and Implicit Contracts.* Berkeley: Center for Labor Economics, University of California.

INDEX

A Collection of Surveys on Savings and Wealth Accumulation, First Edition. Edited by Edda Claus and Iris Claus.
Chapters © 2016 The Authors. Book compilation © 2016 John Wiley & Sons, Ltd. Published 2016 by John Wiley & Sons, Ltd.